THE TRADES UNION CONGRESS

by the same author

NATIONAL WAGES POLICY IN WAR AND PEACE

THE TRADES UNION CONGRESS

1868–1921

BY

B. C. ROBERTS

Reader in Industrial Relations
in the University of London

Ruskin House

GEORGE ALLEN & UNWIN LTD

MUSEUM STREET LONDON

FIRST PUBLISHED IN 1958

PRINTED IN GREAT BRITAIN
in 10pt Times Roman type
by Jarrold and Sons Ltd
Norwich

PREFACE

The Trades Union Congress was founded in 1868, and has, since then, met annually, except for the years 1870 and 1914.[1] Over the course of this time the T.U.C. has grown in status from a yearly demonstration to a powerful and influential institution that speaks in the name of more than eight million members of affiliated unions.

Although the T.U.C. is well on the way towards its centenary, no full history of its development and achievements has been written until now. In this volume the story of the T.U.C. is taken as far as 1921, when the constitution was thoroughly revised and a new era began. This point is a natural one at which to break the narrative, but in some respects it is the middle, rather than the end of a period. The General Strike of 1926 was, in fact, the culmination of many of the ideas that assumed significance in the decade prior to 1921. However, the balance of advantage seemed to lie with concluding this volume in 1921; especially since to extend it to 1926 would have necessitated a substantial addition to its length. Volume II will, therefore, cover the period from 1921 to the present day.

The research for this study was originally started at Nuffield College in 1948, but it had to be suspended for some years. I am grateful to Nuffield College for having given me the opportunity to begin this research. I would also like to express my thanks to the London School of Economics and Political Science for the facilities provided by the Research Division, which have enabled me to complete this study.

The Trades Union Congress has made available its records of the meetings of Congress, and I am grateful to its library staff for their helpfulness.

H. Pelling and F. Bealey have read certain chapters and given me the benefit of their expert knowledge of the origins and early history of the Labour Party. It must, however, be made clear that I alone am responsible for the selection of facts and for the opinions expressed.

Acknowledgments for permission to quote are due to the Passfield Trust, Macmillan and Co. Ltd., Routledge and Kegan Paul Ltd., Ernest Benn Ltd. and the Oxford University Press.

The burden of checking typescript and proofs has fallen upon my wife; she has also compiled the index. Without her help and encouragement this book would not, I am certain, have been completed.

September 1957   B. C. R.
LONDON

[1] This Congress was cancelled at the outbreak of war.

CONTENTS

CONTENTS

*the Mediation Committee—Proposals to Increase the
Authority of the T.U.C.—Bevin Succeeds where Miners
Fail—The Miners Change their Tactics—The New
Constitution Adopted—The Triple Alliance Breaks Down
—Further Changes Proposed in Structure and Functions
of the T.U.C.*

CHAPTER I

THE FIRST
TRADES UNION CONGRESS

The Trades Union Congress was born in the summer of 1868, at a meeting convened by the Manchester and Salford Trades Council, at the Mechanics' Institute, David Street, Manchester. Several attempts had been made to form a national organisation of trade unions before this event. In the decade following the repeal of the Combination Acts in 1824, John Doherty and Robert Owen had tried hard to build nation-wide associations of trade unions.[1] Though both of them managed to found organisations based on a wider appeal than strictly local interests these ventures were not long-lived. The sensational collapse of the Grand National Consolidated Trades Union, immediately after its spectacular growth, brought an end to Owen's chances of reshaping the trade union movement; he went on indefatigably organising socialist congresses, but the unions were too busy coping with the trade depression which threatened their very existence to pay him much attention.

Trade unions in the early 1830s were too precariously established to be in a position to provide a stable basis for a nation-wide organisation. Though they were no longer criminal organisations their legal status was uncertain, and they were subject to considerable political and economic pressure. There were also practical difficulties of another kind to be overcome before trade unions could be effectively organised on a national scale. Whilst the system of communications was slow and uncertain, as it was at the time when Doherty and Owen were making their attempts to set up national movements, the expansion of trade union organisation was immensely difficult. This handicap was removed by the introduction of a cheap and reliable postal system and by the building of a railway network which provided a speedy method of travel between all the major towns in the country.[2]

[1] Cole, G. D. H., *Attempts at General Union, 1918–1834*. Webb, S. and B., *The History of Trade Unionism*, Ed. 1920, pp. 113 *et seq.*

[2] The penny post was started in 1840, and by the end of that decade railways had become established as the main form of long-distance transport.

National Association of United Trades for the Protection of Labour

The next attempt to create a national organisation of trade unions was not made until 1845. At the instigation of the Sheffield Trade Societies a conference was held during Easter of that year and from it came the National Association of United Trades for the Protection of Labour. The name and constitution of the Association betray the influence of the ideas manifested earlier by both Owen and Doherty, but in many respects it foreshadowed the Trades Union Congress. In its adherence to the principle of co-operative production, and the promotion of common action against the attacks of employers on any one of its member trade societies, it reflected the policy of the earlier organisations. However, unlike the Owenite movement of 1833–4, the National Association of United Trades 'was from the first distinguished by the moderation of its aims and the prudence of its administration—qualities to which we may attribute its comparatively lengthy survival for fifteen years'.[1] The Association did not seek to replace the organisations already in existence by a general trades union. 'The peculiar local internal and technical circumstances of each trade', say the rules, 'render it necessary that for all purposes of efficient internal government its affairs should be administered by persons possessing a practical knowledge of them. For this reason it is not intended to interfere with the organisation of existing Trade Unions.'[2] The Association also differed clearly from its forerunners in the emphasis that was placed on its function as a parliamentary committee rather than as a federation for trade purposes. 'Its purpose and duty was declared to be "to protect the interests and promote the well being of the associated trades" by mediation, arbitration, and legal proceedings, and by promoting "all measures, political and social and educational, which are intended to improve the condition of the labouring classes".'[3]

The National Association failed to attract the support of the majority of trade societies; its lack of success was not due to its promoters overreaching themselves in their objectives and organisational design so much as to the fact that most societies were still primarily concerned with the problems of organising their own trades. The trade societies were suffering, in 1846, from the 'effects of an economic depression and could hardly be blamed for their reluctance to support the advanced ideas of some of their number'. Though the aims of the National Association were more in tune with

---

[1] Webb, S. and B., *The History of Trade Unionism*, p. 186.
[2] *Ibid.*   [3] *Ibid.*

the realities of the time than had been the case with its predecessors, the organisation was still premature, the trade societies were neither capable of supporting a central body nor were they willing. The Association did not, however, immediately perish; it lingered on to play a not unimportant part in the passing of the Molestation of Workmen Act in 1859.[1]

Before the trade unions could be linked together by an effective, durable, national body they had to be placed on an efficient business-like basis, and this development in their organisation took place during the 1850s. The story of the steady growth of the trade unions at this time, and the significance of the 'New Model' unionism intro-duced by the engineers, has been told elsewhere.[2] The key to the success of the trade unions lay in the development of a highly industrialised society and in the acceptance by the unions of the fundamental tenets of this society. They sought to modify rather than to overthrow the new economic system, and to protect their members from its vicissitudes rather than to persuade them to reject the system outright. The old ideas of recreating society according to Utopian ideals did not die; they remained deeply fixed in the hearts of many working men; but the unions translated the desires of their members into more immediately realisable aims.

The activities of the unions at this time were by modern standards extremely modest. They sought to redress the balance of bargaining power, then weighted in favour of the employers, and to provide an element of social security for those who suffered the inevitable mis-fortunes of unemployment, sickness and injury. How successfully the unions were able to pursue these aims depended to a large degree on the extent of their funds; to build up their financial strength was, therefore, a task of first priority in every well-led organisation. The leaders of the large unions became imbued with a spirit of thrift and caution, and they tended to grow reluctant to hazard their resources on strike ventures sometimes clamoured for by their followers. If attacked by the employers they would defend, but preferred to husband their funds rather than to use them in aggressive skirmishes.

Strikes and lockouts were not, however, infrequent, and quite

[1] The Webbs were apparently under the impression that the National Associa-tion had been wound up after the passing of the 1859 Act; George Howell states (*Labour Legislation, Labour Movements and Labour Leaders*, 1905), however, that it continued to exist until 1867, but that during its later years it had become solely concerned with advocating the passing of a Conciliation Bill—this was accom-plished in 1867. George Odger referred to its existence disparagingly 'as a perfect myth' in 1866. (*Report of Conference of Trades' Delegates*, Sheffield, July 1866.)

[2] Webb, S. and B., *The History of Trade Unionism*, Ch. IV. Cole, G. D. H., *A Short History of the British Working Class Movement, 1789–1947*, Part 2, Ch. III. Jefferys, J. B., *The Story of the Engineers*, Ch. III.

often financial assistance was given by one union to another. The disturbances in the Lancashire cotton trades produced another attempt, in 1854, to form a national trades federation. Again there was a good deal of talk, and also practical action, in the way of collecting funds for the support of those fighting for the principles of trade unionism, but a national conference held in Manchester, in March 1854, failed to produce any significant advance towards establishing a viable central organisation.

With the disappearance of handcraft methods in the cotton industry trade unionism went into a decline and it was not until the 1850s and 1860s that strong organisations of operatives began to re-emerge. The development of piece-rate price lists by employers led to the vigorous pursuit of collective bargaining by the new cotton unions as they sought to determine the level of earnings enjoyed by their members. They were also ready, unlike some unions, to seek legislation to regulate working conditions in the mills. The cotton unions, were organised, however, on a local basis and their activities were confined to Lancashire. The miners, under the leadership of Martin Jude in the 1840s and under Alexander Macdonald a decade later, were among the first to realise the need to strengthen their movement by organising it on a national basis. They, too, saw the advantage of legislation where they could not achieve results by industrial action.[1] However, not all the miners were convinced either of the need for closer unity within their own ranks, or of the need to influence Parliament to legislate in their favour, and Macdonald had no easy task in holding them to his point of view. While Macdonald was trying to establish a Miners' National Association, events were occurring elsewhere that were to have a bigger impact on the trade union world.

The Builders' Strike

In 1856 the Manchester building trades won a half-day holiday on Saturday afternoon, after a big strike. From 1853 the London building trades had been agitating for shorter hours, but the demand for a nine-hour day was strongly resisted by the employers, who formed their own organisations of master builders to counter the trade unions. The building trade was at this time mainly organised by small craft unions on a local basis, with only loose co-operation between one district and another. The organisation of the employers was a warning to the men, who replied to the threat by forming, in 1858, a joint committee of carpenters, masons and bricklayers to

[1] Webb, S. and B., *The History of Trade Unionism*, p. 300. Arnot, Page, R. *The Miners*, Ch. I and II.

conduct their claims. The moving spirit behind this committee was George Potter, who was to become a leading figure in the trade union world during the next twenty years and play a major part in bringing the Trades Union Congress into existence. Potter was the secretary of a small London union, the Progressive Society of Carpenters and Joiners, and a man of great talent, able to speak and write fluently and evoke tremendous loyalty and enthusiasm from the men he led.[1] Under his leadership the joint committee drew up their demands, and expressed them in polite terms, in the form of a memorandum, which was then submitted to the master builders in 1859. The building employers turned down this claim, whereupon the committee selected four firms by ballot and decided to make an individual approach to each one of them. One of the firms, Messrs. Trollope, reacted by promptly dismissing the man who had presented the committee's memorandum. This high-handed action led very rapidly to the whole of the London building trades coming out on strike in support of the reinstatement of the discharged trade unionist. Before long the men were saying that they would not return to work until they had secured not only the reinstatement of the man, but also the object of their original claim, the nine-hour day. The master builders retaliated by declaring all the men on strike locked out, and presented the notorious 'document' as a condition of re-employment. This action immediately changed the character of the dispute into one in which the unions were fighting, not merely against victimisation and for improved working conditions, but for the right to exist. The other trades, seeing the plight of the builders, and the danger that would be spelled in their defeat, rapidly rallied round, contributing substantial sums of money; especial generosity being shown by the Amalgamated Society of Engineers.[2] The dispute finally came to an end with the employers withdrawing the 'document' and the workers returning to their employment without having achieved their demands.[3]

In spite of the stalemate in which it ended, the struggle was of immense significance in the development of the trade union movement, for it created a new sense of solidarity among trade unionists and emphasised the need for greater unity; in particular it stimulated two important developments, the formation of the Amalgamated Society of Carpenters and Joiners; and the foundation of the London Trades Council.

[1] Born in 1832 at Kenilworth, the son of a carpenter, Potter, after serving an apprenticeship at his father's trade, came to London in 1853 to find work. He became secretary of a small trade society and from 1857 was virtually leader of the London building trades.

[2] Jefferys, J. B., *The Story of the Engineers*, p. 75.

[3] Postgate, R. W., *The Builders' History*, p. 176.

As soon as the trial of strength was over, Potter commenced to regroup his forces, and in the autumn of 1860 he organised a conference of representatives of the building trades societies from all over the country. The conference met in Derby during the first week in January 1861, and remained in session for the whole week. The outcome of the conference was the formation, to continue the struggle on a national basis, of the United Kingdom Association for Shortening the Hours of Labour in the Building Trades.[1] The Association had only a short life, primarily because the employers countered this new move by introducing the hourly system of payment for work, the result being that if the men chose to work an hour less each day they lost an hour's wages. The men tried to resist the change-over from the weekly to the hourly system, but they had neither the organisation nor the financial strength to conduct more than sporadic strikes which soon petered out. The most important result of the Derby conference was that it brought Potter into contact with trade union leaders from other parts of the country and opened the way for his later activities.

Steps Towards Closer Association between the Trades

The London battle had revealed to unionists in the building trades how weak many of their existing organisations were. Most of them were small societies based on local public houses, from which they often took their name; they were organised in a rudimentary fashion and administered so casually that peculation was encouraged and financial resources were difficult to build up. A movement was begun to bring about an improvement in organisation. 'Plasterers, Painters, Carpenters and Joiners and Plumbers formed new organisations altogether. The existing organisation of bricklayers was reconstituted. The half-alive societies of bricklayers, painters and carpenters in the provinces woke up and increased their activities and membership.'[2] The most thoroughgoing reorganisation was undertaken by the carpenters and joiners. Delegates from fourteen of the small societies in London met, together with representatives from the Progressive Society of Carpenters and Joiners and several other trade clubs, and formed an amalgamation committee. After a prolonged and tedious series of meetings the Amalgamated Society of Carpenters and Joiners was launched on 4 June 1860, with a membership of approximately 600. The new society was frankly modelled on the pattern of the Amalgamated Society of Engineers, which had been founded in 1851 and had astonished the trade union world with its

[1] Postgate, R. W., *The Builders' History*, p. 177.
[2] *Ibid.*

ability to donate £3,000 to strike funds during the builders' lockout. William Allan, the secretary of the Amalgamated Society of Engineers, played no small part in giving advice and assistance to the carpenters at the time of the foundation of their new society. J. Lea, who had acted as secretary of the Amalgamation Committee, was the man chosen to be the first secretary of the Amalgamated Society of Carpenters and Joiners, but two years later he was deposed for falsifying the ballot for election to the office.[1] Robert Applegarth, the secretary of a small Sheffield society of joiners, which he had persuaded to join the Amalgamated Society, was elected in his place. Applegarth became a close collaborator of William Allan, and his great ability soon established him as one of the outstanding trade union leaders of his time.

George Potter had little to do with the new Society of Carpenters and Joiners, his Progressive Society having withdrawn before the amalgamation was carried through. Potter was, in fact, unfavourable to the new development of large centralised organisations, preferring a looser form of confederal arrangement of the type he tried to bring about at Derby in 1861. It is unlikely that he disapproved of big amalgamations because they would bring to an end the small societies' dependence on the public house, as has been suggested.[2] His whole career shows that, like the new school of trade unionists who were advocates of the amalgamation principle, he saw the need for closer unity and some form of central machinery. It is more probable that he was against big amalgamations, first because of a dislike of bureaucratic organisation and the strength this gave to rival leaders with whom he was at loggerheads; second, because of the extremely cautious policy they pursued; and third, because he had himself no taste for administration. The leaders of the new amalgamated societies were essentially first-class administrators,[3] whereas Potter's foremost talents were those of propagandist, writer and orator.

The other important development making for greater organisational unity which arose out of the builders' dispute, was the formation of the London Trades Council. Trades councils were already in existence in a few large towns, providing a new link in the developing structure of the trade union movement.[4] The London Trades followed these examples when, at a conference convened by the

[1] Amalgamated Society of Woodworkers, *Our Society's History*, p. 69.

[2] Postgate, R. W., *The Builders' History*, p. 196.

[3] Cf. Webb, S. and B., *The History of Trade Unionism*. 'The special distinction of . . . (the Junta) . . . was their business capacity . . .', p. 237.

[4] One of the earliest was the Liverpool Trades' Guardian Association, founded in 1848; in 1861 the Trades' Guardian Association was replaced by the Liverpool United Trades' Protection Association. See *A Short History of the Liverpool Trades Council, 1848-1948*, by Hamling, W.

London strike committee, they decided to set up a permanent council in May 1860. A year later a constitution was finally adopted which gave the Council the duty of watching 'over the general interests of labour, political and social, both in and out of Parliament', and invested it with the power to give help to societies engaged in disputes by investigating appeals for help and, if these were then considered bona fide, issuing 'credentials' to the London Trades. The Progressive Society of Carpenters were not represented on the provisional committee, and there is no evidence that Potter took any part in the early deliberations, though he probably followed them closely.

At the delegate meetings of the London Trades held in May 1861, called to adopt the constitution of the Council, the Progressive Society of Carpenters was represented by George Potter and W. Tremlett. Potter took an active part in these discussions, proposing several changes in the rules, which were carried; however, he apparently did not choose to be an active member of the Council at this stage, his colleague W. Tremlett being elected as representative of the Progressive Carpenters.[1] Potter was elected to the Council, for the first time, at its annual delegate meeting on 16 June 1863.[2]

Soon after the London Trades Council had adopted its constitution, it was joined by three leaders of metropolitan trade societies, who were destined to become part of a group that was to exercise a powerful influence on the future of the trade union movement. These three included George Howell—who in 1861 was elected secretary of the Council for a year—Edwin Coulson of the Operative Bricklayers' Society, and George Odger, of the Ladies Shoemakers' Society. During the next few years they were joined by the leaders of some of the important national amalgamations, Daniel Guile of the Iron-founders, Robert Applegarth of the Amalgamated Society of Carpenters and William Allan of the Amalgamated Society of Engineers. This group was aptly called by the Webbs the 'Junta'.[3] It came to dominate the London Trades Council and to act as an 'informal cabinet of the trade union world', though the leadership it assumed did not go unchallenged. An unofficial group was bound to provoke hostility since it was responsible to none but its own members, and could not claim to represent the whole trade union movement when there was no national organisation in being.

An incident occurred in 1861, before the Junta really existed, which was an omen of the conflict that was to come. Potter, who was engaged in leading the struggle against the introduction by the master builders of payment by the hour, organised a deputation to the War

---

[1] Minutes of the London Trades Council, 14 May 1861.
[2] *Ibid.*,16 June 1863.
[3] Webb, S. and B., *The History of Trade Unionism*, pp. 233 *et seq.*

Office of representatives of the building trades societies and of the London Trades Council to protest at the use of soldiers as blacklegs in a dispute that was taking place. The deputation secured the withdrawal of the troops, but the assumption of leadership by Potter was resented by the officials of the London Trades Council, who were seeking to make the Council the official voice of the London trade unions. At a meeting of the Council Potter was criticised by George Howell, the secretary, apparently for the manner in which he had behaved.[1] Potter was, however, vigorously defended by his colleague Tremlett, and the matter was allowed to drop, but it pointed to the possibility of a more violent clash in the future.

Potter's aggressive qualities, rather flamboyant manner and tendency to scorn cautious conciliatory methods had won him a considerable following in the building trades, but these traits were not appreciated by the leaders of the Amalgamated societies, who saw in their display a challenge to the ideas on which the 'new model' trade unions were based. They had good reason to be worried about the influence of Potter, for he had started a newspaper in 1861 which brought his name and activities prominently to the attention of the members of all the unions.

The Beehive

The formation by Potter of the Trades Newspaper Company, with a capital of £1,250 and an issue of 5,000 shares at five shillings each, to publish a newspaper with the name of the *Beehive* was a bold venture. Capital was difficult to raise and resort had to be made to the establishment of Beehive Share Clubs, organised by the local trade societies at the public houses which served them as meeting-places.[2] However, in spite of handicaps the paper was launched, and soon proved to be one of the most effective examples of working-class journalism in the nineteenth century.[3] The London Trades Council, when first approached to give their support to the paper were suspicious and demanded more information about it, but some months later, the paper having made its appearance and proved its value, the Council decided to endorse it. Coulson and Odger joined the board of directors and the *Beehive* remained the officially recognised journal of the London trade unions until 1865, when, under

[1] Minutes of the London Trades Council, 21 August 1861.

[2] *Beehive*, 1 November 1862.

[3] Humphrey, A. W., *The History of Labour Representation*. 'It was a very successful and well-conducted Labour newspaper. It was well supplied with Labour and general news, and had live editorial columns. Working men leaders and many middle-class sympathisers contributed, Mr. Frederic Harrison being among the latter', p. 12.

the influence of the 'Junta' the Council decided to withdraw its support from an editor whom the leaders of the Amalgamated societies hated and distrusted. The paper had not been in existence for very long before a conflict began between, on the one side, Potter and his publisher Troup, and on the other, Howell, Applegarth and Odger, over the attitude of the *Beehive* towards the American Civil War.[1] The 'Junta' and George Potter were at one in their belief in the necessity of political reform, and there was no difference of opinion about the function of the *Beehive*, which played a notable part in stimulating support for change.[2] The *Beehive* was, however, Potter's paper and it expressed his ideas; these were not always acceptable to the leaders of the big national Amalgamated societies, who resented the fact that Potter was often regarded as the spokesman of the whole trade union movement.

Under the influence of the new leaders and of the articles of Potter and his colleague Robert Hartwell in the *Beehive*, steps began to be taken to bring about closer unity to achieve political reforms. The growth of the trades councils had led to correspondence between them on matters that were of common interest to members of all

[1] Potter and Troup, the printer of the *Beehive*, had supported the Southern Confederates on the grounds that a victory for the Federalists would not be so much a triumph in the cause of anti-slavery as a triumph for grabbing politicians. The leaders of the North, they stated, were anti-British and wanted to annex Canada; they had erected a system of import duties and were opposed to free trade, which would lead to unemployment and falling wages for British workmen. The *Beehive* was not in favour of slavery, but suggested that it was hypocrisy to be indignant about the South when in British colonies Negroes were being dreadfully exploited by commercial interests.

The other leaders of the London Trades were unequivocally in support of Lincoln and against the slave States. This was the attitude of the majority of British workmen, who saw only the question of slavery and made common cause instinctively with those who aimed at its abolition. Although Troup was still writing in favour of the South in 1864, Potter had by this time turned completely round and the *Beehive* was vigorously supporting the North and denouncing those supporting the secessionists. What had angered the other leaders against Potter was that in supporting the South he had aligned the *Beehive* with the commercial classes in Britain, who were strongly against the North for economic reasons. His turn round was probably due to a realisation that the workers were standing firm not only against the South, but against the business interests in Britain which hoped for a victory over the North. Another factor of considerable importance was the association which had developed between the leaders of the London Trades and Samuel Morley, Frederic Harrison, John Stuart Mill, John Bright and other middle-class radicals, who were ardent champions of Lincoln and the North because they saw that a victory for democracy in America would be a victory for democracy in Britain. Harrison and his friends wrote regularly in the *Beehive* on all manner of subjects and Potter was undoubtedly influenced by their views.

[2] Brand, C. F., 'The Conversion of British Trade Unions to Political Action', *American Historical Review*, January 1925.

trades. The extension of the trades council principle to the national scale was a logical and natural development in trade union organisation, and its culmination was the Trades Union Congress. The Glasgow Trades Council was, perhaps, the first to try and bring about more effective unity in 1861, through a scheme to form a federation of all the trades in Scotland 'into one central association with the view of being the better able to promote, by such organisation, by every legal and constitutional means all measures calculated to forward the interests, and ameliorate the condition of the industrial classes'.[1] These proposals came to naught, but the Council was not deterred, and in the same year it issued an address calling on the trades of the United Kingdom to unite to secure parliamentary reform, a new trade union act and a change in the law of master and servant. The London Trades Council, representing the views of its members before it was joined by Applegarth, Allan and Potter, while in favour of the proposed reforms, would have nothing to do with the suggestions for a 'monster national petition'; this savoured too much of past political failures. Following this rebuff, the Glasgow Trades Council concentrated its attention on securing an alteration in the law of master and servant which the evolving social conscience now declared as monstrously unjust.

The Campaign to Change the Law of Master and Servant

The campaign at first met with a rather cold reception, except from John Bright, who informed the Council that he hoped the trade unions would vigorously pursue this project.[2] Under the leadership of its able founder, Alexander Campbell, and its secretary, George Newton, the Council sent out a circular giving information about the way in which the law operated to the severe detriment of the working class, to all the other trades councils in Britain and Ireland, and asking for their assistance to secure a change in the state of affairs which had been revealed.[3] Following the receipt of favourable replies

[1] Circular filed in the minute book of the London Trades Council, 1861.

[2] Gillespie, G. E., *Labour and Politics in England, 1850–1867*.

[3] As the law of master and servant stood, if an employer broke a contract with an employee, he was liable, if sued, only for damages, or if wages under £10 were involved only to make payment of the amount due when ordered by a court of summary jurisdiction, but if a worker broke his contract, merely by absence from work, he was committing a criminal offence, and on proceedings being taken against him he could receive up to three months in prison. Moreover, under the laws of evidence a workman prosecuted by his employer could not give evidence on his own behalf, whereas in the case of a workman suing an employer, the employer could. Justices had the power, on the evidence of an employer given on oath, to order the summary arrest of a workman for absence from work, and to sentence him to imprisonment; the law allowed no option of a fine or payment of

from London, Bristol, Sheffield, Nottingham, Newcastle and Edin-
burgh, and from several trade unions, a meeting of delegates was
convened at the Bell Hotel, Glasgow, to consider the question.[1] A
committee was appointed to organise, with the London Trades
Council, a further conference in London and this was held during
May 1864. Among those who attended this conference were
G. Odger, who had been elected secretary of the London Trades
Council, Alexander Macdonald, Robert Applegarth, Daniel Guile,
Edwin Coulson, George Potter, T. J. Dunning of the Bookbinders,
Alexander Campbell and William Dronfield, secretary of the
Sheffield Trades Council.[2] The conference was the starting-point for
a parliamentary lobbying campaign which continued under the
direction of the committee set up in Glasgow. The campaign was
carried on with great skill, through public meetings held all over the
country, articles in the Press and with the assistance of influential
members in Parliament.[3]

The culmination of the efforts of the Glasgow Trades Council was
the setting up in 1865 of a select committee to inquire into the law,
and finally, after its report, the carrying of a Bill through Parliament
by Lord Elcho in 1867; the Act remedied the most outrageous aspects
of the legal discrimination against workers in their contractual status
with employers. This campaign, and the way in which it was conducted, was of the utmost significance, for it not only established a
pattern for future political activities by the trade union movement,
but stimulated the development of trades councils, as well as of closer
co-operation between them, and was convincing proof to many who
still doubted the wisdom of engaging in political activities that
substantial reforms could be obtained in this way. The position of the
'Junta' type trade union leaders who deprecated reliance on the
strike as the only weapon by which the trade unions could secure
better conditions and improve the status of their members in the
community, was considerably strengthened.

Potter and the 'Junta' in Conflict

The activities of the trade unions, especially in London, were
intense in 1864, and the year was packed with incident. The friction
between Potter and the Allan, Applegarth, Odger and Coulson
'Junta', which had practically gained control of the London Trades

damages. The Glasgow Trades Council had obtained information showing that
over 10,000 cases came before the courts each year.

[1] *Beehive*, 26 March 1864.
[2] *Ibid.*, 4 June 1864.
[3] Webb, S. and B., *The History of Trade Unionism*, p. 249.

Council, broke out into open hostility. Early in the new session of Parliament, Gladstone, who was then Chancellor of the Exchequer, introduced a Bill to permit the Government to sell annuities to persons of a moderate income at a low cost per week. The small trade union friendly societies at once showed unnecessary alarm and distrust of the Government's intentions. Potter, ever ready to take up what he conceived to be a challenge to the unions, organised a huge meeting of the London Trades societies at the Exeter Hall to protest at this attempt of the Government to ruin the friendly societies by competing with them. From the chair Potter made an admirable statement of Liberal principles, urging the Government to look after its own business and leave the friendly societies to do theirs.[1] However, the promotion of working-class thrift by the Government had become established as a legitimate sphere of Government operations, since the Post Office Savings Bank Act of 1861— of which, following their application, the trade unions had been specially allowed to take advantage. The leaders of the London Trades Council, who boycotted the meeting, were angered no little when Gladstone, in a speech on the Bill in the House of Commons, referred to Potter as the 'far famed secretary of the trade unions', and they at once sent a deputation to the Chancellor to correct this impression. There can be no doubt that on this occasion—as on some others—Potter permitted his enthusiasm to run away with him.

[1] Writing in the *Beehive* on 19 March 1864, Potter stated:

'We, however, oppose the Annuities Bill from a higher stand point than the interest of any particular society. We oppose it on account of its centralisation principle, and from our sincere conviction that, if successful, it will not be industrial assurance companies, and friendly societies only, that will be taken under the paternal care of the Government; Trades' Unions and Co-operative Societies will also be taken under Government patronage, as in France, and will become, as they are in that country, completely emasculated for any practical purpose. We repudiate all Government interference with working men's associations, believing they are able, honest, and intelligent enough to manage their own affairs without the aid of Government officials or red tape. The English working man likes to be appreciated, but not to be patronised, and the wonder is that he has not been altogether spoilt by the hosts of soft-headed, warm-hearted, well-meaning people, who would make a baby of him. Libations of tea and coffee have been freely poured out to the men of the hammer, the trowel, and the loom; bread and butter and plum cake have been laid on the altar in the Temple of Industry; even tobacco has been allowed to send up its fumes, in order that the inexorable powers of the workshop may be mollified; but the divinity of labour has only been slightly conciliated, and has looked somewhat coldly on the blandishments of its worshippers. Granted that all the benefits predicted from the Annuities Bill may come to pass; granted the value of Government security; we are still of opinion that these benefits, and that security, may be purchased at too dear a cost; and that they are not worth the loss of that manly independence, principle, and self-government, which must be the inevitable consequence of the bill.'

George Odger, the secretary of the London Trades Council, did not, however, cut a very impressive figure in this incident. Odger had allowed himself to be billed to speak at Potter's meeting, but, no doubt on finding the attitude of his colleagues to be hostile to the venture, sent a letter of support and apology for non-attendance;[1] this done, he then led the deputation from the London Trades Council to Gladstone to denounce Potter. Though Odger had a reputation for square dealing it looks as if, on this occasion, he was less than completely scrupulous in his readiness to attack Potter. The most important result of the deputation from the London Trades Council lay not in its effect on the Bill, which would not have been withdrawn in any case, but in a statement made by Gladstone during the course of discussion that 'the franchise ought to be extended to the working classes'.[2] This statement created a very favourable impression on the trade union leaders and encouraged their hopes that political reform might soon be realised.

Potter was soon in conflict again with his rivals. When in April the workers in the building trades of Birmingham were locked out and Applegarth tried to persuade them to accept arbitration, Potter intervened, advocating a more militant policy. This brought the wrath of Applegarth down on his head, and he swore to break the *Beehive* for the way in which it had treated him and his handling of the dispute.[3] Later in the year, the Birmingham employers introduced discharge certificates which were given only to men who had been of 'good conduct'. The men at once came out on strike against this system and again Potter and Applegarth clashed over the policy each thought should be pursued. Potter established a strike fund to assist the men, but Applegarth refused to permit the Amalgamated Society to contribute. Eventually the employers withdrew the objectionable certificates, but the men refused to return to work at

---

[1] *Beehive*, 19 March 1864.

'Dear Sir,—To become an apologist when duty calls is far more painful to me than the cold from which I am suffering. I have endeavoured to the best of my ability to recover sufficient stamina to enable me to assist in the good work you have so laudably undertaken, but I regret to say with no good result; in fact I would not be heard over one quarter of the hall and then in the most disagreeable sounds. Under these circumstances you will please excuse me speaking on this important occasion, though with you heart and soul in your just opposition to a government that have manifested in this attempt, their mischievous desire to cripple one of the principled liberties held by working men. That every success may attend your efforts is the fervent wish of yours sincerely, G. Odger.'

The above letter was sent to G. W. Wheeler, secretary of the meeting, who sent it to the *Beehive* for publication.

[2] *Ibid.*   [3] Cf. Postgate. R. W., *The Builders' History*, p. 214.

once. Applegarth's behaviour and indiscreet language brought a storm of angry protest from many trade unionists, and he had to face criticism within the London Trades Council[1] from Potter's supporters.

This affair had hardly had time to blow over when the conflict between Potter and the 'Junta' flared up once more. By this time it had become very difficult for any strike to succeed without the support of the London Trades Council, for the big societies were the only ones with substantial reserve funds, and they could only be appealed to for support through the Council, which was in fact dominated by their representatives. During the winter of 1864–5 the leaders of the Council made it very clear that they would only support strikes in the very last resort and for very special reasons, of which a mere reduction of wages was not one. The Staffordshire iron puddlers had come out on strike against a cut in their wages, with the support of the National Association of Ironfounders. When the employers threatened to call a general lockout if the men did not go back to work, the National Association ordered them to comply; the men, however, refused to listen to this injunction and remained out. At this stage Potter decided to step in to secure help for the striking iron puddlers; he called a meeting of the London societies to raise funds to help the strikers knowing that he would get no support from the Council if he suggested that it should help the Staffordshire men. A special meeting of the Council was called, to chastise Potter for his temerity.[2] He was denounced with impassioned invective and all kinds of accusations were levelled against him. The matter did not end there, for the strike dragged on for some time, and the leaders of the London Trades Council were extremely angry, especially when the intervention of Lord Lichfield with proposals to settle the dispute was rejected by the men;[3] Potter was not in a position to give the strikers real help to win their battle and it was eventually settled by the men having to accept the wage cut, but they managed to retain their union organisation intact. The charges made against Potter by the 'Junta' were obviously inspired by powerful hatred, for they not only accused him of being 'a strike jobber' and of 'pushing his nose into every unfortunate dispute that sprang up', but they also charged him with fraud and misuse of funds. Potter agreed that these charges should be brought before a tribunal of four impartial men, Edmund Beales, the president of the Reform League, Frederic Harrison, Thomas Hughes and Godfrey Lushington. After investigation of the

[1] *History of the London Trades Council*, p. 20. Postgate, R. W., *The Builders' History*, p. 216. See also Humphrey, A. W., *Robert Applegarth*.
[2] Minutes of the London Trades Council, 29 March 1865.
[3] *Sixth Annual Report of the London Trades Council*.

accusations these four judges exonerated him from the most damaging of the indictments.[1]

The 'Junta' were now determined to get rid of Potter, and they packed the annual delegate meeting of the London Trades Council held in August 1865, to make certain of succeeding. William Allan, it was suggested by Potter's supporters, ruthlessly prevented the delegates' credentials from being examined so as to present a challenge to those not properly entitled to vote. After a stormy meeting, the annual report, containing references censuring Potter's conduct, was passed. Potter realised that his influence inside the Trades Council had just about come to an end and refused to allow his name to be presented for nomination to the new Council, but he still had sufficient support to prevent Coulson and Applegarth from being re-elected, after some of the followers of the 'Junta' had gone home owing to the lateness of the hour. The exclusion of Potter from the Trades Council did not mean, as the 'Junta' soon found out, that he had been silenced, or that he ceased to exercise a powerful influence in the trade union movement.

Garibaldi's visit to London

We must now return to the year 1864 and glance at some of the other developments that were taking place, which were to have a profound influence on the progress of the trade union movement. The high spot of that year, in terms of publicity for the democratic cause, was, without doubt, the visit of Garibaldi to London in April. Committees in support of Garibaldi had come into being in the early sixties. The leaders of the working class were not prepared to leave support for Garibaldi to middle-class radicals and, under the influence of Potter, Hartwell and Odger, a Trades Garibaldian Committee had been formed in 1862.[2] The Committee spent two years making preparations for the visit of Garibaldi to England. During this time a large number of meetings and demonstrations were held in favour of the freedom and unity of Italy.[3] When the great day arrived elaborate plans had been made for a huge demonstration of sympathy with the famous Italian. It was one of the greatest processions the

[1] Potter was completely cleared of the six charges of fraud and misappropriation of money, and more or less vindicated on the charges involving the editorial policy of the *Beehive*. See *Beehive*, 24 June 1865. Following Potter's acquittal W. Hamlyn launched a Potter testimonial fund which resulted in £300, and an illuminated scroll being presented to Potter for his service to the working-class movement.

[2] *Beehive*, 1 November 1862. *Reynolds Newspaper*, 5 October, 2 November 1862.

[3] *Beehive*, cf. Howell, George, *Labour Legislation, Labour Movements, and Labour Leaders*.

capital had ever seen and it consisted almost entirely of working men. Every trade had its contingent, with union banners proudly flying. Except for an accident to one of the carriages containing some of the reception committee, the demonstration was absolutely orderly and went off without incident.

The excited crowds and the tremendous interest aroused among the workers by Garibaldi's visit gave the Whigs and Tories cause for alarm, for they knew that the enthusiasm was far more than a gesture of sympathy to the Italian patriot; it was a demonstration of faith in the ultimate triumph of the democratic cause at home as well as abroad.[1] When it was announced that Garibaldi had suddenly cancelled the tour which had been arranged for him of the industrial cities of the north, where the trades committees had prepared receptions similar to the one he had received in London, the news aroused indignation among the radicals. The official explanation of Garibaldi's change of plans was that members of the Government had been afraid that the strenuous exertions entailed by a tour of the north would be too much for a man of his age. It was revealed that Gladstone had been prevailed upon to convey these fears discreetly to Garibaldi; no doubt his motive in doing so was the honourable one of safeguarding his friend's health, but the Government must have been immensely relieved when Garibaldi decided that his presence in this country was unwelcome and cut short his stay.[2] What might have seemed an act of wise statesmanship to the authorities appeared maladroit to the working-class and radical movement and the Working Men's Reception Committee immediately organised a mass meeting of protest at which the leading members of the middle-class radicals were invited to speak. But, as the meeting was about to begin, the police, using force, roughly started to break it up, bringing the meeting to a close. The leaders of the men retired to talk over what was to be done next, and during the course of the discussion the suggestion was made that a National Reform League should be founded.[3] This idea was further stimulated by the reply given by the Home Secretary to a deputation sent to interview him over the breaking up of the meeting, which seemed to contain a threat to the right to hold public demonstrations in the parks of London.

The cause of the freedom and independence of Italy was not the only one followed with intense interest by the leaders of the workers in Britain. The struggle for freedom in Hungary and Poland led to the formation of committees in Britain in their support. In particular

[1] Gillespie, G. E., *Labour and Politics in England, 1850–1867.*
[2] A detailed, though perhaps one-sided, account of this incident is given by John Morley in his *Life of Gladstone,* vol. II, p. 111.
[3] Brand, C. F., *American Historical Review,* January 1925.

the revolt in Poland aroused the sympathy of the radicals, in both the working and middle classes, and it was out of the meetings in the Polish cause that the International Working Men's Association was formed.[1] A further event abroad, which was of considerable significance during these years, was the American Civil War. The British working class rallied magnificently to the cause of the Northern States, and the record of the Lancashire operatives is an unsurpassed example of willingness to sacrifice self-interest for an international ideal, for the cotton famine had plunged the county into deep depression. At a time when the commercial interests had influenced the Government to such an extent that it was on the point of intervening on the side of its friends in the South, it is probable that it was the firm determination of the workers to oppose this step that tipped the balance against intervention.[2] The Government, however, only finally abandoned the idea of intervening when it saw from the course of events that such a step would be a great mistake.[3]

Not all trade unionists were interested in these international issues; the Bookbinders, for instance, withdrew their delegate from the London Trades Council primarily because they disliked the international activities of its leaders. Of course, much of the interest in internationalism was self-interest, for the British trade unionists were concerned to prevent blacklegs from being imported from abroad and they hoped that this could be achieved through the International Working Men's Association. However, the most important result of all this international activity was that it brought the leaders of the trade union movement into close contact with the leaders of middle-class radicalism, thus paving the way for a new parliamentary reform agitation. Co-operation between John Bright and the leaders of the London Trades Council during the days of the American Civil War brought to an end the estrangement of Bright from the working class which had existed since his opposition to the Ten Hours Act in 1847, and encouraged future co-operation in political activities.

Agitation for Political Reform

By the middle of the 1850s Chartism as a movement was dead, and the trade societies were more concerned with building up their

[1] Howell, George: An article on the International in the *Nineteenth Century*, July 1878.
[2] Beloff, M., *History of Mankind*, p. 206. 'The emancipation of the slaves proclaimed by Lincoln in 1862, largely as a military measure, evoked a wave of sympathy from the British working class, even from Lancashire textile-workers hard hit by the cotton-famine, and dispelled any fear of foreign intervention.'
[3] Allen, H. C., *Great Britain and the United States*, Ch. XIII.

organisations than in indulging in political campaigns for the reform of Parliament. Nevertheless, the aims set forth in the Charter were still cherished as a desirable goal by working men all over the country. Individuals here and there, many of them ex-Chartists, continued to work in the cause of reform and hope of eventual success was not allowed to vanish. New organisations began to spring up, and in 1857 the Northern Reform Union was established, with its headquarters at Newcastle; John Kane, secretary of the Ironworkers, who was to play a leading role in the foundation of the Trades Union Congress, was one of its active supporters. During the next decade a great many similar associations were established before their work culminated in triumph in 1867. A National Reform Association already existed in London, and a North London Political Union was formed in 1859, with Benjamin Lucraft, a well-known trade union leader, as its secretary. In 1860 a Midland Counties Reform Association was active, and in the same year it was proposed at a national conference that was held at the Guildhall in London, that a National Reform League should be established on the model of the Anti-Corn Law League, but it was not until later that such an organisation was founded. The reform movement was stimulated by the proposals of Disraeli and Lord John Russell for a reform Act in the House of Commons in 1859. Reform meetings were organised all over the country, but they were sponsored more by middle-class radicals than by working men. The trade societies played no part; it was largely individual trade unionists and especially old Chartists who were active attenders at reform gatherings. In 1862 the leaders of some of the London societies, after a number of meetings, decided to set up a 'Trade Unionists Manhood Suffrage and Vote by Ballot Association' to enlist the support of the trade societies in a new suffrage campaign.[1] The Association succeeded in doing little more than keeping interest in the subject alive, but the events in the sixties, which have already been described, impelled trade unionists to consider the question of reform more seriously.

Following the incident of the Garibaldi protest meeting, related earlier, negotiations were begun to give effect to the suggestion made by George Howell that a Reform League should be established. The trade union leaders were further encouraged by Gladstone's speech in the House of Commons in favour of political reform.[2] A National Reform Union composed mainly of middle-class radicals had come into existence in 1864, with aims of reform more modest than those

[1] *Beehive*, 22 November 1862.

[2] *Ibid.*, 14 May 1864. The deputation to Gladstone over the Annuities Bill (see p. 24), which raised the franchise question, had stimulated him to refer to the need for reform; this speech had a great effect in the country.

desired by the trade unionists, and this undoubtedly encouraged the belief in the necessity of a working-class reform organisation. A small group of middle-class radicals consisting of Samuel Morley, T. B. Potter, P. A. Taylor and Edmund Beales were prepared to support Howell and his friends. Financial assistance was promised and given, but never apparently on the scale of the figures that had originally been talked about.[1] At the suggestion of Beales, George Potter sent out circulars inviting 300 representatives of working men to attend a meeting at St. Martin's Hall, Long Acre, on 23 February 1865, to consider the proposal to form a National Reform League. The League was duly constituted and at a subsequent meeting in March, Edmund Beales was elected president.[2] John Bright supported the League but never became a member because he could not accept the programme of manhood suffrage; he and many other radicals were not prepared to go further than household suffrage. Most of the well-known trade unionists were members of the League's council, including George Potter, who was then already involved in his quarrel with the London Trades Council. Potter dropped out when relations between him and other trade union leaders became increasingly strained, but Robert Hartwell, an old Chartist, and Potter's right-hand man on the *Beehive*, who had presided over the first meeting at St. Martin's Hall, remained prominent in the League. The *Beehive*, however, never failed to lay great emphasis on the activities of the Reform League, and, in fact, on all other reform movements.

After leaving the London Trades Council Potter became increasingly dissatisfied with the policy of the Reform League, which he felt was becoming too deferential to the wishes of Lord Russell and other parliamentarians engaged in the inter-party manœuvring going on over the proposed Reform Bill.[3] Potter wanted to go further than the middle-class radicals who were advising the 'Junta' and on 16 February 1866, he called a meeting of representatives of the trade unions for the purpose of forming an association of working men to obtain a 'lodger clause' in the forthcoming Reform Bill; the Reform League had decided not to press for such a clause until after the Bill had been introduced. Potter pointed out to the meeting that unless a 'lodger clause' was included, a great many workers in London would be unable to benefit from the franchise; 'it was, therefore, their duty, if they desired the vote to agitate determinedly for a lodger suffrage

---

[1] Gillespie, G. E., *Labour and Politics in England, 1850–1867*, p. 251.

[2] *The Times*, 13 March 1865.

[3] The death of Palmerston in 1865 had removed the most powerful obstacle in the way of parliamentary reform, and the issue had become one of immediate political tactics.

and not to wait until the details of the Bill were settled, but to do it at once'.[1] The meeting then went on to consider a resolution proposed by Daniel Guile, leader of the Ironfounders, 'That this meeting, consisting of working men of different trades, hereby form themselves into an association to be called the London Working Men's Association, for the purpose of promoting the interests of the industrial classes; with the introduction of a lodger clause in the proposed government Reform Bill as its immediate object.'[2] This resolution was carried and a committee was appointed to draw up a constitution. At the next meeting, which was held one week later, George Potter was elected president, Robert Hartwell, secretary, F. G. Davis, secretary of the Painters' Council, treasurer, and to the executive committee, Daniel Guile, Mr. Harvey, secretary of the Pattern Makers; Mr. Strong, secretary of the Packing Case Makers; Mr. Jenkins, secretary of the Organ Builders' Society; Mr. Conolly, secretary of the Operative Stonemasons; Mr. Leicester, secretary of the Flint Glass Makers; Mr. Bligh, a shoemaker; Mr. Upshall, a joiner; and Mr. Troup, the publisher of the *Beehive*.[3]

The L.W.M.A. started with only a small membership, but by the middle of 1867 it was claiming 600.[4] It plunged into the struggle for

[1] *Beehive*, 17 February 1866.   [2] *Ibid.*
[3] The following footnote from Mr. A. W. Humphrey's *The History of Labour Representation* is worth quoting here, p. 10.

'In their *The History of Trade Unionism*, Mr. and Mrs. Webb have the following concerning the London Working Men's Association, and George Potter, its chairman: "An expert in the arts of agitation and advertisement, Potter occasionally cut a remarkable figure so that the unwary reader, not of the *Beehive* only, but also of *The Times*, might easily believe him to have been a most influential leader of the working class movement. As a matter of fact, he at no time represented any genuine trade organisation, the Working Men's Association, of which he was President, being a body of nondescript persons of no importance" (p. 238, Ch. 5). 1907 Ed. Mr. and Mrs. Webb were writing *The History of Trade Unionism*, and Potter was, quite possibly—it is not the present writer's business to discuss the question—not a good influence, nor perhaps an influence at all, in the Trade Union world. But the Working Men's Association was—so far as the present writer has been able to ascertain—the first organisation to attempt a national movement for Labour Representation, and in view of this, Mr. and Mrs. Webb's description of the Association appears to be unduly contemptuous. Moreover, Henry Broadhurst and Joseph Leicester were signatories to the manifesto of the Association urging the working class to place Labour candidates in the field; both were rising men in the movement, and should hardly be described as "nondescript persons". That the influence of Potter is not to be judged by the space his doings occupy in the *Beehive* is, of course, quite true. Potter was the leading spirit of the paper and was its editor; and editors are quite human. Perhaps had Potter represented a "genuine trade organisation" he would not have been so much associated with the movement for working-class representation in Parliament. Trade Union work and political work, in that direction, frequently existed in inverse ratio.'
[4] *Royal Commission on Trade Unions*, p. 16, Q. 303.

reform, co-operating with the National Reform League and the Reform Union in the great demonstrations of the next two years. It had much to do with persuading the trade unionists who were suspicious of political action to join in the agitation and was at first more successful than the Reform League in winning the support of the trade unions. In December 1866, the L.W.M.A. organised a huge trade union demonstration in which it was estimated that 25,000 London working men took part, followed on the next evening by a monster meeting at the St. James's Hall which was addressed by John Bright.[1] Two weeks later the *Beehive* reported a demand from the L.W.M.A. for 'a dozen intelligent working men in Parliament'. This aim was modest enough. There was no revolutionary idea of taking over Parliament among the leaders of the working-class reform movement, which was what the upper classes feared would happen if reform were granted. Indeed the reason given for desiring 'a dozen intelligent working men in Parliament' was because it 'would enlighten middle-class opinion and clear away the mist of prejudice in which those classes are now enveloped as to the real motives and conduct of working men generally, but more especially of those, to them, terrible organisations, trade unions'.[2]

There was a good deal of strong language used just at this time in anger at the delays and obstructions being encountered in Parliament. The old Chartist agitation was often recalled and efforts to call a general strike were made. A sharp edge had suddenly been given to the interest of trade unions in bringing about the reform of Parliament by a severe drop in trade which had occurred in 1866.[3] Real wages began to fall sharply; unemployment increased, almost doubling in the year 1866–7;[4] and memories of the hungry forties were revived by bad harvests. The depressed economic situation not only increased the determination of the trade unions to secure reform,[5] it also weakened the resistance of the upper classes, the more intelligent of which had a lively fear of the consequences of refusal to make any concessions. The tremendous demonstrations that were mounted by the reform organisations, and especially the

[1] *The Times*, 4 and 5 December 1866.   [2] *Beehive*, 29 December 1866.
[3] Gillespie, G. E., *Labour and Politics in England, 1850–1867*, p. 265.
[4] Layton and Crowther, *The Study of Prices*, p. 273.
[5] The *Beehive* on the 9 February 1867 published an interesting report from their Lancashire correspondent, 'Arkwright'. '*Beehive* readers will be glad to learn that Lancashire working men are very much alive just now, not merely to questions of wages and foreign competition, and the possibility of maintaining English industrial supremacy, nor yet to the everlasting higgle between work and capital, but to that which evidently lies at the foundation of them all. They are finding out here in the North that the franchise has something to do with wages and with work, and even the very right of the workman to make a free bargain with his employers.'

Hyde Park incident, drove home the lesson that should the temper of the people really turn ugly, nothing short of civil war could prevent Parliament from being reformed.[1]

The onset of a depression usually provokes industrial unrest and 1866 was no exception, being a year in which there was a considerable number of trade disputes. The employers in many trades made a determined attempt to break the rising power of the trade unions by means of lockouts if their terms were not accepted. A bitter struggle ensued when the employers in the Sheffield file industry locked out their workers who were seeking a wage increase; other unions throughout the country came to the assistance of the file trade societies with financial help after an appeal had been made on their behalf.

The Wolverhampton Trades Council passed a resolution urging that 'the time has arrived when the trades of the United Kingdom ought to take action conjointly to rebut the lock-out system now so prevalent with the capitalists; and the dispute and lock-out in the Sheffield file trade affords an excellent opportunity for carrying this into effect'. The resolution went on to suggest that a conference of delegates from the trade societies ought to be held in Sheffield. Potter immediately gave this resolution his support and outlined a scheme for amalgamating the trades in every town in the kingdom into 'one great body, with a responsible and ruling head . . . district labour Parliaments assembling quarterly, and that these district Parliaments should then be represented in one Labour Parliament, to meet annually'.[2] The London Trades Council, which had given its support to the appeal of the Sheffield file trades for financial help, was cool to the Wolverhampton proposal, but it indicated that it would send a delegate, without committing itself to the principle involved, if a conference was held. Other trades councils and trade societies were more favourable in their response and the Sheffield Association of Organised Trades decided to call a conference to establish 'a national organisation among the trades of the United Kingdom, for the purpose of effectually resisting all lockouts'.

United Kingdom Alliance of Organised Trades

The *Beehive* considered the conference one of the most important yet convened by the trades and gave it full support.[3] It was certainly one of the largest; 138 delegates assembled in Sheffield, representing

[1] Cf. John Suart Mill, *Autobiography*, p. 290; *Henry Broadhurst, M.P.—From Stonemason's Bench to Treasury Bench*—for accounts of the breaking down of the railings around Hyde Park, which had been closed to political demonstration by the authorities.
[2] *Beehive*, 12 May 1866.   [3] *Ibid.*, 21 July 1866.

about 280,000 organised workers. George Odger was there, representing the London Trades Council, but the other members of the
'Junta' were not present, probably because of the enthusiastic support
given to the conference by the *Beehive*. Potter could not attend either,
but his associate, George Troup, represented the London Working
Men's Association. The tone of the speeches at the conference was
firm, but conciliatory, and when the delegates decided to establish a
permanent organisation, it was for defensive, not aggressive purposes. The name given to the new organisation was the United
Kingdom Alliance of Organised Trades. Its aim was to build up a
central fund from which to aid members of unions finding themselves locked out by their employers. The Alliance was organised on
a basis of dividing the country into nine regions, each of which sent
a representative to a Judicial Council which had the function of
deciding the merits of a claim for aid, the executive committee,
drawn from the Sheffield trades, being responsible for carrying out
the decisions of the annual conference and the decisions of the
Judicial Council.

The headquarters of the Alliance were in Sheffield and William
Dronfield, secretary of the Sheffield Association of Organised
Trades, was elected secretary. Dronfield, a journeyman compositor,
was an extremely able trade unionist who had been the leading
member of the Sheffield Typographical Society for many years. It
was he who had founded the Sheffield Association of Trades and had
been its representative at the 1864 conference on the law of Master
and Servant. However, Dronfield's abilities and energy were unable
to prevent the Alliance from running into grave difficulties almost
from the start.

With the growth in industrial unrest in the second half of 1866,
the Alliance found itself faced with greater demands than it had
resources to meet, and as a consequence the executive soon became
involved in disputes with those who thought they had a case for help
but had been turned down. Moreover, the Alliance had no control
over its constituent unions and the executive was soon bewailing the
fact that it was difficult to persuade them to carry out their duty when
it was against their immediate interests—a problem of central
organisation in the trade union world which has remained unsolved
to the present day—and pay the levies they had agreed upon. A
second conference in January 1867, when these problems were discussed and rules formally adopted, and a further conference in
September of that year, failed to find a solution for the difficulties of
the Alliance. Support fell off and by the end of 1867 it had lost more
than half its members. The 'Junta' and the London Trades had shown
little interest in the Alliance, so that the organisation was narrowly

based from the first. The factor, however, which contributed most to wrecking the hopes of the founders of the Alliance was an event which literally burst like a bombshell on the trade union world in the autumn of 1866.

Throughout the sixties the trade unions had been acquiring a mantle of respectability and had won the friendship of a large number of middle-class radicals; Gladstone himself, much to the chagrin of employers and diehards, had expressed his support for the work they were doing to ameliorate the conditions of their members. Suddenly, when it was reported on 15 October 1866, that members of the Sheffield Saw Grinders' Union had attempted to coerce a non-member by dropping a keg of gunpowder down his kitchen chimney, the trade unions were threatened with a nation-wide revival of animosity towards their activities. The leaders of the London Trades Council realised at once the dangers in the situation and immediately dispatched Odger and Danter to Sheffield to make an investigation. They returned with a report which exonerated the Sheffield unions from responsibility for the crime, but denounced some of the methods which had become common practice in the Sheffield trades.[1] The whole trade union world was anxious that its name should be cleared, and supported the demand of the London Trades Council that a full inquiry should be held, not only into the Sheffield outrage, but also into the way in which the trade unions were generally conducted, so that they could be completely acquitted of the horrid crimes with which they were now besmirched. When in due course it was revealed that the man mainly responsible for the dreadful crimes that had been committed in Sheffield was also the treasurer of the Alliance, the organisation suffered a severe blow, from which it never recovered.

On 16 January 1867 the trade unions received a second shock; one which brought with it more immediate danger than the first. On that day the Court of the Queen's Bench handed down a decision in an action brought by the Boilermakers' Society against its Bradford secretary for wrongfully withholding a sum of £24 from the union.[2] The Court held that because a trade union was at Common Law a body in restraint of trade it was an unlawful organisation, and, therefore, could not secure the protection of its funds. The unions had previously enjoyed this protection under the Friendly Societies Act, by depositing their rules with the Registrar of Friendly Societies, but it was now held that the unions were not covered by this Act. The effect of the decision was not only to deny to the trade unions the right to use the law courts to recover their members' money from

[1] Cf. Webb, S. and B., *The History of Trade Unionism*, p. 260.
[2] *Hornby* v. *Close*.

a defaulting official; it meant they could not, apart from the existence of a statute, 'invoke the aid of the law for any purpose whatever'.[1] All the careful work which had gone into building sound trade union administration and accumulating funds was jeopardised by the decision, and could only be retrieved by a Parliament that contained no trade union representatives, and was not even elected by the class that now stood in such dire need of its help. Not unnaturally the decision stimulated the trade unions in their demands for reform and made them more than ever conscious of the need to act politically, and it brought over to this point of view many of those conservative trade unionists who were still frowning on the idea of trade unions taking part in political campaigns of any kind.

The leading members of the London Trades Council, William Allan of the Amalgamated Society of Engineers, Robert Applegarth of the Amalgamated Society of Carpenters, Edwin Coulson of the Operative Bricklayers, Daniel Guile, of the Friendly Society of Iron-founders and George Odger, secretary of the London Trades Council, decided to form a private conference of Amalgamated Trades to undertake the defence of the trade unions from the Hornby v. Close decision; this group met for the first time on 28 January 1867.[2] The leaders of the Amalgamated Trades took this step almost certainly because they had no desire to be trammelled by carrying with them other delegates to the London Trades Council which still included quite a number of Potter's followers. Although there was no question of their integrity in wishing to see the trade union movement free from the menace which threatened it, their conspiratorial action did betray a contempt for the rest of the trade union movement, which led, in fact, to a strengthening of the influence of their detested rival, George Potter.

A Royal Commission Inquires into Trade Union Activities

The Government announced, through the Queen's Speech at the opening of the parliamentary session during the first week in February, the establishment of the expected Royal Commission to inquire into the Sheffield outrages and the activities of the trade unions. George Potter, never allowing the grass to grow under his feet, immediately organised a deputation to the Home Secretary from the London Working Men's Association to plead for the appointment of a working man on the Commission, or, if the Government would not agree to that, of one of that group of middle-class gentle-

<hr>

[1] Slesser and Baker, *Trade Union Law*, p. 17.
[2] Minutes of the Conference of Amalgamated Trades. Webb Collection, vol. XVIII, British Library of Political and Economic Science.

men who had for long been friends of the trade unions. The Home Secretary informed the delegation of the names of the members of the Royal Commission which included Thomas Hughes, one of the staunchest allies of the unions, and the Earl of Lichfield, who was known to be sympathetic to them, and said if that would meet the wishes of the deputation, the Government would consent to the appointment of Mr. Frederic Harrison—a frequent contributor to the *Beehive*—in addition.

It was not until a week later that the Conference of Amalgamated Trades, cautious and ponderous as ever, considered the establishment of the Royal Commission and also decided to send a deputation to the Home Secretary to try and persuade the Government to appoint a working man. They failed to move the Government on this point, but later they did succeed in persuading the Royal Commission when it sat to admit a representative of the trade unions to witness the proceedings.[1]

Meanwhile George Potter who was a superb opportunist, acting through the L.W.M.A., did what the London Trades Council might have done had not its leaders preferred to act as a 'clique'. He organised, with the support of Alexander Macdonald, John Kane, and most of the leaders of the provincial trades councils the largest and most representative gathering of trade union leaders ever held.[2]

[1] Minutes of Conference of Amalgamated Trades, 14 February and 21 February 1867.

[2] The Webbs' description of the conference and the events which followed it is rather misleading, owing to their inability to give Potter credit for any activity which he undertook. They wrote, 'The effective though informal leadership of the movement which the Junta had assumed during the sittings of the Royal Commission had not gone entirely unquestioned. Those who are interested in the cross-currents of personal intrigues and jealousies which detract from the force of popular movements can read in the pages of the *Beehive* full accounts of the machinations of George Potter. The *Beehive* summoned a Trade Union Conference at St. Martin's Hall in March, 1867, which was attended by over one hundred delegates from provincial societies, Trades Councils, and minor London clubs. The Junta, perhaps rather unwisely refused to have anything to do with a meeting held under Potter's auspices. But many of their provincial allies came up without any suspicion of the sectional character of the conference, and found themselves in the anomalous position of countenancing what was really an attempt to seduce the London Trades from their allegiance to the Junta and the London Trades Council. The Conference sat for four days and made no little stir. A committee was appointed to conduct the Trade Union Case before the Commission, and Conolly the president of the Operative Stonemasons, was deputed to attend the sittings. But although special prominence was given in the *Beehive* to all the proceedings of this committee, we have failed to discover with what it actually concerned itself. An indiscreet speech by Conolly quickly led to his exclusion from the sittings of the Commission; and the management of the Trade Union Case remained in the hands of Applegarth and the Junta', *The History of Trade Unionism*, p. 272.

This Conference of Trades met at St. Martin's Hall on 5 March 1867, and a committee was set up by it to watch over trade union interests in the proceedings of the Royal Commission. It also passed resolutions in support of the movement to secure the amendment of the Master and Servant Law.

At a meeting of the London Trades Council on 7 March 1867, twenty-five delegates, who were attending the St. Martin's Hall Conference, were present by invitation. Mr. Austin (Sheffield Trades Defence Committee) said that a difference appeared to exist between the convenors of the trades conference and several of the London trades that were not represented and he asked for the co-operation of the Council to heal this difference. Alexander Macdonald said that as a representative of 36,000 men he did not care who convened the conference as long as all the trade unionists joined in action. Although the conference as constituted was determined to go on with their great objects, still they desired the co-operation of the larger trades that were not represented at the conference. W. H. Wood, representative of the Manchester and Salford Trades Council, said, as one of those who were responsible for convening the meeting, that he felt it was due to himself to say that they had no idea of creating any division in any organisation. Applegarth, replying for the Trades Council, said it had been the intention of the Council to support Mr. Neate's Bill[1] and then they had thought of calling a meeting of provincial delegates to discuss that matter, but abstained on the ground of expense, and also because any agitation would play into the hands of the ironmasters and large manufacturers. He also said that Potter had attacked him in the *Beehive*, that the L.W.M.A. was not representative of trade unionists and that, therefore, he would have nothing to do with anything promoted by them.

Daniel Guile, following Applegarth, said that his views did not coincide with those of the previous speaker. Another delegate asked Applegarth to name the opponents of trade unions in the L.W.M.A., whereupon William Allan intervened to make a vigorous and rather abusive reply, but found it difficult to supply a convincing answer. Applegarth then cited Hartwell, Troup, a man named Blythe and a Mr. Brock, who was, he claimed, not a trade unionist but a meat salesman. Not surprisingly this answer did not seem to the provincial delegates to be adequate, and they appealed to the Trades Council not to allow feelings of personal jealousy to interfere with the work for a great cause. Whetstone, of the Amalgamated Society of Engineers', executive committee, then strongly defended the

---

[1] The Bill Mr. Neate proposed to introduce was a temporary measure to protect the funds of trade unions until the Commission had reported. Cf. *The Times*, 13 February 1867. *Beehive*, 16 February 1867.

L.W.M.A., saying that if the London Trades Council did not choose to invite the provincial delegates, he did not consider it right to censure the Association for doing so, and that it was time these petty jealousies were dropped. John Kane also said that he had had his fill of recriminations and asked the Council to act with them on the Committee. A resolution was moved to this effect by William Dronfield, but the meeting was closed without it being put to the vote, and Allan asked a deputation from the provincial trades to meet the Conference of Amalgamated Trades on the following day. When this meeting occurred, Allan launched a fierce attack on the sponsors of the St. Martin's Hall Conference, and stated that the Amalgamated Trades would have nothing to do with those 'meddlers' but would gladly co-operate with any trade society that was prepared to co-operate with them, and there the matter ended for the time being.[1]

The committee elected by the St. Martin's Hall Conference nominated Tom Conolly, president of the powerful Society of Operative Stonemasons, as their representative to report the proceedings of the Royal Commission. These reports were printed at length in the *Beehive* and provided a valuable service to the trade unions in keeping them informed of the doings of the Commission. Potter's committee, although it met regularly, had unlike the 'Junta', no clear conception of its purpose, and when, some weeks after the Commission had started taking evidence, Conolly was excluded from its sittings, it became rather futile and died of its own inanition. The dismissal of Conolly, much to the glee of the Conference of Amalgamated Trades, was a rather despicable incident and in other circumstances would have led to a protest from a large section of the working-class movement. Investigations of the Sheffield outrages had revealed that a prominent Sheffield trade unionist, named Broadhead, who was leader of the Saw Grinders, was culpable. Conolly at a public meeting of the L.W.M.A., held to protest against the criminal behaviour of the leaders of the Grinders, had foolishly said: 'What could be expected from a town that returned such a man as Mr. Roebuck to represent it.' Roebuck, the 'man who had passed from Chartism to Whiggery', was a member of the Commission, and at its next sitting he asked that Conolly should be excluded because of his remarks. Eventually it appears that Conolly was told that he could remain if he would sign a statement to the effect that he had not meant what he had said but had been misrepresented by the Press. This Conolly refused to do, and as a consequence he found himself refused admission to future sittings of the Commission.[2] Roebuck,

[1] Minutes of the Conference of Amalgamated Trades, 8 March 1867. *Beehive*, 9 March 1867.   [2] *Ibid.*, 6 July 1867.

although sitting in a judicial role, did not check his own violent denunciations of the trade union movement during the time the Commission was sitting, and it was no secret that he was intent on finding evidence to support his hostile opinions.

The elimination of the representative of Potter's Conference of Trades left Applegarth a clear field to organise the defence of the trade unions.[1] The leaders of the Amalgamated Trades collected evidence and supplied it to Harrison and Hughes who used it to the maximum effect. Assisted by Professor Beesly, A. J. Mundella, Henry Crompton and other middle-class friends, they were able to prove that the great amalgamated trade societies were far from being the aggressive instruments of mob rule, bent on coercing the working man to make destructive attacks on the fabric of society, which they were imagined to be by great sections of the employing class.[2]

On 20 June, as the Commission was collecting evidence in London, the news burst that William Broadhead had confessed to playing a leading part in instigating the crimes of which the trades in Sheffield were accused. Public indignation rose to a fresh height and the Press was practically united in its denunciation of the trade union movement, clamouring for indiscriminate action by the authorities.[3] All over the country the trade unions held urgently convened meetings to condemn Broadhead and dissociate themselves from his activities. The London Working Men's Association demanded that the executive of the United Kingdom Alliance of Organised Trades should be removed from Sheffield in order to free it from the taint upon it.[4] The report of the Sheffield investigation, published a few days later, showed in fact that the vast majority of trade societies in that town had not been concerned in the outrages, but this blow was one from which the Alliance never recovered.

Fortunately for the trade union movement the confidence placed in it by men like Beesly, despite the personal attacks which they had to suffer, never wilted.[5] Although there could be no excuse for Broadhead and his confederates, the evidence obtained in Sheffield showed that the methods they had employed had arisen orginally as a result of the appalling working conditions in the cutlery trades, and the lack of a proper status for the trade unions.[6] To fair-minded

[1] Humphrey, A. W., *Robert Applegarth.*
[2] See Minutes of Evidence and Reports of the Royal Commission. In his *Autobiographic Memories*, vol. I, p. 322, Frederic Harrison writes: 'They were well supplied with facts and figures by the masters' agents, but not nearly so well supplied as we were by Applegarth, Howell and Allan, the Union Secretaries.'
[3] Cf. *The Times*, 25 June 1867.
[4] *Beehive*, 29 June 1867.   [5] *The Times*, 4 June 1867.
[6] Minutes of Evidence—*Royal Commission on Trade Unions.*

men these revelations emphasised the importance of securing legislation which would permit the trade unions to carry out their legitimate functions without the constant fear of imminent destruction through the hostility which they encountered especially in the courts. The loyal friends of the trade unions continued with their work of addressing meetings and writing articles putting the case for the recognition of trade unions as essential organisations for the protection of labour, and for setting them free from the restrictions which inhibited their rightful activities.

Effects of the 1867 Reform Act

The outburst of anti-trade unionism might have gone much further had it not been for the campaign for the extension of the franchise which was then rising to its climax with the Reform Bill before Parliament. The attention of important sections of the middle class was concentrated on this event, and the association which had developed with the working-class movement discouraged attacks on trade union leaders they had come to know personally and for whom they had some respect. After the Reform Bill had been carried— with the lodger franchise[1] for which Potter had consistently fought —the report of the Royal Commission was bound to appear in a different light; since politicians of both parties were interested in canvassing the working-man's vote they could not easily accept the advice given by the most bitter opponents of the trade union movement. The arrival on the Statute Book of the Reform Act of 1867, was, therefore, of tremendous significance to the trade union movement, for it ensured that in future the interests of the trade unions could not be ignored by the legislature, and that in turn the trade unions would become increasingly concerned with what went on in Westminster and Whitehall.

Though the Reform Act was an accomplished fact, the London Working Men's Association was not prepared to rest content; its leaders then wished to see that the vote won for working men was used by them to secure the return of some of their own class to the House of Commons. The question of Labour representation had already been raised several times by the secretary, Robert Hartwell, but it was not until October 1867, after the Reform Act had been carried, that the Association passed resolutions which called upon workmen to unite to procure the return of working men to Parliament; to create a Working Men's Parliamentary Election Fund; and urged co-operative societies, trades councils, and other working-class organisations to join together to find and contest winnable seats.

[1] Cf. Woodward, E. L., *The Age of Reform, 1815–1870*, p. 180.

These resolutions were followed a month later by the issue of a manifesto on the 'Direct representation of Labour in Parliament'. One of the aims of the manifesto was to dispel the idea that there was any intention of setting up a working-class party. What the signatories of the manifesto had in mind was the return of a few men who understood the working men's point of view from experience, and who would co-operate with such middle-class radicals as Thomas Hughes, Henry Crompton and John Stuart Mill. The contents of the programme of the Association published in the manifesto as 'Our Platform' were largely such as could be supported by most of the radicals; there was nothing revolutionary or socialist about them. The programme included demands for the extension of the franchise to manhood suffrage; the ballot; the return of working men to Parliament; the abolition of class legislation and the evils it had engendered; the termination of Church rates; an improvement in the relations between landlord and tenant; a national and unsectarian system of education; legal protection for trade union funds; reduction in the hours of labour; the development of co-operatives; improved housing for the working class; and emigration to the colonies.[1] Most of these demands reappeared in resolutions after the Trades Union Congress was founded, remaining constantly near the heart of the policy of social reform that was to be pursued by the leaders of the trade union movement for the next twenty years.

As the London Working Men's Association made preparations to put working men in the field when the first election after the Reform Act should take place, Potter, still smarting under his defeat by the Conference of Amalgamated Trades over the Royal Commission, launched two new projects in an attempt to recapture the leadership of the trade societies. Early in 1868 he put forward a scheme for a meeting between twelve representatives selected by the leading trade societies, and twelve representatives selected by the employers, who would try to arrive at a national agreement that would put an end to strikes and lockouts. At the same time, in an editorial in the Beehive, he offered the olive branch to the Conference of Amalgamated Trades, asking them to appoint one of the representatives.[2] The Conference of Amalgamated Trades would have nothing to do with the idea, for tactically it would have been entirely to Potter's advantage if they had accepted, and after a certain amount of initial support the plan seems to have collapsed. Potter's second

[1] Beehive, 16 November 1867.

[2] Ibid., 14 March 1868. The change in Potter's attitude was probably brought about by difficulties into which his paper had fallen. The Beehive had never been free from financial worries and the enterprise was running short of capital. Potter no doubt hoped to restore its fortunes by winning back some of the support that he had lost.

scheme was to call a 'National Parliament of Labour' in London during May; however, shortly after he had propounded this idea it was learnt that the Manchester and Salford Trades Council had already taken steps to do precisely the same thing. Thereupon, after correspondence with W. H. Wood, the secretary of the Manchester and Salford Trades Council, Potter decided to postpone the calling of the Labour Parliament until after the Royal Commission had reported, and in the meanwhile to support the Trades Congress to be held in Manchester.[1]

The 'Junta' was doing a most effective job in presenting the case of the trade unions to the Royal Commission, but little was known of this by the remainder of the unions. The northern trade societies, in particular, had little trust in the leadership of the 'Junta'. The Committee appointed by the St. Martin's Hall Conference, which represented a considerable section of the trade unions, had, in fact, severely criticised the 'Junta' for the arrogant manner in which it sought to impose its leadership on the movement and for its refusal to make common cause with the rest of the unions in a united body. The attitude of the 'Junta' was not determined by purely egocentric motives; there was a genuine distrust of Potter and the northern trade union leaders, and a strong fear that if they were not pushed into the background the case of the unions might be jeopardised before the Royal Commission.

The conflict between the 'Junta' and Potter and the provincial union leaders went deeper, in fact, than a difference of opinion over the tactics to be used in presenting the union case to the Royal Commission. The 'Junta' disapproved of militancy and were concerned lest their members should be stimulated by a desire to emulate the strike activities of other unions, and so endanger their carefully accumulated funds. The other unions were in turn critical of the pacific, conciliatory policy of the 'Junta' which seemed to them to savour of defeatism. This difference in basic attitudes led to a sharp disagreement over the Bill prepared in 1867 by Mr. Neate, and supported by the 'Junta', which sought to give protection to the funds of the unions. Potter and his friends wanted to see legislation that would also protect the unions from legal decisions that had made the right to strike extremely dangerous to exercise.[2] The 'Junta' felt that an attempt to extend the Bill at that juncture might

[1] *Ibid.*, 11 April 1868.
[2] It had, for example, been held in *Rex* v. *Druitt* (1867) that 'abusive language and gestures' and acts 'calculated to have a deterring effect on the minds of ordinary persons, by exposing them to have their motions watched, and to encounter black looks', would be criminal offences. See Hedges and Winterbottom, *The Legal History of Trade Unionism*, p. 51.

undermine the impression of the unions that they were seeking to give the Commission, and the public.

Neate's Bill did not succeed in passing the House, and the 'Junta' then sought to promote a Bill drawn up with the help of Beesly, Harrison and Crompton which was designed to establish firmly the legal status of the unions and so make impossible prosecutions based on the doctrine of conspiracy; the Bill also contained provisions which would give the unions the legal protection they desired for their funds. This Bill also aroused controversy among the leaders of the unions, since to some of them it did not go far enough in protecting the right to strike. In the event it proved too late in the session to achieve much success with the Bill; the text was, however, circulated to the trades and they were urged to bring it to the attention of candidates in the forthcoming parliamentary election on the new franchise.

The 'Junta' indicated that they would be prepared to call a national conference to consider the situation as soon as the Royal Commission had presented its report, or the Government had introduced a Bill. Neither Potter nor the provincial trade union leaders were willing to wait until the 'Junta' in its wisdom deemed that the time was ripe for a conference; indeed it would have been surprising if they had been prepared to place much faith in the intentions of a group that had consistently shown its contempt for their wishes.

Manchester and Salford Trades Council Organises Trades Congress

There were good reasons for calling a conference of the Trades in 1868. More than a year had elapsed since the St. Martin's Hall Conference. Much had happened in the meantime; the Reform Bill had been passed, an election on the new register would soon be held, and the Royal Commission was approaching the end of its labours. The idea that the Manchester and Salford Trades Council had in mind when it issued its invitation to the trades was the establishment of an annual Congress of the unions rather than a special conference along the lines of those that had been summoned in the previous few years.

The purpose of the proposed new organisation was not to strengthen the industrial bargaining power of the trade unions, nor were the Manchester and Salford Trades Council intent on establishing a political body similar to that of the London Working Men's Association, on a national scale. Their aim was to found a Congress at which unionists would meet annually and discuss those questions which were of outstanding importance to the trade union movement, thus clarifying their own minds and, at the same time, through the publicity which they hoped their deliberations would receive, enlighten the public as to the objects of trade unions and the intelligence and respectability of their leaders. The invitation circular sent to the trades stated that:

> the Congress shall assume the character of the annual meetings of the British Association for the Advancement of Science and the Social Science Association, in the transactions of which societies the artisan class are almost excluded; and that previously carefully prepared papers shall be laid before the Congress on the various subjects which at the present time affect the trade societies, each paper to be followed by discussion upon the points advanced, with a view of the merits and demerits of each question being thoroughly ventilated through the medium of the public press.[1]

The Social Science Association had been founded in 1856 by a group of lawyers, clergymen, doctors and a few figures well known for their public works. It held annual proceedings in a different town each year, papers being presented by authorities to the various sections into which it divided itself. The Social Science Association secured a good deal of publicity during its annual conference and published voluminous reports of its proceedings—which are a mine of information on social problems in the middle decades of the nineteenth century. Its *Report on Trade Societies and Strikes*, published in 1860, was widely noticed and served the trade unions well, for its conclusions were that they were not so dangerous to the health of society as middle-class opinion had in the past assumed. In the early years of the Association well-known Labour leaders such as William Newton, Alexander Campbell and George Jacob Holyoake had been asked to present papers, but by the middle sixties this practice seems to have been given up, probably because the trade unions were becoming increasingly politically conscious.[2]

One of the last trade unionists to read a paper before the Association was William Dronfield, but his contribution was omitted from the report of its proceedings and so were the speeches of several trade society members who took part in the discussion, although a paper strongly critical of unions was published. It appears that Dronfield resented this discrimination and told the story of the way in which

[1] This circular was printed in the *Beehive* on the 21 March 1868. Since this chapter was written Mr. A. E. Musson, *The Congress of 1868*, has discovered a copy of the original circular in the files of the Manchester Typographical Society. The Webbs reprinted what they believed to be the only surviving copy of the original circular which they had found in the *Ironworkers' Journal*. It is clear that they had not carefully read the *Beehive*, or they would have noted that the version which they printed was a subsequent and slightly altered one, which had appeared in the *Beehive* on 25 April.

[2] Cf. *Annual Proceedings of the Social Science Association*.

he had been treated to Nicholson and Wood, president and secretary of the Manchester and Salford Trades Council, and also, like Dronfield, journeyman compositors. It was apparently Nicholson who, having heard Dronfield's account of the hostile attitude of the Social Science Association, suggested that the trade societies ought to hold their own congress.[1] The proposal received the immediate support of Nicholson's colleagues and preparations were at once begun to organise the first working-men's trades union congress. It was originally proposed to hold the Congress on 4 May 1868, but it was subsequently decided to postpone the gathering until 2 June, which fell in Whit-week. The first invitation had merely invited Trades Councils and Federations to send delegates, but, probably owing to a fear of inadequate support, the second circular extended the invitation to individual societies as well. Following the practice of the Social Science Association, a list of subjects for discussion was set out in the invitation and papers were solicited from the delegates.

When the Trades Union Congress assembled at the Mechanics' Institute in Manchester, on 2 June 1868, W. H. Wood, secretary of the Manchester and Salford Trades Council, was elected president and he announced that there were present thirty-four delegates representing 118,367 members. Most of the important Trades Councils except Glasgow and London were represented along with the Ironfounders, Malleable Ironworkers, Masons, a number of small trade societies and the London Working Men's Association. The only well-known individuals there were William Dronfield from Sheffield, John Kane of the Ironworkers, T. J. Wilkinson of the Flint Glassmakers and George Potter. The Congress was ignored by the 'Junta' and the London Trades Council. It was not by any means as representative a gathering as the famous St. Martin's Hall Conference in 1867.

The suspicions entertained by the provincial trade societies of the self-appointed London Conference of Amalgamated Trades were made crystal clear by the opening address of the president, W. H. Wood. The president expressed the fear that the Royal Commission might not have been given a full picture of the rights to which the unions were entitled. Wood said:

> Although a Royal Commission had been sitting for some time taking evidence as to the operations of the various trade societies of this country, they conceived neither the Royal Commission, nor the press, nor the public of this country had been enabled to ascertain thoroughly the claims on which these trade unions were founded, the principles they sought to initiate, and the objects for which the various associations were established.

[1] See Musson's account of this incident: *The Congress of 1868*.

It was thought that the deliberations of the Congress would help to remedy this situation.

It had been conceived that the amount of intelligence possessed by the working classes would tend to dispel the ignorance which had hitherto prevailed in reference to their operations, and place trade unionists before the public in that position which they believed they merited.[1]

After the Congress had listened to the president's address, it discussed a paper by Potter on the necessity of trade unions; the second day was devoted to considering the regulation of the hours of labour, and the third day technical education. The Royal Commission was not discussed until the fourth day of the Congress and then John Kane severely attacked the composition of the Commission, which he described as a body of 'lawyers, landed proprietors and manufacturers' and declared that it was not 'worthy of the confidence of trades unionists'. Other delegates spoke in the same vein and a resolution of no confidence in the Commission was prepared by a committee elected by the Congress, but George Potter said that:

it would place them in a very wrong and false position throughout the country if they were to pass a direct motion of want of confidence. Some of the Commission were respected by trade unionists and they had done some things which trade unions approved of, therefore they could not consistently pass a resolution entirely condemnatory of their proceedings. They should wait until the report of the Commission was presented, and if it proved to be unsatisfactory, then would be the time to pass a vote of censure and ignore them altogether.

He ended this statesmanlike speech with a redrafted version of the original resolution which was carried by 25 votes to 6.[2] The point most disliked by the delegates was the refusal of the Commission to admit the Press to its hearings—its operations being likened to the Star Chamber. No attacks were made on the Conference of Amalgamated Trades but the delegates were critical by implication that they had been kept in the dark as to what was occurring at the sittings of the Commission. The feeling of the delegates was that they had no choice but to support the Conference of Amalgamated Trades and this view was embodied in a resolution moved by John Kane:

That this Congress pledges itself in the names of the respective societies represented to aid and assist the London Committee of Amalgamated Trades in their laudable efforts to secure the legislation and protection of trade union funds, and hereby declares its determination to continue

[1] *Beehive*, 13 June 1868.   [2] *Ibid.*

the agitation, and to make the support of this measure a condition for candidates for parliamentary honours before giving any pledge or vote at the ensuing election.[1]

There is no evidence that Potter either spoke or voted against this resolution, which was carried; thus he tacitly agreed to support the Conference of Amalgamated Trades. Another resolution a short time later, moved by Peter Shorrocks of the Manchester Trades Council, following his paper on the law of conspiracy, intimidation and picketing, resolved that 'the influence of this Congress shall be directed to aiding the London Conference of Amalgamated Trades to alter the third section' of the Combination Act of 1825. Thus, although the Manchester Congress had been ignored by the leaders of the Amalgamated Trades, it played an important part, through the attitude it adopted, in furthering the process of healing the breach in the trade union movement which had existed since 1864.

During the week of its sitting the Trades Union Congress heard and discussed papers given under the following titles, 'Trade Unions an Absolute Necessity', 'Trade Unions and Political Economy', 'The Effects of Trade Unions on Foreign Competition', 'Regulation of the Hours of Labour', 'Limitation of Apprentices', 'Technical Education', 'Courts of Arbitration and Conciliation', 'Co-operation', 'The present inequality of the Law in regard to Conspiracy, Picketing, Coercion, etc.', 'Factory Acts Extension Bill', 'The Legalisation of Trade Societies'. The quality of these papers was of a high standard and showed that there was no lack of ability among these ordinary working men, who were the leaders of their trade societies.

There were strong demands from the Congress for every effort to be made to reduce the hours of work, and all trades were recommended 'to adopt the apprenticeship system, and in all cases to limit the number of apprentices if found desirable to protect the interest of any trade'. A scheme of voluntary arbitration devised by Mr. A. J. Mundella was described by the delegate from Nottingham and received the warm approbation of the rest of the delegates, who decided, however, that to make it perfect it should be made compulsory in all trades by Act of Parliament. The Congress was not satisfied with the Factories Act of 1867, and wanted to see the principle of compulsory inspection extended so that it would apply to all places where women and children were employed.

These demands for legislative action indicate that although the idea behind Congress of a working-man's Social Science Association

---

[1] The *Beehive* and the *Manchester Guardian* gave fairly full reports of the daily sessions of the Congress, but the main London papers practically ignored it, and none of them recognised it as having any significance.

was accepted by most of the delegates, they were too near the core of life to allow it to remain merely that. They could not dispassionately and remotely consider questions of immense importance to their everyday lives without also considering practical steps to remedy the social evils from which they suffered. When the proposal to hold a congress annually was discussed they passed a resolution which pointed clearly in the direction in which the Trades Union Congress was to move in future years. It stated: 'That it is highly desirable that the trades of the United Kingdom should hold an annual congress for the purpose of bringing the trades into a closer alliance, and to take action in all *parliamentary*[1] matters pertaining to the general interests of the working classes.'

The delegates to the first Congress, having decided that the gathering should be an annual event, then agreed that the second Congress should be held in Birmingham and be organised by the Trades Council of that town with the help of a committee of five, which they elected.

Though the delegates to the first Trades Union Congress were not aware of it they had created a national trade union organisation that was to have a life span far exceeding that of any of its predecessors. The National Association of United Trades, founded in Sheffield in 1845, and its successor, the United Kingdom Alliance of Organised Trades, founded in 1866, had petered out because they were mainly concerned with pooling the resources of the trade unions to provide mutual aid against 'lockouts'. This eminently sensible idea was in practice, however, extremely difficult to carry out. Small trade unions were ready enough to receive aid when in difficulties, but only too often they were reluctant to pay their dues. The larger and more powerful societies, while not opposing central organisation for industrial bargaining purposes, were suspicious of them, and preferred to maintain their autonomy, fearing that they might find themselves dragged along by a small union into activities for which they had no relish.

The increase in the bargaining strength of the trade unions which became apparent in the 1850s and 1860s stimulated the employers to counter-measures by the use of the 'lockout' and the 'document', which in turn led the smaller unions to seek greater unity for their self-protection. The larger unions were inclined to be more cautious and preferred to follow as far as possible a policy of non-provocation and so avoid the need to fight a battle unless it was forced upon them. The first Trades Union Congress had been mainly concerned with questions that were of a political nature, but as might have been expected this did not entirely meet with the approval of George

[1] My italics.

Potter and his friends. Commenting on the Congress a week later the *Beehive* regretted:

> that the Congress separated without the adoption of a resolution recognising the necessity of a National Labour League, to include all trades societies throughout the kingdom, in a federated system something similar to that now in existence amongst the States of North America . . . we hold that no trade society, however powerful, can, by itself, successfully resist the united action of the employers in that trade, backed as that combination always is by capital and sustained, as it generally is, by the press and public opinion.[1]

Potter, as usual, was wanting something of both worlds. He still hankered after the powerful central organisation that could defeat the employers by militant strike action, and, at the same time, saw that events had opened new opportunities. In his demand for a strong federal organisation, he was in fact posing a problem for the trade union movement which is still unsolved, and is of major importance at the present day.[2] Ought the common interest of the whole movement to override the sectional interest of each union, and if so, how could this be accomplished? Since the movement is empirical the abstract answer has never really mattered; the significant question has always been whether some sectional autonomy should be surrendered to the T.U.C. in order to overcome this or that particular problem facing the trade unions. The results have been the consequence of many factors, the least important of which has been that of following any particular theory of organisation.

The Trades Union Congress was made possible as a permanent institution by the development in trade organisation and the change in the political climate that brought in its train the Reform Act of 1867. The passing of the Reform Act and of the Master and Servant Act in the same year were tangible proofs of the power of political organisation; they provided visible evidence of the new status that had been attained by the working class. Political reform opened up the prospect of working men becoming Members of Parliament and laid the foundations of mass democracy in which the pressure-group tactics of mass organisations such as the trade unions assumed an entirely changed significance. Nothing marks more clearly the advance in social importance of the trade unions than the Sheffield

[1] *Beehive*, 13 June 1868.
[2] Bell, J. D. M., *Industrial Unionism: a Critical Analysis*. 'In short now that the long-awaited social transformation is upon the trade unions they must effect greater co-ordination of their activities . . . in the looser and more acceptable form of something approaching a "British Trade Union Federation". Flanders, Allan, *British Trade Unionism*. "What is needed is the application of the federal principle to the whole Trade Union World."'

Outrages in 1866. This incident, which suddenly blew up like a storm cloud, threatened to deluge the trade unions with a flood of public hostility and seriously hinder their progress, but caused instead only a momentary disturbance and had in the end exactly opposite consequences. A decade before this could not have happened, for such a passion of hatred would have been unleashed that the trade unions would have been set back a long way. The Royal Commission, which was ordered to investigate the activities of the trade unions, proved to be not so much a menace as an opportunity, which was quickly grasped, to display to the world the civic virtues and economic desirability of organised labour.

The Royal Commission compelled the leaders of the trade unions to examine their own tactics and immensely strengthened the policy of the leaders of the Amalgamated Trades, whilst at the same time it emphasised the need for political action to impress on Parliament and the public the need for providing a legal framework in which the trade unions could function in a legitimate way to protect the interests of their members. Thus the stage was set for the coming into being of a new type of central trade union organisation which would exercise a different function from that of the old type trades alliance; one that was mainly political and propagandist in orientation, rather than one which had as a primary objective the pooling of resources to fight the employers on the industrial battle front. Nor were its objectives the reorganisation of society on revolutionary lines. The fundamental principles of Victorian capitalism were accepted; the organisation strove, not for Utopian goals, but for practical reforms that appealed to the good sense of progressive citizens of all classes.

CHAPTER II

THE FOUNDATIONS LAID

In the months that followed the first Trades Union Congress the attention of the leaders of the working class was concentrated on the impending dissolution of the old House of Commons and the first electoral combat on the reformed registers. The London Working Men's Association, under Potter's leadership, worked hard to see that those entitled to vote for the first time should not lose the opportunity by failing to ensure their inclusion on the electoral roll.

A more difficult problem, however, was that of finding constituencies where working-men candidates would have some chance of winning. Wherever it was proposed that a working-man candidate should stand, the local Liberals refused to accept him. 'No sooner did a working-man's candidate make his appearance before any constituency than he was either directly snubbed by the pseudo Liberal politicians and journalists or damned with faint praise' wrote the *Beehive* with some justifiable anger. In the event, the trade union movement failed to rally the necessary support to put many working-class candidates in the field and only three went to the polls.[1] W. R. Cremer, one of the founders of the Amalgamated Society of Carpenters and Joiners, fought Warwick, but was defeated by a combination of Liberals and Tories. George Howell, with the support of the local working-men's association, stood at Aylesbury, but came bottom of the poll against a Liberal and a Tory. The third candidate, Edward Owen Greening, did not really rank as a trade union nominee, but was, however, well known in the Co-operative movement. He suffered the same fate as the others, being defeated by the Liberal. The other working-class candidates, George Odger, Alexander Macdonald, and Robert Hartwell, were either edged out by the Liberals, or had to retire before polling day because of a lack of funds. This election, in fact, ended the career of Hartwell, who had to take money from his opponents because his supporters failed to raise the funds necessary to pay his election expenses.

The unfortunate fact was that the working-class movement was ill prepared for the election. The trade unions had shown considerable

[1] For the full story of the working-class candidates in this election see Humphrey, A. W., *The History of Labour Representation*. Cole, G. D. H., *British Working Class Politics, 1832–1914.*

apathy and reluctance to find the funds necessary to support independent candidates in the face of opposition from the official Liberals. The election resulted in a heavy defeat for the Tories, to whom the newly enfranchised working-class voters felt no particular gratitude for passing the Reform Act. The leaders of the working class were not under any illusion, however, as to the meaning of the substantial Liberal majority. The *Beehive* editorial, reviewing the result of the election, stated: 'At present as in the past, the only interest unrepresented in the new Parliament will be that of the industrial or labour interest', and went on to draw the moral that working men should learn a lesson and be better prepared at the next election.[1]

Some weeks prior to the election, Peter Shorrocks, who had acted as secretary to the first Trades Union Congress, circulated to the trade societies the accounts of the Manchester Congress, accompanied by a statement urging them to do everything possible to put 'men of your own class' up for election. 'Few, too few, are at present before you as candidates ready to fight your cause in the only place where you can look for justice. It is your duty to support them in their struggle with unswerving fidelity; let not party politics turn you from your duty.'[2] It was not 'party politics' which let the working-class candidates down so much as the fact that there was no real organisation to support them and no strong belief that they stood any chance of winning. It would have required far more than this single exhortation in the name of the T.U.C.—which, of course, at this stage of its development was not strong enough to lead a campaign —to have defeated the vested interests of both parties, against which the working-class candidates had to struggle.

The healing of the breach between Potter and the 'Junta' was carried a stage further when, after the Congress of 1868, the leaders of the London Working Men's Association approached the Conference of Amalgamated Trades and the London Trades Council with the suggestion that a joint meeting should be held to consider the passing of a Trade Union Bill to rescue the unions from the insecure position in which they found themselves as a result of judicial decisions. After considerable hesitation, the Conference of Amalgamated Trades agreed to sponsor such a meeting with the L.W.M.A. and the London Trades Council, the conference was eventually held in October. It discussed the Bill drawn up by Henry Crompton and Professor Beesly for the Conference of Amalgamated Trades which had been moved in the Commons late in the last session. There was a good deal of opposition to the third clause, which dealt with violence and intimidation, and the representatives of many of the trades wanted further time for consideration. On Potter's suggestion

[1] *Beehive*, 28 November 1868. [2] *Ibid.*, 19 September 1868.

the conference was adjourned for a week. When it reassembled, there was still uneasiness on this clause and a committee was set up to go into the question with the sponsors of the Bill. The committee subsequently reported that they had agreed to support the Bill as it stood, but the general election prevented any progress being made with it.

Report of the Royal Commission

Early in the new year there were rumours that the report of the Royal Commission would soon be published, but it was not until March 1869 that it made its appearance. The Majority Report was much less damaging to the trade unions than they could have expected when the Commission began its work, and was a tribute to the effective way in which the trade union case had been conducted by the Conference of Amalgamated Trades and by their friends on the Commission. The Majority Report recommended that legal recognition should be given to the trade unions on condition that they eschewed action that would lead to breach of contract or to discrimination against non-unionists. It also recommended that protection should be given to the funds of a trade society provided that it did not permit its rules to contain clauses involving the limitation of apprentices, or the use of machinery, or place any ban on the introduction of contract or piece work.

In contrast, the Minority Report produced by Harrison, Hughes and the Earl of Lichfield, advocated the sweeping away of all legal discrimination against working men and their trade unions. In principle, the minority argued, the treatment of a workman before the law should be no different from that of any other member of the community. Nor should any act done by more than one person in combination be a crime if the same act when done by a single person would not be a crime. The Minority Report was backed up by a masterly analysis of the trade union movement and the changes necessary in the law to put this report into effect. Frederic Harrison rendered further service to the trade unions by drafting a Bill which avoided the disputed third clause of the old Bill and which, would, if carried, have put into practice all the proposals which he and his colleagues had made in their Minority Report.

The Conference of Amalgamated Trades had promised to call a national conference when a Trade Union Bill was before the House, but they failed to do this, circulating instead a memorandum explaining their intentions with respect to the Bill. Though Potter was now anxious to promote the unity of the Labour movement, he and his friends decided to convene a meeting of those trade societies which had been present at the St. Martin's Hall Conference in 1867. Hughes, Harrison and Crompton, who were in attendance to explain the Bill to the assembled delegates, had urged the 'Junta' to co-operate with Potter in the interest of securing the desired legislation. The 'Junta' refused to take second place to Potter, but a letter was received from Robert Applegarth, inviting all the delegates at this meeting to attend a further meeting the following week, convened by the Conference of Amalgamated Trades, to secure united action in support of the Bill, which was to be introduced in the House of Commons by Hughes and Mundella, and the invitation was accepted by all those present.[1] William Allan took the chair at this next meeting and a committee of five was elected by the delegates, including Potter, to act with a committee of five from the Conference of Amalgamated Trades to secure the passage of the Bill.[2] This meeting can be taken as marking the end of the feud between Potter and the Conference of Amalgamated Trades; it was reported in the *Beehive* with complimentary remarks about Allan, and from then on there are no more references to the 'clique'. However, the same cannot be said of the attitude of the 'Junta', which, although no longer one of overt criticism, was marked by an extreme caution and suspicion of the activities of the other trade societies and their leaders.

The Government had no intention of accepting the Hughes-Mundella Bill and did everything they could to resist it without actually committing themselves to outright opposition on principle. In June a huge demonstration was held by the trade societies at the Exeter Hall, presided over by Samuel Morley, M.P., and supported by many other radical members of Parliament. At this meeting George Potter said the 'Government might find itself in trouble if this Bill was not supported . . . the working men who had supported the Liberal Party deserved to have this measure passed.'[3] This meeting was followed up by a deputation to Mr. Bruce, the Home Secretary, of 150 trade union leaders representing, they claimed, over 600,000 organised workers. The Minister, however, insisted that only the Government could deal with the problem, and urged that the Hughes-Mundella Bill should be withdrawn, so that the matter could be considered during the recess.[4] In face of growing pressure from the trade unions, and after the second reading of the private Bill, the Government agreed to introduce a temporary measure to protect union funds until it was ready with its proposals for a comprehensive Trade Union Act in the next parliamentary session. Hughes and Mundella agreed, on the firm promise of Government action, to press their private Bill no further.

[1] *Beehive*, 24 April 1869.   [2] *Ibid.*, 1 May 1869.
[3] *The Times*, 24 June 1869.   [4] *Beehive*, 3 July 1869.

The Second Trades Union Congress

Meanwhile, as all this activity, concerned with the promotion of the Trade Union Bill was going on, preparations were being made for the second Trades Union Congress to be held in Birmingham. The date originally arranged was 23 May, but this had to be changed to 23 August because of the trades' meetings in London in support of the Bill. When the second Congress opened at the Oddfellows Hall, Temple Street, Birmingham, there were present 47 delegates, representing 40 trades councils and trade unions, with a combined membership of over a quarter of a million. The leaders of the Amalgamated societies again remained aloof, but on this occasion the London Trades Council was represented by George Odger, and George Howell was present as delegate from the Number 4 Lodge of the Operative Bricklayers. There were also a number of delegates from non trade union working-class organisations including the Labour Representation League, the Marylebone Working Men's Association and the Birmingham Barr Street Reform Association.

T. J. Wilkinson, of the Flint Glass Makers' Society, was elected as president of the Congress, and the procedure followed was roughly the same as that of the year before. Papers which had been prepared by representatives of the various societies were read and then discussed. The Congress assumed more of a political shape than it had done at Manchester, as more attention was given to formulating and passing resolutions expressing the policy the delegates desired the trade union movement to pursue.[1]

George Potter was called upon to deliver the first paper, which was entitled 'The disorganisation of Labour' and was largely devoted to the evils of drink, an unusual subject for Potter, and one which earned him a certain amount of criticism from W. H. Wood who thought it inappropriate—though other delegates seemed to appreciate it. *The Times* avidly seized on the opportunity to point out in a leader on the Congress that if working men curbed their inclination towards drink there would be little need for trade unions to improve their conditions of life.[2] This theme, which was a common one in the Press of that time, was part of the obdurate middle-class belief that it was through individual action alone that a workman could raise his standard of living, and that by placing his faith in combination he was acting under a dangerous illusion. That too much drink was a menace, not only to individuals, but to the effectiveness of trade unions, was recognised by most of the leaders,

[1] For full reports of this Congress see *The Times*, *Beehive*, and the *Birmingham Daily Post*.
[2] *The Times*, 30 August 1869.

many of whom were staunch abstainers and fully supported the Club and Institution Union, which, under the leadership of the Reverend Henry Solly, was endeavouring to rescue the working class from the public houses; they would not, however, accept the view that it was drink and drink alone that condemned the workman to his lowly economic and social status.

William Owen, secretary of the Operative members of the Potteries Board of Arbitration, then read a paper on the subject of Arbitration and Conciliation. There was at this time a strong sentiment in favour of these procedures as an alternative to strikes and lockouts, but there was also a good deal of scepticism as to their results. The resolution moved in support of the establishment of 'Courts of Arbitration and Conciliation' was strongly attacked by Conolly of the Stonemasons, who said: 'that arbitration would more surely than anything else degrade working men to the lowest possible level'. This view was regarded by the 'Junta' type trade unionist as an old-fashioned opinion—it became modern again later when trade unions learned that arbitration did not yield the results for which they had hoped—and it was not acceptable to the other delegates, who proceeded to pass the resolution.

Owen, who was also the editor of the *Potteries Examiner*, one of the outstanding working-class newspapers in the country, read a second paper on 'Working Class newspapers and the best means for their establishment'. During the discussion Potter revealed that the circulation of the *Beehive* had fluctuated since its foundation between 4,000 and 9,000 copies per week and that the total capital expended over the eight years of its life to that date was no more than £2,500. The sales of the paper were tiny, by modern standards, but it was surprisingly widely read and there can be no doubt that its influence had been far greater than the modest scale of its circulation would suggest.

Peter Shorrocks introduced what was perhaps the main subject of the week; the Royal Commission and the legislation on its report. He suggested that the only legislation the trade union movement required, with the exception of a law to protect trade union funds, was legislation to bring about the total abolition of all laws affecting combinations. This sweeping opinion received a certain amount of support from Kane, Wood and Potter. However, George Howell, realising that such a policy would leave the trade unions at the mercy of unlimited interference from the courts, moved an amendment on the lines of policy advocated by Frederic Harrison, and adopted in the Trade Union Bill, precisely to prevent this danger. After a discussion which showed that there was a good deal of mental confusion among Shorrocks' supporters, who were not, it seems, strongly opposed to the Trade Union Bill, both resolutions were passed. It was then proposed by Owen (Potteries Trade Council) and Howell (Operative Bricklayers) that a committee should be formed 'to prepare a statement in accordance with this and other resolutions to go out to the world, to the Trades Unions and legislators. . . .' Shorrocks, Owen, Howell, Clare (Dublin Association of Trades) and Bailey (Preston Trades Council) were elected, together with the officers, Kane, Wilkinson and McRae. Odger was also proposed but he declined the invitation to stand: 'because at the time he was afraid its interests would clash with the amalgamated trades'.[1] The committee does not appear to have carried out even the modest task which was assigned to it, since there is no record of its achievements. W. R. Cremer thought that Congress should go much further and appoint a committee to watch and report upon any measures introduced into Parliament which were likely to affect the unions, and after Congress had decided to support the miners' demand for a new Mines Regulation Act, Odger, Conolly, Potter, Harry, Cremer and Howell were appointed, according to the *Beehive*, on the last day of Congress, as a Parliamentary Committee to watch the progress of a Bill through the House if one were introduced in the next session.[2] No reference was made in the report to the attitude of Odger towards this committee. There is, however, no evidence that the committee held any meetings or did anything to forward the resolutions carried by Congress. In the circumstances there can be little doubt that the failure of both committees was due to the suspicious attitude of the 'Junta'. Nevertheless their election was another step forward in the evolution of the Trades Union Congress, and presaged the establishment at a future Congress of a Parliamentary Committee that really became an effective body.

One of the most interesting papers delivered during the week had been given by A. A. Walton, an old Chartist and secretary of a Co-operative Building Society, on 'The best means to secure the Direct Representation of Labour in the Commons House of Parliament.' George Howell and W. Harry of the Chelsea Working Men's Association also contributed papers on this theme. Walton was the first person to suggest to the Trades Union Congress that working men should form their own party; however, he apparently considered that it should be under the aegis of the Liberals.

The Session of the Reformed Parliament [said Walton] was allowed to pass without a single member having suggested an enquiry into the cause of more than a million and a half working men in England being

[1] Davis, W. J., *The British Trades Union Congress—History and Recollections*.
[2] *Beehive*, 4 September 1869.

in a state of compulsory idleness. That he viewed as an unmistakable proof of the want of sympathy in the House for the wants of the working classes. . . . The conditions of the working man had been neglected, and not a single working man had been permitted to enter Parliament in the labour interests. What therefore should they do? They should unite, form a working man's party, and at all future elections where two Liberal candidates had to be elected they should insist upon nominating one, allowing the middle class to choose the other. . . . They should in future disregard the delusive cry, 'Don't divide the Liberal interest,' but having one object in view, nothing should divert them from its accomplishment.[1]

Although the Congress accepted the principles of Walton's paper in a resolution, several years elapsed before the first trade union members were elected to the House of Commons and it was thirty years before the T.U.C. really put Walton's advice fully into practice.

A resolution was also proposed in support of Sir Charles Dilke, who had given notice that he intended to introduce a Bill in the Commons to secure the payment of members. A number of delegates, however, considered that it would not be appropriate for working men to ask for their representatives to be paid, and the resolution was withdrawn on grounds of impropriety. The leaders of the unions were not willing to admit to a standard of political morality any less strict than that which the middle class had adopted. They were, however, anxious to increase their political influence and a resolution was then moved and carried in support of the Labour Representation League.

This body had been established earlier in the summer of 1869, following the dissolution of the National Reform League in the previous March. Discussions between the leaders of the Amalgamated Trades, Potter and his followers, and W. R. Cremer and his associates, had led to the formation of a united body with R. Marsden Latham, a barrister, as its president, William Allan as its treasurer, and Lloyd Jones as its secretary. The policy of the Labour Representation League was:

> to secure the return to Parliament of qualified working men . . . (and) . . . where deemed necessary, recommend and support as candidates from among the other classes such persons as have studied the great Labour problems and have proved themselves friendly to an equitable settlement of the many difficult points which it involves.

The formation of the Labour Representation League was another fruit of the reconciliation that had taken place between Potter and the leaders of the Amalgamated Trades. It was also part of the

[1] *The Times*, 30 August 1869.

general trend towards the Liberal-Labour alliance which profoundly influenced the working-class movement during the next twenty years.

Other questions of importance considered by the Congress were education, emigration and co-operation. On the first it carried a resolution 'That this Congress believes that nothing short of a system of national, unsectarian and compulsory education will satisfy the requirements of the people of the United Kingdom. . . .' Emigration was another cause which Potter advocated with ardent zeal, having formed the Workmen's Emigration Society, which had the object of ameliorating the condition of the working class at home by persuading the Government to assist in transporting unemployed men of good character overseas to people the Empire. Mass unemployment led the trade unions to give strong support to emigration as a means of removing surplus labour and of bringing supply into line with demand. After listening to papers on the benefits of co-operation and industrial co-partnership, read by Howell and Holyoake, Congress passed an ambiguous resolution, to meet the criticism of those who demanded a more militant policy from the trade unions, to the effect that strikes had secured advances in wages and shorter hours of work, but that at the same time they had brought poverty.

Before Congress adjourned it was decided that the expense of holding it would be met by an equal levy on each society represented, R. McRae, the secretary, announcing that the Congress the year before only cost each body represented six shillings and eightpence —which was indeed a modest sum even in those days. It was further decided after discussing the merits of Nottingham and London, that the venue of the next Congress should be London and that the London Trades Council should be asked to undertake the responsibility of organising it. The reason for the choice was that the delegates desired to lobby Members of Parliament to obtain their support for the resolutions carried by Congress. The Trades Union Congress was beginning to assume the political leadership of the trade union movement and it wanted to assert its authority at the heart of affairs. There was still, however, a good deal of suspicion and dislike among the provincial delegates towards the leaders of the Amalgamated Trades. They felt they were being led by a group of autocratic, aloof Londoners, who cared little for the desires of the small provincial societies. In an interview with the Webbs, William Owen told them that Allan and Applegarth rather looked upon the Trades Union Congress as an intruder upon their preserves; that they were individualists, in favour only of legislation to remove the disabilities under which labour suffered, and strongly against special legislation for work people.[1] They felt that skilled working men were of an equal social status with the middle class, and should, therefore, not seek special privileges which would single out the working class as different and, by implication, put them into a lower category than other sections of the community.

The Trade Union Bill

Towards the end of the parliamentary session of 1869 the Government rushed through, as promised, a temporary Trade Union Funds Protection Act as a stop-gap measure, but the trade union movement had to wait until 1871 before the Government revealed its full intentions. The Trade Union Bill, when it finally appeared, had been in all but one aspect, worth waiting for. It admitted the case made out by the minority report and made proposals to change the law in all the major aspects this report suggested. The objects of a trade union would not, henceforth, because they were in restraint of trade, render any member of a union liable to a criminal prosecution for conspiracy or, for that reason, render void any agreement or trust. Every trade union would be allowed to register its rules, unless they were in violation of the criminal law, and the unions would be given protection for their funds without any alteration in their fundamental legal status. Thus the unions were given the legal standing they required, but they were protected from irresponsible litigation by Clause 4 which prohibited any court from entertaining legal proceedings instituted with the object of directly enforcing, or recovering, damages for the breach of internal agreements and those made between two unions. The weakness of the Bill, from the point of view of the trade unions, was in the 'third clause'. This was the clause which dealt with threats or the use of violence, intimidation and molestation, persistent following, and watching and besetting. This clause at once raised the deepest apprehension in the trade unions, for the terms in the Bill were undefined and unlimited in their application, which immediately suggested that any form of picketing during a strike might be interpreted by the courts in such a way as to make it impossible.

Up to the time the Bill was published the London Trades Council, under the domination of the Conference of Amalgamated Trades, had fought shy of convening the Trades Union Congress. The Council had decided in June 1870, that it would wait until the Bill came before Parliament in the following session.[2] There can be no doubt that the leaders of the Amalgamated Trades were reluctant

[1] Webb Collection, Section A, vol. I.
[2] Minutes of the London Trades Council, 15 June 1870.

to convene the Congress because they preferred to hold the reins of power in their own hands. The minutes of the London Trades Council reveal that it was pushed into summoning the Congress in 1871 because of the insistent demands that were coming from the provincial trades councils.[1] It was finally summoned in such a hurry that complaints were made at the short notice given. The leaders of the Amalgamated Trades had reluctantly realised that the 'third clause' could only be fought by rousing the whole trade union movement to undertake a nation-wide campaign for its elimination.

The Congress met on 6 March 1871, in the Portland Rooms off Tottenham Court Road (not far from the site of the new headquarters of the T.U.C.). Fifty-seven delegates assembled, from 49 societies, representing a membership of almost 300,000. Among the delegates were all the leading figures in the trade union world, and it was for the first time a really fully representative Congress. Daniel Guile took the chair and welcomed the delegates on the first day until the Congress elected George Potter chairman. It was not the Potter of yesterday, but the Potter who had made his peace with the great trade union 'bosses'; who had in fact bowed to their power and wisdom.

Potter's Final Triumph

The election of Potter as president of the 1871 Trades Union Congress was his final triumph in the trade union movement, although he continued to attend as a delegate for some years. The leaders of the Amalgamated Trades could afford to let him have this success since Potter no longer wielded the same influence as of old; he was not even master any longer of his own creation the *Beehive*, for he had had to seek the assistance of the 'Junta' to rescue it from financial difficulties. The leaders of the Amalgamated Trades had agreed to help on condition that they appointed as joint managing editor the Reverend Henry Solly who, with Potter, was made responsible to a managing committee with William Allan as chairman. The price of the paper was reduced and its format changed. The new *Penny Beehive*, which appeared for the first time in February 1870, was a very different production from the old *Beehive*. Under Solly's influence the paper adopted a patronising tone; peddling the panaceas of abstinence and religion, with virtue as its main stock in trade, it came more and more to look and read like a cross between a parish magazine and *Tit-Bits*. Sales fell and Solly was dropped; with Potter once more in sole charge, the *Beehive* improved, but though it survived until 1878, it never again became quite the same

[1] Minutes of the London Trades Council, 27 January 1871.

vigorous working-class paper as of old. Potter's editorial ability seemed to have considerably deteriorated, but that may have been due to the fact that he no longer had as his assistant Robert Hartwell, who had done much in the old days to make the paper the success that it had been.

The militancy for which Potter was famed had mellowed with experience and now there was little difference between his outlook and that of the leaders of the Amalgamated Trades. He had always held fundamentally the same Liberal-Labour beliefs as most of his contemporaries in the trade union world, but his rivals had realised the importance, and grasped the technique of building up strong trade unions earlier than he. Potter, at the head of a tiny union, looked to a united trade union movement rather than to sectional strength as the salvation of trade union weakness. He had supported almost every strike in the past, partly out of idealism, partly because the tradition of aggressive action was deeply ingrained in the building trades, but mainly because, with his unbounded energy, wherever anything was happening he wanted to be in on it. With no great problems of organisation to worry about, responsibility did not weigh heavily on his shoulders. Potter's style, on the platform and in the Press, inclined towards the flamboyant—later it often became verbose and obscure—when compared with that of Allan or Applegarth. As editor of the *Beehive* it was his business to comment on every event of interest to the trade union world; it is not then surprising that he was accused of 'pushing his nose into every unfortunate dispute that sprang up', especially since he could not resist taking a more active part in any event than that of a mere commentator. It should not be forgotten that when Potter first achieved fame he was only in his middle twenties, and he was only twenty-nine when he founded the *Beehive*. Like other young men he was impatient, and with his ability and taste for the dramatic, he found it difficult to keep out of the public eye. William Allan and George Odger were much older men than Potter, although Applegarth was a year his junior. The difference between Applegarth and Potter was clearly one of personality as well as outlook. Applegarth was the most able trade union leader in the country, and most certainly had a better brain than Potter, or any of his contemporaries; he thought more clearly and was cool and calculating in his methods. The hatred he cherished for Potter, for he never forgave him,[1] was mainly the result of a rather intolerant contempt for what he regarded as weakness in Potter's character.

The conflict between Potter and the leaders of the Amalgamated

[1] Applegarth in the 1890s described Potter to the Webbs as 'a fraud from the first'. Webb Collection, Section A, vol. I.

Trades ended in one sense with the victory of the latter but in another sense it continued long after they had passed from the Congress scene. Throughout the history of the trade union movement there have been those who put more faith in militant strike action than in careful organisation and cautious administration. Both types have their place and their value, and have a healthy effect upon one another. Potter's great contribution to the development of the trade union movement has been overshadowed by the limelight thrown on the leaders of the Amalgamated Trades. The significance of the policy pursued by Allan and Applegarth has undoubtedly been great in the growth of the trade union movement, but so, too, have been the qualities possessed by Potter, which have done much to maintain a spirit of drive and vigour.[1]

Potter's presidential address to the Congress had both a prophetic and a valedictory ring about it when he said that he did not think he would be far wrong if he were to say that on that day they entered upon a new epoch in the history of trade organisations.[2] By the time the Congress was over it had consolidated itself as the national organisation of the trade union movement.

The main item on the agenda was, of course, the Trade Union Bill, and Congress spent a good deal of time discussing the report of the Conference of Amalgamated Trades, which was read to the delegates. Feeling was running high, and some of the delegates in their dislike of the 'third clause' would have been prepared to oppose the whole Bill. A deputation was sent to the Home Secretary to protest against the objectionable section of the Bill and the Congress adjourned early each day so that the delegates could attend the House of Commons in order to lobby members.

Although the Trade Union Bill was the most momentous topic discussed during the week the Congress dealt with many other important questions. The Mines Regulation Bill was considered and amendments to it proposed. The truck system was condemned and a demand for its abolition made; taxation, unemployment, education, limitation of apprentices, arbitration, convict labour, emigration,

---

[1] The Webbs, in concentrating on the achievements of the 'Junta' dismissed Potter as unimportant. R. W. Postgate in his study of the Builders gives a more objective account of Potter, but his remark that 'No clear-minded revolutionaries supported Potter; only the old worthies of trade unionism who carried on their lodge business mainly in the bar', is misleading. Closely associated with him in many of his activities were such nationally important trade union leaders as Alexander Macdonald, John Kane and Daniel Guile; those middle-class radicals who did so much for the trade union movement at this time respected his ability and gave him their support as readily as they did the 'Junta'. Moreover, Potter had also a great following among provincial trade unionists.

[2] *Beehive*, 11 March 1871.

shorter hours, the employment of women and children in agriculture, co-operation, Labour representation in Parliament and the international fraternisation of labour were all topics that came before Congress during the week. Samuel Plimsoll was permitted to address the delegates on the need for legislation to protect the lives of British seamen sailing in unseaworthy ships. He received the full support of the Congress, and an appeal was made to all the trade unions to make a contribution towards Plimsoll's campaign.

The Parliamentary Committee

The most outstanding progress made by this Congress lay in the election of a Parliamentary Committee that was empowered to co-operate with the London Trades to watch over the passage of the Trade Union Bill and if necessary to convene another Congress. The members of the Committee were Alexander Macdonald, Lloyd Jones and Joseph Leicester, with George Potter as chairman and George Howell as secretary. William Allan, who had been elected treasurer of the Congress, was later appointed treasurer of the Parliamentary Committee.[1] On the Tuesday following the end of the Congress, the Parliamentary Committee met and drew up a letter embodying the resolution passed by Congress threatening to oppose the whole Bill unless the obnoxious clause was withdrawn. The resolution read:

> That this Congress having reconsidered the Trades Union Bill in connection with the explanations and representations of the Home Secretary, hereby resolve that, whilst they are anxious to obtain from Parliament any legislation that may enable them to carry forward their efforts on behalf of the legitimate interests of their fellow workmen, refuse in any way to sanction any Bill that, in its provisions, pre-supposes criminal intentions or tendencies on the part of English workmen, as a class.[2]

The letter, signed by Potter, Howell, Macdonald, Leicester and Jones, was printed and in the hands of every M.P. by the following Thursday. The result of this letter and the deputation that had been sent to the Home Secretary by Congress the week before, led to a Government decision to split the Bill into two parts.[3] The first part contained all the positive proposals supported by the trade unions, and the second the criminal clauses. This prompt action by the

[1] Howell Papers, Ref. 331·88.

[2] Report of Congress Committee. *Beehive*, 18 March 1871.

[3] This concession by the Government did not give much satisfaction to the trade unions, but it proved to be of considerable significance and greatly helped them in the long run.

Parliamentary Committee led to some protest from the Conference of Amalgamated Trades on the ground that before any action was taken they should have been consulted. Not wishing to create any further friction, the Committee sent an explanatory note to the Conference of Amalgamated Trades, and the secretary, George Howell, was instructed to arrange a meeting between the two committees. The leaders of the Amalgamated Trades revealed that touch of arrogance and spite, which occasionally marked their actions, by all failing, with the exception of Daniel Guile, to turn up at the meeting after it had been arranged; a message was sent instead to say that they accepted the explanation of the Parliamentary Committee. Eventually a joint meeting was held and a second statement issued, which was practically a replica of the first, signed this time by Allan, Applegarth, Potter and Howell.

These published protests were followed up by the lobbying of Members of Parliament. The Committee was, however, taken by surprise by an amendment introduced in the House of Lords which aimed at making all picketing impossible. An immediate interview was requested with the Home Secretary, who was, however, unable to receive a deputation owing to illness, but the Committee was met by the Under Secretary of the Home Office, with the result that the Government agreed to oppose the amendment when the Bill was reported back to the House of Commons. In spite of the intervention of the Government the Lords amendment was sustained by the Commons, most of the business interests on both sides of the House voting for it. In those days, party whips had much less control over members than they have today and a government could not then count on party discipline to push any of its proposals through.

The result of this debate on the amendment and the division list were published in the *Beehive*, which commented:

> We leave the list to the judgment and concerted action of the trade societies in those constituencies whose members spoke and voted against us, and that too after the Government had moved to disagree with the Lords Amendment, thus voting against their party in the interest of their class, and decidedly to the detriment of trades societies instead of striving once for all to do even scant justice to the great mass of the intelligent and industrious artisans of the country. . . .[1]

> The analysis of the voting lists shows that nearly all of the representatives of the great centres of industry either voted for the Lords' amendments or absented themselves from the division lists. Let the organisations note this fact and compare it with the professions of the hustings where most of them promised to vote an honest Trades Union Bill.[2]

[1] *Beehive*, 15 July 1871.   [2] *Ibid.*

This was the first time in which the division lists had been published with the specific intention of influencing the way in which the working class would vote at the next election, and it marked a new stage in the growth of democratic government in Britain. It was a warning to the Liberals that they could no longer ignore the demands of the trade unions now that working men had been given the vote.

As soon as the two Acts reached the Statute Book the Conference of Amalgamated Trades decided formally to wind up. The Conference no longer had any *raison d'être* now that the unions had been given the legal protection for their funds which they had set out to achieve. Moreover, the Trades Union Congress was by then well established, and its Parliamentary Committee, responsible to the whole trade union movement, would in future be doing the kind of work which the Conference in its more limited field had done so well since 1867. There was need to end the division in the trade union movement between the metropolis and the provinces, in order to mobilise the full strength of the movement to secure the repeal of the Criminal Law Amendment Act, and this could only be done through the Trades Union Congress and its Parliamentary Committee, which was now representative of trade societies throughout the country.

After the passing of the Acts the Parliamentary Committee secured the services of the barristers, Henry Crompton and Rupert Kettle, who in the past had often proved their friendship for the trade unions, to report and analyse the cases that might occur. The new Acts took effect from 1 January 1872, and the Committee thought that the movement ought to take stock of its position so that it would be prepared to meet the problems that were likely to arise. It was, therefore, decided that the next Congress should be called— only nine months after the previous one—to coincide with the beginning of the new era in the legal status of the unions. It was also thought that January was a good month in which to meet because it coincided with the opening of a new session of Parliament, and the Committee was anxious for a brief on its future activities.

Congress Adopts Legislative Programme

At the fourth Congress, which was held in Nottingham, 77 delegates were present, representing 63 societies whose combined membership numbered over 250,000.[1] W. H. Leatherland, president

[1] The number of delegates and societies they represented had increased, but the total membership was apparently some 35,000 smaller. This fall in membership was fortuitous, since no proper system of affiliation had been devised; if, therefore, a society was unable to be represented by a delegate its membership was not counted.

of the Nottingham Trades Council, was elected president of Congress. This was the commencement of a custom that was to last for twenty-eight years. It was thought that as the Trades Council of the Town where Congress met was responsible for making all the organisational arrangements for the hospitality of the delegates during the week of their stay, it was only fitting that the Council should have the opportunity of proposing one of its outstanding members as the president of the Congress, thus conferring an honour on the Council and the man.

An interesting aspect of the Parliamentary Committee's report was the statement of income and expenditure since the previous Congress.[1] The Committee had established its main duties during the year, carrying out the instructions of Congress by lobbying members, deputations to ministers and publicity campaigns. All these activities had been carried out at the minimum cost, and the work of the officers and also of the Committee had been entirely voluntary without even any recompense for personal expenditure in which they might have been involved. Important steps towards remedying this unsatisfactory situation were taken by the Nottingham Congress.[2]

The introduction of the Committee's report, which had not been circulated at this stage, gave rise to a question as to how it was that it had been printed in a newspaper before the delegates had been made aware of its contents. The delegates were angry at what they considered to be a breach of faith on the part of the Committee in

[1] Report of Congress Committee. *Beehive*, 13 January 1872.

EXPENDITURE TO 8 JANUARY 1872.

		£	s.	d.
By Cash.	1,000 Circulars to M.P.s and others, Postage, Envelopes, etc.	3	11	4
,,	Printing ditto	1	7	6
,,	Trade Union Bills and Digest	5	0	0
,,	Deputations, etc.	1	1	0
,,	Stationery, Postage and Transit	1	7	10
,,	Kenny's Printing Bill (last Congress)	1	15	0
,,	Arbitration Bills, Reports	3	4	0
	Total Expenditure	17	6	8
	Balance in hand		4	8

4 January 1872.

George Potter, *Chairman.*
William Allan, *Treasurer.*
George Howell, *Secretary.*
Alexander Macdonald.
Lloyd Jones.
Joseph Leicester.

[2] Howell Papers, Ref. 331·88.

permitting a hostile paper to comment on the report before it had been endorsed by the Congress. They were only quieted when the president explained that a copy had been given to a reporter in confidence on the understanding that nothing would be published until after Congress had accepted it. A lively discussion then followed on the report, which was finally approved.

The delegates empowered the Parliamentary Committee to raise the necessary funds to carry out the tasks laid upon them by Congress and in future to pay the secretary an honorarium for his services. Congress then considered how it could improve the conduct of its business. Complaints had been made the year before about the nature of the subjects chosen for discussion, and the unnecessary length of some of the papers read. At the 1869 Congress it had been decided to restrict the time for reading any paper to twenty minutes, but this was not easy to carry out in practice. It was now decided that it was a waste of the time of Congress to listen to papers on such subjects as 'The Necessity of Trade Unions'. In future papers should be few in number and it was agreed that before one could be read it must be first submitted to the Parliamentary Committee for approval. The delegates made it clear that they had no intention of allowing Congress to be a mere debating society; it was to be a genuine Parliament of Labour that legislated for the trade union movement and not simply a talking-shop. Although the practice of reading papers was to continue, the conception of the Trades Union Congress as a working man's 'Social Science Association' was about dead. It would still be the place where the voice of the working man was heard; but it would be the place where it was heard democratically deciding the policy that his representatives on the Parliamentary Committee would endeavour to carry out.

Congress had not yet permanent standing orders to govern the way in which it conducted its business, and much time was squandered each year in the tedious discussion of procedure. To prevent an annual repetition of this petty squabbling the Parliamentary Committee was instructed to draft permanent standing orders for the approval of the next Congress.

After these details had been settled the Congress turned its attention to the Criminal Law Amendment Act, and the Trade Union Act. Mr. Mundella and the Honourable Auberon Herbert, at the request of Congress, both addressed the delegates. They outlined the action they had taken whilst the Bills were before Parliament, and gave the unions' representatives some advice as to the course of action which they should follow in the future. All the leading figures at Congress took part in a rather lengthy debate and a resolution by which 'this Congress pledges itself to use every legal means to secure the repeal of the Criminal Law Amendment Act' was carried. Then John Kane, supported by George Howell, proposed:

> That to give practical effect to the resolution moved by Mr. Walton and adopted by this Congress we recommend that united action shall be taken by Trades Societies and working men generally to resist the return to Parliament of any candidate who may refuse to pledge himself to vote for the repeal of the enacting clauses of the Criminal Law Amendment Act, and in the meantime this Congress recommends the working class electors of the United Kingdom to use their influence with their present members of Parliament to vote for the repeal of the enacting clauses of the Criminal Law Amendment Act.[1]

In addition to passing these resolutions, Congress, at the suggestion of Alexander Macdonald, agreed that a petition should be laid with the House of Commons and a memorial on the question sent to the Prime Minister.

A subject which aroused almost as much interest as the Criminal Law Amendment Act was that of workmen's compensation. The legal position of workers injured during the course of their employment was such that, owing to the doctrine of 'common employment', it was impossible for them to obtain compensation from their employers, even when it was shown beyond a shadow of doubt that an accident had occurred because of the negligence of the employer or of one of his agents. The position of the worker was intolerable under these circumstances; an employer could expose his servants to the greatest risk of life and limb without the least worry about the consequences. The law in mid-Victorian times often failed utterly to give the workman elementary justice, but this was one of the worst examples. It was assumed that a man was not compelled to take a job and that he undertook employment with his eyes wide open; therefore, that when he accepted the contract of employment, he accepted with it the risks the work entailed. The very suggestion that employers should be liable for accidents that occurred in their workshops aroused a storm of indignation from outraged industrialists, and generally throughout the Press. Every kind of argument was used to justify the freedom from liability enjoyed by the employers. It was suggested that if the Government should be so foolish as to interfere with the situation, as it existed under the Common Law, it would bring ruin to British industry. Manufacturers would be unable to meet overseas competition, profits would fall to zero and unemployment would mount, thus throwing the economic life of the country into the depths of depression. The argument was seriously advanced that discipline would disappear and employers would be

[1] *T.U.C. Annual Report*, 1872.

at the mercy of the demands of the mob. It was implied, and it was perhaps believed, that on the morrow of a Workmen's Compensation Act, workmen everywhere would rush to injure themselves simply in order to secure compensation. The resolution carried by the 1872 Congress in favour of a change in the law marked the beginning of a campaign that was waged for many years against these prejudices before the validity of the case made out by the trade unions was acknowledged.

When the Nottingham Congress came to a close it had been decided by the delegates that the Parliamentary Committee should be charged with the pursuit of the following legislative programme during the next session: a Bill to repeal the Criminal Law Amendment Act; a Mines Regulation Bill to improve safety measures; an Abolition of Truck Bill, to include the enforcement of weekly wage payments without deductions; and support of the Conciliation and Arbitration measure recently drafted for the Committee by Mr. Kettle. On the last day of the Congress Alexander Macdonald moved the following resolution embodying the main decisions of the week,

> That a Committee be appointed by this Congress to be called the Parliamentary Committee, for the purpose of taking any action that may be necessary to secure the repeal of the penal clauses of the Criminal Law Amendment Act, the Truck Act, the getting of a proper Compensation Act and to watch over the interest of labour generally in the proceedings of Parliament, the Committee to continue in existence till the next meeting of Congress. That the Committee shall consist of nine members. Further, that it be remitted to the constituencies to see if they will make a levy per member or pay voluntarily such a sum as will maintain the action of the Committee, and that the answers of the Trades Councils and Trades Societies be returned to the Secretary of the Committee, within four weeks from the close of the proceedings of Congress, so that the Committee may take the action necessary to realise the objects of their appointment.[1]

Congress accepted his resolution with the addition that the treasurer, William Allan, should also sit on the Committee.

The problem of the influence of the platform over the delegates is a serious one in all democratic assemblies; it is apt to rouse strong passions, which provide a healthy check on the dictatorial tendencies inherent in all executives. It is apparent that the Congress had had the benefit of firm guidance throughout the week from its Standing Orders Committee, which met nightly to discuss the next day's session. The minutes of the Standing Orders Committee show that it had decided, in private, who it wanted on the Parliamentary Committee, and had then suggested to Congress that the choice should be

[1] *Ibid.*

endorsed. The suggestion that the delegates should simply accept, without alteration, the list of names proposed to them, led to some resentment, which was expressed in a long discussion. It was finally decided that others should have the right to be nominated and that an election ought to take place. Eventually eleven names were submitted and voted upon. George Potter and Thomas Birtwistle[1] were at the bottom of the poll and so were not included in the Parliamentary Committee for the forthcoming year, those elected being A. Macdonald, W. Hicking, W. H. Leatherland, W. Leigh, J. Kane, D. Higham, G. Thomas, T. Halliday, G. Howell. Following the election it was agreed that William Allan, the treasurer, should also have a seat on the Committee. Later in the day, when the Parliamentary Committee met for the first time, it elected Alexander Macdonald as its chairman for the following year. Though in the nature of things it was inevitable that the work of the Parliamentary Committee had to be administered from London, the lasting distrust of the provinces had to be assuaged by the election of a provincial secretary, W. Hicking, as well as a corresponding London secretary, G. Howell.

Two precedents were set at Nottingham, one spiritual and the other social, which soon became part of the tradition of the annual meeting of the Trades Union Congress. The Reverend F. Morse, a Nottingham clergyman, was asked to give a short religious address to the delegates; the Congress sermon became thereafter a regular annual feature. It was at this Congress, too, that the delegates were accorded the first municipal reception, the Mayor of Nottingham inviting them to a banquet at the Town Hall. The occasion was not without incident, for a few delegates were republicans and refused to rise to drink to the Queen, much to the horror of some newspapers.[2]

The growing national importance of the Trades Union Congress was reflected in the greatly increased attention paid to it by the Press. A large number of reporters were present, including two from the Paris Press, and most of the leading morning and weekly papers carried lengthy reports of the main debates.

By the time the next Congress came round—it was held in the New Assembly Rooms, Leeds, in January 1873—the Parliamentary Committee was able to present a report to the delegates which showed a substantial increase in support from the trade societies. Including a small balance left over from the 1872 Congress, income, as a result of the appeal sent out to all the unions, had increased from

---

[1] Birtwistle was to become well known as a powerful leader of the cotton operatives.

[2] George Howell recorded that the majority responded to the loyal toast with fervour.

£41 10s. 0d. in the previous year to £295 16s. 6d., and expenditure had gone up from £16 11s. 4d. to £200 12s. 10d. Of this the honorarium paid to the secretary, including an allowance for his expenses and office rent, accounted for £113 17s. 0d.

The delegates attending the Leeds Congress numbered 132, representing 140 societies with an aggregate membership of 750,000, compared with 77 delegates, representing 63 societies with an aggregate membership of 255,710 at the 1872 Congress. This great increase in the strength of the Trades Union Congress reflected the tremendous expansion of trade unionism that had taken place throughout the country during the past few years. This growth rested primarily on the 'great cyclical expansion from 1868 to 1873',[1] but the successful political action of the trade unions, and the passing of the 1871 Trades Union Act, with all the publicity these events occasioned, undoubtedly contributed to the rapid rise in membership. Although the boom petered out towards the end of 1873, real wages continued to rise and trade union membership went on climbing for another year before it was halted. 'It is possible', say the Webbs, 'that between 1871 and 1875 the number of Trade Unionists was more than doubled.'[2]

As the Webbs have pointed out, there was a certain similarity in this trade union boom and that of 1832–4, but there were also considerable differences. In both cases trade union organisation was carried to agricultural labourers and women workers; in both cases attempts were made to supersede the private capitalist by the establishment of co-operative enterprises. The significant difference between the two periods lies in the fact that in the 1870s the trade union movement had become well established as a national institution. It no longer sought, as in the earlier period, to overthrow the State through the abolition of the capitalist employer; it was now content to confine its activities to securing a more equitable share of the good things that the mid-Victorian economy had to offer. The efforts to establish co-operative enterprises by some unions in the seventies were isolated examples and attracted few imitators, and although the Trades Union Congress had gone on record as being in favour of co-operative production, it did nothing to stimulate the advance of the trade union movement in that direction. With the onset of depression the trade union experiments in co-operative production came to an end; the downward turn of the trade cycle was also fatal to the National Agricultural Labourers' Union, whose delegate, Joseph Arch, claimed 40,000 members at the 1873 Congress, and 100,000 at the Congress of 1874; numbers which thereafter dwindled rapidly.

[1] Rostow, W. W., *British Economy in the 19th Century*, p. 24.
[2] Webb, S. and B., *The History of Trade Unionism*, p. 326.

Standing Orders Adopted

Together with its report, the Parliamentary Committee presented to the 1873 Congress the standing orders which it had drawn up as instructed. After some discussion these were adopted. Rule One read: 'The Congress shall consist only of Delegates representing bona fide Trades Societies, and Trades Councils, and similar bodies, by whatever name they may, for the time being, be called.' By this rule the Credentials Committee, which under the new standing orders was the Trades Council of the town in which the Congress was held, was given the responsibility of deciding whether an organisation came within the definition of bona fide. It is no longer left to the local trades council to scrutinise credentials, but the bona fide test has remained in the constitution of Trades Union Congress ever since; no attempt has been made to add to its definition, but over the course of time the decisions of Congress have given it a fairly concrete meaning.

The duties of the Parliamentary Committee were limited to (1) watching over 'all legislative measures directly affecting the questions of labour, and (2) initiating, whenever necessary, such legislative action as Congress may direct, or as the exigencies of the time and circumstances may demand'. No regular income was guaranteed to the Committee in the form of an affiliation fee fixed by Congress. It was simply left to the officers, who were given authority under the direction of the Committee 'to solicit subscriptions, donations, or levies, for the purpose of defraying the expenses incurred by such Committee; but the mode of payment shall be left optional with each society as to whether it shall pay by levy or donation'.[1]

This loose form of organisation did not meet with the approval of all delegates; some desired to see the trade union movement placed on a federal basis, and others were jealous of the growing authority of the Parliamentary Committee. The London Trades Council, which had resuscitated its activities after the dissolution of the Conference of Amalgamated Trades felt that its natural right of leadership in matters that concerned Westminster was being undermined, and suggested that the Congress should merely appoint provincial delegates to co-operate with it, thus avoiding the need to appoint a Parliamentary Committee. Provincial trade union leaders, however, had no intention of abandoning their control over the Parliamentary Committee to a purely London body and the suggestion was dropped.

The Parliamentary Committee was able to report that the Mines Regulation Bill was now an Act of Parliament. It was not all that the

[1] *Report of Trades Union Congress*, 1873.

miners desired, but it introduced new principles of State intervention that could be developed in the future. The Committee detailed the other work it had done with each of the Bills it had been instructed by the previous Congress to promote. The report provided a useful source of information for the delegates and served to guide them in framing their instructions to the Parliamentary Committee for the coming year. George Howell was able to read to the delegates a letter which the Committee had received from the President of the Board of Trade, informing them that the Government was preparing a Bill to amend the law relating to compensation for injuries to workmen. Congress was, on the whole, well pleased with the efforts made by the Parliamentary Committee, and at the conclusion of the discussions on the report a resolution of thanks was carried unanimously.

The trade unions were anxious to consolidate the gains made by the Engineers and other trades in achieving a nine-hour day, after a struggle in 1872, and instructed the Parliamentary Committee to press during the next session of Parliament for a nine-hours Bill, to cover women and children. Congress again spent a good deal of its time on the Criminal Law Amendment Act. The determination of the delegates to secure the repeal of this Act had been reinforced by the sentences passed by Mr. Justice Brett, shortly before Congress assembled, on striking London gas stokers.[1] It was decided, as an immediate step, to send a petition to the Home Secretary, praying for the mitigation of the sentences imposed on these men.

Preparations for a General Election

The feeling manifested by delegates over the action of Mr. Justice Brett, and the threat contained in the resolutions passed by the Trades Union Congress that, in the general election that was bound to be held soon, trade unionists would vote against the candidates who had supported the Criminal Law Amendment Act, caused the Government to try and placate them by releasing the gas stokers from prison soon after Congress ended. No steps were taken, however, to introduce legislation to protect the unions from the severe punishment the courts might impose if they exercised their legal right to strike.

[1] The attitude of the judges, as the Webbs have pointed out (*The History of Trade Unionism*, p. 284) almost nullified the right to strike which it was generally thought had been conceded by Parliament in the 1871 Act. Lord Justice Brett found, for example, that the striking gas stokers were guilty of conspiracy to coerce or molest their employers by preparing to strike; and since the conspiracy was also criminal he was able to impose the drastic penalty of twelve months' imprisonment.

The Gladstone Government badly needed the support of the trade unionists, as it had been gradually losing its popularity since 1870. Forsters's Education Act had outraged the sensibilities of the radical Nonconformists; surrender to the claims of Russia in the Black Sea, at the London Conference, had irritated others; and the Jingoes had been inflamed by Gladstone's wise, but apparently weak policy over the Alabama claims; Lowe's match duties had raised a storm about his ears, and Bruce's licensing laws had driven the brewers over to the Tories. Congress, though well aware of the impending election, did not do much to ensure that better preparations were made to meet it than had been made before. A resolution moved by George Potter was carried, calling upon:

> the various trade societies, councils, and committees, and all active friends of labour, to organise the voting power of the working classes, with a view to opposing vigorously and determinedly every candidate for Parliament who does not pledge himself to vote for the abolition or alteration of any law affecting injuriously the character and freedom of Trades Unions, especially the Masters and Servants Act, the Criminal Law Amendment Act, and the law of conspiracy as applied to trade societies, under which the gas stokers had been convicted.[1]

A second resolution:

> That it be an instruction to the Parliamentary Committee, in the event of an election, where application is made to them, to give advice and assistance in organising Trade Societies in any borough where a fair prospect of returning representative working men to Parliament is apparent, and to give such advice and assistance as in their judgement may appear best calculated to ensure the return of as many competent representative working men as possible at the next election

was also carried, though it met with some opposition. The cause of the opposition lay partly in personal jealousies and partly in a fear that the Parliamentary Committee was usurping the rights of the trades councils. The London Trades Council, now dominated by George Shipton, sought to delete all reference to the Parliamentary Committee and to recommend that electoral organisation should be on a local basis only, but this was not accepted by the delegates.[2]

The new Parliamentary Committee contained more big names than the previous one, the delegates electing Macdonald, Guile, Allan, George Odger, Peter Shorrocks, John Kane, William Owen, Thomas Plackett, and George Howell. The officers were Macdonald, chairman, Guile, vice-chairman, Allan, treasurer, and Howell, secretary. The Leeds Congress was the first for which an official report was

---

[1] *T.U.C. Annual Report*, 1873.   [2] *Ibid.*

made, and the new Parliamentary Committee was instructed to make arrangements for a proper record of the contributions to the debates and the decisions arrived at, to be kept for future reference.

The rapid growth of the trade union movement, coupled with the publicity which had attended the holding of the Trades Union Congress and the activity of the Parliamentary Committee to secure from the Government the repeal of the Criminal Law Amendment Act, and of all penal legislation which discriminated against workmen, led the employers to form in 1873 a National Federation of Associated Employers of Labour. This body was avowedly called into being as a consequence 'of the extraordinary development . . . and elaborate organisation of the Trades Unions'.[1] According to the rules the object of the Federation was to 'promote and maintain such relations between Capital and Labour as will secure perfect freedom to both and conduce to the welfare of the whole community'. To attain that end the Federation was empowered to watch over all legislation affecting industrial relations between employers and employed; to collect and disseminate information to its members; and to endeavour to secure unity of action in resisting demands made by combinations of workmen in so far as they affected the Federated Trades as a whole. Following the example of the Parliamentary Committee of the T.U.C., the National Federation of Associated Employers presented a memorial to the Home Secretary giving reasons why the Government should not accept the case submitted on behalf of the trade unions for the repeal of the Criminal Law Amendment Act, amendment of the Master and Servants' Act and amendment of the Law of Conspiracy. Subjected to pressure from both organised workers and employers, the Liberal Government was unable to make up its mind which way to act; it simply remained inert until the Prime Minister made the inevitable decision to dissolve.

Speculation as to the moment when Gladstone would cease to reflect on destiny and call the throw was intense in 1873. It was a year full of election alarms, and little progress was made by the Parliamentary Committee with the Bills it was concerned to promote. The Government gave the election crisis as the reason why it could not fulfil its promise to introduce a workmen's compensation measure during the session, but it was still clinging to office when the Sixth Annual Trades Union Congress met at Sheffield, in January 1874. The Congress was the most impressive yet held; 169 delegates representing 153 societies with a membership of 1,191,000 were present;[2] but it was also more divided than any before. In its report

[1] See Appendix 1. Webb Collection, Section B, vol. XXIII.
[2] *T.U.C. Annual Report*, 1874. Caution needs to be exercised in the use of these figures, as they contain duplication and may not have been accurately compiled.

the Parliamentary Committee drew the attention of Congress to the refusal of the Government to repeal the Criminal Law Amendment Act, and the fact that many members of the Government had voted against the Committee's Repeal Bill, moved by Mr. Mundella in the House of Commons.

The most interesting and lively discussion followed a paper by Henry Broadhurst, delegate from the Stonemasons' Society, on the Direct Representation of Labour.[1] He suggested that if one million trade unionists were levied one shilling each, it would raise a fund of £50,000, or, if only half that number contributed, £25,000.

> If [said Broadhurst] the next general election is to carry a dozen working men into that legislative chamber—more notorious for its massive golden Bar, than for its intellectual calibre—the trades unions must commence in earnest to prepare the funds, without which all efforts will be wasted, and those who make the sacrifices thoroughly disheartened.[2]

Broadhurst's paper was followed by one given by Mr. Wrigley of Sheffield, who also made an eloquent appeal for more positive trade union political action. On its conclusion a large number of resolutions on the subject were put forward, and at the president's request an attempt was made to agree upon a composite draft but this was not achieved and a resolution and an amendment were finally agreed upon. The resolution stated that:

> it is the opinion of this Congress that the duty of all trades societies and the industrious classes generally should be to exert themselves in the most strenuous manner for the support of labour candidates at the coming election. We therefore recommend that trade societies should be asked to contribute at least sixpence per member towards raising a fund to secure the return to Parliament of as many working men at the next general election as possible, and that the money be placed in the

[1] Henry Broadhurst was born at Littlemore near Oxford in 1840, one of a large family of eleven or twelve children. After leaving school at the age of twelve and having spent a year in a blacksmith's forge he was apprenticed at the shop in which his father, a journeyman stonemason, was employed. After working in various parts of the country, including six years in Norwich, Broadhurst moved to London in 1865 where he was employed as a stonemason on the new Government buildings in Whitehall and on the stonework of the House of Commons. He joined the London Working Men's Association and the Reform League and was active in the great demonstrations of 1867, taking part in the famous Hyde Park incident when the demonstrators pulled down the railings. In the same year he was elected to the Committee of the Stonemasons' Society and in 1873 was sent as the Society's delegate to the Trades Union Congress. In 1873 he was appointed Secretary of the Labour Representation League, and from that time onwards became one of the leading figures in the trade union world.

[2] *T.U.C. Annual Report*, 1874.

hands of such a committee as in the opinion of the members of Congress might meet the exigencies of the case; and, further, such committee be empowered to render such assistance and advice as in their judgement may appear best calculated to attain the objects we have in view.[1]

This resolution was too far-reaching in its implications for those who were suspicious of the Parliamentary Committee and of the accumulation of power in its hands, and an amendment was tabled: 'That this Congress believes that local efforts are most desirable and the best means of securing the return of working men to Parliament, and recommends all trade unions in all trade districts to amalgamate and go in common council for the said object.'[2] But even this was too much for a majority of delegates, for it was amended in turn by the following: 'That in the opinion of this Congress, it is unwise and undesirable to pledge itself to any course of action in respect to labour representation in Parliament, and that each representative be at liberty to take what action he thinks proper in the town or city in which he resides.'[3] This final amendment was eventually carried and became the official policy of the T.U.C.

The division of opinion within the Congress was again brought out by the attempt of the London Trades Council to turn it into an industrial federation on the pattern of earlier types.[4] A motion moved by J. D. Prior, secretary of the Amalgamated Society of Carpenters and Joiners, to form a federation of trades councils to act with the Parliamentary Committee, had been rejected by the Congress in Leeds the year before, but in the meantime the National Federation of Associated Employers of Labour had come into existence, mainly, according to the statement issued, for the purpose of countering the growing power of the trade unions. Fear of what this body might be able to do to injure the trade unions persuaded the delegates to instruct the Parliamentary Committee to draw up an address on federation and to ask each trade union to take a vote on the desirability of forming such an organisation.

The Parliamentary Committee received a rebuff when, seeking to improve the conduct of Congress and enhance its own influence, it proposed that the delegates should amend the standing orders so as to cancel the preference given to a local man to become the president of Congress. By a large majority they refused to agree that the chairman of the Parliamentary Committee should, by virtue of his office, preside over the next Congress. It was agreed, however, that the size of the Committee should be increased from nine to eleven members.

[1] *Ibid.*   [2] *Ibid.*   [3] *Ibid.*

[4] A meeting of the representatives of the trades councils during the week of Congress to discuss the question of forming a 'federation' had resulted in the passing of a resolution in favour of the principle of federation.

During the week the secretary read a letter which had been received by the Parliamentary Committee from the Ligue Universel des Corporations Ouvriers of Geneva, a body which had risen out of the wreck of the First International, asking for co-operation in the setting up of a new international organisation. A lengthy discussion brought out all the distrust of continental labour movements felt by most of the leaders of the trade unions in Britain, who had been horrified by the events of the Paris Commune and disliked the revolutionary tone adopted by the I.W.M.A.;[1] and it was agreed to let the question stand adjourned until the next Congress, so that the Parliamentary Committee could obtain more information meanwhile.

No sooner had Congress terminated than the long-awaited dissolution of the House of Commons was announced and a general election was under way. Owing to the reluctance of the trade unions to take effective action, the working class was only a little better prepared for this election than it had been for the previous one. During 1873 the Labour Representation League had made attempts to create some sort of electoral organisation, but it was only of the most primitive kind. With the help of a small number of trade unions, including the miners and the ironworkers, which had voted financial help for working-class candidates, the L.R.L. was able to put forward thirteen well-known trade unionists. Among these were John Kane, George Howell, Henry Broadhurst, George Odger, Alexander Macdonald and Thomas Mottershead, all of whom were members of the Parliamentary Committee. Most of the working-men candidates were opposed by both Liberals and Tories. Alexander Macdonald and Thomas Burt, the leader of the Northumberland Miners, had straight fights and managed to win. The success was small, but since trade unionists were entering the House as members for the first time it was a significant milestone in the history of the Labour movement.

Another Royal Commission

How much the refusal of Gladstone to do anything to remove the grievances of the workers had to do with his defeat it is not possible to say, but candidates had been closely questioned on their attitude towards the repeal of the Criminal Law Amendment Act. Disraeli had indicated that if he was returned the Act would be amended, and the Parliamentary Committee assumed when the Tories took office that steps to implement this promise would be immediately undertaken. Grateful, however, as Disraeli might have been for the support

[1] Karl Marx had annoyed the British trade union leaders by a speech in Holland, in which he suggested they were all in the pay of Disraeli or Gladstone.

of the working class in helping to bring about the downfall of the Liberals, and Tory democrat that he claimed to be, he was not over-anxious to reward the trade unions by repealing the Act. Instead he sought to postpone an immediate decision by setting up a Royal Commission and offering places on it to the newly elected members of Parliament, Macdonald and Burt, and the well-known friend of the trade unions, Thomas Hughes. As soon as the Parliamentary Committee heard about Disraeli's plan to set up a Royal Commission it held a special meeting on 17 March, to which A. J. Mundella, Frederic Harrison, Thomas Hughes and several other middle-class supporters of the trade unions were invited. After a lengthy discussion, a statement was issued, deprecating the establishment of the Commission and declaring that it was the opinion of the Committee that the time had arrived for immediate legislation. On the evening of the same day Thomas Hughes and Thomas Burt received telegrams from Mr. R. A. Cross, the Home Secretary, asking them to call on him at 11 a.m. the next day. On meeting Mr. Cross the following morning they were offered seats on the Royal Commission. When they asked for time to consult their colleagues before giving him their answer, they were told by the Home Secretary that he was starting off for Windsor at once to deliver the names of the Commissioners into the hands of the Queen that day, and that they would have to send their answer by telegraph to arrive at the latest by 3 p.m. that afternoon. There being no time to call the Parliamentary Committee, Hughes and Burt immediately sought out Macdonald, and after discussion it was decided, with the full concurrence of Burt, that Hughes, with Macdonald instead of Burt, should agree to take their places on the Commission.[1] As soon as this decision was revealed to the London members of the Parliamentary Committee it was decided to summon each member by telegram to an emergency meeting to be held on 20 March. At this meeting Hughes and Macdonald explained why they had accepted the Home Secretary's invitation. Although the Parliamentary Committee had decided to have nothing to do with the Commission, and they had been associated with that decision, Hughes and Macdonald considered they had acted in the best interests of the trade unions, because Cross had promised that legislation would be introduced that year if they accepted the invitation to join the Royal Commission. Secondly, the Government was determined to instigate an inquiry before it introduced legislation, and, therefore, they felt that

[1] The Home Secretary had in the first place invited Macdonald to serve on the Royal Commission, but the letter had not reached him owing to the fact that he was at the time moving around the country on his trade union duties. Cf. Macdonald's speech to the T.U.C., January 1875.

it was desirable that there should be persons on the Commission who could ensure that the trade unions' case would be taken fully into consideration. This explanation was not convincing to the Parliamentary Committee, which had been strongly advised by Harrison, Beesly and Crompton not to assist the Commission in any way, whereupon Macdonald resigned from his position as chairman of the Committee. A resolution passed immediately afterwards stated:

> that this meeting of the Parliamentary Committee elected by the Trades Union Congress representing more than one million working men, especially convened, consider the action of the Government in appointing a Royal Commission to be a mere excuse for delay, and we adhere to the resolution already passed deprecating the appointment of the Commission, and we pledge ourselves to continue to protest against the whole scheme as being a surprise, an intrigue, and a fraud; and we further recommend the whole Trade Unions of the country to refuse to have anything to do with the Commission . . . in any way. . . .[1]

The London Trades Council seized the opportunity to attack the Parliamentary Committee for its attitude and a statement was issued that it would take 'such action with reference to the appointment of the members of the proposed Royal Commission as it may deem desirable'.[2] At a later meeting the Trades Council appealed to the Parliamentary Committee to change its attitude and to be prepared to give evidence before the Commission.[3] This criticism by the London Trades Council seems to have been a part of the campaign it was waging against the Parliamentary Committee, under the leadership of its secretary, George Shipton, who later was one of the few trade unionists to give evidence before the Royal Commission. George Odger, who was both a member of the Trades Council and on the Parliamentary Committee, moved one of the Council's resolutions and appears to have been playing a double game, for he also supported the Parliamentary Committee's resolution against the Royal Commission. The intrigues of the London Trades Council led to an attack on it by Thomas Halliday, leader of the Amalgamated Association of Miners, who suggested that the representatives of trades councils should not have the right to sit on the Parliamentary Committee.[4] The *Beehive* also delivered a justifiable rebuke to the Trades Council;[5] this led Professor Beesly to write a letter, in an endeavour to pour oil on troubled waters, in which he regretted the asperity of the article when there was need for the trade unions to

[1] *Report of the Parliamentary Committee*, 1874.
[2] Minutes of the London Trades Council, 12 March 1874.
[3] *Ibid.*, Special Delegate Meeting, 24 March 1874.
[4] *Ibid.*, 21 April 1874.
[5] *Beehive*, 21 March 1874.

show a united front.[1] He feared that the Government might make use of the dissensions to delay legislation still further.

The repeal of the Criminal Law Amendment Act was still the major item on the agenda at the next Congress which was held at Liverpool, in January 1875, and it gave rise to an acrimonious debate. After Henry Broadhurst had moved a resolution regretting that 'the obnoxious Criminal Law Amendment Act still remains unrepealed' and pledging Congress 'to use all the constitutional means in its power to obtain the repeal of this class-made law', later speakers criticised Macdonald's action for 'helping the Government in its reprehensible policy of delay'. This theme was taken up by W. R. Cremer who charged that members of the Parliamentary Committee were not sincere in their opposition to the Royal Commission, and went on to allege that a number of them had given their support to non-working-class candidates at elections because they had been well supplied with the 'needful'. This statement created an uproar and several delegates demanded that a committee of inquiry should be at once set up to investigate these allegations. This was carried after Mr. Burt and Mr. Macdonald had been given an opportunity to defend their own actions. They both made it clear that they would be satisfied with nothing less than the total repeal of the Criminal Law Amendment Act, and fully supported Broadhurst's resolution; the matter was then dropped until the investigation had taken place.

When the Committee of Inquiry reported, Congress was informed that Cremer, who had been called to give evidence, had been completely unable to sustain his allegations; thereupon Macdonald moved that he be expelled from Congress and not allowed to take a seat again until he had withdrawn 'the whole foul and unwarrantable charges'. This proposal was carried by an overwhelming majority. The next day Cremer sent a letter of apology withdrawing what he had said; the apology was accepted and it was agreed that Mr. Cremer would be permitted to attend future meetings of Congress. This was the end of the incident, but not the end of the suspicions entertained against the Parliamentary Committee. Many northern delegates thought that the Committee was influenced too much by the London Trades Council. Reference had been made in the debate to the 'London clique' on the Parliamentary Committee, an echo of Potter's charge against the 'Junta', and another delegate had remarked 'wherever there was a number of London delegates there was always a row'.[2] To this George Odger replied 'there was more confusion imported into London by country delegates than they ever knew before they came'.

[1] *Beehive*, 28 March 1874. [2] *T.U.C. Annual Report*, 1875.

Developments at Congress

When George Howell introduced the Parliamentary Committee's report it was found to contain a section on the thorny subject of federation, which might have been expected to raise a good deal of discussion, but in the event raised hardly a murmur.

> The Committee have felt [stated the report] that they could not take any active steps with regard to the question of federation of trades unions, as it was a subject which should rather arise out of the necessities of individual trades than be pressed by your Committee . . . The Committee, however, have considered that some advance towards some kind of federation has been made by the new constitution which they have proposed to Congress, at the same time they are fully aware that this has reference to extended and more definite parliamentary action than to questions of disputes arising between employers and employed.[1]

There, for the moment, the idea of federation was allowed to rest, as the delegates endorsed the Committee's report, and attention was concentrated on the constitutional proposals.

These proposals were concerned mainly with the basis of representation at Congress and the payment of an affiliation fee of a farthing per member. They aroused a good deal of controversy, for they threatened to deprive the small unions of the voting strength they had enjoyed from the first Congress. It was now suggested that societies with less than 2,000 members should be permitted only one delegate, the number of delegates rising with the membership. As things stood there was no rule governing representation and the small society could send as many delegates as the large, which resulted in a substantial attendance from those societies with headquarters in the town where Congress was being held. As voting was simply by a show of hands the large unions felt they were at the mercy of irresponsible decisions taken by the delegates of the small ones. Another controversial suggestion made by the Committee was that trades councils should be allowed to send delegates 'only for such societies as may not otherwise be specially represented in any other form'. This proposal was an attempt to curb the influence of the trades councils at the Congress and was, no doubt, a consequence of the recent activities of some of them, which were resented by the Parliamentary Committee. The proposals of the Parliamentary Committee were not, in the event, accepted, but this was not to be the end of the conflict between it and the trades councils. The upshot of the debate was that the proposals were referred back to the Parliamentary Committee, 'in order to elicit during the year the opinions of the trades societies throughout the country'.[2]

[1] *T.U.C. Annual Report*, 1875.   [2] *Ibid.*

Most of the time of Congress was devoted to protesting at the failure of the Government to introduce legislation to repeal the Criminal Law Amendment Act, to amend the Master and Servant Act and to protect the trade unions from the Common Law charge of conspiracy, but the delegates were equally as emphatic on a number of other issues. Congress reiterated its full support for the work of Samuel Plimsoll, M.P., to prevent the loss of life at sea due to the over-loading of unseaworthy vessels. It demanded a revision of the laws governing the conduct of magistrates and the selection of jurymen. At this time workmen were almost debarred from serving on juries because of the qualifications necessary, and cases involving trade unionists were invariably tried by middle-class individuals who were anything but well-disposed towards organised workers. Support was given to a Bill to shorten the hours of children, young persons and women employed in shops and factories.

A trade union for women had a representative at Congress for the first time, albeit a man. The thought of women trade unionists and their presence at Congress was too much for some of the delegates, and a protest was made. Congress was not, however, disposed to accept this extremely sectarian point of view, and a letter from Mrs. Emma Paterson, the founder of a trade union for women employed in the bookbinding trade, read by the president, was listened to sympathetically.[1] At the next Congress held in October 1875, women delegates took their seats for the first time. They were Miss Simcox of the Society of Shirt and Collar Makers, and Mrs. Emma Paterson, representing the Society of Woman Bookbinders, and the Society of Women Upholsterers.

[1] Mrs. Emma Anne Paterson was born in 1848 and died in 1886, but in this relatively short life she accomplished a great deal for women workers. Daughter of a headmaster, she had early become interested in social problems, and at the age of nineteen was appointed secretary of the Working Men's Club and Institute Union. In 1872 she became secretary of the Women's Suffrage Association, but in the next year she resigned on marrying Thomas Paterson, a cabinet maker. After a honeymoon spent in the United States she returned to found the Women's Protective and Provident League with the object of assisting working women to form trade unions, to improve their conditions of employment—a scheme which had been suggested to her by the Female Umbrella Makers' Union of New York. The first union founded by the League was among women employed as book-binders, and this was followed by unions of shirt-makers, tailoresses and dress-makers. Five years after her death the organisation founded by Mrs. Paterson changed its name to the Women's Trade Union League; by 1895 30 societies were affiliated to it. From 1875 to 1886 she was a regular attendant as a delegate to the Trades Union Congress, and on a number of occasions was nominated for the Parliamentary Committee. Mrs. Paterson, though coming from a middle-class environment, was the pioneer of trade unionism for women, and by her tact and ability overcame the prejudices of the men in trade unions who were almost as conservative as the employers in their attitude towards the organisation of women.

During the 1874 Congress Alexander Macdonald had somewhat grandiloquently announced that he was offering a cash prize of £50 for the best essay written on Trade Unionism to be submitted before the next Congress, and it produced a result for which he had not bargained. The winning essay having been chosen, the President opened a sealed letter containing the candidate's identity, which had been concealed under a pseudonym, and read it to the delegates. This was followed by an interlude of embarrassed silence, for the name was that of one of the most implacable haters of the trade union movement, a John Wilson of Sheffield, who was notorious for both his written and spoken utterances against them.[1] Within a few moments the delegates had recovered sufficiently to laugh at the audacity and ability of a man who was capable of turning his opponents' arguments to such good account—he was sent the prize of £50, but it must have irked the delegates to reward his insolence so well.

The election of the Parliamentary Committee was closely contested from a large number of nominations and provoked another commotion. A snap resolution had been carried just before the election took place, that not more than one member from any trade could be on the Committee at the same time. When T. Halliday of the Amalgamated Association of Miners and W. Brown of the Miners' National Union were both elected, it was moved that Brown withdraw. This step gave rise to a fierce argument followed by resolution and counter-resolution, the outcome being that Macdonald led the delegates of the Miners' National Union out of the Congress in disgust when the final decision went against his colleague. There was a good deal of rivalry between the two Miners' organisations, and it must have been galling to Macdonald to find his organisation unrepresented, after he and Burt had refused to stand for election because they felt that membership of the Parliamentary Committee would be improper now that they were Members of Parliament. Macdonald's ability was recognised by the delegates, but he was not a popular figure among them. He was imperious in his manner and tended to lecture Congress in a way that aroused resentment.

On the last day it was decided to alter the month in which Congress met from January to October, so as to give the Parliamentary Committee more time to prepare its legislative programme before each new session of Parliament opened. This meant that there would be

[1] Wilson was a pen-knife blade-grinder and had been a member of the Pen-Knife Blade-Grinders' Society of Sheffield. He was the reader of a paper attacking the unions at the meeting of the Social Science Association in 1865, which was also addressed by William Dronfield. It was the publication of Wilson's paper and omission of his own that so aroused Dronfield's anger and caused him to complain of the bias against the unions shown by the Social Science Association.

two Congresses in one year, which was, in part, a compensation for the failure to hold a Congress in 1870.

One great trade union leader was absent from this Congress: William Allan, who had died towards the end of 1874.[1] William Allan had stamped his ideas on the trade union movement over the past quarter century, but he was not a great success at Congress. A dour, somewhat taciturn Scot, he was a poor debater, and had a contempt for the more flashy platform oratory, but he could be blunt to a degree that had a devastating effect on his opponents. He was respected not for his brilliance, but for his solid strength and reliability. Although Allan played an important part in carrying through a revolution in trade union organisation, he was a conservative at heart, and deeply suspicious of new ideas and new movements. The Amalgamated Society of Engineers, which he had methodically built up into a powerful organisation with great financial resources, was a testimony to his determination and organising ability. The death of Allan, following the departure of Robert Applegarth from the trade union movement the year before, brought to an end that formidable combination of trade union leaders in London which had had such an influence over the course of trade union affairs.

The Royal Commission on Labour Laws reported soon after the Congress was over, in February 1875. The Majority Report stated categorically 'That in a free country men should be at liberty to combine for the protection of their common interest, so long as they do not interfere with the rights of others, and are guilty of no breach of the law, ought not to admit of question.'[2] The majority of the Commission, however, saw no reason to repeal the Criminal Law Amendment Act or the Master and Servant Act, though they did recommend a number of slight modifications. These did not meet the objections of the trade unions and Alexander Macdonald entered a dissent from the findings of the majority, in which he called for the repeal of the Criminal Law Amendment Act, drastic change in the Master and Servant Law, and a revision of the law of conspiracy so as to protect the trade unions in future from decisions of the kind made by Mr. Justice Brett in the case of the Gas Stokers.

The Work of the T.U.C. Considered Completed

The Parliamentary Committee made it clear to the Government that they would not be content with the proposals made by the Royal Commission on Labour Laws, and the Government, alive to the importance of the working-class vote from the recent election,

---

[1] Daniel Guile was appointed treasurer of the T.U.C. in Allan's place.
[2] *Royal Commission on Labour Laws*, 1874–5.

decided that it would be politically expedient to go much further than recommended by the majority of the Royal Commission, so that when Congress assembled again at Glasgow the Parliamentary Committee was able to report the passage of the Conspiracy and Protection of Property Act, which, *inter alia*, repealed the Criminal Law Amendment Act; and of an Employers and Workmen Act. The report recorded how the Committee had skilfully mobilised full support in the House of Commons to improve the Bills submitted by the Government. They had agreed with their friends in the House that they would accept the leadership of Robert Lowe, who less than a decade before had been an arch opponent on the Liberal benches of the aspirations of the trade unions, 'so that there would be no appearance of division in our ranks'. Then 'your committee sent out a special "whip" requesting members to support Mr. Lowe's instruction. . . .' This section of the report concluded 'workmen are no longer under an exceptional criminal code, *the work of emancipation is full and complete*'.[1] There was cause for jubilation, but this statement, as events proved, neglected the lessons of past experience; it failed to remember that an Act of Parliament was interpreted by courts which were influenced by a Common Law that was still hostile to the existence of trade unions.

Indeed, so grateful were the Parliamentary Committee to Mr. R. A. Cross, the Home Secretary, for having introduced the Bills and piloted them through the House of Commons, that they moved that a vote of thanks be sent to him. A vote of thanks to a Conservative Minister was an unprecedented event and aroused some criticism from a few delegates who were not sure 'that the labouring classes had reached such a land of milk and honey' as a result of the legislation of the last session. One after another, however, leading members of the trade unions supported the resolution, but the point was made that the vote of thanks to Mr. Cross should not, 'be construed into a vote to the Conservative Party. . . . But they should thank Mr. Cross for having the moral courage in the face of his party, to do justice to working men.'[2] The intention of the Parliamentary Committee was laudable but it was rather naïve of them to imagine that the Conservatives would not construe the vote as one in support of the party. In terms of strategy the vote could be regarded as a clever move, for it again indicated to the Liberals that the trade union would give their support to any party supporting their objects, but there is no evidence that such subtle considerations were in the minds of the members of the Parliamentary Committee. Perhaps more than anything else the resolution was a product of a belief that the major

[1] My italics. *T.U.C. Annual Report*, 1875.
[2] *Ibid.*

work of the Parliamentary Committee had been accomplished; that, at least, was the view of George Howell, its sponsor.

Howell, who had been the secretary of the Parliamentary Committee since 1871, was so convinced that henceforth the trade union movement would have little further need of the Trades Union Congress and its Parliamentary Committee, that he handed in his resignation.[1] There was certainly an air of complacency about this Congress, not detectable in its predecessors; but other delegates, especially those from the provinces, were not prepared to abandon the instrument they had created. A number of slight changes were made in the standing orders of Congress, the most important of which was that henceforth the secretary of the Parliamentary Committee would be chosen by a vote of the whole Congress, and not by the Committee as hitherto. Congress then proceeded to elect a new secretary.

George Odger refused to accept nomination, leaving the delegates to choose between Henry Broadhurst and George Shipton, the other two candidates. The former was elected by 74 votes to 27, and then endorsed by a unanimous vote of Congress. The defeat of Shipton prevented the London Trades Council from securing the influence it desired over the Parliamentary Committee. Broadhurst was, like most of the other trade union leaders, a radical liberal in his views. Although living in London, he was not regarded as one of the 'London clique', and in earlier days he had been closely associated with George Potter in many of the latter's activities. Broadhurst, a mason by trade, had in common with other leaders in the building trades, such as Harnott, been a critic of the policies of the leaders of the Conference of Amalgamated Trades, but as time went on had gradually come to accept their outlook as superior to the doctrine of militancy, of which the Builders had been the most vigorous supporters. During his tenure of office as secretary of the Parliamentary Committee, Broadhurst was to carry the policy of practical caution, for which the leaders of the Amalgamated Trades had been well known, to the extent of provoking a revolt against his leadership.

With the Glasgow Trades Union Congress, one phase in the history of the organisation came to an end and a new one began. Looking back over the eight years of its existence the record was impressive. It had succeeded in securing the removal of legal bonds which had threatened to choke the life out of the trade union movement, and these results had been achieved by sagacious leadership which earned for the trade union movement increased public respect. A new relationship had been developed between the trade unions and the State.

[1] Davis, W. J., *The British Trades Union Congress—History and Recollections.* Howell was also ill and wanted to devote time to writing, which may have affected his decision.

The trade union movement was no longer tainted with the odour of a criminal conspiracy, but had been recognised by Parliament as a legitimate agency for the protection of its members' economic interests. When Parliament accorded the trade union movement this recognition, after many hesitations and half-hearted concessions, it did so having been converted to the belief that it was acting in conformity with the prevailing social philosophy. The trade union movement, when urging its demands on Parliament, was not seeking to overthrow the economic system of free competition; it was, it believed, merely insisting that workers and employers should be placed on a basis of equality. What the trade unions did, as the Webbs point out, was to turn the weapon of the employers—freedom of contract—to their own account. 'What they demanded was perfect freedom for a workman to substitute collective for individual bargaining, if he imagined such a course to be for his own advantage.'[1] It seemed to the trade unions that it was palpably illogical of the employers to argue that they should have the right to hire and fire without constraint, but that workers should not have the right voluntarily to withdraw their labour in concert—or that employers should insist on the non-interference of the State with them in the conduct of their business activities, and yet demand that everything should be done by the State to suppress trade unions when established by workmen.

Neither trade unionists nor employers were consistent in their attitude towards State interference. Both sides wanted to secure the advantages of *laissez-faire*, but they were prepared to jettison theory when its logic was discomfiting. They were genuinely sincere in their demands, and a charge of inconsistency would have been indignantly refuted. However there was no virtue in clinging to an impossible position at the dictate of abstract logic, for the test of policy was in the result it achieved. Most of those politicians who gave their support to the trade unions did so not to betray their principles, but to save them. Speaking in the House of Commons, on the Employers and Workmen Bill, A. J. Mundella said:

> He had with him an extract from a foreign journal, which states that every foreign working man was a socialist and desired to be a Robespierre. But you would not find a socialist or an Internationalist in the United Kingdom. Why was that? Because our working men had a respect for property, and what they wanted was only equality. If this Parliament should put masters and men on an equality, the result would be the best possible for the interest of capital and labour and for the promotion of harmony in the whole nation.[2]

[1] Webb, S. and B., *The History of Trade Unionism*, p. 294.
[2] *The Times*, 29 June 1875.

Even if this statement was a little sweeping it expressed what was profoundly believed by the leaders of the trade unions and their middle-class friends, and it was accepted, though a little uneasily, by Parliament. The ultimate implications of the doctrine of equality aroused little apprehension, for they were beyond the range of vision of most people.

Faced by an acute conflict of interest, Parliament had sought reconciliation and found it at the expense of the doctrinaire. The fact was that the trade unions had become a major political influence in the country, and that their interests could only be ignored by politicians at their peril. By bringing the trade unions 'within the pale of the constitution', the danger of their adopting revolutionary ideas was practically eliminated. The role of the Parliamentary Committee was of considerable significance, for through it the attention of the organised workers was focused on reform through Parliament. Moreover, the Trades Union Congress, consisting of representatives from independent constituencies, with its procedure modelled on Westminster, and its function mainly to secure legislative reforms, in itself contributed towards educating working men to seek advancement by democratic constitutional means.

The acceptance, however, of much of the ideology of *laissez-faire* by the trade union leaders, was to prove to be not only a help, but also a handicap to the development of the trade union movement. The Parliamentary Committee, under its new leader, Henry Broadhurst, was to grow in status, but to lose its dynamic. Its objectives narrowed, its policy lacked political imagination and when it was in doubt it sometimes sought to evade rather than to face up to its problems. It is true that the difficulties which beset the trade unions during the next decade, and after, were, in part, due to the absence of a clear policy. Had the union leaders known, however, exactly where they wanted to go, that fact would not have ensured their getting there. The next period was one in which immense changes in the social organisation of the country were taking place and it is evidence of the strength and flexibility of the trade union movement that it was able to adjust itself to these changes and at the same time to increase its importance in the State. If the trade union movement had been hidebound by a doctrinaire theory, its difficulties would have been greatly increased, and it would not have exercised the influence it did over social and political events. As we shall see, in spite of weaknesses, the Trades Union Congress and its Parliamentary Committee were responsible for securing considerable advances in the economic status of the working class.

Even if this statement was a little soothing it expressed what was profoundly believed by the leaders of the trade unions, and their middle-class friends, and it was accepted, though a little uneasily, by Parliament. The ultimate implications of the doctrine of equality aroused little interest. Such doctrines remained a privilege of a few people.

Faced by an acute conflict of interest, Parliament had sought

CHAPTER III

THE BROADHURST ERA

The depression which followed the trade boom of the early seventies falls into two periods. In the first, unemployment and falling wages were concentrated in a few major industries, spreading later to others. A temporary recovery then took place, but soon gave way to a second severe collapse of employment, and employers sought to offset falling revenues by drastic reductions in their wages bills. The cuts in wages put the trade unions in a difficult situation, for many of them were firm supporters of arbitration, and a number were tied to sliding scales; they were, therefore, in a weak position to offer strong resistance to the reductions in wages which were imposed upon them. Nevertheless, bitter opposition to the policy of the employers rapidly sprang up, and a spate of strikes and lockouts occurred between 1875 and 1880. In 1875 the miners of South Wales were on strike for almost five months against reductions made in their wages by colliery owners.[1] In the following year, 20,000 miners came out on strike in South Yorkshire, and 'Strikes and wage cuts from 7 to 15 per cent were reported from every district connected with the coal and iron industries.'[2] In 1877 the Clyde shipwrights were locked out for three months for demanding an increase in wages, and in the same year a fierce struggle began between the stonemasons and the master builders. The stonemasons had asked for an increase in wages, as the building industry was still booming, owing to a shift in investment from overseas to home projects. 'The general position of labour became seriously worse in 1878. Average unemployment, rising through the year, announced the final phase of the depression. Pauperism moved decisively upwards, consumption of food and beer slumped.'[3] Throughout the year strikes and lockouts continued, the whole of Lancashire being convulsed by the lockout of weavers in the Burnley and Blackburn districts for refusing to accept a reduction of their wages by 10 per cent. 'During 1878, four trade societies, the engineers, the carpenters, the ironfounders, and the boilermakers, whose aggregate membership was only 93,714, paid in out-of-work

[1] "The most remarkable event in our industrial history during the past year was the lockout in South Wales, whereby it was computed about 10,000 persons were deprived of their means of living.' *T.U.C. Annual Report*, 1875.

[2] Rostow, W. W., *British Economy in the 19th Century*, p. 217.

[3] *Ibid.*, p. 219.

benefit considerably over a quarter of a million pounds.'[1] The nadir
was reached in 1879; during this black year unemployment reached
the average figure of 12 per cent, but some unions recorded more than
25 per cent of their members as being without work. 'The Iron-
founders had a considerable capital to begin the year with, but at the
end the society was in debt. The Engineers expended, in addition to
its income from 45,000 members, £111,000 in providing the various
benefits to which its members were entitled.'[2]

The Impact of Depression

The mounting unemployment and falling wage levels, which the
trade unions were unable to prevent, placed a tremendous strain on
the resources of the weaker societies, many of which simply collapsed.
Most of them, however, held on grimly, and came through the crisis
with depleted funds and a much lowered membership. The number
of unions affiliated to the T.U.C. fell in 1879 to 92, the smallest
number since 1872. Affiliated membership, which had been over
1,000,000 in 1874, slid down until it was less than 500,000 in 1880.
That the movement weathered this economic blizzard relatively
intact was evidence that the foundations of the trade unions, which
had been relaid in the previous two or three decades, were soundly
constructed. With the recovery of trade in the early eighties union
membership began to rise once more and continued to rise despite
the onset of large-scale unemployment again in the mid-eighties.

By 1882 the level of unemployment, which had begun to fall sharply
in 1880, was below 3 per cent, but this recovery lasted only until
the end of the following year, over 8 per cent being unemployed in
1884, 9 per cent in 1885, and 10 per cent in 1886. This was the
bottom of the cycle and the climb out of the trough of the depression
began again until unemployment fell to 2 per cent in the prosperous
years of 1889 and 1890.[3] Money wages, which had fallen during the
earlier depression, remained practically stationary between 1880 and
1887; but real wages, which had barely held their own up to 1880,
rose steadily thereafter throughout the eighties owing to the continuous fall in prices.[4]

By 1889 membership of trade unions affiliated to the T.U.C. had
risen from less than 500,000 at the beginning of the decade to 885,055,
but the severe depressions had revealed weaknesses in the organisation of labour. The struggle to remain in existence had encouraged

[1] Davis, W. J., *The British Trades Union Congress—History and Recollections*,
p. 75.   [2] *Ibid.*
[3] Beveridge, W. H., *Full Employment in a Free Society*, Appendix A.
[4] Bowley, A. L., *Wages and Incomes in the United Kingdom since 1860.*

the large unions to pursue their own sectional policies with little regard for any common industrial strategy. A number of attempts were made to persuade the unions to bind themselves together in a federated organisation, but each attempt foundered on the refusal of the unions to relinquish their autonomy. The situation as the Webbs saw it was as follows:

> The annual Trades Union Congress, the Parliamentary Committee, and the political proceedings of these years constitute practically the only common bond between the isolated and often hostile sections. In all industrial matters the Trade Union world was broken up into struggling groups, destitute of any common purpose, each, indeed, mainly pre-occupied with its separate concerns, and frequently running counter to the policy and aims of the rest.[1]

The philosophy of the leaders of larger unions affiliated to the T.U.C., represented on its Parliamentary Committee, was that of safety first; their aim to avoid provoking the employing class to attack the unions. The policy followed by the Parliamentary Committee was essentially the same as that which had been pursued at an earlier stage by William Allan and his friends; cautious pressure on Members of Parliament to secure legislative reforms that would place working people on a basis of equality with other sections of the community on matters of importance to their social and economic well-being. The trade union movement had embraced the doctrines of the Liberal Party, and, in the decade after 1875, the programme of the Parliamentary Committee contained little that was more advanced than the radical measures proposed by Mr. Chamberlain. But as, in the past, the policy of the leaders of the Amalgamated Trades had been challenged, and to some extent modified, by Potter and his friends, so this policy of the Parliamentary Committee was also severely criticised by the more militant spirits. The depression administered a shock to the whole nation and sharpened conflict in society. During the depressed years social tensions were masked by the immediate effects of this shock, but underneath they were building up, and when prosperity returned after 1886 they began to burst out. The Parliamentary Committee could not immunise itself from these pressures, though the leaders of the old and well-established trade unions tried to isolate them from the worst effects. New ideas or, more truly, old ideas revived and given a new twist and development, could not be kept where they started, outside the trade union movement and the T.U.C. They rudely intruded and internal harmony was disturbed by bitter conflict between the entrenched leaders of the unions on the Parliamentary Committee and the rising

---

[1] Webb, S. and B., *The History of Trade Unionism*, p. 357.

younger generation of trade unionists who brusquely challenged the old traditions with new socialistic ideas.

The Trades Union Congress continued to meet annually, but the membership it represented remained for the ten years following 1875 only one half of the peak figure registered in 1874. Doubts were expressed as to the value of Congress, and the suggestion was made that it was a luxury the trade unions could no longer afford to maintain. This view was not entertained by the more far-sighted of trade unionists, but J. D. Prior, the chairman of the Parliamentary Committee felt it necessary to go out of his way, when addressing the delegates to the 1876 Congress, to answer these critics and to emphasise why there was a continuing need for the Trades Union Congress and its Parliamentary Committee.[1] The reasons given by Prior were important ones, but the wider aims of the trade union movement seemed of relatively little consequence to many a rank and file member struggling to eke out a living and menaced by unemployment and reduced wages.

The Parliamentary Committee refused to have anything to do with the economic battles being fought by the unions, and when it referred to the state of the economy in its annual report to Congress in 1877 it did so with a certain insular satisfaction that cannot have brought comfort to the unemployed. 'Amidst the general depression of European industries it was some consolation to know that their own country was the best employed of any nation which is considered to have a place in the race of manufacturing production.'[2] It is not necessary to search far for an explanation of this attitude. The trade unions and their representatives on the Parliamentary Committee did not believe that there was anything which they could do to overcome the depression in trade. They found comfort where they could and naturally hoped that recovery was on its way. Meanwhile it was best for the trade unions to be as conciliatory as possible. The rank and file were not so ready to accept such advice as some of their leaders were to give it, and trade union leaders found themselves pushed into leading strikes for which they had little heart. The failure of one strike after another was proof to a good many of them that inexorable economic laws could not be altered by strike action, but the demand for a radical change in policy could not always be resisted.

Attempts to persuade the Parliamentary Committee to pursue a more militant course met with strong opposition, not only because its members held these views, but also because they realised that if they attempted to carry such a policy out, it would probably wreck the Trades Union Congress. A proposal that the Parliamentary

[1] *T.U.C. Annual Report*, 1876.   [2] *Ibid.*, 1877.

Committee should have the power to give advice to trade unions involved in trade disputes or difficulties was rejected by Congress in 1877, but the Parliamentary Committee was instructed to examine the problem of demarcation between skilled and unskilled workers. When the Committee issued its report to the following Congress it was made clear that the Committee was not going to have anything to do with such a dangerous idea as accepting responsibility for preventing the occurrence of demarcation disputes. Henry Broadhurst, replying to criticism of the timidity displayed by the Parliamentary Committee, said 'that the less their annual Parliament interfered with the differences arising between trade and trade, and industry and industry, the better would it be for the success of their great undertaking.'[1] He went on to suggest that it was not very sensible to ask the Parliamentary Committee to undertake such a task when it had not the power to see that its conclusions were carried out. At the 1879 Congress, the question of the Parliamentary Committee taking more effective steps to help the individual unions was once again raised. On this occasion Robert Knight, secretary of the Boilermarkers' Society, introduced the proposal that the Trades Union Congress should be reorganised as a federation, thus giving the Committee the authority to carry out a policy in the interests of the whole of the trade union movement. The delegates, spurred on by the knowledge that unemployment had exposed the weakness of their unions, passed the resolution by a majority of two votes, more as a gesture of despair than of conviction as to its value.[2] When, however, the Parliamentary Committee subsequently ignored the resolution, no vote of censure was moved against it.

A Limited Programme of Social Reform

The parliamentary programme adopted by Congress between 1875 and 1880 was mainly concerned with employers' liability for accidents, the reform of magistrates' courts, the abolition of imprisonment for debt, the extension of household suffrage to the counties and redistribution of seats, the extension of polling until 8 p.m. in provincial boroughs, the payment of Returning Officers' expenses out of the rates, the reform of the patent laws and the appointment of 'practical men' as factory inspectors. This programme of important, but, unfortunately, minor reforms, ignored almost completely the basic social and economic problems of the working class. It reflected the ideas of trade union leaders who were broadly content to accept the social organisation of society and saw no

[1] *T.U.C. Annual Report*, 1878.   [2] *Ibid.*, 1879.

reason to challenge it fundamentally. This point of view was a product of the status enjoyed by their members, who were for the most part skilled craftsmen with an established position in the industrial life of the country and who were, in spite of the depression, steadily improving their standard of living.

The demand for an Employers' Liability Bill had been in the Parliamentary Committee's programme since 1872. In 1873 the Liberal Government had promised to introduce legislation on the subject, but had refrained because of an impending election. In 1875 Alexander Macdonald introduced a private member's Bill, which had the support of the Trades Union Congress. This Bill was resisted by the Tory Government, but as a result of sustained pressure from the two working-men members and the Parliamentary Committee it set up a select committee of the House of Commons to inquire into the problem. The select committee produced both a Majority and a Minority Report, but both fell far short of what the T.U.C. desired.[1] Clause One of Macdonald's Bill ran:

> Where any action or proceeding is brought for recovery of damages or of compensation in respect of bodily injury or loss of life, alleged to have been occasioned after the passing of this Act, to any person, it shall not be any ground of defence that the person by whose negligence the injury or loss of life is alleged to have been occasioned was employed in common employment with the person injured or killed, or that the risk of injury or loss of life was knowingly or voluntarily incurred by the person injured or killed in the course of his employment.[2]

The Majority Report, however, only recommended that accidents directly caused by negligence on the part of an employer's head manager should rank for damages, the doctrine of common employment remaining otherwise untouched. The Minority Report made a little further concession to the case of the trade unions by recommending that an employer's liability should be extended to cover acts of negligence committed by foremen and their deputies, as well as managers. The Trades Union Congress refused to accept either of these meagre proposals and continued to support Macdonald's efforts to persuade Parliament to pass his Bill. The defeat of the Tories in the election of 1880 removed the main obstacle, and one of the first measures of the new Liberal administration was an Employers' Liability Bill. The Lords, dominated by Tories, and ever ready to spike Liberal legislation, tried to wreck the measure, but the Parliamentary Committee quickly organised a large-scale demonstration against their action, and the Government stood firm behind

---

[1] *Report of Select Committee on Employers' Liability for Injury to their Servants*, Parliamentary Papers, 1877, vol. x, p. 551.

[2] *Employers' Liability for Injury Bill*, Parliamentary Papers, 1876, vol. I, p. 353.

its Bill. The Act passed was not all that the trade unions wanted, but it did mark a considerable advance in social legislation and challenged the individualist theory that respect for property rights had a priority over the welfare of working men and women. The deficiencies in the Act, which permitted employers to contract out, and did not abolish the doctrine of 'common employment', soon became apparent, but this did not prevent the trade unions from recovering thousands of pounds in compensation for accidents suffered by their members. At the same time the trade unions, and in particular the miners and railwaymen, of whom an appalling toll of injuries and death was taken each year by industrial accidents, continued their agitation for an improved Act.

The emphasis given to the reform of the judicial system, by the Parliamentary Committee during this period, can be traced to the influence of that small group of barristers who had been closely associated with the trade union movement since the sixties.[1] The Positivists, Frederic Harrison, Henry Crompton and Professor Beesly, in particular, devoted a great deal of attention to the trade union movement.

> The policy of the Positivists had been to secure complete legal independence for workmen and their legitimate combinations; to make them more respected and more conscious of their own worth; to lift them to a higher moral level; that they would become citizens ready and desirous to perform all the duties of citizenship.[2]

From the foundation of the *Beehive* in 1861, Harrison and Beesly were regular contributors, writing mainly on general and foreign politics. During the campaign to secure the reform of the law as it affected trade unions, Crompton wrote many brilliant articles analysing their legal position and indicating the changes which they should demand. At times the *Beehive* carried three main articles in one issue from Harrison, Beesly and Crompton, but they were usually careful not to push their own particular creed too hard, seeking to influence the workers by enlisting their support for political policies in which they had immediate interest. The Positivists were never really able to extend their influence over the leaders of the working man beyond the programme of popular radicalism. After the legislation of 1875, and the Trade Union Amendment Act of 1876, the influence

[1] The passing of the Justice's Clerks Act, in 1877, enabling magistrates to grant costs, and of the Summary Jurisdiction Act of 1879, which permitted a defendant to claim the right to be tried before a jury when the penalty which could be inflicted exceeded three months, owed a good deal to the pressure of the Parliamentary Committee.

[2] From a statement by Henry Crompton quoted by the Webbs, *The History of Trade Unionism*, p. 362

of the Positivists diminished, and their interest in the trade unions gradually declined. The trade unions, hard hit by the depression, grew sectional and insular in their outlook, as they concentrated their attention on their own problems. They were no longer moved by the enthusiasm of the Positivists for the freedom of subject minorities in far-off countries as they had been in the 1860s, and almost equally ignored their call for support of Home Rule in Ireland. It was over the Irish question in 1881, that the Parliamentary Committee made it clear to the Positivists that they would no longer accept their advice. Harrison, Beesly and Crompton wanted the T.U.C. to oppose Gladstone's policy of coercion in Ireland on the grounds that the Government was using the same policy there as had been used against trade unions in England, and which might be used again to crush them, but the union leaders were indifferent to this argument.[1]

By this time the Parliamentary Committee had become conscious of its own strength, and of its importance to the Liberal Party. Broadhurst and other members of the Parliamentary Committee had political ambitions, and at the 1880 election Broadhurst was returned to Parliament under the aegis of the Liberals; moreover he had a great personal reverence for Gladstone, who was later to reward him for his loyalty. They believed that there was more chance of the unions securing from the Liberals the practical reforms that the Committee was sponsoring if it acted in alliance with them, than if it continued aloof and constantly critical. It had always been the policy of the Positivists to advocate support for the Liberals, but not to be too closely identified with one party, since that would destroy the ability of the T.U.C. to hold the balance between the parties and thus, in exchange for its support, to dictate its own terms. The Parliamentary Committee no longer agreed with Henry Crompton that: 'The condition of this effective force was that, while it was being used in furtherance of political action, it should be kept clear and independent of political parties.'[2]

Compared with the advantages which Broadhurst and his colleagues on the Parliamentary Committee hoped would accrue from their association with Liberal statesmen, the Positivists now had little to offer. Their atheistic and aridly intellectual philosophy was not congenial to Broadhurst, and most of his colleagues, who had a narrow *bourgeois* outlook, and the estrangement from the Positivists developed into a complete divorce after Harrison had been refused permission to speak in a debate at the 1883 Congress.[3]

During the years of Disraeli's premiership the Trades Union

[1] See Henry Crompton's statement to the Webbs, *ibid.*, p. 363.
[2] *Ibid.*
[3] Cf. Ensor, R. C. K., *England 1870–1914. The Prominence of Religion*, p. 137.

Congress gave no consideration to the momentous issues raised by his foreign policy. No resolution appears on the agenda, nor in the debates is reference ever made to any aspect of the 'Eastern Question', in spite of the fact that during these years Gladstone was rousing radical opinion against the Tories with his campaign on the Bulgarian atrocities.[1] Disraeli's imperialist wars in Afghanistan and South Africa were not mentioned, but the Parliamentary Committee invited a Lancashire industrialist in 1879 to read a paper on the potential markets offered to British exports if the continent of Africa was opened up to foreign trade. Henry Crompton, who was present at this Congress, asked the delegates not to support such a scheme, which would involve England in the crimes and horrors of wars of conquest; he received some support, but Congress, with mass unemployment in mind, gave the paper a cautious approval.[2]

Little preparation was made by the Trades Union Congress in the late seventies for the next election. On the initiative of Adam Weiler,[3] an old supporter of the International Working Men's Association, resolutions were carried in 1878 and 1879 calling on the Parliamentary Committee to draw up a list of questions to be submitted to candidates, but nothing was done until the last minute. The election programme put forward by Congress[4] was based on the resolutions

[1] Broadhurst and other trade union leaders were privately active in support of Gladstone's foreign policy. Cf. *Henry Broadhurst, M.P.*, p. 19.

[2] *T.U.C. Annual Report*, 1879.

[3] Adam Weiler was a prominent member of a group of German socialist *emigrés* who had settled in London. He was a disciple of Marx and had played an active part in the International Working Men's Association. A cabinetmaker by trade, Weiler for many years represented the Alliance Cabinetmakers' Society at the Trades Union Congress. In 1878 he read a paper on the limitations of hours of work by law, and he regularly moved resolutions in support of this aim. Land nationalisation was another subject that he urged on the delegates to the Congress.

[4] The candidates were asked whether they would support:

A Bill to amend the law of compensation in cases of accidents, so that workmen, or their families, may recover from an employer in the event of injury or death from accidents due to negligence?

A Bill to reform the administration of justice by limiting summary jurisdiction of magistrates, especially in securing the right of appeal and trial by jury?

A Bill to extend the Employers and Workmen Act (1875) to English seamen whilst in British waters?

An increase in the number of factory and workshop inspectors?

A Bill to reform the Patent Laws?

A Bill for the abolition of imprisonment for debt?

A redistribution of political power, by extension of household suffrage to the counties, and rearrangement of the division of seats?

The extension of the hours of polling until 8 p.m. for provincial boroughs?

The payment out of the rates of the returning officers' charges at Parliamentary elections?'

carried in 1879, and was in marked contrast to the speeches of Gladstone during his famous Midlothian campaign. The leader of the Liberal Party concentrated almost entirely on foreign affairs, but the manifesto of the Parliamentary Committee was concerned exclusively with domestic issues.

Each year resolutions were moved and perfunctorily carried urging the trade unions to 'do the utmost in their power to return competent men of their own class to Parliament'. At the 1876 Congress the resolution stated that it was 'the imperative duty of the delegates present to make a decided stand in this direction by forming committees or associations in their respective districts to carry out the same'.[1] An amendment demanding 'manhood suffrage' was withdrawn after a strong speech by Broadhurst, who argued that this was a 'red herring'. In the following year Congress readopted manhood suffrage as its aim, but it did not appear in the election programme of the T.U.C. in 1880; the Parliamentary Committee contented itself with what it considered to be the limit of practical reform, the extension of household suffrage to the counties. Although Broadhurst had strongly supported the 1876 resolution, and was secretary of the Labour Representation League, he did nothing to see that it was really put into effect. The Labour Representation League was practically moribund, and Broadhurst was too immersed in his duties as secretary of the Parliamentary Committee, as well as busy looking after his own constituency of Stoke (where he had the support of the local Liberals), to be prepared to galvanise it into life. The Labour Representation League was by then little more than an appendage of the Liberal Party, and had abandoned any pretext of running a large number of independent Labour candidates. The radicals had not much use for the League, for under the leadership of Chamberlain the National Liberal Federation was organising the radical wing of the Liberal Party in the political machines that were being created in the constituencies on the Birmingham model. Only Benjamin Lucraft, Joseph Arch, Alexander Macdonald, Thomas Burt and Henry Broadhurst went to the polls in 1880 as direct Labour candidates, the first named, facing Liberal as well as Tory opposition, suffered defeat, as did Joseph Arch, who stood as a Liberal—whilst the other three were successful.

The first Congress after the return of the Liberals to power in 1880 was held in Dublin. Apart from the fact that Congress had not met before in Ireland, it was almost uneventful. The delegates listened to papers read on the difference in the Poor Law of England and Ireland, Work and Workmen, and the Irish Land Laws. This last paper led to a resolution in favour of land reform and peasant

---

[1] *T.U.C Annual Report*, 1876.

proprietorship, which the Parliamentary Committee subsequently urged on Gladstone as a remedy for the Irish problem. The next Congress, held in London in 1881, was made memorable by the expulsion of several delegates who it was found were paid advocates of 'protection'.

Free Trade or Protection

The trade depression and the growth of overseas competition had begun to stimulate here and there second thoughts about the universal merits claimed for free trade. In the late seventies the sugar refiners and merchants began to agitate for measures to be taken against the bounties paid by foreign Governments on exports of sugar, which were hitting the home trade. They sought to gain the support of the trade unions by paying the expenses of any workmen who were willing to advocate their cause in working-class organisations. The vast majority of workers were firm adherents of the principles of free trade, but the propaganda of the protectionists had some effect, and a deputation was sent from Birmingham to interview Joseph Chamberlain, the President of the Board of Trade. Chamberlain, at this time a free trader, 'succeeded in convincing them that a "countervailing duty", if imposed, would mean the thin end of Protection, and be a great danger to the Free Trade principle which had done so much for the commerce of Britain'.[1] The 'fair traders', however, found a number of individuals who were prepared to advance their views at the Trades Union Congress, and the issue came to a head in 1881.

It was found that there were six delegates present who had not had their expenses paid by the societies they purported to represent, but had received them from the 'sugar interests'. Each of the six was given an opportunity to explain his position, but Congress found these explanations unconvincing and decided to expel them. In anticipation of the need to take this step Congress had passed a new standing order early in the week, 'That in the opinion of this Congress, no one should be eligible as a delegate to Congress whose expenses are paid by private individuals, or by institutions not bona fide Trades Union or Trades Council.'[2] The expelled delegates made a scene and one of them had to be ejected bodily. Immediately after Congress terminated, the three main agents of the 'protectionists', T. M. Kelly, S. Peters and P. Kenny, launched a campaign of abuse against Broadhurst, circulating to trade unions and trades councils letters of a defamatory character, alleging that he was personally corrupt and in collusion with capitalist interests. These attacks led

[1] Davis, W. J., *The British Trades Union Congress—History and Recollections*, p. 86.   [2] *T.U.C. Annual Report*, 1881.

the Parliamentary Committee to issue a special statement in denial of the charges.[1] Strong resolutions condemning the behaviour of Kelly, Peters and Kenny were carried by the next Congress. Far from damaging Broadhurst's reputation these slanderous attacks strengthened it, for his accusers had themselves extremely unsavoury reputations, Kelly and Peters having been expelled by the Bristol Trades Council, and Kenny by the London Trades Council, because of their reprehensible behaviour.

There were further attempts to convert the Trades Union Congress to protection in the eighties, and the agitation for 'fair trade' continued, making some headway in the London Trades Council with the connivance of George Shipton. Shipton was not in favour of protection, but he was hostile to the sugar bounties, and seems to have been prepared to accept expenses for his work from the National Anti-Bounty League.[2] In March 1887 Shipton organised a conference of trade union delegates to protest against the sugar bounties. He then circulated the resolution passed to the trades councils, and 220 of them carried similar resolutions. This activity was followed by a deputation, said to represent 500,000 members, to the Prime Minister. But with the return of prosperity and the advent of new unionism, interest in the sugar bounties rapidly dissipated, leaving free trade—for the time being—the unchallenged orthodoxy of the trade union movement.[3] Support for the abolition of the bounties was a perfectly logical policy for free traders, but mixed up as the agitation was with the issue of protection, it seemed to the Liberal trade union leaders to be the thin end of the wedge—as indeed it was.

Nationalisation of the Land

At the Fifteenth Congress, held in Manchester in 1882, there were faint signs of revolt against the narrow, timorous policy of the Parliamentary Committee. An amendment to a resolution regretting the failure of the Royal Commission on Land Law Reform to propose any important changes in land tenure, stating 'That no reform will be complete short of nationalisation of the land', was carried by 71 votes to 31.[4] However, it was probably personal jealousy rather than desire for a change that led Thomas Ashton of the Cotton Spinners to move that no member of the Parliamentary Committee should be eligible to hold office for more than two years consecutively. As the subject was not raised until late on the last day of Congress,

[1] T.U.C. Annual Report, 1882.
[2] For a detailed account of the attempts to win organised Labour for tariff reform, see History of the London Trades Council, p. 52.
[3] Brown, B. H., The Tariff Reform Movement in Great Britain, 1881-95.
[4] T.U.C. Annual Report, 1882.

it was agreed to hold it over until the next year,[1] and when it was raised in 1883 it was narrowly defeated. Although the voting on this issue showed that there were many delegates who were not content with the Parliamentary Committee, they were unable to provide any real opposition to the domination of Broadhurst, as the revived debate on land reform also illustrated. When the same delegate as the year before, H. W. Rowland, a London cab driver, again moved an amendment asking Congress to reaffirm its support of 'nationalisation of the land', to a much weaker resolution on land reform, proposed by Joseph Arch, and supported by the Committee this was defeated after a long debate by 97 votes to 34.[2] 'This decision was important', writes W. J. Davis, 'as in effect it declared that the Parliamentary Committee would be compelled to withdraw from its declared intention to urge the nationalisation of the land in Parliament.'[3] Although Davis criticised the Webbs for stating that 'when Congress insisted on passing a resolution with which the Parliamentary Committee found themselves in disagreement it was silently ignored',[4] there is no evidence to show that the Parliamentary Committee did more than wait until the 1883 Congress to get the nationalisation resolution reversed.

At the Congress of 1882 and 1883 the subject of young girls employed in chain-making was raised, the Parliamentary Committee having sponsored a Bill to prevent girls under fourteen years of age working at the forges. This attempt to secure protection for these girls called forth angry speeches from the women delegates who were violently opposed to special legislation for their sex. They urged that there should be no legislation at all, but if legislation there must be, it should also include boys.[5] The fear of the women delegates was that discriminatory legislation would reduce the employment opportunities for girls, and thus lead to greater hardships than those inflicted by the wretched working conditions at Cradley Heath. The women delegates were against special legislation to protect female labour as such, on feminist grounds, allied to which they were stern advocates of the pure Liberal doctrines of voluntary action. In the following year Miss Wilkinson, one of the women delegates who had spoken so passionately in the debate on the chain-making girls, raised the question of the franchise for women, reminding the delegates that Gladstone had said that he would consider giving women the vote when this became a popular question, and urged the men to help in this struggle for women's rights.[6] Later in the week a

---

[1] *T.U.C. Annual Report*, 1882.   [2] *Ibid.*, 1883.
[3] Davis, W. J., *The British Trades Union Congress—History and Recollections.* p. 99
[4] *Ibid.*, p. 96.   [5] *T.U.C. Annual Report*, 1883.   [6] *Ibid.*, 1884.

resolution was carried which asked, 'That the franchise should be extended to women on the same conditions as men.'[1] At the 1885 Congress Miss Wilkinson moved an addition to the manifesto that was to be issued to the workers by the Parliamentary Committee before the forthcoming parliamentary election, in support of votes for single women. This was carried by 70 votes to 10.[2] One of the arguments used by the women delegates was that single women and widows had a right to the vote as a compensation for not having a husband. In reply to the protests of the men delegates, Mrs. Paterson said she would agree that if all married women had husbands like the delegates who had spoken they did not need a vote—an argument which male vanity could hardly resist.

Extension of the Franchise

The demand, which the trade unions had been making for some time, for an extension of the franchise to the counties, bore fruit in 1884. The radical wing of the Liberal Party was bent on destroying Tory control of the countryside through the squirearchy, and lent their support to the demand for a new Reform Act. On 31 January 1884, the Parliamentary Committee sent a delegation to interview Gladstone, and present a memorial on County Franchise Reform; the delegation was so large that the reception had to be held at the Foreign Office, no room being big enough to accommodate it at No. 10, Downing Street. The delegates were mightily pleased with Gladstone's statement to them, which hinted at legislation on the lines demanded by the T.U.C., and later in the day a special vote of thanks was sent to the Prime Minister expressing appreciation of his words. The following day Gladstone replied, stating that the delegation from the T.U.C. had made a deep impression on his mind, but whether this was from the weight of argument or weight of numbers is not clear. When the 1884 Congress met in September, the Franchise Bill had been before Parliament, but was being held up by the House of Lords. A resolution condemning the Peers was moved by Joseph Arch, and the feelings of the delegates were expressed in bitter speeches.[3] The Parliamentary Committee, however, was concerned with being 'statesmanlike' and the more strongly worded amendments to the official resolution were resisted. A country-wide agitation led by Joseph Chamberlain under the war cry of 'Peers against the People' convinced the Conservatives that it would be prudent to make concessions. After negotiations between Gladstone and the leader of the Opposition, Parliament was recalled and the Reform Bill was carried, receiving the Royal Assent on 6 December 1884.

[1] *Ibid.*   [2] *Ibid.*, 1885.   [3] *Ibid.*, 1884.

The scene was now set for a general election, but this did not come at once, for when the Government was defeated in the House on the Budget and Gladstone resigned, Salisbury took office and his Government lasted for five months before he dissolved Parliament. When the 1885 Congress met at Southport, it was realised that a general election could not be far away, and the Parliamentary Committee submitted an election manifesto for the approval of the delegates which contained the following points:

1. A Bill to amend the Employers' Liability Act of 1880.
2. An increase in the number of factory inspectors.
3. An increase in the number of mine inspectors.
4. A Bill to prevent further loss of life at sea.
5. An extension of the Employers' Liability Act to shipping.
6. A Bill for the better regulation of safety on the railways.
7. A Bill to make a certificate of competency compulsory for all those who have charge of an engine.
8. The removal of unnecessary obstacles to the appointment of workmen to the civil and magisterial service.
9. The abolition of the property qualification in local government.
10. Such reform of the land laws as was best calculated to set free the springs of natural industry and to promote home consumption of manufactured goods.
11. The restitution of educational and other endowments to the service of those for whom they were originally intended.[1]

A good deal of criticism was forthcoming when this rather insipid document was presented to Congress, and the Parliamentary Committee was attacked for its timidity. Broadhurst, replying to the critics, told the delegates, in his most unctuous manner, that he was in favour of many of the things they wanted, but asked whether they would be justified in embodying in that address such questions as free education, the payment of returning officers' charges, and the payment of Members of Parliament. The delegates appeared to think so, for they promptly moved and carried a resolution instructing the Parliamentary Committee to insert clauses covering these three items, to which was added the demand for the franchise for women.[2]

Lib-Labs and Conservatives

Although in the preamble to the manifesto there was mention of the 'labour party', this meant no more than the desirability of having a few working men in the House who could put a working-class point of view from their personal experience, and there was only the mildest of references to the return of 'labour representatives'.[3]

[1] *T.U.C. Annual Report*, 1885.   [2] *Ibid.*   [3] *Ibid.*

When the manifesto stated that it was not their intention to put forward a policy 'which is not in harmony with the highest and best interests of the nation', the Committee was trying to reassure Liberal voters that Labour members would not demand revolutionary changes. The main theme of the preamble was that the Parliamentary Committee's programme was above party politics. Broadhurst would probably have preferred to have given outright support to the Liberal Party, but the influence of the Lancashire representatives, who were Conservatives, was particularly strong at this stage. It was undoubtedly the influence of Mawdsley and Birtwistle, representatives of the Spinners and Weavers on the Parliamentary Committee, that led to the manifesto stressing the importance of electing a Parliament to govern 'this, the greatest Empire in the World'.[1] The need to send to Parliament workmen who held Conservative political opinions, if they would make good Labour representatives, was emphasised by speakers from the floor of Congress during the week.[2] In a comment made to the Webbs in

[1] *Ibid.*

The Liberal Party was not, of course, opposed to the Empire, but its leaders thought of it in rather different terms. The British Empire was the theme on which Lord Rosebery chose to speak, when he was invited by the Parliamentary Committee to address Congress in 1884. His speech was of fascinating interest both for its shrewd appraisal of the achievements of the trade union movement, and its far-sighted appreciation of the evolution of the Empire. Rosebery compared the structure of trade unionism which he described as 'detached self-management, with a common centre in this Congress', with the organisation of the British Empire. 'Now, many of us would like to see this principle of federation far more applied than it is to the concerns of the British Empire. Each of you here feels, I take it, that what makes every separate trades union powerful and prosperous makes a union of all the trades unions such as that which is here today and that while every union is strong, every bond which, while respecting the individuality of the separate unions, draws them in their common object closer together makes these unions stronger themselves. . . . Suppose there was only one trades union which comprised all the trades—bookbinders, saddlers, nailmakers, and so forth—it would be a weak organisation because it could not respect and consider sufficiently the individualities of the different callings, whereas, if it kept clear of all these individualities and distinctions, it would be altogether colourless and powerless. If it attempted to override them, it would simply be an endless source of irritation and jealousy, and would probably break up in a very short time. Now your present organisation, if I rightly understand it, avoids both these difficulties. It combines strength for mutual objects with separate management for separate objects; and what I have said to you about trades unions is exactly true of the British Empire. . . . The British Empire seems to me to steer and waver between the two dangers which I have indicated.' Rosebery saw the need to develop the Empire as a federation of equals and he appealed to the Congress to make the future development of the Empire one of its prime interests.

[2] The influence of those who sympathised with the Conservatives was shown when the attitude of Broadhurst towards the Royal Commission on the Trade Depression was severely criticised. Broadhurst had been invited to sit on this Commission, but he had refused on the grounds that it was a Tory manœuvre to

1894, with reference to their *History of Trade Unionism*, Broadhurst attributed the hesitancy of the Parliamentary Committee at this period to the fact that 'every new move was looked upon by Tory workmen as making for Radicalism'.[1] This was an attempt, *post facto*, by Broadhurst, to counter the strictures of the Webbs on his leadership of the Parliamentary Committee, but it is clear that the prolonged depression had caused a significant number of workmen, especially those employed in the export industries, to support the Tory policies of imperialism, and, to some extent, protection. There was, in fact, a long-established following for the Conservatives in Lancashire and Yorkshire that stemmed back to the ten-hours agitation and the famous Richard Oastler, who was a Tory radical.

The 1885 Congress was extremely placid, and neither the Parliamentary Committee nor the delegates entertained a suspicion of the storm that was soon to break about them. The same resolutions were passed as in previous years, but if the delegates were content with the minor gains which the Parliamentary Committee was able to record during the year, the appointment of four trade union leaders as magistrates of Lancashire, and the agreement of the Stationery Office to use only trade union firms to do their printing, these were not sufficient to satisfy the rank and file, which was suffering acutely from mass unemployment and reductions in money wages.

Not very long after Congress was over came the general election. As a consequence of the extension of the franchise and the redistribution of seats by Gladstone in the previous year, eleven Lib-Labs were returned to Parliament. These were T. Burt, B. Pickard, C. Fenwick, J. Wilson, W. Crawford and W. Abraham, all miners, and J. Arch, J. Leicester, George Howell, W. R. Cremer and Henry Broadhurst. As a reward for his consistent support of the Liberal Party, Henry Broadhurst was given a post in the new Government, formed after Salisbury's resignation in February, as Under-Secretary to the Home Office.[2] George Shipton was appointed secretary of the Parliamentary Committee in his place. The appointment was only temporary, however, as before the next Congress the Liberals, who had secured a majority of 82 over the Conservatives, were defeated in the House, following the disaffection of a section of the Liberal

win working-class support. Birtwistle and Drummond, secretary of the London Society of Compositors, however, accepted invitations and Broadhurst condemned their action in the Parliamentary Committee's report. As a result of the debate on this item, Broadhurst was compelled to delete the offending sentences from the report.

[1] Webb Collection, Section A, vol. I.

[2] This was in recognition of the work that Broadhurst had done for the Eastern Question Association, Gladstone told him. See *Henry Broadhurst, M.P.* by himself, p. 188.

dissentients on the Home Rule for Ireland Bill. Gladstone dissolved and went to the country, and this time the Tory Unionists were returned with a majority of 118, including the Liberal dissentients. The Lib-Lab group was reduced to nine, Joseph Arch, John Wilson and Joseph Leicester being defeated, but James Rowlands,[1] well known in connection with the London reform associations, was elected in addition to the other Lib-Labs who retained their seats.

Not only was the Liberal Party defeated on the Irish question, but the radical movement disintegrated over the issue of Home Rule. The unfortunate elimination of Dilke from politics and the revolt of Chamberlain left the Liberal Party bereft of the most important leaders of its radical wing just at a time when, if the problem of Ireland could have been settled, they might have gained control of the party. The confusion imported into the political scene by these events, and by the breakdown of the two-party system, encouraged the development of a demand for independent Labour representation. At the 1885 Congress a resolution had been carried welcoming the formation of Labour Associations at various places in the country, but no further action had been taken. The increase in the number of Lib-Lab members as a result of the Reform Act stimulated further efforts to enlist the aid of the trade unions to secure the return of a larger number of Labour representatives. At the 1886 Congress, George Shipton moved that funds should be created in each district for the support of working-class candidates.[2] A lengthy discussion followed, during which all the arguments heard before, that this proposal would involve the trade unions in politics, and that support should be given equally to members of both political parties, were put forward. Finally, T. R. Threlfall, secretary of the Southport Trades Council, who had been president of the 1885 Congress, and for long known as a supporter of direct Labour representation, moved an amendment calling upon Congress to establish a Labour Electoral Association, which would have the object of securing more Labour representatives in Parliament and on local governing bodies. The amendment further proposed that there should be an annual

---

[1] G. D. H. Cole appears to have confused James Rowlands, whom he describes as a 'cab driver' with H. W. Rowland, secretary of the Cab Drivers' Union. Cf. *A Short History of the British Working Class Movement, 1789–1947*, p. 231. James Rowlands, having served his apprenticeship, became a watch-case maker and was made a freeman of the Goldsmiths' Company. Formerly a student at the Working Men's College, Great Ormond Street, Rowlands was one of the founders of the Leaseholds Enfranchise Association and was active in a number of Reform organisations. He was born in 1886 in East Finsbury, the constituency which he won as a Lib-Lab. He had contested the division in the election of the previous year, but without success.

[2] *T.U.C. Annual Report*, 1886.

conference of delegates from affiliated associations, and a minimum subscription of five shillings per society, and that the Association should be governed by a Labour Electoral Committee, to be set up by Congress to work in conjunction with the Parliamentary Committee. The amendment was eventually carried by a substantial majority, and Congress then chose a Committee on a regional basis, England being divided into six divisions, and Ireland, Scotland and Wales each counting as a single division. The number of members on the Committee from each district varied according to the organised strength of the division. The Committee met immediately after it had been chosen, and elected John Wilson of the Durham Miners as its president, W. Abraham, M.P., of the South Wales Miners and J. M. Jack, secretary of the Scottish Ironmoulders, as vice-chairmen, F. Harford, secretary of the Amalgamated Society of Railway Servants as treasurer, and Councillor T. R. Threlfall as secretary.[1]

When the Labour Electoral Association and the Committee were established it seems to have been assumed that they would come under the control of the Parliamentary Committee. This was the object of the promoters of the scheme, says W. J. Davis, but 'leading members thought it best . . . to set it up in business as it were "on its own account" '.[2] It is clear, as Professor Cole has pointed out, that the 'creation of an elaborate organisation, with a full list of officers quite independent of those of the Trades Union Congress itself indicated that from the outset the L.E.C., even if it reported its proceedings to Congress, meant to act independently of Henry Broadhurst and the Parliamentary Committee'.[3] The difference, however, between Threlfall and his associates and Broadhurst was only one of degree; Threlfall wanted to build up a Labour Party with a programme of its own, but he was by no means a socialist, and in the event the Labour Electoral Association soon became tied closely to the Liberals.

New Ideas Intrude

The year 1886 saw the depression become almost as bad as it had been in 1879, and the Congress was held against a background of incidents that warned of the transformation that was taking place in the atmosphere of working-class politics. The Trafalgar Square riots, the unemployed agitation, the speeches of H. H. Hyndman, William Morris, John Burns and Tom Mann were heralds of a new force that was taking shape—a force that would soon batter itself

[1] *T.U.C. Annual Report*, 1886.
[2] Davis, W. J., *The British Trades Union Congress—History and Recollections*, p. 119.
[3] Cole, G. D. H., *British Working Class Politics, 1832–1914*, p. 103.

against the practical, cautious Liberalism of the old men, and cause them to fight a stubborn defensive battle. In 1886, there was relatively little support inside the trade unions for the policies of radical socialism, but the 'new' ideas were beginning to take root. Hyndman had started the Democratic Federation in 1881; it adopted a socialist policy in 1883, and added the prefix Social in the following year. The S.D.F. campaigned with missionary zeal to make converts to Marxist socialism and Hyndman secured nation-wide publicity for his ideas through his public debates, first with Henry George, whose book *Progress and Poverty* had made a great impression on the Labour movement, and later with Bradlaugh, whose fame as a radical was then at its peak. The S.D.F., however, diminished its immediate effectiveness by accusing the leaders of the trade unions of treachery to the working class, and by calling upon the rank and file to rise and overthrow their supine leaders. In 1884 the well-known split occurred in the ranks of the S.D.F., William Morris and others leaving Hyndman and forming the Socialist League. Then, in the following year, came the affair of 'Tory Gold', when the S.D.F. ran two candidates in the 1885 election on money supplied by an agent of the Conservative Party, in order to split the Liberal vote. This fiasco led to a vehement denunciation of the S.D.F. from every other section of the Labour movement. Despite these blunders, and also the arrogant, doctrinaire opinions of Hyndman, the S.D.F. had a big influence on some of the younger trade unionists who were eager to receive a philosophy of life more purposeful than that of the Parliamentary Committee.[1]

It was evident at the 1886 Congress that whatever the attitude of the Parliamentary Committee might be the trade unions could not be isolated from the socialist ideas that were emerging from the political ferment going on in the country. The president, F. Maddison, of the Hull Trades Council, posed the issues that were coming to the fore in a vigorous opening address, that by implication was highly critical of the policy pursued by the Parliamentary Committee. He advocated the eight-hour day, nationalisation of the land, the payment of Members of Parliament, a far more vigorous attack on capitalism, and concluded by deploring the division between skilled and unskilled workers. *Reynolds Newspaper* praised Maddison's speech in the editorial: 'This is the way to talk to capitalists. Call the doctrine socialistic, revolutionary, or what name you will.'[2] The same paper bitterly attacked Broadhurst for his middle-class ambitions and lack of activity on behalf of the workers, but such sentiments as yet cut little ice with most of the delegates to Congress and

---

[1] Beer, M., *History of British Socialism*.
[2] *Reynolds Newspaper*, 5 September 1886.

it was no surprise when, after a few months' absence as a junior Minister of the Crown, Broadhurst was re-elected secretary to the Parliamentary Committee. Broadhurst's appointment in the Government had been excellent ammunition for his critics, but the more far-sighted realised that it had a much greater significance than some would allow. 'This was an event the importance of which cannot be exaggerated. For the first time in our history an honoured worker in the field of labour was raised to an office of power.' So stated Maddison in his presidential address, and he went on,

> We had also an additional honour conferred upon us as unionists by the appointment of Mr. Burnett to the post of Labour correspondent to the Labour Bureau, which has been very wisely formed in connection with the Board of Trade. Now I think these are significant signs of the times, and reflect great credit upon the ministers who brought them about. But we must not stop here. These should not be regarded as concessions, but as a recognition of the just right of the workers to a share in the government of the country. Personally I shall not be satisfied until we have a representative of unionism within the charmed circle of the Cabinet.[1]

Signs of new ideas intruding on the Parliamentary Committee were to be seen in the discussion at the 1886 Congress on a resolution on international trade unionism. Ever since 1872, when the International Working Men's Association had become discredited in the eyes of British trade unionists, the Parliamentary Committee had been extremely suspicious of all continental trade unions. The Universal League of Working Men, which had been in communication with the secretary of the Parliamentary Committee in 1874, sent a letter in 1878 drawing the attention of the T.U.C. to a resolution which had been passed by the Standing Orders Committee of the League, regretting that the French Government had prevented the League from convening an international conference of working men in Paris, and proposing that the T.U.C. should consider holding an international congress in London at an early date. Broadhurst read this letter to the delegates at the 1878 Trades Union Congress, but it evoked little interest. A year later, at the 1879 Congress, Adam Weiler moved a resolution that the Parliamentary Committee be instructed to carry as far as possible a constant correspondence with Labour organisations of other countries for the purpose of establishing friendly relations and preparing the way for an international

---

[1] *T.U.C. Annual Report*, 1886. The Bureau of Labour Statistics was started by A. J. Mundella when he became President of the Board of Trade in Gladstone's third Government, as a section of that department, and John Burnett, secretary of the Amalgamated Society of Engineers, and treasurer of the T.U.C. Parliamentary Committee, was appointed its first head.

congress. This resolution was carried, but little or nothing was done by the Parliamentary Committee to see that it was implemented. In 1883 the subject of an international congress again arose when the Parliamentary Committee, in its annual report, informed the Trades Union Congress that 'an important communication has been received from Paris, in reference to an effort to bring about a better understanding between trade organisations of Great Britain and the Continent'. The report went on to say with typically British superiority that, 'The letter will be laid before the Congress, and it is satisfactory to know that it affords evidence of a more practical tone than many previous communications of the kind.'[1] Before reading the letter Henry Broadhurst described the various measures which had been taken to check the bona fides of the senders. Broadhurst said that, as Mr. Mundella had not been unfavourably impressed by the letter, he would not ask Congress to reject the invitation to send representatives to attend an international congress to be held in Paris, but he was clearly anything but enthusiastic about the idea.[2] The outcome of the discussion on the question was that the appointing of delegates to attend the Conference in Paris should be relegated to the Parliamentary Committee . . . but further inquiries as to the bona fides of the sponsors should be made before the deputation was appointed.[3] Following this cautious approval the Parliamentary Committee went ahead and sent a delegation composed of A. W. Bailey,[4] John Burnett and Henry Broadhurst.

These three worthy British Trade Union leaders were horrified by many of the discussions they attended in Paris, but the report which they presented to the next Congress was on the whole fair and balanced. The writers showed a certain amount of insular conceit when they stated 'the position we assumed was that we were so well organised, so far ahead of foreign workmen, that little could be done until they were more on a level with ourselves'.[5] The report however, also showed a good deal of understanding of the differences between the Labour movement in France and Britain, and it goes on to say,

> As to France we are assured that since the Conference a marked advance has been made in the organisation of the trades, and the number of syndical chambers has largely increased. As the chief object

[1] *Ibid.*, 1883.

[2] Mundella had advised against Congress giving approval to the letter from the League of Working Men in 1874.

[3] *T.U.C. Annual Report*, 1883.

[4] President of the Amalgamated Society of Tailors. Had been a member of the Parliamentary Committee almost from its foundation.

[5] The Webbs, by quoting only this sentence, give an inaccurate picture of the delegation's report. Cf. *The History of Trade Unionism*, p. 396.

of the French Workman's Socialist Federation is, however, to work through Parliament, their chief increase of strength is to be looked for in electoral returns. In Paris alone they have tripled the organised voting power they possessed three years ago, and a corresponding development of their power is claimed in the provinces, where many workmen have been elected to the municipal chambers. These facts show that the Conference has not been without result, and they point the moral that other conferences may lead on to further progress. They also teach us that a compact labour party, working steadily for itself, may not be out of place in this country.

The report concluded

> With these facts before it, the Congress will be able to form its own conclusions as to the desirability or otherwise of placing in the hands of its committee any special or general power in respect to international meetings that may be proposed or questions that may arise during the year.[1]

Congress, in fact, did nothing beyond merely accept the report, which is no doubt what the Committee desired.

Correspondence continued between the Parliamentary Committee and continental trade unions and also with trade unions in the colonies. Early in 1886 an invitation was received from Paris inviting the T.U.C. to send a delegation to an international conference to be held in August. 'Your Committee, recognising the increasing influence of international competition upon British trade and labour, resolved to send their president to the Paris Congress.'[2] Fresh from his visit to the capital of France, James Mawdsley, the Conservative chairman of the Parliamentary Committee, told the delegates to the Trades Union Congress that he had gone to Paris full of prejudices against foreigners but he had come back with changed opinions. He moved and was seconded by C. J. Drummond, that Congress should adopt the resolutions passed in Paris. The resolution subsequently carried marks an enormous shift in the policy of Congress from its obsession with reforms of the legal system to demands that the State should interfere to give every workman better conditions of employment, and an improved standard of life. This was a jump from *laissez-faire* to collectivism with a vengeance, and it was hardly surprising that Broadhurst soon had second thoughts about the wisdom of its adoption.

The complete resolution called for:

1. Interdiction of work done by children under 14 years of age.
2. Special measures for the protection of children above 14 years and of women.

[1] *T.U.C. Annual Report*, 1884.　　　　[2] *Ibid.*, 1886.

3. The duration of the day's work to be fixed at eight hours with one day's rest per week.

4. Suppression of night work, excepting under certain circumstances to be specified.

5. Obligatory adoption of measures of hygiene in workshops, mines and factories, & etc.

6. Suppression of certain modes of manufacturing injurious to the health of the workers.

7. Civil and penal responsibility of employers with respect to accident.

8. Inspection of workshops, manufactures, mines, & etc., by practical inspectors.

9 The work done in prisons not to compete disastrously with private enterprise.

10. A minimum rate of wages to be established which will enable workmen to live decently and rear their families.

11. The propriety of holding an International Congress in England during 1887.[1]

Clause Ten raised most criticism, the wisdom of trying to obtain a legal minimum rate of wages being called into question; nevertheless in spite of this and other misgivings that were voiced, the resolution was carried *in toto*. Although the Parliamentary Committee did not advise Congress to reject the resolution, and they could hardly do so when Mawdsley was chairman of the Committee, their subsequent action demonstrated they were not yet converted to the kind of collective action by the State which was part of the resolution proposed.

In the early part of 1887 the Committee, as instructed, issued a long memorandum to the trades on the question of holding an International Congress in England that year. The burden of this lengthy document was that the delegates to the 1886 Congress were not really aware of what they were doing when they passed the international resolution. To hold an International Congress would involve spending an enormous amount of time and money. The real reason, however, why the Parliamentary Committee was against holding the International Congress was that they were afraid of allowing 'advanced ideas' to be given a popular platform. The memorandum stated:

Our present object is merely to point out that the late International Congress was not a Trade Union Congress in the sense in which we understand one to be. If representatives from Socialistic bodies were to be admitted to a Trade Union Congress held in England, delegates from all the co-operative societies, working-men's clubs, political clubs of both parties and other social and political associations should in common

[1] *Ibid.*

fairness be also admitted. This may, perhaps be an extreme view to take of the matter, but it is, nevertheless, a logical one.[1]

The Parliamentary Committee, after issuing this statement, referred the whole matter back to Congress. Mawdsley, having been persuaded to withdraw from the previous position, moved a fresh resolution at the 1887 Congress, merely instructing the Parliamentary Committee 'to take every available means to bring about united action on questions directly affecting the interests of labour'. This watering down of the previous year's instruction to the Parliamentary Committee to organise an International Congress in London, did not meet with the approval of the delegates, who were increasingly influenced by socialist ideas being propagated outside the Congress, and Mawdsley's resolution was amended to instruct the Parliamentary Committee to hold an International Congress in London during the following year. The Parliamentary Committee was thus compelled to make arrangements for a Congress, to which Broadhurst and many other members of the Committee were strongly opposed.[2]

The Parliamentary Committee Attacked

The 'new radicalism' was gaining momentum and the Parliamentary Committee were not to be allowed to remain oblivious to it. The Committee had few tangible gains to record at the 1887 Congress for its year's work, as most of the Bills it had sponsored had been refused passage through Parliament. There was hope that a new Truck Act would soon become law, but the Committee could hardly claim much credit for that, as most of the work inside the House had been done by Bradlaugh; and outside it was the report of Mr. Alexander Redgrave, Chief Inspector of Factories, a report which the Government had tried to suppress because it was so damaging to the employers, which had drawn attention to the need for a new Act. The remarks at the end of the Parliamentary Committee's report indicate how far out of touch it was with a considerable section of the working class. After noting that unemployment existed in many industries—it could hardly have done otherwise—the report went on to say: 'We are pleased to notice, however, that so far as we are aware, there has been no general attempt to reduce the rate of wages

[1] Circular sent out by Parliamentary Committee, 1887.

[2] John Burns, in a powerful article in *Justice*, 3 September 1887 had violently attacked the P.C. for not organising the International Congress and called for the expulsion of the 'Broadhurst Gang'. *Reynolds Newspaper*, 4 September 1887 published an article in a similar vein.

in any part of the country.' This was followed in the next paragraph by the statement that:

> One of the redeeming features of the present time is the enormous supply of food for the people. Of course, however cheap a loaf may be, it is outside the range of purchase of a penniless man, but, if bread and other necessaries of life were much dearer, they could not be obtained by vast numbers of people who can and do purchase them now.[1]

For those in employment real wages were rising;[2] it was, however, the large numbers of penniless men, for whom the Parliamentary Committee offered no crumb of comfort in its complacent message to Congress, who were in the minds of the new radical movement.

If President Maddison introduced a breath of fresh air into Congress in 1886, the speech of Mr. W. Bevan, president in 1887, must have made Broadhurst and members of the Parliamentary Committee shiver. It was a tremendous contrast to the Committee's report, and was couched in language that presaged a new era in oratory at Congress. One thing was certain, he said, and that was 'this labour movement is the inevitable outcome of the present condition of capital and labour'; capital had used the House of Commons for its own ends, and why should not labour

> lighten its burdens and generally secure for itself a happier condition of things? Of course we shall be told that State interference in these matters is injurious. . . . It is very singular that this objection to State interference is only urged when questions of labour are brought forward. When the landowners with the help of Parliament, were filching the land from the people, we did not hear many objections to State interference, and when Parliament passed laws punishing seamen for disobedience or not fulfilling their articles we did not hear much about State interference. Gentlemen, we can do with State interference if the homes of the people can be improved, or work to the unemployed be given, or bread to the hungry, or hope and succour to the uncared for poor of our large towns. State interference has assisted wealth, monopoly, and privilege long enough. Let it be now used to help the poor, the down-trodden, and the ill-paid and over-worked toilers. These desirable results can only be obtained by the organisation of the masses, and by running labour candidates wherever possible.

He went on to say: 'Gentlemen, Socialism has lost its terrors for us. We recognise our most serious evils in the unrestrained, unscrupulous and remorseless forces of capitalism.'[3]

[1] *T.U.C. Annual Report*, 1887.
[2] See Beales, H. L., 'The "Great Depression" in Industry and Trade', *Economic History Review*, October 1934. Phelps Brown, E. H. and Hopkins, Sheila V., 'The Course of Wage Rates in Five Countries', *Oxford Economic Papers*, June 1950.
[3] *T.U.C. Annual Report*, 1887.

With a speech from a Welshman, and a socialist, too, to set the tone, the Congress was almost certain to be lively, and so it proved. The first clash came when Keir Hardie, who was attending his first Congress as a delegate from the Miners' Union of Ayrshire, moved an amendment to the Parliamentary Committee's report, calling for an eight-hour day. Hardie was clearly out of order and he was strongly attacked for trying to rewrite the report. After this little scene was over Hardie again tried to amend the report; a statement by the Committee that the trade unions were powerful enough to protect the workers without State assistance arousing his anger. This amendment, like the previous one, was overwhelmingly defeated. Hardie was again in the limelight when S. Uttley, of the Sheffield Trades Council, moved a resolution, the purpose of which was to enlist the support of Congress to secure an increase in the number of local Labour Electoral Associations. Hardie devoted most of his speech in this debate to a fierce attack on Broadhurst, accusing him of supporting an employer with a very bad trade union record, simply because this man had stood as a Liberal candidate, and implied that he was prepared to sacrifice the interests of the workers for those of the Liberal Party. Broadhurst's reply to Hardie's accusations was equally demagogic and consisted mainly of an attack on Hardie's personal character. This Congress 'scene' distracted attention from the main point of the discussion and from the declarations of Threlfall and John Wilson, both of whom unreservedly advocated the formation of a separate and distinct Labour Party with a programme of its own. An amendment to the resolution, demanding that election expenses should be met by subventions from the rates, and that Members of Parliament should be paid by the State, was moved by Robert Knight, secretary of the Boilermakers' Society. This was accepted; then the resolution as amended was put and carried with only one vote against. Although the Lib-Labs did not vote against the resolution, Charles Fenwick and Ben Pickard, both Lib-Lab M.P.s, voiced, during the debate, their hostility to the conception of an independent Labour Party which was beginning to take root in the trade unions.[1]

A further instance of the new radical tendencies which were influencing Congress could be seen when the delegates passed an amendment to a feeble resolution, moved by George Shipton on land-law reform, in favour of imposing an immediate tax on the land, but ultimately to make it the property of the nation. Charles Freak, of the Boot and Shoe Operatives, seconding the amendment, commented that it was better to support nationalisation than the 'shapeless proposition originally moved'. But the Broadhurst group

[1] *T.U.C. Annual Report*, 1887.

dug in their heels when an attempt was made to instruct the Parliamentary Committee to sponsor an 'Eight Hours Bill'. After a long debate in which Broadhurst poured scorn on the limitation of hours of work by legislation, he was finally forced to concede that:

the Parliamentary Committee be . . . instructed . . . to obtain a plebiscite of the members of the various trade unions of the country upon this important question, and whether, if approved, such reduction of hours shall be brought about by the trade unions themselves or by means of an Eight-Hours Labour Bill.[1]

The Parliamentary Committee had been defeated on a number of key issues, but the composition of the new Committee elected for the ensuing year showed little change. The new radicals were not yet strong enough to affect decisively the policy of Congress, and until they could secure representation on the Parliamentary Committee they were prevented from exercising their influence at the point where it could most effectively be used.

During the following year the Parliamentary Committee sent out invitations to the International Conference it had been ordered by Congress to hold. It also took a poll, as instructed, of the trade unions on the question of the eight-hour day. Whether by accident or design the Committee framed the questions ineptly, and omitted to give clear instructions to the unions as to how the poll should be conducted. Not unnaturally, the result was ambiguous and the report presented by the Parliamentary Committee to the 1888 Congress was extremely unsatisfactory. James Mawdsley, speaking on behalf of the Committee, suggested that Congress ought to let the matter drop, but Keir Hardie proposed that the Parliamentary Committee should be instructed to hold a fresh poll with the question reduced to two simple issues. 'Are you in favour of an eight-hour day?' and 'Are you in favour of it being obtained by an Act of Parliament?' This was carried by 42 votes to 22.[2]

The 1888 Congress was the occasion of Keir Hardie's second clash with Broadhurst, Fenwick and Pickard. In supporting an amendment moved by John Hodge of the Steel Smelters, which was designed to pledge Congress to the principle that Labour representatives should act independently of either of the main political parties, Keir Hardie reiterated the charges which he had made in the previous year. Again Hardie met with a sharp rebuff, for the proposal which he had supported was defeated by 82 votes to 18. Hardie at this time was actively concerned with the formation of a Scottish Labour Party, which was successfully launched shortly afterwards, but

---

[1] *Ibid.*   [2] *Ibid.*, 1888.

similar attempts in conjunction with Tom Mann and H. H. Champion, during Congress, to interest the trade union leaders in founding a British Labour Party, met with practically no response.

Broadhurst and his Lib-Lab friends were completely dominant at the 1888 Congress, and any premature hopes that might have been aroused the year before were dispelled. Although Hardie was successful in persuading Congress to instruct the Parliamentary Committee to hold a fresh plebiscite on the question of an eight-hour day, a resolution asking the Committee to sponsor an Eight Hours Bill for the mines and the railways was overwhelmingly defeated. The old hands of the Parliamentary Committee were still strongly entrenched, and defeating them inside Congress was no easy matter. The real struggle was, in fact, going on outside Congress.

One resolution that was carried unanimously at the 1888 Congress proved to be of considerable importance as a practical measure of assistance to the trade unions. In 1885 the Stationery Office had agreed to give its contracts for printing only to firms which accepted trade union standards. The resolution demanded that this principle should be extended by the Government to other departments. Before the next Congress came round the London School Board, under the influence of Stewart Headlam, Annie Besant and A. G. Cook, who had been elected as an advocate of 'fair wages', had announced that in future the Board would only give contracts to firms that paid trade union rates. This policy was soon followed by the newly created London County Council. In 1891 the House of Commons granted the trade unions their case when it passed the 'fair wages resolution', and by 1894 150 local authorities had adopted some kind of 'fair wages' resolution.[1]

An International Congress

The long-delayed International Congress opened on 6 November 1888, and lasted for five days. There were 123 delegates present, of whom 81 were British, 19 French, 10 Belgian, 10 Dutch, 2 Danish and 1 Italian.[2] As soon as the Congress started trouble began over the appointment of the Standing Orders Committee and some

[1] Webb, S. and B., *The History of Trade Unionism*, p. 399.
[2] *Official Report of the International Trades Union Congress.* German delegates had been excluded on the grounds that they would not have sent genuine working men, though more probably it was due to the attack made on Broadhurst by the German representative, Grimpe, at the Paris Congress, 1886, for having entered a capitalist Government and, it was alleged, having deserted the cause of labour. The fact that Germans were forbidden to leave their country to attend international congresses was probably also a consideration which weighed in the decision not to invite them.

British delegates suggested that the British delegation should quit the Congress; then objections were raised against a number of delegates on the grounds that they were not genuine workers. A letter from the secretary of the Amalgamated Society of Engineers stated that John Burns did not represent the A.S.E. at the Congress. However, as Burns had been sent as the delegate of the West London Branch of the A.S.E., the Standing Orders Committee had no choice but to agree with Burns that his credentials were in perfectly good order. The worst fears of the Parliamentary Committee were realised, for its critics had not been kept out of the Congress. The sympathies of the foreign delegates were shown when all of them, together with nine British delegates, voted for John Burns as president. Perhaps it was for this reason that George Shipton, who was elected president by a majority of thirteen over Burns, delivered an address which dealt with trade unionism from the time of Edward the Third, and took so long to complete it that most of the delegates must have wondered whether the Congress would ever get past the opening stage. Eventually the delegates began their real business. The Danish representatives presented a vague resolution in favour of the abolition of all laws hampering the freedom of association and combination. Keir Hardie and Charles Freak put forward as an amendment more concrete proposals, including the holding of an International Congress at regular intervals. 'Mrs. Besant opposed it in a defiant protest against the narrowness and pettiness of the British trade unionists.'[1] She moved an amendment of her own calling on 'all workers to organise themselves into different syndical chambers and groups'.[2] Mrs. Besant had made herself famous by organising that year the strike of match girls at Bryant and May's factory, and she delivered a scathing attack on the British trade unionists who had left it to her, 'a woman of the middle class' to organise these unskilled workers. Other British delegates rose and protested against Mrs. Besant's remarks, and her resolution was defeated, as was the amendment moved by Keir Hardie; the Danish resolution was carried ultimately with a substantial majority. On the eight-hour day question Mr. Parnell, delegate of the Cabinetmakers, moved a resolution which stated that 'it is impossible to further reduce the hours of labour without the aid of the State, and in every case eight hours shall be the maximum number of hours worked'.[3] This completely divided the English delegation, but after an acrimonious debate, during which John Burns made a powerful speech, and several amendments were defeated, the motion was carried by a majority of four votes, all the continental delegates except the Italian voting for it.

[1] *Official Report of the International Trades Union Congress.*
[2] *Ibid.*   [3] *Ibid.*

The feeling of the Parliamentary Committee about the International Congress is evident from the content of the few paragraphs which were devoted to it in the Committee's annual report to the 1889 Congress.[1] That the Parliamentary Committee had had enough of international trade union gatherings was made clear by its refusal to send a delegate to an International Congress organised by the French trade unions, in the summer of 1889. This decision led to a great deal of criticism and the Committee had to send out several circulars to the unions explaining to them why it refused to participate; the reason given was that it had no instructions from Congress. This was constitutionally correct, but the Committee had not waited for instructions from Congress to send Mawdsley to Paris in 1886, and it carried little conviction.

Upsurge of New Unionism

The year 1889 brought a sudden and dramatic change to the trade union world. The victory of the match girls the year before was the catalyst which stimulated the unskilled workers into activity. It demonstrated that trade union organisation was of benefit, not only to the skilled artisan, but could also, given resolute leadership, secure better wages and working conditions for the unskilled labourer.

The economic climate was vastly different from that of only two or three years before. Trade was no longer depressed, and gone was the mass unemployment which had been over 10 per cent in 1886. It was suddenly realised that the nation was prosperous again. Early in the year John Burns, who had become one of the best-known figures in the Labour world, turned his attention away from the London County Council, to which he had just been elected, to aid Tom Mann and Will Thorne in organising the gas workers. In May 1889 the Gas Workers' and General Labourers' Union was launched, and soon members were streaming in. So quickly did they join that only a few weeks later the union's leaders judged the time was ripe for them to submit their demand to the London Gas Companies. To everybody's surprise the companies, after a slight hesitation capitulated without a struggle and agreed to reduce the standard working day from twelve hours to eight.[2] This swift success electrified the Labour movement and within no time the dock labourers were emulating the gas workers. From 1887 Ben Tillett had been trying to

[1] *T.U.C. Annual Report*, 1899. 'As to whether the Congress was successful and of value to the Labour movement, opinions may differ . . . we can only hope that, although no immediate or demonstrative good has resulted, yet the Congress may not be without great effect in the future. . . .'

[2] Thorne, W., *My Life's Battles*.

build up a Tea Workers' and General Labourers' Union, but had achieved only limited response from the dockside workers. Suddenly a small dispute over a bonus paid on the general rate of 5*d*. per hour broke out in the West India Dock and Tillett, sensing that this was the moment to act, called on every docker to support the claims of the men for a basic rate of sixpence per hour. Within a matter of days thousands of workers had spontaneously joined the strike and the whole Port of London was idle.[1] Burns and Mann hastened to range themselves alongside Tillett, and together they brilliantly organised the inchoate mass of unskilled dockside labourers who poured into the union, welding them into a fighting force which exhibited splendid discipline and unity throughout the struggle with the Port Employers. Public sympathy was with the dockers, as it had been with the match girls during their strike, and 'finally the concentrated pressure of editors, clergymen, shareholders, ship-owners and merchants enabled Cardinal Manning and Sydney (afterwards Lord) Buxton, as self-appointed mediators, to compel the Dock Directors to concede practically the whole of the men's demands. . . .'[2]

Broadhurst Fights Back

At the time the 1889 Trades Union Congress was being held the Dockers' struggle was at its height. It was referred to by George Shipton, then chairman of the Parliamentary Committee, as 'a very lamentable labour dispute',[3] but he thought that Congress would like to give an expression of their feeling and render help without delay to the class now struggling in the metropolis. 'Thousands of pounds were subscribed from all over the world to help the dockers, but the best that the Trades Union Congress could do was a donation of £10 which was collected from the delegates.'[4] The annual report of the Committee contained no reference to the organisation of the unskilled workers and the remarkable victory of the gas workers. Instead it denounced the critics of the Parliamentary Committee for sowing 'the seeds of disruption'.[5]

This section roused R. Newstead of the London Society of Compositors, to move its deletion from the Committee's report. These paragraphs were nothing more, he declared, than a 'series of indirect attacks, base insinuations, and insults on those who had endeavoured to push the wheels of progress, and make clear their

[1] Smith and Nash, *The Story of the Dockers' Strike*. Mann, Tom, *Memoirs*.
[2] Webb, S. and B., *The History of Trade Unionism*, p. 404.
[3] *T.U.C. Annual Report*, 1889.   [4] *Ibid.*
[5] *The Labour Elector*, edited by H. H. Champion, and managed by a committee consisting of Mann, Burns, Hardie, Bateman and Parnell, had conducted a vehement, personal campaign against Broadhurst throughout 1889.

position in contra-distinction to the retrogressive action of the Parliamentary Committee and its secretary'.[1] The result of the debate was a triumph for the Parliamentary Committee, for the amendment was defeated by 142 votes to 18.[2]

After this indication of support for the Parliamentary Committee, John Wilson immediately moved a motion of confidence in the Parliamentary Committee's secretary, to which Keir Hardie straightaway moved an amendment that Henry Broadhurst was 'not a fit and proper person to act as Secretary of the Parliamentary Committee'.[3] Hardie repeated the charges which he had first made two years before, alleging that Broadhurst had supported unfair employers, and that he held shares in a public company where men were overworked and underpaid. After the amendment had been seconded, delegate after delegate rose and defended Broadhurst. The secretary himself made a masterly 'I have been stabbed in the back' speech in which he paraded his honesty and loyalty to the trade union movement.

> I have refused subscriptions, I have refused friendly aid, I have refused all approaches in years past when they were made to make friends in the Congress, and if today you discharge me from my position (loud cries of 'No, no')—I shall leave your service with clean hands. I shall leave your reputation untarnished and unblemished.[4]

When Broadhurst sat down, having spoken for an hour, it was to terrific applause, and the result of the debate was a foregone conclusion.[5] He had given an impressive demonstration of his formidable qualities as a debater at Congress. Hardie, as a miner and a trade unionist should have known that the trade union movement, built as it was on working-class solidarity, and intensely loyal to its leaders, would not easily repudiate Broadhurst. Hardie's error was to make his attack personal. Many delegates would have agreed that Broadhurst was conservative, that he had made mistakes, and that he ought not to hold shares in Brunner Mond, but that was no reason for charging him with the most heinous of all crimes to a trade unionist; deliberate treachery to his brother members. It was perhaps inevitable that the clash was bitter, for both sides saw the difference between them not as a question of political opinion and strategy, but as a deep moral issue. The old unionists saw the new as enemies within, wantonly trying to smash the movement which had been so carefully and painstakingly created since the days of Allan and Applegarth, and they could not understand such folly except as the manifestation of base and perverse minds.

---

[1] *The Labour Elector.*   [2] *T.U.C. Annual Report*, 1889.   [3] *Ibid.*
[4] *Ibid.*   [5] Cf. *Manchester Guardian*, 4 September 1889.

The new unionists regarded the old as having grown fat and selfish, concerned only to retain their power and to enjoy what was granted to them by their allies, the industrialists and the Liberal Party, from the exploitation of the mass of unskilled and unorganised workers. Both sides were convinced of the virtue of their policy and could not understand the unwisdom of the other in not recognising it, and they tended, therefore, to seek for an explanation in one another's motives. Fortunately, deep as the division appeared to be, it was gradually bridged over by the common sense displayed on both sides. The British trade union movement was too empirical by nature to elevate doctrine, whether old or new, to rigid dogma, and to follow the continental pattern of splitting into rival organisations wedded to conflicting theories.

The Eight-Hour Day Issue

The eight-hour day question, which had become one of the key issues between the old and the new unionists, again provoked a long debate in 1889. The retaken ballot had resulted in 39,629 votes in favour of the eight-hour day, with 62,883 against.[1] This result, although only one-eighth of the membership of the Trades Union Congress had voted, was another victory for the Parliamentary Committee. Having been forced to retake this ballot the secretary of the Parliamentary Committee had so worded the instructions supplied with the voting papers as to induce a bias against voting for legislation; it was, thus, not surprising that the result did not deter Hardie from proposing that Congress should, nevertheless, accept the principle of an eight-hour day. After a serious debate, in which all speakers applied themselves to the merits of the issue and avoided rancorous personal references, Hardie's resolution was lost by 88 votes to 63.[2]

In spite of the defeat of the general proposal there was little opposition to the representatives of the Lancashire Miners' Federation when they moved that the time had come for an Eight Hours Bill for the mines and asked the Parliamentary Committee to sponsor one. The miners at this time were divided into two main groups, mainly over the issue of the sliding scale, to which Durham, Northumberland and South Wales adhered, but which other districts had abandoned. In 1888 the districts which had abandoned the sliding scale decided to sever their connection with the old National Union of Miners, and formed a new Miners' Federation of Great Britain.[3]

[1] T.U.C. Annual Report, 1889.   [2] Ibid.
[3] Arnot Page, R., The Miners, Ch. III, p. 91.

The leaders of the Federation, which had started with only 36,000 members and had grown rapidly to 200,000, threw its weight behind the demand for more legislative action. The Federation soon began to exercise an important influence in Congress; its leaders were not socialists, as many of the new unionists claimed to be, but practical opportunists ready to make use of the State when the failure of voluntary negotiations made this necessary.

When Congress met in 1890 the Parliamentary Committee reported to it that the Committee had not been able to carry out its instructions to prepare an Eight Hours Bill for the mines. At its first meeting after the 1889 Congress, the Committee had been unable to agree on the details of a Bill and decided to ask W. Crawford, M.P., to prepare one, although they knew that as a representative of the Durham Miners he was opposed to a legal eight-hour day and was almost certain to refuse, as he did. The subject was not considered again by the Committee until the following February, when a convenient excuse presented itself, since the Miners' Federation had held a public conference and decided to sponsor a Bill themselves. Transparent as this excuse was the Parliamentary Committee survived a motion of censure condemning them for 'failing to carry out the definite instructions given to them by the Congress . . . last year'.[1]

The New Men Make an Impression at Congress

The atmosphere at this Congress was considerably changed from that of previous years. First of all this was because Congress was far larger than it had ever been before. At Dundee in 1889 there had been 211 delegates present, representing 885,055 members; this year there were 457, representing a combined membership of 1,470,191, an increase of 600,000 over the year before. During the past two years workers had poured into the trade unions in a wave comparable with the other great expansions of trade union organisation in the 1830s and 1870s. Keir Hardie was no longer practically a lone challenger of the 'old gang' on the Parliamentary Committee, for he was joined by three men famous for their recent achievements, John Burns and Tom Mann, both of whom had been sent as delegates— much to the displeasure of the General Secretary—by the old and aristocratic Amalgamated Society of Engineers, and by Ben Tillett. John Burns was loudly applauded by the delegates on the first day of the Congress when he rose to move a resolution expressing the sympathy of Congress with the workers of Australia, who had supported the dock strike so magnificently, and were now themselves on strike, and pledging Congress to do everything possible to raise

[1] *T.U.C. Annual Report*, 1890.

funds in Britain in reciprocal aid. The resolution was carried unanimously.

The great moment for the new unionists arrived when, speaker after speaker having put their points for and against the legal enactment of an eight-hour day, the resolution in favour was carried by the narrow majority of thirty-eight votes. One of the most dramatic incidents in the debate occurred when the representative of the Operative Society of Stonemasons, Broadhurst's own union, declared that he had been authorised to advocate a legal eight-hour day.[1]

John Burns boasted in a speech soon after Congress that the delegates had passed sixty resolutions and 'Forty-five out of the sixty resolutions were asking for State or Municipal interference on behalf of the weak against the strong.'[2] This statement, however, gives a very misleading impression of the 1890 Congress. It is true that the influence of the new unionists was greatly felt there, but it could hardly be said that they dominated the proceedings, as Burns implied. The rejection by Congress of several amendments directly critical of the Parliamentary Committee and of James Macdonald's amendment in favour of 'the nationalisation of land, shipping, railways and all other means of production' is evidence of this, but an even clearer demonstration of the strength of the old unionists was the election of Charles Fenwick as the new secretary of the Parliamentary Committee, over George Shipton and T. R. Threlfall, after Henry Broadhurst had announced his resignation. Fenwick, who had been a Member of Parliament since 1885, was a representative of the Northumberland Miners, a strong advocate of Gladstonian liberalism and deeply opposed to State intervention. He had been one of Broadhurst's most constant supporters.

The election of J. H. Wilson, S. Uttley, W. Matkin and John Burns to the Parliamentary Committee promised greater support for new ideas, but the Committee was still preponderantly composed of old unionists. Had it not been for the refusal of Thomas Birtwistle to serve on the Parliamentary Committee, because he could not accept the instructions of Congress to sponsor an Eight Hours Bill, and the refusal, out of pique, of the next man on the list, John Burns would not have been a member of the Committee. Certainly those attending the 1889 Congress would have found it difficult to believe that twelve months later Broadhurst would have resigned and that John Burns, the arch-agitator would be a member of the Parliamentary Committee. This indeed was a great change, but it was far from being a decisive victory for the socialists.

[1] *Ibid.*
[2] Quoted by the Webbs on p. 408 of *The History of Trade Unionism* as evidence for stating that the Liverpool Congress was a decisive victory for the socialists.

Broadhurst Resigns

Broadhurst gave illness as the reason for his resignation. He was a sick man, and the responsibility and work of the secretary to the Parliamentary Committee was heavy, for no other paid help was employed, but it is doubtful if this was the sole reason, although he strongly denied that there was any other. It is more probable that after the victory of the dockers, and the repudiation of his policy by his own society, he realised the ideas of the new unionists were rapidly gaining ground, and, as he was the main target for their criticism, he preferred not to suffer the ignomy of being defeated in the election for secretary, after being the unquestioned choice of Congress for fifteen years.

Broadhurst was undoubtedly an extremely capable trade union politician; among the long line of leaders who have made an impression on the evolution of the trade union movement he stands out as one of the most powerful and influential figures, and his resignation marks the end of an era in the history of the Trades Union Congress. The Webbs severely criticised Broadhurst's policy, and it would be difficult not to agree to a large extent with them that the Parliamentary Committee 'failed either to resist the new ideas or to guide them into practicable channels'.[1] It must, however, be counted to Broadhurst's credit that under his leadership the Trades Union Congress became firmly established as part of the fabric of social organisation in Britain. The alliance with the Liberals, which he diligently pursued, contributed in no small measure to the significant advance in the status of the trade union movement which took place during his period of office. Its Parliamentary Committee was recognised as an authoritative body on all matters of political importance to the movement. The Trades Union Congress, however, throughout Broadhurst's secretaryship, was representative of little more than half a million skilled artisans. The remainder of the working class, the millions of unskilled workers, were, with the exception of the cotton industry and a few other rare exceptions, unorganised, and for the most part barely taken into consideration by the Parliamentary Committee. Its policy reflected the philosophy of unions whose members were craftsmen, conscious of their skill and standing in the community as worthy, respectable and independent citizens. The unskilled workers were regarded as being of another class; as uneducated, undisciplined and lacking in the moral character to overcome the vices engendered by chronic poverty. They could not pay the high subscriptions necessary to secure the elaborate system of friendly benefits which consolidated the craft unions, and protected

[1] Webb, S. and B., *The History of Trade Unionism*, p. 397.

their standards as well as giving their members a measure of assistance in times of distress. They had no apprenticeship system and demarcation rules to restrict the flow of applicants for their jobs, and they suffered most from unemployment and low wages. For these reasons it was believed that the unskilled workers could not be organised in trade unions; moreover it was feared that if they were organised they would constitute a threat to the standards established by the craft unions.

The End of an Era

It is not surprising that the organisation of the unskilled workers coincided with the rebirth of British socialism, for the conception of trade union organisation and functions had to be widened before there was any possibility of organising them effectively. To the old unionists the establishment of trade unions without friendly benefits, which were prepared to rely principally on the strike weapon and political activity to secure improved wages and working conditions was courting disaster, not only for the organisations founded on such a basis, but for the whole trade union movement. They pointed to the failure of such ideas in the past, and could not believe that the recrudescence of them would produce results any better than before. But the situation was not the same as they had found it a generation ago. Then the problem was to build and consolidate unions among those who were ready to be organised. It was inevitable that when the skilled workers adopted the model of Allan and Newton they had virtually to turn their backs on the poorest section of the workers, but their achievement in establishing strong unions, securing parliamentary reform and 'practical' legislation helped to produce the conditions that made possible a further expansion of trade union development. Though the old unionists were responsible for the success of the trade unions and the new status of the skilled worker in society they only dimly perceived the ultimate social implications of their activities, and failed to understand their significance for the unorganised non-craftsmen who sought to advance themselves from the indignity and discomfort of grinding poverty. Social myopia is not a unique characteristic of any one section of the community and trade unions have often had more than their fair share of blame for it.

Institutions—economic, political, religious, educational—once established in society tend to live on as perpetuations of certain social attitudes at the time of their origin, fortified as they grow older by a bureaucracy which has grown up around the translating of these attitudes into action. Institutions, except in their early stages when they have something to win through social change, are not in themselves primarily oriented towards awareness of or adaptation to new social developments. Intruding events from without or dissident individuals or minority blocs from within may force change. But any firmly established institution tends to be a preserving and stabilising, not a creative influence.[1]

Whilst it is certain that economic conditions alone do not determine social change, it is clear that they exercise a profound influence. The prolonged depression was, perhaps more than any other factor, responsible for the new radicalism and the outdating of much of the philosophy of the Parliamentary Committee.

> This slump of the eighties following so soon after that of the seventies and linked to it by the unlifted depression in agriculture, gave Victorian courage and optimism the severest shock that it had yet received. Among its by-products were a Lord Mayor's Fund (memorably maladministered); a circular from Chamberlain at the local government board to the local authorities urging relief works (an experiment chiefly valuable for its negative results); a Royal Commission 'on the Depression in Trade and Industry', which buried itself under the pile of its own blue books, and a hot stirring of social thought. . . .[2]

The depression caused established modes of thought and behaviour to be questioned by all sections of the community. As prices fell and profit-making became more difficult the assumptions on which the *laissez-faire* economy rested began to be questioned by industrialists, and they sought to protect themselves by combination. Britain, supreme in the markets of the world, began to feel the effects of competition from France, Germany and the U.S.A.; here and there voices were raised challenging the sanctity of free trade. Liberal economic doctrines no longer seemed quite so perfect in their purity; the assistance of the State was called for not only by socialists, but also by industrialists who wanted their trade protected from the effects of 'unfair' competition. Gradually the notion of State intervention grew less fantastic and the chorus in favour of collectivist policies swelled as the eighties passed by.

The prolonged depression had stimulated social thought, but it was the return of prosperity which focused attention on to the most exploited workers, for it enabled them to rise and demand better conditions. The massive demonstrations of 1888 and 1889 stirred the conscience of the middle class and the striking men and women found a public sympathetic to their claims for an improvement in their conditions of employment, which materially assisted them to secure their modest demands.

[1] Lynd, Helen, *England in the 1880's*, p. 421.
[2] Ensor, R. C. K., *England, 1870-1914*, p. 111.

The self-righteous beliefs of the mid-Victorian middle class were dealt severe blows by rebels from their own social stratum. H. H. Hyndman, H. H. Champion, William Morris, R. B. Cunninghame Graham, Mrs. Besant, Steward Headlam, the Webbs, Bernard Shaw and the rest of the Fabians, were all middle-class intellectuals who had identified themselves with the interests of the poorest section of the community and sought its regeneration through the propagation of socialist doctrines.

The trade union movement could not isolate itself from this social flux. Its leaders might fulminate against those who spread socialist ideas, or, as they preferred to say, sowed 'the seeds of dissension in our ranks', but they could not ignore them as they had the unorganised workers in the past. The new alliance between trade union activists of the calibre of Hardie, Burns and Mann, and middle-class socialist intellectuals was as significant as that of the orthodox trade union leaders and their middle-class political allies, and was to have equally far-reaching consequences.[1]

The inability of Gladstone's second Liberal administration to take any serious steps to alleviate the social problem supplied convincing arguments to illustrate the futility of the working class placing much reliance on the Liberal Party to deliver it from economic exploitation. Tied intellectually and politically to the Liberal Party, the Parliamentary Committee was in a difficult position to exert to the limit the kind of pressure that socialists demanded. Broadhurst and his friends might wring minor concessions from the Liberal Party, but they were not sufficiently influential to bring about a drastic change in its policy. In any case they had no desire to do this, for it would have meant abandoning many of their own beliefs, which were more in harmony with the Liberals than with the socialists. Nor did they wish to give support to the Tories by attacking the Liberals. Hardie had at first thought that if a sufficient number of Lib-Lab members of Parliament were returned, pressure could be put on the Liberal Party to adopt a policy more in keeping with the interests of the working class, but the mid-Lanark by-election convinced him that this was a mistake, and from then onwards he concentrated on the task of persuading the trade union movement to establish its own independent Labour Party.[2] Before this could be achieved, the

[1] The Progressive Party which controlled the London County Council from 1892 to 1907 was another manifestation of a fruitful alliance between middle-class Liberals, radicals, socialists and trade unionists.

[2] Hardie had offered himself to the Liberal Association as a Labour candidate, but had been rejected in favour of a young lawyer, whereupon he fought the Liberal and Tory candidates on an independent Labour platform. The Liberal Party with the connivance of Threlfall, the leader of the Labour Electoral Association, tried to buy Hardie's withdrawal with the promise of a safe seat at the next

Trades Union Congress had to be wooed away from its allegiance
to the Liberal Party, which meant first capturing the control of the
Parliamentary Committee.[1] It was the formation of the new unions
that really made this possible. Their advent was a tremendous
advertisement for the ideas of their founders, and strongly influenced
the rank and file of the old-established unions. The existence of the
new unions ensured a vigorous challenge to the policies of the
Parliamentary Committee; how the challenge developed and influenced the Trades Union Congress is evident in the history of the
next decade.

general election. This suggestion was indignantly refused, and the mid-Lanark
by-election became an intensely bitter three-cornered contest which resulted in
Hardie being at the bottom of the poll, but profoundly convinced that the time
had now come when the working class should break with the Liberals, and have
its own political party. See Stewart, W., *James Keir Hardie*, p. 45.

[1] 'Some method must be devised to capture that Congress.' Tom Mann to
John Burns, in 1888. Burns Collection, British Museum (46286-2).

CHAPTER IV

NEW RADICALISM; REACTION; NEW ORGANISATION

The 'New' Unionism had been carried to its successes in 1889 and 1890 on the crest of a prosperity wave. The following year brought an abrupt change in the economic situation. Unemployment rose again and the upward trend of money wages turned downwards.[1] The effect of this recession on the trade union movement was to cause many of the recently won members to abandon their union cards. The new unions suffered a greater loss of membership than the older ones, since they were unable to offer friendly benefits as an inducement to stick to the union. The leaders of the old unions were not slow in pointing out that this decline in membership was exactly what they had forecast but any secret hopes they might have cherished that the 'new' unions would be swept away were disappointed. Membership of the trade unions affiliated to the Trades Union Congress fell from the peak figure of almost 1,500,000 in 1890 to only 900,000 in 1893; thereafter, however, as trade revived, membership began to creep up again. Fortunately for the 'new' unions this slump was neither so steep as its two predecessors nor so prolonged; by 1896 recovery was almost complete and trade boomed during the next four years.

The slump, together with technical changes in industry, sharpened the conflict in industrial relations and a number of disputes occurred in the next few years. The recession in trade did not, as might have been expected, worsen the relationship between the old unionists and the new; if anything it had the opposite effect, drawing them closer together in the common struggle to prevent working-class standards of living from being cut by wage reductions. Some of the 'new' unions soon forgot their opposition to friendly benefits as their members indicated they would appreciate them, though, compared with the old unions, these were only on a modest scale owing to their low rates of contributions. As the practical needs of their members were asserted, the revolutionary sentiments that were often on the lips of the founders of the 'new' unionism in the late eighties gave way to more realistic trade union demands. The 'new' unions were compelled to adopt the well-tried methods of trade union organisation, on which they had previously been inclined to pour scorn. This,

[1] Money wages had risen sharply after 1886.

133

however, was not all triumph for the old unions, whose supporters were infected by the feverish burst of energy generated by the 'new' unions. Not only did the former rapidly increase their membership; they also widened their scope of recruitment and commenced to assist in the organisation of the unskilled workers. The clash between the old unionists and the new was real enough, but the lines of demarcation became rapidly blurred; many of the differences of opinion manifested in the Labour movement during the nineties cut right across trade union boundaries, whether they were in origin new or old.

The successful establishment of the new unions increased the influence in the trade union movement of those like Keir Hardie who desired to break from the Liberals and organise an *independent* Labour Party. The ascendancy of the Liberals was not, however, easily supplanted; the victory of those who desired a Labour Party took a long time to achieve and when it came it was something of a surprise.

The movement for independent Labour representation found a voice in a number of Labour newspapers which had come into existence, the most noticeable of them being Joseph Burgess's *Workman's Times*, Keir Hardie's *Labour Leader*, and Robert Blatchford's *Clarion*. Of these, the *Clarion*, founded by Blatchford in 1891, was the most influential, and became the rallying point of a propaganda movement which carried the message of socialism with missionary zeal to towns and villages all over the country. While the *Clarion* socialists appealed to the heart and sentiment, the Fabian Society used facts and logic to drive home the case for social reform. At this stage the Fabian Society was not in favour of an independent Labour Party, but sought to permeate the Liberal Party with its ideas. Until 1890 the Society had no contact with the working-class movement and few workers had any idea of the existence of the Fabians. During that year the Society organised a propaganda campaign in Lancashire, its speakers giving over sixty lectures at meetings organised by Radical Working Men's Associations, Co-operatives, S.D.F. and Socialist League Branches.[1] This campaign brought the leaders of the Society into personal contact with the men and women playing an active part in the industrial movement and had an important influence on their future policy and activities.

The tracts which the Society was churning out on many of the administrative problems facing social reformers were assisting the movement towards independent Labour political organisation because they blue-printed the practical content of a political programme and demonstrated the feasibility of its application.

[1] Pease, E., *History of the Fabian Society*.

One of the products of the expansion of trade union activities was a growth in the number of trades councils. These bodies, composed of local trade union officials, were a natural forum for socialist propagandists, and many of them, though not without a struggle, became strongholds of support for the establishment of an independent political party to represent the interests of Labour in the House of Commons. In 1891 the London Trades Council formed a Labour Representation League to secure the return of more working men to Parliament, and in Bradford, after a clash with the supporters of the Liberal Party, a Labour Union was set up to sponsor independent Labour candidates, an example which was followed elsewhere.

Although events were moving in favour of an independent Labour Party, and the Trades Union Congress had gone on record in support of reforms which neither of the main parties was likely to introduce, it was reluctant to take the next step and break with the Liberal Party to form a party of its own. At the 1891 Congress, Keir Hardie moved an amendment to a resolution urging the return of more working men to the House of Commons, to the effect that each trade union should contribute a penny per member to create a Parliamentary Fund which would be administered by the Parliamentary Committee for the assistance of working-class candidates. The amendment mustered a certain amount of support, but was easily defeated by 200 votes to 93.[1]

Reference was made by a number of delegates, during the course of the 1891 Congress, to the prospect of an early election, but little preparation was made for it. The Labour Electoral Association, founded in 1886, had built up a large number of local committees, but had increasingly fallen under the influence of the Liberals. The national body was reluctant to support candidates who were socialists, but many of the local committees repudiated this policy and some adopted independent Labour candidates.[2] When the general election was held, in July 1892, the L.E.A. managed to put more than twenty Lib-Lab candidates into the field, of whom ten were eventually returned.[3] This was not a good showing when account was taken of the effort which the L.E.A. had made and of the fact that a Liberal majority was returned by the electorate. The independents fared no better, only Hardie, Burns and Havelock Wilson being elected out of the sixteen or seventeen candidates put forward by the

---

[1] *T.U.C. Annual Report*, 1891.

[2] Humphrey, A. W., *The History of Labour Representation*, p. 96.

[3] The sensation of the election was the defeat of Henry Broadhurst. The defection of the Miners, who refused to vote for Broadhurst because of his opposition to the Eight Hours Bill was an important factor in his defeat. Cf. *Henry Broadhurst, M.P.*

S.D.F., Scottish Labour Party, and independent Labour committees. The Liberals, under the skilful prodding of the Fabians, had adopted the 'Newcastle' programme which, if not exactly a bold programme made some concessions to the need for a number of social reforms.[1] If not fully consistent, the programme was sufficiently wide and sufficiently radical to win the seats from the Conservatives and Liberal Unionists which gave Gladstone an overall majority of 46, and a fourth term as Prime Minister.

The 1892 Congress assembled shortly after the new Government was installed, and the relatively poor results of the L.E.A. campaign in the general election influenced the delegates sufficiently for them to accept a proposal by Keir Hardie that the Parliamentary Committee should be instructed to prepare a scheme of Labour representation 'dealing especially with the financial difficulty' to be submitted to the unions in time to be considered before the next Congress.

Conflict in Congress over the Eight-hour Day

The annual Trades Union Congress continued to provide opportunities for a clash of opinion between those who wanted to break with the traditional alliance with liberalism and those who were against supporting the development of State socialism. The suggestion that the working day should be limited by law to eight hours had become a symbolic issue in the conflict, and the lively dispute that had become a regular feature of Congress often ranged far beyond the merits of the proposal. In 1891, after one of the longest Congress debates on record, an amendment by Keir Hardie 'That legislation regulating hours of labour to eight per day shall be in force in all trades and occupations save where a majority of the organised members of any trade or occupation protest by ballot voting against the same', was carried.[2] Congress was faced for the second time with the same issues when the resolution calling on the Parliamentary Committee to use every means in its power to secure the passage of an Eight Hours Bill for the mines was debated. Immediately after the vote, which went overwhelmingly in favour of the Bill, a Congress 'scene' occurred. A good deal of lobbying had been going on, and Keir Hardie and another delegate had decided to have leaflets printed listing the men they desired to see on the Parliamentary Committee, and calling on all 'eight hours men' to vote for them. Hardie and King were severely censured by delegate after delegate, including those whose names had been cited, for using their names without permission, and an attempt was made to have both men

[1] Shaw, G. Bernard, *The History of the Fabian Society*—a Fabian Tract.
[2] *T.U.C. Annual Report*, 1891.

expelled, but the good sense of the president and Congress prevailed and the matter was dropped. Apart from this episode and a row over the new standing orders, of which more will be said later, the 1891 Congress had been free from the bitter personal note sounded sometimes in previous years.[1]

At the next Congress a vote of censure was moved by Sam Woods of the Miners' Federation against the Parliamentary Committee and the action of its secretary, Charles Fenwick, for not carrying out the instructions of Congress to give full support to the Miners' Eight Hours Bill, which had been moved in Parliament. The Committee's method of promoting the Bill had been deliberately maladroit; and Fenwick had actually spoken and voted against it. The Committee was also accused of having omitted the words 'eight hours' from the report of the resolution passed the previous year, the wording of

[1] An extremely vivid picture of the debate on the 'Eight Hours Question' is given in the contemporary account printed in the *Trade Unionist*, 19 September 1891, from which the following extracts are taken.

'From Tuesday afternoon, when Mr. Matkin rose with his resolution on the international aspect of the question, to Wednesday afternoon, the discussion was sustained, the speaking throughout being at a remarkably high level, and characterised by intense feeling, well kept in hand. It is true that few new arguments were adduced, but it may be questioned whether in any other assembly in the world a more brilliant presentment of the case could have been obtained. There was a comparative absence of the desire for making points, and scoring off the other side, whilst an intensity of personal conviction was thrown into the discussion from both sides. With all the strong emotions aroused by the debate, the absence of fierceness and bad feeling was notable, and there was an almost complete dearth of the lower features of discussion, of the imputation of unworthy motives and personalities. Each man spoke for himself, was more concerned to express the convictions that burned in him than to deal with the arguments of the other side, so that the speaking partook the form of an experienced meeting rather than a debate.'

'The Federation men sat together in the gallery, on the right of the platform, their stalwart leaders looking down from the front seat upon the Northumberland and Durham Pitmen. When a division came out favourably for the Federation, the whole hall resounded with their cheers. They were a demonstrative set of lads. But before they had well sat down, up would jump the Northumbrians and Durhamites and wave their hats at the gallery, cheering defiantly, but with a good-natured look on their faces.

'When the first permissive amendment came on there was great excitement and eagerness to see how the result would go. The textile representatives voted for it almost to a man. . . . "Shortly after it became rumoured abroad that Mr. Keir Hardie's friends inside and outside the room were dissatisfied with the resolution, and that another amendment would come on later, with the support of the Miners' Federation. This was the motion in the form of trade exemption, which was finally carried amidst great enthusiasm and so ended the eight-hours debate, amidst a flourish of hats, umbrellas, walking sticks, and the handkerchiefs of those whose headgear is not adapted to demonstrative purposes—the women delegates to wit."'

which had appeared to give them some loophole. Fenwick defended himself by pointing out that he was elected as a Liberal, and that as a Member of Parliament his first responsibility was to his constituents, the majority of whom were not in favour of eight hours legislation. He claimed that when he had been elected as secretary of the Parliamentary Committee the delegates knew exactly where he stood on this question. There had been no question of deception and he challenged any delegate to show when he had neglected his duties as secretary. He concluded by pointing out that the problem was inevitable if they had Members of Parliament on the Committee.

The problem raised by the representation of sectional interests is a fundamental one in a parliamentary democracy. There is no easy solution to it—indeed it remains an equally difficult problem at the present day—and the serious tone and high level of the speeches in Congress bear witness that this was understood by the delegates. The issue was clearly put by Ben Tillett when he said:

> Here is a Congress pledged to eight hours by legal enactment, and you are electing to the most responsible position a man you know to be an honest man who will vote against it. . . . They had got a lesson, and instead of passing a vote of censure they should put an eight-hours man in the place of Mr. Fenwick.

The motion was rejected by a large majority, and the delegates confirmed this expression of confidence in Fenwick by re-electing him as secretary with a majority of one hundred votes, over an 'eight hours man'.[1] This result, though inconsistent with the declaration of Congress in favour of the Bill, was a magnificent expression of the delegates' ability to appreciate both sides of a great issue.

The question of the accuracy of the report of the previous year's Congress resolution raised more disquiet, and it was agreed that a special committee of inquiry should be set up to investigate the charge. After the Committee had examined all involved it reported 'that no disclosures reflecting on any of the persons concerned have been made'.[2] The official minute book showed the resolution as omitting the operative words 'eight hours'. Unfortunately the original written amendment as submitted could not be found. It was revealed that the Parliamentary Committee had made up its report 'of the Newcastle Congress proceedings in the way established by precedent—from newspaper reports of the proceedings of Congress corrected from the official minute book'. The report exculpated the secretary, and was accepted with a recommendation that in future all resolutions and amendments should be filed and preserved for

[1] *T.U.C. Annual Report*, 1892.   [2] *Ibid.*

reference. Congress then went on, notwithstanding its affirmation of faith in Fenwick, to pass a resolution instructing the Parliamentary Committee to give full support to the Miners' Eight Hours Bill; and another resolution calling upon the Committee to convene an international congress to discuss the eight-hour day.[1]

A year later, the 1893 Congress listened to a vote of censure once more being moved on the behaviour of the Parliamentary Committee over the Miners' Eight Hours Bill. After a debate identical with the one which had taken place the year before, Fenwick and his colleagues were again vindicated; and Fenwick was re-elected as secretary; this time by a huge majority over Keir Hardie, the only rival candidate.

Keir Hardie seeks to persuade Congress to support Independent Labour Representation

Congress was not prepared to elect Hardie to the most important post in the trade union world, but it did take some important steps along the road he was urging the trade unions to travel. As a result of his resolution the year before calling on the Parliamentary Committee to undertake an examination of the problem of Labour representation, the Committee submitted a scheme for the establishment of a political fund 'for the purpose of assisting independent labour candidates in local and Parliamentary elections'. Contributions were to be optional, but each society desiring to affiliate with the movement, 'shall subscribe annually to the election fund the sum of five shillings per hundred members'. The administration of the fund was to be in the hands of a committee elected annually at Congress by the delegates representing the contributing societies. 'The selection of candidates in every case to rest with the localities in the first instance. . . .' Most important 'all candidates receiving financial assistance must pledge themselves to support the labour programme as agreed upon from time to time by Congress'.[2]

The proposals met with a good deal of opposition from the supporters of the Labour Electoral Association, but Congress not only rejected their point of view, it accepted an amendment moved by James Macdonald, to insert that candidates should pledge themselves 'to support the principle of collective ownership and control of all the means of production and distribution' as well as the current programme of Congress. When, however, Keir Hardie tried to persuade the delegates to go one step farther, and say:

> That in the opinion of this Congress the claims of labour in Parliament should be asserted irrespective of the convenience of any political

[1] *Ibid.*   [2] *Ibid.*

party; and to secure this it is necessary that the labour members in the House of Commons should be unconnected with either the Liberal or Tory party, and should sit in opposition to any Government, until such time as they are strong enough to form a Labour Cabinet,

he was narrowly defeated.[1] Hardie was never a popular or trusted figure at Congress; many delegates, including some who agreed with his aims, feared that he was over-ambitious and would vote against him when they thought that he had gone too far.

While Hardie was unable to succeed by personal persuasion, growing unemployment and impatience at the failure of the Government to tackle the social problem were gradually winning support for his policy. Any hopes that might have been entertained about the willingness of the Liberals to act vigorously when they were returned to power had been dissipated in the early nineties. After the revelations of the House of Lords Committee on Sweating, which issued a series of reports between 1888 and 1890, the Conservative Government had appointed a Royal Commission on Labour, under the Chairmanship of Lord Hartington, on which seven Labour representatives were appointed. For a Royal Commission it had not been long at its labour when the Conservatives were turned out, and Gladstone seemed content to shelter under this hoary device for avoiding action on problems of concern to labour when he again took office. The rank and file, discontented with the worsening economic situation, turned to direct action and in 1893 there were strikes all over the country against reductions in wages. Although in nearly every case the workers had to go back on worse terms, those in employment were relatively well off, as there had been a substantial fall in prices of consumer goods. It was the out-of-work who suffered most, and when Keir Hardie drew the attention of Parliament to their plight the Parliamentary Committee had to report 'we regret the negative and hostile manner with which the question was met by both parties in the House of Commons'.[2] Even the Liberal majority on the Parliamentary Committee was finding it increasingly difficult to distinguish Tweedledum from Tweedledee in the House of Commons.

The defection of a number of local committees from the L.E.A., and the formation, all over the country, of independent Labour groups which came together at Bradford, in January 1893, under the leadership of Keir Hardie, to found the Independent Labour Party, had created some alarm amongst those who were opposed to social-ism, and jealousy in others. John Burns, in 1893, was in the latter

[1] *T.U.C. Annual Report*, 1892.
[2] *Report of the Parliamentary Committee*, 1893.

category and stated to Congress that he supported both the plan of the Parliamentary Committee to set up a fund to promote Labour candidates, and also Macdonald's socialist amendment. 'Till the independent labour party are put out of existence there is nothing between trade unionism on one side and trade unionism plus a Socialist labour party on the other. These parties are at present separate, but if they are blended together they would be invincible.'[1] He was not, therefore, in favour of the establishment of an independent Labour Party but of a united trade union and socialist party. This had always been Keir Hardie's theme, but Burns was soon to forget that he had ever supported it.

With the passing of the resolution in support of a parliamentary fund under the control of the Parliamentary Committee the socialists had scored a success, but they had left a loophole through which the Parliamentary Committee could escape its responsibilities. When the Committee reported to the 1894 Congress it stated 'that no committee had been appointed by Congress to take charge of the organisation and administer its funds'.[2] The Parliamentary Committee had considered that it had discharged its obligations by sending out a circular to the unions drawing their attention to the passing of the resolution; as only two replies were received it had done nothing further in the matter. The reason for the Parliamentary Committee's change of heart was undoubtedly, as Professor Cole has suggested, the fact that the passing of James Macdonald's amendment committed them to a socialist policy.[3] But this was not the only reason. The great increase in unemployment had resulted in a serious drain on the resources of the unions. It was not therefore surprising that on more sober consideration, even many of those who had given it their support let the matter drop. There was little likelihood that the rank and file, who were too concerned with bread and butter questions of industrial policy, would strongly press trade union executives at such a time to embark on any expensive political schemes. The plan could only have gone ahead if a vigorous lead had been forthcoming, and without this it was bound to be stultified.

The Miners' Eight Hours Bill had received a second reading in the House of Commons, but on reaching the committee stage it had been amended by the insertion of a clause permitting local option, whereupon it had been withdrawn. This clause had been carried by a majority of only five votes, one of which had been cast by Charles Fenwick. This was the last straw, and the delegates to the 1894 Congress decided to put an end to the anomaly of having such a diehard

[1] T.U.C. Annual Report, 1893.
[2] Report of the Parliamentary Committee, 1894.
[3] Cole, G. D. H., British Working Class Politics, 1832–1914, p. 111.

opponent of Congress policy as its secretary. W. E. Harvey, one of the leaders of the Miners' Federation, speaking on the report, said: 'He believed the time had come when the opinion of the Congress in favour of an eight-hour day would be carried into effect by the appointment of an eight hours man as its chief official.'[1] Pete Curran, of the Gas Workers' and General Labourers' Union, described Fenwick as a 'round peg in a square hole', but every speaker paid tribute to Fenwick's honesty of purpose, and right to speak and vote according to his conscience in the House of Commons. When it was announced that Fenwick had been defeated, his successor, Sam Woods of the Miners' Federation, made a speech in which he said that the change would make no difference to his personal regard for Fenwick; the defeated secretary replied in a similar vein, offering to give every assistance to Woods in the carrying out of his job.

Keir Hardie secured another resounding propaganda victory when, by 219 votes to 61, his amendment adding the words 'and the whole of the means of production, distribution and exchange' to a resolution calling for 'the nationalisation of the land, mines, minerals and royalty rents', was carried. On this occasion Harvey spoke against Hardie's amendment. Although Harvey was a prominent figure in the Miners' Federation, which had been founded in opposition to the conservative Miners' National Union, he was, like so many others among its leaders, by no means a socialist. He was in favour of collectivist policies up to a point, but he wanted no more than to use the State as a prop to bolster up the activities of the trade unions. He was in favour of the State regulating working conditions in the mines; he was even ready to see the ownership of the land vested in the State, because he did not believe that landlords had a right to levy a toll on every ton of coal dug out of the earth.

> But [he said] the majority of the Congress did not believe they were going to dispense with the ideas of thought and enterprise. However old and fossilised trade unionism might be, it had done more for the country than all the Socialist policy had propounded.[2]

The real strength of the socialists was clearly shown in the voting for the new secretary of the Parliamentary Committee, when Tom Mann, who was their candidate, received somewhat less than one-third of the total votes cast; the passing of the nationalisation resolution was more a gesture of annoyance at the failure of the Government to tackle seriously the nation's economic and social problems than a real conversion of Congress to socialism.

[1] *T.U.C. Annual Report*, 1894.   [2] *Ibid.*

Revision of the Standing Orders

A rather innocuous sounding resolution, to amend the standing orders of Congress, which proved to have far-reaching consequences unforeseen by the delegates, was passed during the week. Trouble had occurred over the standing orders on a number of occasions. For several years past lengthy discussions had taken place on the standing orders and a number of important revisions had been made. Many of the changes proposed were not from entirely disinterested motives as everybody knew, and so they were usually regarded with a good deal of suspicion. Up to 1890 voting had been by a show of hands, on the simple principle of one man one vote, and there was nothing in the standing orders to prevent an organisation sending as many delegates as it pleased, so long as they were its bona fide representatives. At the Congress of that year an amendment was moved to the standing orders that votes should be allocated on the basis of the number of members for whom the societies had paid. The principal supporters of this change were the large unions, especially the Miners' Federation, which, with 150,000 members, was the largest union affiliated to Congress. The basis of representation under the new standing order was that each society with 1,000 or less members would, on the payment of £1, be entitled to one vote. On the payment of £1 for each additional thousand members, or fraction, they would be entitled to one extra vote. When the chairman attempted to apply this formula at the 1891 Congress, a tremendous row ensued. The trades councils representatives objected strongly to the introduction of the new method, the Glasgow delegate pointing out that it would cost his council £40—about one-third of its annual income—to obtain its vote. After a long and confused discussion it was agreed to issue voting cards to the delegates, which took one hour to do, for them to vote on whether they would suspend the new standing order in favour of the old method of one man one vote. It is doubtful if the delegates knew what they were voting on. One observer commented: 'The scene of "distributing the voting cards" was certainly unique in the annals of labour parliaments. Somebody said it looked the Dutch Auction in Petticoat Lane, others that it resembled a scene at the Stock Exchange on an exciting day. . . .'[1] The result of the voting proved to be overwhelmingly in favour of a return to the older and simpler method. This was not to the liking of the Miners' Federation, which 'had paid up £150 so as to secure the full quota of votes'.[2] The correspondent wrote: 'Mr. Pickard will now have to give up a

---

[1] *The Trade Unionist*, 12 September 1891.
[2] *Ibid.*

technical advantage out of deference to public feeling.'[1] This was not the end of the matter, however, for Congress spent the best part of another day wrestling with one ingenious amendment after another, the passing of which only served to further complicate the issue, until, in exhaustion, they finally agreed to refer the matter to a committee to examine the question and report to the next Congress.

This Committee did its job and presented to the 1892 Congress a revised version of the standing orders. Clause Four, after being slightly amended was adopted by Congress and provided that

> Trade societies, by whatever name they may be known, shall be entitled to one delegate for every 2,000 members or fraction thereof; provided always that they have paid £1 for every 1,000 or fraction thereof towards the expenses of the Parliamentary Committee for the past year, and 10s. for each delegate attending the Congress, and forward their names and addresses fourteen days prior to the date fixed for the meeting of Congress.

> Trades Councils or like organisations made up of a number of branches or trades shall only send representatives, and be called upon to subscribe as aforesaid for those members who are not directly represented through their own respective trade or associations. No credential card shall be issued to any society or trades council not having complied with the foregoing conditions.

Nowhere in this new version of the contentious clause in the 1891 standing orders, is there any reference to the question of the number of votes to be wielded by the delegates. Congress dropped the subject with the tacit consent of all concerned. In the second part of the new clause the attempt is ostensibly made to prevent dual representation; the covert aim, however, was to cut down the strength of the representation of the trades councils.

In the eighties the trades councils had been strongholds of Liberal radicalism, but they had increasingly come under the influence of the new unionists. It was largely through the trades councils that the socialists were putting over their policy direct to the rank and file. The importance of using the trades councils as a means of counteracting the conservatism of many of the trade union leaders was stressed by Tom Mann and his friends.

> Already [said Mann in 1892] the London Trades Council has subdivided itself so as to give the necessary attention to the requirements of the kindred groups of trades; and a special department is now dealing effectively with the citizenship side of the labour question, under whose

---

[1] Ben Pickard, leader of the Yorkshire Miners and president of the Miners' Federation, was a staunch Liberal. His authority over the Yorkshire miners was almost absolute and for years he was the greatest obstacle to the spread of I.L.P. influence among his followers.

auspices lectures and addresses will be given to enable all concerned to get a sound education upon the industrial question.[1]

The new clause was not entirely successful in preventing the trades councils from having an effective voice at Congress, and it merely presaged the more drastic policy that came three years later.

An important result of the new clause was that Congress could now rely on obtaining a regular income from its affiliated organisations, proportionate to their membership. Up to this date the Parliamentary Committee had been compelled to issue an annual appeal for funds, and the unions had contributed what they felt to be reasonable, according to their financial situation.

The standing orders were further revised in 1893. The size of the Parliamentary Committee was increased from eleven to thirteen members, including one representative from a trade union or trades council in Ireland. An attempt to make the chairman of the Parliamentary Committee, president of Congress, at the end of his year of office, was made by W. C. Steadman, secretary of the Barge Builders' Union, on the grounds that 'they generally found that the man who could pull most wires was selected as president' under the existing system; but this was defeated. Under the new Clause Four an important ruling was made that no union could affiliate only part of its membership, but had to affiliate on all its membership roll. It had been found that a number of unions had affiliated only part of their membership, and then by simply paying the delegates' fees had sent their full quota of delegates to Congress.

These changes did not quell dissatisfaction with the standing orders, and another spate of amendments faced the 1894 Congress. Most of them were rejected, but one proposed by W. J. Davis, which sought to improve the way in which the annual Congress was conducted, was accepted. It read,

> That on account of the increase in the number of matters placed on the agenda paper for the consideration of the Congress and the limited time available for their proper discussion, this Congress is of opinion that the various subjects should be grouped, and remitted to Grand Committees or sections of the delegates, on the lines of the Grand Committees in the House of Commons, or Sections as in the British Association. Such Committees, having arrived at a decision on the questions remitted to them, shall report to Congress for confirmation. The Parliamentary Committee being instructed to carry out the terms of this resolution, which shall come into operation at the next Congress.

[1] *The Trade Unionist*, 6 February 1892. In the same speech Tom Mann urged the need for closer relations between the trade unions and the Co-operative movement, and the need for the Government to set up a Ministry of Labour.

On the last day of the 1894 Congress a number of resolutions, principally dealing with matters of organisation, remained to be dealt with and it was decided, on the proposal of Keir Hardie, to remit these to the Parliamentary Committee for consideration.

A Coup d'État

At a meeting of the Parliamentary Committee on the 10th October, at the suggestion of John Burns, the following resolution was passed,

> That in accordance with the resolution of Congress remitting a number of resolutions and amendments to the Standing Orders of the Parliamentary Committee, it is hereby agreed that a sub-committee be appointed to revise the Standing Orders, which said Standing Orders shall be submitted for approval to a meeting of the full Parliamentary Committee, and after adoption they shall be sent out to the trades, and shall become the Standing Orders governing the proceedings of Congress next year.[1]

The sub-committee elected consisted of John Burns, James Mawdsley and J. M. Jack[2] with the addition of the chairman and secretary of the Parliamentary Committee, David Holmes[3] and Sam Woods. It was not until the 20th November, when the sub-committee presented the result of its work, that the rest of the Parliamentary Committee realised what Burns had in mind when he moved to set up the sub-committee to consider the standing orders.

The recommendations of the sub-committee were mainly threefold, (1) to end the representation of trades councils at Congress; (2) to reintroduce the Miners' Federation plan of voting in Congress, which was dropped at the 1891 Congress;[4] (3) to exclude as a delegate to Congress anyone who was not either working at his trade, or employed as a permanent salaried official of his society. Realising, that as a result of the suggested changes, he himself would be excluded from the Trades Union Congress in the future, Broadhurst, who had continued to attend Congress as a delegate after his resignation as secretary and had been elected a member of the Parliamentary Committee in 1893, put up a strong resistance to them. The struggle on the Parliamentary Committee went on for three days, with the Committee evenly divided, six for the changes and six against, until David Holmes, the chairman, gave his casting vote in favour of the Burns proposals.[5]

[1] *Report of the Parliamentary Committee*, 1895.
[2] Secretary of the Scottish Iron Founders.
[3] Secretary of the Cotton Weavers.
[4] See p. 143.
[5] *Report of the Parliamentary Committee*, 1895.

Burns and Holmes, who had been elected as the first fraternal delegates to the annual convention of the American Federation of Labour[1] left for America two weeks after the Parliamentary Committee had accepted the new standing orders. It had been Burns's intention to hold back the new standing orders until near the date of the next Congress, but Broadhurst seized the opportunity to have them circulated to the trades immediately after Holmes and Burns had left the country. As soon as Keir Hardie learned the details of the changes he published a lengthy article in the *Labour Leader* attacking them. After severely criticising the way in which the revision of the standing orders had been engineered, and the constitutional validity of the procedure, he went on to say that the clause restricting delegates to working members and permanent paid officials,

> is the great masterpiece stroke of policy, and but for the supposed urgency of securing the immediate enactment of this, the Parliamentary Committee would not have rushed so incontinently into unconstitutional ways. The object of the proposal is plain. It is meant to exclude from the Congress those who are neither working at their trade, nor paid officials of their trade unions. Anyone who will take the trouble to go through the list of delegates to the last Congress will find that the only change such a rule would make would be the exclusion from future Congresses of the following: Henry Broadhurst, John Burns, Thomas Burt, Keir Hardie and Tom Mann. I understand Mr. Burns claims to be a paid official of the Amalgamated Society of Engineers, since that body pays him £100 a year for representing their interests in Parliament. He would, therefore, if this is correct, be still eligible to go to Congress. Mr. Burt is still an official of the Northumberland Miners' Union, and would be a paid official again were he to lose his present position as Under Secretary to the Board of Trade. The new rule, therefore, has been framed for the express purpose of excluding Broadhurst, Mann and myself.

Hardie went on to write,

> By a strange combination of circumstances he (Burns) secured the co-operation of a stronger and abler man than himself. Mr. James Mawdsley was but recently a Tory. He is now to all intents and purposes a Socialist with sympathetic leanings towards the Independent Labour Movement. . . . Mr. Mawdsley sees in Mr. Henry Broadhurst a paid tool of the Liberal Party, who is rapidly regaining a position in the Congress, and who may one day again be its secretary.[2]

Hardie's analysis of the situation seems to have been substantially correct, but his opinion of Mawdsley was too much influenced by

[1] Congress had received Mr. John Lloyd, the first fraternal delegate to the T.U.C. from the A.F. of L. in 1894.
[2] *Labour Leader*, 29 December 1894.

the fact that he had signed the minority report of the Royal Commission on Labour, which had been drafted by Sidney Webb,[1] and called for the 'substitution as fast as possible of public for capitalist enterprise'.[2] He had also supported State intervention, for example, in the extension of the Factory Acts, and voted with the progressives on other issues, but he was no socialist. He was an avowed Conservative with a cautious sympathy for certain collectivist schemes; this was no more a contradiction of his politics than was Shaftesbury's work for the miners a denial of his Toryism. When Mawdsley later found the money to enable James Sexton to stand as an I.L.P. candidate in Lancashire, at the 1895 election,[3] this was probably determined more by a shrewd belief that it would take away votes from the Liberal and let in the Tory, than an indication that his sympathies were leaning towards the I.L.P.[4] That the new standing orders were a triumph for Mawdsley was patent enough, for they gave the Cotton Operatives and the Miners almost a third of the votes in Congress.

Shortly after writing the article Hardie wrote to Broadhurst, asking him to write something to follow it up, so as to stimulate interest in the issue. He also asked

> Do you intend, in the last resort issuing a minority report? I don't well see how you can avoid it. I will treat as confidential anything you say which is not for publication. My summing up of the situation is, I know, correct.[5]

Whether Broadhurst replied to Hardie is not known. However, no article appeared under his name in the columns of the *Labour Leader*. Broadhurst did, however, act on Hardie's suggestion of a minority report, for Mrs. Webb records in her diary how he visited them in order to get their help and advice, on the 15 January 1895; two weeks after Hardie's letter had been dispatched. After listening to Broadhurst's account of the *coup d'état* she writes, 'Then we set to, and discussed the whole constitution of Congress. Broadhurst had evidently come, not only to get Sidney's advice, but to get him to draft alternative "standing orders" to be submitted to Congress.'[6] Later Mrs. Webb writes 'Sidney virtually agreed to Broadhurst's request to draw up suggestions for his private use.' And a little further, on, after a gleeful analysis of the pros and cons of the situation, 'it

[1] Cf. Webb, B., *Our Partnership*, p. 40.

[2] *Minority Report, Royal Commission on Labour*.

[3] *Sir James Sexton—Agitator* p. 146.

[4] Mawdsley stood as a Conservative candidate at later elections.

[5] Broadhurst Correspondence in the British Library of Political and Economic Science.

[6] Webb, B., *Our Partnership*, p. 50.

will be almost impossible for us to refuse Broadhurst's appeal to help him carry out our views'. There is no evidence that the Webbs carried out their promise, and drafted alternative standing orders for Broadhurst, or if they did, that he made any attempt to use them. Nor is there any evidence to show that the Webbs had any influence on the Parliamentary Committee where, in fact, they were highly distrusted.

Curiously, following the appearance of Hardie's article in the *Labour Leader*, hardly any further reference to the new standing orders was made. No campaign against them was organised by either Hardie or Broadhurst, and the issue was completely dead until the 1895 Congress, when they came into force. Hardie apparently decided that the fight against the new standing orders was a hopeless one, for he accepted an invitation to go to America on a lecture tour and to visit the Chicago Labour Congress, which was held at the same time as the Trades Union Congress.[1] Hardie probably gave up the idea of attempting to stir up widespread opposition to the new standing orders when he realised the extent of the apathy on the question, and that Broadhurst was not going to make a real fight against them. With a general election in the offing he was more concerned with organising the I.L.P. in preparation for it; the return of a strong contingent of Hardie's supporters to the House of Commons would have enormously strengthened his position. In the event the severe defeat of all the I.L.P. candidates and the antagonisms created by its 'abstain from voting where there is no socialist candidate' policy, strengthened the position of Burns and Mawdsley. Broadhurst's dislike of socialism was a sufficient reason to explain his reluctance to join in a campaign, which, if it had been successful, would have redounded to the benefit of Hardie and his followers. He preferred to wait until Congress and to make a personal appeal to the delegates not to pass the standing order which would expel him from their midst. The suggestion made by David Holmes, that Broadhurst had not opposed the changes until he realised that he would be excluded, although he indignantly denied the imputation, is plausible in view of his opposition to the socialists.

The determination of the majority of the Parliamentary Committee not to take any steps that would provide the socialists with an opportunity to attack the Liberals was illustrated by the circular which they issued to the trade unions in June. This called upon trade unionists to write to their M.P.s urging them to support the Factory and Workshops Bill, which was being wrecked in committee by amendments. The circular stated that:

> The Government have in the main endeavoured to stand by the chief provisions in the Bill as read a second time in the House of Commons,

[1] Stewart, W., *James Keir Hardie*, p. 115.

but have been compelled by the overwhelming force of opposition to agree to modifications of a nature which may be calculated to seriously affect the efficiency of some of the clauses, especially with regard to young persons and women.[1]

The circular, out of tenderness for the Liberal Party, failed to mention that the Home Secretary, Asquith, had given way on the sixteen-year-old limit, to a deputation of manufacturers, before the Bill came in front of the committee, or that the greatest opposition was, in fact, coming from Liberal industrialists in the House of Commons. To have mentioned these facts would, of course, have strengthened the movement for independent Labour representation, and opposition to the new standing orders.

When the 1895 Congress opened at Cardiff everyone knew that the great issue would be the new standing orders. The delegates had a foretaste of what was to come when the president, Councillor Jenkins of Cardiff, delivered his address. Much of it was devoted to a slashing attack on the leaders of the I.L.P. Reference was made to the recent election and the tactics which had put no less than twenty-eight I.L.P. candidates in the field.

> They knew [said the president] that those candidates were not approved by the Congress, nor, except in very few instances, by the local trades councils and unions; and they knew also that adherents of the Independent Labour Party harassed and opposed genuine trade unionist candidates who happened also to be Liberals.[2]

Hardie and his associates were scornfully criticised for misleading Congress in previous years by persuading the delegates to vote for resolutions that charged the Parliamentary Committee 'with an amount of legislative work beyond hope of being dealt with in any one session of Parliament'.[3]

As soon as the preliminaries were over and the Congress was under way, J. Havelock Wilson moved the suspension of the standing orders so that a resolution would be put censuring the Parliamentary Committee for exceeding their instructions

> from the Norwich Congress in putting into force the new standing orders without first submitting the same to the Cardiff Congress . . . further . . . that it is contrary to the constitution of the T.U.C. and all other public bodies for any committee to deal with the constitutional rules of an association, and to put them in force without submitting the same to a duly convened meeting of delegates.[4]

Havelock Wilson argued that the resolution moved by W. J. Davis and carried, which had been cited by the Parliamentary Committee

[1] *The Factory and Workshops Bill*, 12 June 1895.
[2] *T.U.C. Annual Report*, 1895.   [3] *Ibid.*   [4] *Ibid.*

as giving them authority to introduce the new standing orders before they had been approved by Congress, was concerned only with the grouping of Congress into Committees to facilitate business, and gave them no mandate to introduce any further changes. It was in order for the Parliamentary Committee to propose alterations in the standing orders, but it was entirely unconstitutional to put them into effect before they had been voted on by Congress. Wilson was supported by George Barnes of the Amalgamated Society of Engineers, Paul Weighill of the Stonemasons, W. Matkin, General Union of Carpenters and Joiners, Ben Tillett, John Hodge and a number of others, but Mawdsley and Holmes were able to make great play of the fact that Broadhurst, Thorne, Tillett and Wilson had all agreed to the sub-committee being set up to revise the standing orders. The real reason for the new standing orders was apparent in John Burns's speech, which made little attempt to defend the constitutionality of their imposition on Congress. They were in the interests of labour he was reported to have said:

> because the gate through which they (Broadhurst and he) passed every impostor could go, and (he) affirmed that real independent labour and real socialism could only succeed by sending *bona fide* working men and honest officials to represent the working men of the country.[1]

When the resolution was put the president said that the voting would be according to the new standing orders. Immediately a tremendous uproar broke out. Attempts were made to move the president out of the chair, but, backed by the standing orders committee, he refused to budge. The commotion eventually subsided and the vote was taken, 357,000 votes being cast for the resolution, and 604,000 against. Even had the voting been on a show of hands the Parliamentary Committee would still probably have just got a majority, for they had carefully organised the maximum support in the lobbies of the Congress.[2]

The new standing orders could, as a matter of principle, be defended on their merits in all three cases where they introduced a major change. It was anomalous to allow trades councils to send delegates and, in effect, make policy decisions, when the trade union branches of which they were composed also decided the policy of Congress through their direct union representatives. It was not undemocratic to give due weight to the greater numbers organised in

[1] *Ibid.*
[2] Samuel Gompers, the founder of the A.F. of L. was a fraternal delegate; he was himself no mean practitioner of the art of manipulating a Labour Congress and he must have admired the ruthless way in which the opposition was bludgeoned by the leaders of the T.U.C.

the big unions. Nor was it anything but sensible, in a movement which was not primarily political, to keep out persons who were not representatives of a bona fide trade union, and were merely interested in using Congress for political ends. But these arguments were not answers to the charge that the Parliamentary Committee had acted unconstitutionally in introducing the new standing orders before they had been considered by Congress, or that the reason for their introduction in this unprecedented manner was due more to personal and political animosities than to desires to perfect the constitution of Congress. Mawdsley was quite candid about what they had done. 'We saw our opportunity and took it,' he told an interviewer from the Press; and when asked: 'But would Congress have given you a mandate had they known how you were going to exercise it?' he replied, 'That is their look out. We saw that the Congress was losing whatever influence it had, and we were determined to pull it back again into the old paths.'[1]

John Burns Enjoys his Triumph

The motives of John Burns were more complex. He was a man possessed of many advantages. He had intelligence and courage, and was gifted with immense histrionic ability. His reputation stood high, for he had done as much as any man to stimulate the advance of the working class during the past decade. Unfortunately his character was warped by a streak of meanness and personal vanity. His intense egotism was manifest in the suspicion, jealousy and hatred he displayed for his erstwhile socialist colleagues. He could not bear to think that others stood equally with him in the struggle to convert the working class to socialism. He quarrelled with Ben Tillett in 1891[2] over the conduct of a dock strike for which he had no responsibility. Although Hardie had a great admiration for Burns and would loyally have agreed to his leadership of the independent Labour movement, had Burns been willing to accept it in 1892, Burns reciprocated by treating Hardie first with suspicion, then with derision and contempt which left Hardie bewildered. Among the papers of Burns, deposited in the British Museum after his death, there are a large number of letters from Keir Hardie which indicate that he wanted to be on the friendliest terms with Burns and could not understand the cold

[1] *Daily Chronicle*, 31 August 1895.
The Webbs, although they had qualms about the way in which Mawdsley's victory had been achieved, were not displeased with it. They believed they could use Mawdsley (*Our Partnership*, p. 48), and knew they had no influence over Keir Hardie, whom they utterly despised.

[2] Burns Collection, British Museum (46286–5), Letter to Tillett, 20 October 1891.

response which he received.[1] The election of 1892 seems to have been the point when Burns moved decisively away from Keir Hardie. He had promised to make a speaking tour in support of the candidates of the Scottish Labour Party, and then for some reason decided at the last minute not to go, in spite of the pleading of Hardie not to let them down.[2] Immediately after the election he wrote to Hardie complaining that Hardie had made a declaration of the policy that would be pursued by the 'Labour Party' in the House of Commons without any authorisation, and again in 1893 he was making the same complaint.[3]

Elected to Parliament by the citizens of Battersea, undisputedly the favourite son of the Borough's working class, Burns had no need for the support of any party, nor any inclination to be trammelled by responsibility to one. He firmly believed that the working men of England should look to John Burns for leadership, not to a lot of 'cranks, fools and faddists'. With his reputation and brilliant demagogic abilities he was always a formidable platform figure, but that alone was not sufficient to give Burns the power as well as the plaudits which he craved. Burns had no real power in the trade union movement, in the sense that he could count on the solid support of a great organisation, like James Mawdsley, the secretary of the Cotton Spinners, or such new unionists as Will Thorne and Ben Tillett. He saw his future as a leader of men, in the House of Commons and on the London County Council, not as a trade union secretary. Having turned against the I.L.P. and allowed his hatred of Keir Hardie to reach 'the dimensions of mania',[4] he was determined at all costs to prevent the socialists from capturing the trade union movement. The fact that in the process he would lose his seat on the Parliamentary Committee was a sacrifice Burns enjoyed making and turning to account against his opponents. When asked by a reporter if he had not committed suicide by his action:

> Not a bit of it [said John, his face all smiles]. On the contrary, I am in the position of a man who has been in an overloaded boat and has jumped overboard, not to drown himself, but to lighten the ship. I am strong enough to swim ashore unaided. Some of the rats that have been thrown overboard with me have not got that strength, and will inevitably go under.[5]

[1] *Ibid.*, Letters from Keir Hardie, 1890, 1891, 1892, 1893.
[2] *Ibid.*, Letter from Keir Hardie, 25 May 1892.
[3] At the 1893 Trades Union Congress Burns referred to Hardie and the I.L.P. candidates as 'literary deadheads' and 'journalistic blacklegs'. 'He denounced the arrant frauds that, in the name of independent labour and socialism were going about the country doing everything to disintegrate labour and trade-unionism.'
[4] Webb, B., *Our Partnership*, p. 39.
[5] *The Star*, 4 September 1895.

As for Broadhurst, Burns considered him to be an out-of-date old fogey, and cruelly described him to Congress as a 'superfluous veteran'. The fact that Broadhurst had been a central figure at the Trades Union Congress for twenty years, had held the position of Under Secretary to the Home Office, and was, 'next to Mr. Gladstone, . . . admitted by the highest authorities to be the most successful vote-maker at elections on the Progressive side',[1] was enough to incense Burns's insanely jealous nature. Burns always denied in public that he coveted for himself a place in the Government, but it would have been most unlike him, once inside the House of Commons, not to have imagined himself on the front bench. When the day of his elevation to a ministry arrived, he characteristically remarked to a friend, 'I am going to be at the top of the tree or nowhere. I will hold no subordinate position.'[2] Commenting on a speech made by Burns to his Battersea followers, early in October 1894, Keir Hardie had made a prophetic observation about 'honest John's' future career.

> If Mr. Burns contemplates entering the movement at some future time [he wrote] this speech has made it more difficult than ever to do so; if he intends to remain outside until the end it is quite within the limits of possibility that the year 1905 may find him a member of the Individualist Cabinet formed by an alliance with Liberals and Tories, to make a last stand against the triumphant advance of the ever conquering army of Collectivists.[3]

As Hardie was writing this piece Burns was taking the steps to carry out the *coup d'état* against the I.L.P. which was an important stage in his journey from a roistering advocate of working-class revolt to a Liberal Cabinet Minister.

Before the 1895 Congress came to an end it confirmed the charge that the Parliamentary Committee had acted unconstitutionally by carrying an amendment to the new standing orders which read: 'And no alteration can take effect, except by the express desire of the delegates assembled in Congress. The Parliamentary Committee to have no power in framing new orders.' This somewhat shamefaced concession to scruple, was, of course, in part self-protection, for Mawdsley and his friends were not going to let their defeated enemies repeat the manœuvre, should they once more gain the ascendancy. There was, however, little immediate danger of this, for the socialists were routed when it came to the election of the Parliamentary Committee for the following year. Of the collectivists only John Hodge and Will Thorne were successful, Ben Tillett losing his seat.

[1] Davis, W. J., *The British Trades Union Congress—History and Recollections*, vol. II, p. 57.
[2] Quoted by Kent, William, in *John Burns—Labour's Lost Leader*, p. 147.
[3] *Labour Leader*, 13 October 1894.

The pendulum had, indeed, swung back a long way from the days when the new unionists, flushed with their victories, imagined they had revolutionised the Trades Union Congress.[1] So angry and disappointed were the representatives of the trades councils, who had gone along to the 1895 Congress in the vain hope that the new standing orders would be rejected, that they moved to set up a rival organisation of their own. Tom Mann and Ben Tillett warned them of the unwisdom of this course, and, lacking leadership, the idea fell through.[2] Mann saw clearly that unless the social question was dealt with by radical measures, the policies which the I.L.P. were recommending would gain ground, and that the changes in the standing orders could not prevent the trade union movement from adopting them. Summing up the situation, three weeks after Congress, he wrote:

> It is an altogether mistaken view to suppose that by narrowing the basis of representation at the Congress, that therefore, either Socialism or Socialists will be kept out. Both the cause and the men will continue to make themselves felt. It is amusing to those who know the facts of the situation to find friends discussing the subject as though the unions classed by some as the 'New Unions' were essentially Socialistic, and the older unions were not so. There is as large a proportion of carpenters, masons, engineers and cotton operatives avowed Socialists, as is to be found amongst the gas workers, dockers, chemical workers, and general labourers. Some think that it's a case of skilled men who are anti-Socialist, and the unskilled who are Socialists. This is not so. The position in which the miners' delegates found themselves when considering the Collectivist resolution is indicative of what may be expected from all the large unions at an early date, viz., as many for Socialism as against it.[3]

Under a Conservative Government

The advent of the Conservative Government to power in 1895 marked the beginning of a long period of Conservative rule. Their victory was due mainly to the failure of the Liberal Government to deal effectively with the social question during its period of office

[1] Congress reversed the resolution it had carried in 1894 in favour of 'the nationalisation of the means of production, distribution and exchange', being content to say that it thought the land, minerals and railways should be the property of the nation.
[2] The Scottish trades councils showed more determination; they decided to form a Trades Union Congress for Scotland and succeeded in securing sufficient support to meet for the first time in 1897. The Scottish T.U.C. proved a viable organisation, but it has never achieved an influence comparable with the original body; to this day it gives trades councils the right to affiliate and to send delegates to its annual Congress.
[3] *Labour Leader*, 28 September 1895.

from 1892 to 1895. The Liberals lost the election because the working class refused to vote for them as they had in 1892. The I.L.P. had put twenty-eight candidates into the field, but since the workers did not turn to socialism, all of them were defeated. Nor did the Lib-Labs improve their position, only nine of them being returned. The leadership of the trade unions, rent by internal dissension, was unable to give any clear direction to the rank and file, which was more concerned with immediate problems of work and wages than with politics.

Unemployment, which stood at about 6 per cent in 1895, gradually declined during the next few years. Of those in employment over a quarter were earning less than 20s. per week in 1894, but with the improvement in trade the vigorous industrial activity of the unions succeeded in securing advances in wages which offset the rise in prices which started in 1896. The loss of trade union members sustained by the movement during the early nineties was gradually made up by fresh recruitment as economic conditions improved.

In their attitude towards the working class the Conservatives were divided. On the one hand, Chamberlain and the Radical Unionists, supported by a number of young Conservatives, were in favour of social reform of a mild sort. On the other, the industrialists were pressing for an all-out attack on the trade union movement. They had watched with growing fear the rising strength of the movement; they were determined to rid themselves of the restrictions which the trade unions placed on their ability to employ whom they pleased at what rates they pleased, and were furious because their continental competitors were not compelled to negotiate with workers enjoying the same degree of bargaining strength.

During its first year of office the Conservative Government carried out the recommendation of the majority report of the Royal Commission on Labour by passing the Conciliation Act. This gave the Board of Trade power to encourage the formation of voluntary Joint Conciliation Boards, and to use its 'good offices' to bring the parties in a dispute together and appoint conciliators or arbitrators if that were desired. This Act proved to be significant in so far as it brought the State into industrial disputes with a positive role to play. It was not, however, an auspicious piece of legislation from the workers' point of view, and they showed not the slightest interest in it. It was not even mentioned in the annual report of the Parliamentary Committee to the 1896 Congress, which commenced with the opinion that,

> The past year has almost been a barren period so far as progressive legislation is concerned in the direct interest of the workers. It has been usual when new Governments have come into power to expect, especially during the first year of such Government, measures of rather a startling

character to be introduced in the interests of the working class community; but although the present Government have been in office for fifteen months, it would be difficult to point out any one really tangible and beneficial measure passed in the interests of labour, and while other measures of a retrograde and questionable character, such as the Education Bill and the Agricultural Rating Bill, have been fully occupying the time of Parliament, measures which were promised in such large profusion during the last Parliamentary Election by candidates seeking the suffrages of the electors—such as the Employers' Liability Bill, the shortening of the hours of labour, old-age pensions, measures to increase greater confidence among the commercial classes of the country with a view to bringing about a better state of trade, and also work for the unemployed—have been grossly neglected.[1]

The following year the Parliamentary Committee were able to report, though with no great enthusiasm, the passing of a Workmen's Compensation Bill. It was under the influence of Chamberlain that the Government had introduced this Bill, which was described by the Parliamentary Committee as of 'a novel and experimental character'. Congress had drawn the attention of succeeding Governments to the weaknesses of the Employers' Liability Act of 1880. After many years of effort Gladstone was prevailed upon, in 1893, to place before Parliament a Bill, on the lines of the one which the T.U.C. promoted year after year, to remedy the evil of contracting out and bring to an end the use of the doctrine of common employment. After it had passed through the House of Commons the Government's Bill was wrecked by amendment in the House of Lords, and was withdrawn. It was this behaviour of the Lords that led to one of Gladstone's famous denunciations of the Upper House, which was, incidentally, his last speech in the Commons, for he handed his resignation to the Queen immediately afterwards. Chamberlain's 1896 Workmen's Compensation Bill departed from the earlier legislation by introducing entirely new principles. The Bill proposed, instead of giving the trade unions the right to claim compensation if it could be proved that an accident had occurred because of the negligence of an employer or one of his servants, that all accidents occurring at work in certain industries should be eligible for compensation, the employer being compelled to insure each worker to cover his liability.

When the Act reached the Statute Book it was received with mixed feelings by the T.U.C., and the Parliamentary Committee was divided in its attitude towards it. A luke-warm resolution supporting the Act was passed by Congress in 1897 'regretting its very limited application'; servants, shop assistants, seamen and agricultural

[1] *T.U.C. Annual Report*, 1896.

workers were excluded from its provisions. The Parliamentary Committee continued unsuccessfully to press its own Bill on employers' liability, and the Government made a partial concession to the trade unions in 1903 by extending the Workmen's Compensation Act to cover agricultural workers.

The 1896 Workmen's Compensation Act was based on legislation that had been enacted in Germany, and for a time it looked as though, under the leadership of Chamberlain, the Conservatives might carry through a programme of social reform on the lines followed by Bismarck—a programme which Chamberlain greatly admired. Together with an almost useless Truck Amendment Act, and a few other minor reforms, this was, however, the extent of social reform carried out by the Conservatives during the last years of the nineteenth century. Chamberlain's reforming zeal gave way before his encroaching enthusiasm for the Empire. The old age pensions, which he had promised if elected in 1895, were forgotten just at the time when they had been introduced in New Zealand and were being urged at home by social investigators such as Charles Booth.

The Employers Counter-Attack

The attention of the skilled workers' unions was much occupied with events in industry at this time. Several industries were going through rapid technical developments, which were threatening the established position of skilled craftsmen. Composing machines were widely introduced by printing firms in the 1890s; mechanical presses were improved and their use extended. These developments led to a continuous battle between the employers and the unions over apprenticeship rules, wages and hours of work.[1] In the boot and shoe industry the introduction of new methods of machine production resulted in a breakdown, in 1895, of the system of conciliation and arbitration that had been established to settle disputes over wages and working conditions. A national lockout followed and the crisis was only resolved by the reorganisation of the procedure for the settlement of disputes. It was, however, in the shipbuilding and engineering industries that new machines, new techniques and new methods of management were to have the most significant consequences.

Whilst the old-established craft unions were endeavouring to impose some control on these developments, principally by resisting changes in established practices, the new unions were seeking to extend their organisations and gain wider recognition. The increased industrial activity of the trade unions was fought by the employers in several different ways. One of the most important of the develop-

[1] Musson, A. E., *The Typographical Association.*

ments that occurred was the growth of employers' federations. Employers in a number of industries had, in earlier years, set up organisations for mutual support, but it was in the 1890s, following the successful establishment of the new unions, that a considerable expansion of employers' organisations occurred. In the gas industry, led by the South Metropolitan Gas Company, a number of employers introduced co-partnership and profit-sharing schemes in an attempt to wean away the allegiance of their workers from the unions.[1] Another section of employers, the Shipowners' Federation, launched a counter-attack on the trade unions, after an attempt to form a company union had failed, by opening 'Free Labour Registries', in 1893. This policy led to a strike in Hull which threatened to spread to the rest of the country. The London Trades Council declared its support for the dockers, and endeavoured to persuade the Government to withdraw the troops and police which it had sent to Hull. After a seven weeks' stoppage, the strike was settled through the intervention of John Burns, with nothing gained by the workers. In the cotton districts the operatives were locked out for twenty weeks, and in the same year the coal owners tested the strength of the unions by locking out the miners, and attempting to impose a wage cut of 25 per cent. This struggle lasted fifteen weeks and only ended when the Government intervened. On this occasion the employers were frustrated, for the miners returned to work at little below the old rates, and gained in addition the principle of a minimum wage, which would be a first charge on the industry.

Trade unionism had existed among railway workers since the 1870s, but the companies refused to recognise the right of their employees to organise.[2] In 1896 'a determined attempt was made to root out Trade Unionism' by the London and North Western Railway.[3] The dismissal of men for belonging to a union led to public criticism of the company, and encouraged the Amalgamated Society of Railway Servants to seek an improvement in working conditions for all grades. The Society's demands were contemptuously ignored and it was not until years later that the companies were compelled to recognise the unions. Employers in other industries were not so well placed to resist the pressure of the unions, and they were glad to make use of a strike-breaking organisation.

In 1893 a renegade trade unionist and dissatisfied adventurer, named William Collison, had founded the National Free Labour Association, with the aim of crippling the power of the unions.[4]

[1] *Ministry of Labour Report on Profit Sharing and Co-partnership*, 1920.
[2] Webb, S. and B., *The History of Trade Unionism*, p. 525.   [3] *Ibid.*
[4] See *The Apostle of Free Labour: The Life Story of William Collison*, told by himself.

The main purpose of the Association was to provide a reserve of 'blackleg' labour for the employers, willing to be sent anywhere to be used for strike-breaking, and to be used as 'evidence' that the workers were not satisfied with their trade unions. The employers were only too ready to make use of this organisation, but it had little success; the workers owed too much to the unions to be deceived by a device of this kind.

In 1895 the engineers employed in the shipyards on the Clydeside and Belfast came out on strike for the eight-hour day. The struggle lasted for three months, and ended with the workers going back empty-handed. Two years later the Amalgamated Society of Engineers claimed a reduction of hours to eight per day in London, and a number of firms agreed to this demand, but the large firms refused. The A.S.E. called its members out on strike against these employers, who, in turn, asked the Employers' Federation to declare a lockout of 25 per cent of the men employed in engineering throughout the country. The dispute rapidly widened from the original question of an eight-hour day to one in which the whole principle of trade unionism was at stake.

For a long time the A.S.E. had been resisting the introduction of labour-saving machinery. Experience had taught the engineers that the installation of such machinery would result in the replacement of skilled by unskilled workers who would be paid at a lower rate. The Employers' Federation were determined, not only to refuse to grant the eight-hour day, but also to impose conditions which they hoped would destroy the strength of the trade union. This was the real objective of the employers, who were bent on showing that they would brook no interference with the right of management to manage as it saw fit. The question of prerogative was, at bottom, the fundamental issue in all the major disputes at this time. As a condition of lifting the lockout the engineering employers insisted on the men accepting overtime and piece-rate work, the abolition of apprenticeship rules and the right of the trade unions to bargain for them. Faced with such terms, the A.S.E. had no choice but to fight to the bitter end. The men eventually went back to work with the 'kitty' empty, after being locked out from July 1897 to January 1898; but their union was still intact in spite of the assistance rendered to employers by the National Free Labour Association. They were forced, however, to accede to many of the demands made by the employers.[1]

The engineers had suffered a severe defeat, but the employers would have had less cause for elation had they been gifted with an ability to look ahead a few years. One consequence of the lockout

[1] Jefferys, J. B., *The Story of the Engineers*, p. 144.

was that it shook the whole world of labour from top to bottom. The serious implications of the lockout were recognised by the Trades Union Congress, when, in 1897 the standing orders were suspended and Pete Curran of the Gasworkers' Union moved:

> That this Congress desires to express its entire sympathy with the Amalgamated Engineers and others now struggling to obtain an eight-hour working day. We fully recognise the importance of the struggle which is now being waged, and how seriously the principle involved in the dispute affects the whole of our industries. We sincerely trust that all the trades represented at this Congress will come to the aid of those affected, both morally and financially.

Later in the week a further resolution was carried instructing the Parliamentary Committee to undertake the collection and distribution of money supplied by the other unions.

The result of this resolution was that the T.U.C. Parliamentary Committee established a fund for the collection and distribution of aid to the engineers.[1] This 'was a new departure from the ordinary work of Congress, there being no precedent during the past thirty years' the Committee stated in its report the following year.[2] A number of trade unionists had asked the Parliamentary Committee to call a special conference of all trades to consider what action could be taken to give further support to the engineers. The Parliamentary Committee had refused to do this on the grounds that it would be setting a precedent for which they had no authority; no trade union had asked for such a conference, and further, the cost of holding such a conference would be great and the money could be better used by the A.S.E. The upshot of this ultra-cautious attitude of the Committee was that Ben Cooper, of the Tobacco Workers' Union, moved a vote of censure at the Congress of 1898 on the Parliamentary Committee.[3] This was rejected by the delegates, but many thought with W. C. Steadman that Cooper's resolution had 'done good, if only in the way of directing attention to the necessity of amending the Standing Orders, in order to give the Parliamentary Committee power to call such a meeting in the future'.[4]

[1] *Report of the Parliamentary Committee*, 1898. £23,500 was collected and disbursed through this fund.

[2] *Ibid.*

[3] The Congress of 1898 was held in Bristol and it met in one of the city's most famous buildings, the Colston Hall. This gathering was made memorable by a great fire which started in the middle of Wednesday night, in a clothing factory next door, and spread rapidly to the hall, which was completely burnt out. When the delegates assembled next day they found only a ruin and all the documents that had been left in the hall overnight had been destroyed. However, emergency arrangements were made and the Congress was able to complete its business in spite of having been burnt out.

[4] *T.U.C. Annual Report*, 1898.

The frustration felt by many delegates on the floor of Congress at the wary policy of the Parliamentary Committee was expressed by speakers who criticised Congress for not being a real 'Parliament of Labour', and who gave vent to their feelings by passing a resolution stating that, 'Congress is of opinion that the agenda is over-crowded ... and that in order to give opportunity for discussion the practice of the Parliamentary Committee in placing resolutions of their own on the agenda be discontinued.'[1]

The T.U.C. Produces an Offspring

Since 1874 the Trades Union Congress had been talking about the need to turn itself into a federation, and any number of constitutions had been drawn up and conferences held, but always the interests of the trade unions had been too diverse for this ideal to be realised. With the advent of the 'new' unionism, interest in the idea revived more strongly than ever before. In 1890 the Parliamentary Committee drew up a constitution for a federation of trade unions, as instructed, but it remained a paper project. At the 1893 Congress the subject came up for an airing again, with references to the American Federation of Labour, which was quoted as a suitable pattern to follow. In the following year a Committee was set up to draft a fresh scheme to overcome financial difficulties that had been apparent in the earlier attempts. This Committee's report was rejected on a card vote in the highly charged atmosphere of the 1895 Congress, after it had been carried on a show of hands.[2] The engineers' lockout brought the matter to the fore again, and Congress passed a resolution calling on the trade unions of the United Kingdom to form a federation 'to render mutual assistance in disputes, strikes and lockouts affecting any trade unions affiliated to the federation. . . . A committee of thirteen to be elected from this Congress for the purpose of taking into consideration the best means of federating the trade unions.'[3]

This Committee, under the chairmanship of Robert Knight, secretary of the Boilermakers' Union, and for many years a staunch advocate of federation, reported to the 1898 Congress the result of its work, and it was agreed that the Parliamentary Committee should call a special conference, not later than January 1899, to which all trade unions affiliated to the T.U.C. should be invited to send

[1] *T.U.C. Annual Report*, 1898.

[2] *The Clarion* took up the question of federation with vigour and a series of articles written by Blatchford and P. J. King appeared in 1897 as a pamphlet, which had a wide sale.

[3] *T.U.C. Annual Report*, 1897.

delegates. This special conference was held in Manchester, and after sitting for three days the rules of the new organisation were finally agreed upon.[1] The Parliamentary Committee constituted itself the provisional executive committee of the Federation, but decided that it would be safer not to have any responsibility for the new organisation. It, therefore, called a council meeting of representatives of the unions which had joined the Federation in the following July. At this meeting the Parliamentary Committee presented a report and then retired, leaving the Council to elect its officers and make arrangements for the conduct of future activities of the Federation. Pete Curran was elected president and Isaac Mitchell of the A.S.E., secretary.[2]

The name given to the new organisation was the General Federation of Trade Unions, but this was more a designation of hope than reality. At the outset only 44 societies joined with an aggregate membership of 343,000—about one quarter of the total number of workers organised in trade unions affiliated to the T.U.C. Moreover, it was very far from being a federation; it was in fact merely a collection of loosely bound autonomous unions. The idea in the minds of the most ardent advocates of a trade union federation was to create a powerful organisation that could carry out the industrial functions that were, as they saw it, shirked by the Parliamentary Committee, and meet the growing challenge of the employers' organisations.[3] However, the crucial issue of the power to be granted to the central organ, the Management Committee, over the constituent units, was burked, as a delegate to the inaugural congress pointed out. The leaders of the large unions had no desire to see established a strong, centralised organisation which would diminish their own authority, and they took care to see that this did not happen. They refused to join even the emasculated federation that was founded, so that it consisted mainly of the smaller and financially weak unions. Without the necessary power at the centre it was hamstrung from the very beginning as a militant body aimed at directing the entire trade union movement against the employers.

The constitution of the General Federation of Trade Unions stated that:

(1) The objects shall be to uphold the right of combination of labour, to improve in every direction the general economic position and status of the Workers by the inauguration of a policy that shall secure to them the power to determine the economic and social conditions under

---

[1] *Report of the Special Trades Union Congress*, held on 24, 25, 26 January 1899, at the St. James's Hall, Manchester.

[2] *First Annual Report of the G.F.T.U.*

[3] Cf. *The Clarion Federation Scheme.*

which they shall work and live, and to secure unity of action amongst all Societies forming the Federation.

To achieve this object the G.F.T.U. was:

(2) To *promote* Industrial Peace, and by all amicable means, such as Conciliation, Mediation, References, or by the establishment of Permanent Boards, to *prevent* Strikes or Lock-outs between Employers and Workmen, or disputes between Trades or Organisations. Where differences do occur, to assist in their settlement by just and equitable methods.

The final object was:

(3) To establish a Fund for mutual assistance and support and for carrying out the foregoing objects.[1]

The functions of the Federation were to be, as the constitution emphasises, defensive mutual insurance, and so funds had to be built up. It could not, therefore, embark on an offensive policy which would at once bring it to financial ruin, and, as a mutual insurance society, it soon became more concerned with preventing strikes, whatever ideas some of its founders may have had, than with promoting them.

The Legal Challenge to Trade Unionism

The most dangerous challenge to the trade unions came, at this time, not from the direct activities of the employers in the shape of lockouts, which the Federation had been set up to deal with, nor from the Government, but from the law courts. The 'new' unionism, with its socialistic creed, the great increase in numbers and financial strength of the trade unions, and the rebirth of their fighting spirit put fear into the upper classes. Reflecting this emotion, the Judicial Bench, in a series of judgments from 1893 to 1901, gradually whittled away the ability of a trade union to strike. In 1893 it was decided that it was an actionable offence to refuse to handle the goods of a 'blackleg' firm;[2] in 1895, that to publish a black list of either workmen or employers was using illegal means if the court considered the motive was to compel;[3] in 1896, that to use pickets to try and persuade men not to work for an employer whose men were on strike, even if done peaceably, would be an offence;[4] in 1901, that to strike, or threaten to strike in order to coerce an employer to discharge non-union employees was illegal.[5] Finally, in 1901, Mr. Justice Farwell's famous

[1] *Code of Rules Adopted by the Special T.U.C.*, 1899.
[2] *Temperton v. Russell.*   [3] *Trollope v. London Building Trades' Federation.*
[4] *Lyons v. Wilkins.*   [5] *Quinn v. Leatham.*

Taff Vale Judgment, that a trade union could be sued for tort, was upheld by the House of Lords. This last decision was the heaviest blow, for it made the strike into a useless instrument of trade union policy, and was a threat to the lifeblood of a trade union—its funds.

Prior to the Congress of 1901, the main duties of the Parliamentary Committee, as laid down in the standing orders, were confined to watching and initiating legislation of concern to the trade unions. No reference was made to organising financial support to assist unions and their members in legal cases where it was in the interest of the whole trade union movement that they should be taken, if necessary, to the House of Lords. The Parliamentary Committee sought to overcome this limitation on its authority, and the relatively slender financial resources at its disposal, by securing permission from Congress to issue an appeal to the affiliated organisations asking them to contribute to special funds to assist the unions and persons involved. The Lyons *v.* Wilkins case revealed the weakness of the Parliamentary Committee in this respect. An extraordinary feature of this case was the lapsing of the appeal to the House of Lords owing to a combination of circumstances which included an error on the part of a solicitor; the failure of Mr. Wilkins, because of legal debts already incurred, to give the necessary instructions until the very last moment; and the length of time that it took the T.U.C. to raise the money to finance the appeal. This incident, together with the Taff Vale Case, led the Parliamentary Committee to recommend an alteration in the standing orders that would enable the Parliamentary Committee to levy the affiliated unions on a *pro rata* basis in order to meet the expenses necessary to test a legal decision of importance to the whole trade union movement, by taking it, if required, to the House of Lords. Though there was some reluctance on the part of a few delegates to accept this proposal, since it extended the power of the Committee to act without the express sanction of the Congress, eventually the idea was adopted unanimously and it has remained an important feature of the work of the T.U.C. ever since.

The Case for Independent Political Representation Accepted

The danger from the courts, together with the hostility of the employers, the indifferent attitude of the Conservative Government to the claims of the workers and the weakness of the Liberal opposition, stimulated demands from the unions that the T.U.C. should seek to secure a larger number of Labour representatives in Parliament, even before the decision in the Taff Vale Case had occurred.

At the 1899 Congress, P. Vogel, delegate of the Waiters' Union and James O'Grady of the Furnishing Trades Association, wanted Congress to establish a Parliamentary Fund by compulsory levy for the purpose of running candidates who, if successful, would have been paid a salary by Congress. Will Thorne, who had no wish to see the predominantly Lib-Lab Parliamentary Committee in undisputed control of a political organisation, quickly moved the next question. Moreover, he was aware that a far more important resolution was on the agenda, dealing with political representation. This resolution was moved by J. H. Holmes, a delegate of the Amalgamated Society of Railway Servants, and it read:

> That this Congress having regard to its decisions in former years, and with a view to securing a better representation of the interests of Labour in the House of Commons hereby instructs the Parliamentary Committee to invite the co-operation of all Co-operative, Socialistic, Trade Unions, and other working class organisations to jointly co-operate on lines mutually agreed upon, in convening a Special Congress of representatives from such of the above named organisations as may be willing to take part to devise ways and means for securing the return of an increased number of Labour members to the next Parliament.

The resolution was supported by the Dockers, General Labourers, Railway Servants and Shop Assistants, and opposed by the Miners' Federation and the Cotton Spinners on the ground that it was of an impracticable character. After a debate which lasted most of the afternoon the resolution was put and carried by 546,000 votes to 434,000.[1]

The immediate reason for the resolution coming up in 1899 was the approaching general election. It was passed, though only narrowly, because the situation had changed quite considerably during the previous five years. There was no longer the same fear in Congress that the I.L.P. was going to take it over. Nor was Congress the battleground of powerful personalities, identified with rival organisations and theories, as it had been in the days of Hardie, Burns and Broadhurst. The strength of the employers had shown that only limited gains could be made by striking, and the decisions of the law courts threatened to render even those nugatory. The Conservative Government, primarily concerned with foreign policy, colonial expansion, and the Boer War, seemed indifferent to social questions at home, and the Parliamentary Committee, after detailing the lack of progress made by a long string of Bills it had been instructed to promote stated to the 1899 Congress, 'Your Committee again wish to point out that with the present mode of procedure of the House of Commons it is almost impossible to get any useful Bill through the

---

[1] *T.U.C. Annual Report*, 1899.

House unless the Government allow it to pass by withdrawing its opposition, and in their opinion, if any remedy is to be effected it must be done by the working classes at the polls.'[1]

The Parliamentary Committee agreed to the setting up of an informal sub-committee with the representatives from the Fabian Society, Independent Labour Party and Social Democratic Federation to consider the resolution and prepare for the conference. A suggested outline agenda was drawn up by this committee, but it was subsequently redrafted by the full Parliamentary Committee before publication. The revisions made by the Parliamentary Committee, though they retained the substance of the original proposals, did not meet with Hardie's approval since he feared that the Committee was out to water down his aim of securing a completely independent Labour group.[2] It is obvious that the Parliamentary Committee was reluctant to break completely with the Liberals, since many of its members had little confidence in the political effectiveness of the I.L.P. and the other socialist groups, but the agenda did state that a resolution advocating the formation of a distinct Labour group with its own whips would be placed before the delegates.[3]

The conference was eventually held on the 17 February, at the Memorial Hall, Faringdon Street, and lasted two days, under the chairmanship of W. C. Steadman; 129 delegates were present, representing more than 500,000 members; this was only a little over a third of the number affiliated to the T.U.C. Fortunately for those who wanted a Labour Party on the lines advocated by Hardie, the coal and cotton unions, with a few minor exceptions, ignored the conference. Among the larger organisations, only the Railway Servants, the Engineers, Gasworkers and the Boot and Shoe Operatives sent representatives. These four organisations had, between them, over one-third of the votes at the conference, and, since they held 'advanced' views, Hardie and Ramsay MacDonald were assured of a large block vote so long as they pursued a cautious and tactful policy. The I.L.P. leaders realised that they could not afford to alienate the trade unions, and they worked in very close harmony to defeat the more extreme proposals of the S.D.F. A resolution moved by the S.D.F., which sought to compel the new body to adopt full-blooded socialism, including a recognition of the class war, as its creed, in fact helped Hardie to achieve his main objective. The resolution was strongly opposed and in its place an amendment, moved by Alexander Wilkie, a member of the Parliamentary

[1] *Report of the Parliamentary Committee*, 1899.
[2] *The Labour Leader*, 13 January 1900.
[3] *Conference on Labour Representation. Programme of Proceedings and Standing Orders*, 27 December 1899.

Committee, was adopted. This merely called for the establishment of a Labour Group in Parliament, and a pledge that the members would act together on a Labour Platform of 'four or five planks, embracing questions upon which the vast majority of the workers in the country are agreed'. On 'purely political party questions', the Labour representatives were to be left entirely free. This was precisely the kind of policy that Hardie was afraid the delegates might be persuaded to accept. Hardie at once proposed a further amendment, which by comparison with the S.D.F. proposal appeared mild, but which contained the heart of what he had long been trying to obtain. It went further than the Parliamentary Committee really wanted to go, but Wilkie was persuaded to withdraw his amendment in favour of Hardie's, which was then carried unanimously. The finally adopted resolution provided for the establishment of 'a distinct Labour Group in Parliament who shall have their own whips, and agree upon their policy', though it went on to satisfy those who doubted the wisdom of this step by asserting that the group must be prepared to co-operate with any party for the promotion of legislation in the interests of Labour. Thus Labour members would be free to enter into collaboration with the Liberals whenever they might decide that this was desirable.

On the second day the conference decided to establish an executive committee composed of seven trade union representatives, two from the I.L.P., two from the S.D.F., and one Fabian, making twelve in all, and it agreed that the duty of the Committee should be to prepare a list of candidates, administer the funds, convene an annual conference and keep in touch with the trade unions.[1]

The Labour Representation Committee, which was an alliance between trade unionists and intellectual socialists, embraced individuals, through their organisations, from all sections of the community. It was committed to no abstract political theory, but existed simply to obtain the legislative measures which working-class organisations believed would improve the standard of life of the wage earner. The trade union movement, on which the alliance was based, would have accepted nothing more than a policy of practical reform, and this was realised by the leaders of both the I.L.P. and the Fabian Society, who were prepared to enter the alliance on those terms. The S.D.F., too rigid and doctrinaire to be associated for long with a body so pragmatic in its attitude to socialism, soon withdrew to preserve its doctrinal purity.

The new century thus started with the organised workers being

[1] For full accounts of the founding of the Labour Party see Cole, G. D. H., *British Working Class Politics, 1832–1914*; Williams, Francis, *Forward March*; Pelling, H., *The Origins of the Labour Party, 1880–1900*.

represented by three separate, independent national organisations, or four if the Co-operative movement is included. The General Federation of Trade Unions and the Labour Representation Committee had been set up by the Trades Union Congress, primarily because the Parliamentary Committee was reluctant to extend its functions in the directions represented by the two new organisations. The marked distaste shown by the Parliamentary Committee towards increasing the powers of the Trades Union Congress stemmed fundamentally from the history of the trade union movement, which was a product of *laissez-faire*, and, despite growing adherence to collectivist policies, was saturated with the philosophy of liberalism. Each trade union was, and, for that matter, still is, an autonomous organisation established to protect the interests of its own members, and it was prepared to agree only to a minimum of collectivism in respect of its own organisation. The Trades Union Congress had been established to represent the collective aspirations of the trade union movement to the Government of the day, and the functions of the Parliamentary Committee were conceived in the narrow framework of watching and promoting legislation both specific and general in the interest of Labour, agreed upon by the unions assembled in Congress. The fear of going beyond these functions was grounded not only on differences of political ideology, but on the deeply held belief that such a development would endanger the position of the Trades Union Congress.

The tenuous hold which the Parliamentary Committee had over the constituent unions was illustrated by the disaffiliation of the Amalgamated Society of Engineers in 1898. Under standing order number twenty, the Parliamentary Committee was authorised to appoint arbitrators, should either party to a dispute between two unions request this to be done. In 1898 the Co-operative Smiths' Society of Gateshead charged the Amalgamated Society of Engineers with filling the places of their members when they were out on strike, and asked the Parliamentary Committee to intervene. After a careful investigation of the circumstances surrounding the dispute, the arbitrators appointed by the Parliamentary Committee found in favour of the Co-operative Smiths' Society, and recommended that the A.S.E. withdraw its members at once. Every effort was made to persuade the A.S.E. to accept the findings of the Committee, but it refused, and preferred to leave the T.U.C. rather than give way.[1]

This incident emphasises the wisdom which Congress showed in not attempting to burden its organisation with tasks which, in practice, it would have proved impossible to carry out. Had Congress turned itself into a gigantic, highly centralised federation, it

[1] *T.U.C. Annual Report*, 1899.

would have run into difficulties that would almost certainly have led to its complete breakdown. By establishing the G.F.T.U. as a separate body, it avoided this danger to a considerable extent. Similarly, when an attempt was made to turn the T.U.C. into a political party, the delegates showed their intelligence by rejecting the resolution. Had Congress taken this step, the T.U.C. would have been rent by political dissension on a far greater scale than has been the case. The position of the trade union movement in the State, and its relations with the Government would have been entirely altered.

The creation of the G.F.T.U. and the L.R.C. did not, of course, settle all the problems with which the T.U.C. and Parliamentary Committee were faced; on the contrary, the very fact of their existence created new problems. The links that existed between the three organisations rested on the nature of their origin and common interest rather than on well thought out formal arrangements.[1] None of the three organisations had strictly defined functions, and it was not long before they were entertaining suspicions of one another and demands for their co-ordination were being heard. Speaking as a fraternal delegate from the G.F.T.U. to the Congress of 1900, I. Mitchell, its secretary, attempted to allay some of the fears that had been aroused since it came into being. He said that to obviate any possibility of rivalry the Parliamentary Committee had been invited to send representatives to the general council of the G.F.T.U. and continued,

> The Federation had decided to confine themselves entirely to trade matters. The Trades Union Congress was a political body, or they dealt essentially with political questions. They were perfectly willing in the Federation to allow the Congress to look after the political interests of the workers, and had decided not to interfere with any political question of any description.[2]

Relations with the Co-operative Movement

The establishment of a satisfactory relationship between the T.U.C. and G.F.T.U. and L.R.C. was largely a matter for the future at the turn of the century, but links between the T.U.C. and the Co-operative movement had been in existence for a long time when the two former organisations were founded. Management committees

[1] One of the resolutions passed at the Memorial Hall Conference, stated that the L.R.C. should report annually to the 'T.U.C. and annual meetings of the national societies represented on the Committee'. Although the T.U.C. exercised no control over the L.R.C., the constitutional relationship was not finally made clear until 1904.

[2] *T.U.C. Annual Report*, 1900.

of Co-operative societies—most of whom were trade unionists—were generally in favour of their employees joining a trade union, but this did not mean that on the whole they received much better conditions of employment than was provided by good private employers. The Co-operative movement, though originally based on socialist principles, had long before tended to put them on one side so far as its employees were concerned. The movement was beset by a dilemma which was never satisfactorily solved. On the one hand, societies had to pursue commercial success to provide good dividends for the benefit of their members; on the other, Co-operative employees felt that Co-operative principles ought to mean more than the pursuit of dividends, and many of them believed that they were being cheated out of their expectations because the movement had succumbed to capitalist influences.

In their attitude towards the Co-operative movement, the delegates to the Trades Union Congress were often far from unanimous. For many years complaints about the Co-operative movement had been raised, and rebuttals made on the floor of Congress. Sometimes the charges appear to have been exaggerated, but, whatever their merits, disputes were common between trade unions and Co-operative societies over matters of wages, hours and working conditions. The Co-operative movement was looked upon by most trade unionists as an integral part of the Labour movement, and they felt that it ought to conduct its employment practices on a higher level than was usual with ordinary commercial enterprise. When allegations of 'sweating' and hostility to trade unionism were made, many delegates were shocked and bitter in their reproaches and others, reluctant to concede the validity of such grave indictments, rallied to defend the Co-operatives. In 1892 a resolution had been passed by Congress urging closer unity between the two movements, and as a result the Parliamentary Committee, in conjunction with the Co-operative Union, established a joint committee which drew up rules for the guidance of both movements in trade disputes.

The rules, which were accepted by both sides and put into operation, provided for a permanent committee which was given the duty of making a full inquiry into all disputes brought to its notice, and was empowered to offer its services as an arbitrator to the disputants. A trade union label scheme was also approved to provide a distinctive mark on goods supplied by the Co-operatives and made under trade union conditions. The adoption of these recommendations improved the relations between the two movements, but sharp conflicts continued to occur, and resolutions condemning Co-operative societies for not accepting trade union conditions came up year after year.

It was not until 1898 that the Parliamentary Committee sent

fraternal delegates for the first time to the annual Co-operative Congress; representatives from the co-operative movement had been attending the Trades Union Congress for a number of years, but it was not until the middle of the nineties that an address from them became an annual feature. In his address to the 1900 Congress, Mr. H. Vivian, representing the Co-operative Union, emphasised the importance of the co-operative movement to the trade unions in times of industrial conflict, and instanced the miners of South Yorkshire, who, when on strike, had drawn over £40,000 out of the Barnsley Society. It was not, however, until many years later that a concerted attempt was made to organise this potential source of reserves for the trade union movement on a more specific basis.

CHAPTER V

TAFF VALE TO TORY DEFEAT

Within a few months of its formation the L.R.C. had to plunge into an election, when Salisbury, under the influence of Joseph Chamberlain, decided to take advantage of the nationalist feelings which had been aroused by the victories over the Boers in the South African War. The Conservative administration was returned with practically the same majority as it had had before the dissolution. The L.R.C. had little time to put many candidates in the field; out of the fifteen which they managed to run, two were returned—Keir Hardie, and Richard Bell, secretary of the Amalgamated Society of Railway Servants. It is doubtful, even if the L.R.C. had been in a position to support more candidates, whether they would have achieved much greater success. The plain fact was that the Labour movement had no clear policy to put against the appeal to patriotism which swept the Conservatives back into office. The I.L.P. and the S.D.F. were absolutely opposed to the South African War; the Fabian Society and the Trade Union Movement were divided. In 1899 a resolution urging the Government to settle the dispute by peaceful means was carried by Congress against a good deal of opposition. In 1900 a more forthright resolution attacking the Government's policy as dictated by capitalist imperialism scraped through with a narrow majority, a large number of delegates refusing to vote.

The L.R.C. aroused no great enthusiasm among trade unionists, and its relatively poor showing in the election led to plenty of 'I told you so' remarks. If the Liberals had not been paralysed by the South African War, which divided them as much as the Labour movement, and could have agreed to the dynamic programme of social reform which they attempted a few years later, the Labour Representation Committee might have petered out, but fortune decreed otherwise. The House of Lords' decision to uphold the Taff Vale Judgment and the equivocal attitude of the Liberals towards this decision was an important factor in the consolidation of the L.R.C.[1]

---

[1] The hostility of the Supreme Court to the trade unions was underlined almost immediately afterwards by its decision against the unions in *Quinn* v. *Leatham*.

In 1892 the House of Lords had decided that a shipowners' cartel was legally entitled to use such measures as the boycott and the black-list to eliminate competition, but when the same means were used by a trade union, nine years later, to protect the interests of its members, it was found that the officials concerned had offended against the law of civil conspiracy. To the members of the unions

Mr. Justice Farwell's judgment had been made during the week that Congress was sitting, in 1900; its significance was immediately realised and standing orders were suspended to permit a discussion on this new menace to the trade union movement. A resolution was carried instructing the

> Parliamentary Committee to call the attention of the trade societies of the country to the above judgment, pointing out the absolute and urgent necessity of the case being fought right through to the House of Lords, and, seeing that this case equally affects every society in the country, that the Parliamentary Committee obtain from each society their consent to a contribution, pro rata, for the purposes of prosecuting the appeal.[1]

Ben Tillett, however, 'hoped that Congress would not get into a condition of alarm and panic'. 'He did not think that the effect of the decision on the legal world would have such an influence as some of the delegates anticipated. . . . He did not believe . . . that judges would be so silly as to take the course suggested by some of the members there.'[2] The reason for Ben Tillett's new-found confidence in the benevolent disposition of the judges was that he had become a convert to the merits of compulsory arbitration. He could not easily advocate on the one hand, 'That in view of the increasing number of lockouts and refusals by employers to arbitrate, we urge the Government to pass a Compulsory Conciliation Arbitration Act, and the appointment of judge and court, with authority to enforce awards by fines and imprisonment of persons refusing to accept award of such court. . . .',[3] and at the same time condemn the judges when they made a bad decision. Tillett's argument that the fate of the workers would be better in the hands of the law courts than in the hands of the employers was hardly convincing in the light of past experience. There was a strong body of opinion in the trade unions in favour of voluntary arbitration, but Tillett regarded this as a failure; compulsion appealed to him as the only way awards could be enforced on the tough port employers, many of whom refused to recognise his union. His resolution was rejected by a large majority, and the defeat of Tillett's motion became an annual event during the next seven or eight years, until he was converted by circumstances once again to the principle of direct action.

The legal decisions made during the nineties, culminating with the Taff Vale Judgment, had created a situation of great difficulty and

---

this decision was an obvious case of applying one standard to the rich and another to the poor; a view that modern legal authority upholds. See Kahn-Freund, O., *The System of Industrial Relations in Great Britain.*

[1] *T.U.C. Annual Report*, 1900.   [2] *Ibid.*   [3] *Ibid.*

uncertainty for the trade unions. They could no longer be sure that a strike would not involve them in costly legal actions, even, perhaps, make them liable for heavy damages. As long as it could ignore the problem, this situation was not unwelcome to the Conservative Government, but a complacent attitude was precisely what the trade unions were determined to make impossible. Soon after the House of Lords' decision in favour of the Taff Vale Judgment, the Parliamentary Committee, carrying on the tradition of the Conference of Amalgamated Trades, consulted its legal friends in the House of Commons, H. H. Asquith, Sir Robert Reid, R. B. Haldane and Sir Charles Dilke. The result of this conference was not altogether encouraging. Some wanted to return to the position before the legal decisions had been made; others thought this would be unsatisfactory and considered that changes in the law were necessary. The difficulty was that interpretations differed as to what the law had been before the judges had changed it. The outcome of this conference was the drafting of a Bill by Mr. Edmund Browne, Standing Counsel to the Parliamentary Committee,[1] which did little more than redefine the right to picket, and which Richard Bell, M.P., general secretary of the A.S.R.E. undertook to introduce in the House of Commons. Another proposal made by the lawyers was that the trade unions should separate their benefit funds from their general funds by forming subsidiary companies to operate the 'friendly' side of trade union activities. This plan was circulated to the unions by the Parliamentary Committee, but it did not commend itself to them.

On the 19 April 1902, the Parliamentary Committee interviewed Sir Henry Campbell-Bannerman, leader of the Liberal Party, who promised the services of the Liberal whips in support of a resolution to be moved in the House of Commons, 'That legislation is necessary to prevent workmen being placed by judge-made law in a position inferior to that intended by Parliament in 1875.'[2] The Committee carefully prepared to obtain the maximum support for the resolution by organising a conference of Labour members and the friends of Labour legislation, appointing lobby representatives, sending out two whips to all members to support the resolution, and urging all the unions to press members in their constituencies to give their support. The debate in the Commons on the resolution was something of a triumph for the Parliamentary Committee, for weighty speeches were made in favour of fresh legislation, and when it came to the vote, the Liberals and the Irish group as well as the handful of Labour members voted for the resolution, so that the Government

[1] Mr. Browne was appointed in 1900.
[2] *T.U.C. Annual Report*, 1902.

found its majority reduced to only twenty-nine; a warning to them of the political implications of the question.[1]

All the time the South African War continued it was difficult for the trade unions to obtain public attention for the campaign they were waging against Taff Vale and other constricting legal decisions, but as the war dragged on the imperialist fever died down and home economic and social problems began to loom large. Besides doing nothing significant to improve the lot of the working class, the Government declared that wage earners must share the cost of the war; it imposed taxes on bread and raised duties on beer, spirits, tea and tobacco. Real wages had begun to fall at about the turn of the century; prices rose, and the Government's policy intensified this trend. With the end of the war unemployment also began to increase. W. J. Davis, commenting on the attitude of the Government, wrote, 'The Government thought itself serene and acted as though it was almost supreme when dealing with Labour questions.' 'It would fain have the working classes believe that because the national sentiment in favour of the South African War had given the Government a new lease of power that it had a mandate to baulk and thwart all labour aspirations.'[2] By 1902, Beatrice Webb was, not surprisingly, writing in her diary of the Trades Union Congress, 'Dominant note of the Congress is determination to run Labour Candidates on a large scale, and faith in the efficacy of this device for gaining all they require.'[3]

As soon as the war was over things began to go in favour of the Labour alliance. Within a matter of weeks the Labour Representation Committee had increased its members in the House of Commons, David Shackleton being returned unopposed in a by-election at Clitheroe. Half a year later the Labour Representation Committee had a much more significant triumph; Will Crooks was returned at the Woolwich by-election, a safe Conservative seat, with a majority of over 3,000; and Arthur Henderson vanquished both the Liberal and Tory candidates in a three-cornered fight at Barnard Castle. The conference of the L.R.C., held in 1903, showed that membership was rapidly increasing, having risen by 300,000 in the previous year to a total of 750,000. The conference agreed to a voluntary levy of a penny per member per year, to finance the running of candidates and to pay them a salary if elected. Although the trade unions had received considerable support from the Liberals in Parliament on the

---

[1] The weakness of the debate was that the Liberal lawyers had no clear policy to put forward and their legal arguments were also often confusing and contradictory. *Parliamentary Debates*, 14 May 1902.

[2] Davis, W. J., *The British Trades Union Congress—History and Recollections*, vol. II, p. 222.

[3] Webb, B., *Our Partnership*, p. 245.

Taff Vale question, the conference displayed an increasing resistance to Labour candidates identifying themselves with any other party.[1]

A Royal Commission Again

Meanwhile the Parliamentary Committee of the T.U.C. had organised several conferences jointly with the Management Committee of the G.F.T.U. and the Labour Representation Committee to consider what should be done next in the fight for a new Trade Union Act. The Liberal lawyers, as well as Edmund Browne, the Standing Counsel to the Parliamentary Committee, were usually present at these conferences to give their advice. It was decided to draft a Bill that would go much further than the one drafted the year before, to deal with the law of conspiracy and the conduct of trade disputes, though not, however, seeking to restore the trade unions to a position where they could neither sue, nor be sued as a corporate body. Partly owing to a division of opinion regarding the type of legislation that ought to be sought, but mainly in order to obtain the maximum public support for the Bill, a special delegate conference was called in London on the 11 March 1903. The conference unanimously adopted the Bill, and this was the signal for a tremendous agitation to commence in its support throughout the country. M.P.s were lobbied, and thousands of letters and resolutions were sent to them from every part of the British Isles.

David Shackleton moved the second reading of the Bill on the 9 May, and it was defeated by only twenty votes. This uncomfortably narrow victory, in conjunction with the general political situation, which for the Conservatives had deteriorated considerably since the end of the South African War, made it plain to Balfour that, much as he disliked action, he could no longer ignore the problem. He therefore set up a Royal Commission on Trade Disputes, hoping by this means to shelve the issue. The Government appointed no trade unionist to the Commission, although the chairman of the Parliamentary Commission submitted two names on his own initiative, but Sidney Webb was invited to be a member; an appointment which gave the Labour movement no satisfaction.[2] According to Beatrice Webb this was Haldane's doing, and she wrote in her diary, 'The job is eminently one for him to do, and will have the incidental advantage of bringing us again into communication with the trade union world.'[3]

[1] Report of Third Annual Conference of the Labour Representation Committee, 19–21 February 1903.

[2] Labour Leader, 29 August 1903, described the Commission as 'bogus' and all its members as 'interested in the capitalist class'.

[3] Webb, B., Our Partnership, p. 268.

Her satisfaction was rather misplaced, for the Webbs were regarded with mistrust by practically all the leaders of the trade union
movement, not only for their criticisms of the Parliamentary Committee, as Beatrice rather egotistically thought, but also because of
their superior, snobbish attitude. The Webbs had poured scorn on
the Labour Representation Committee and were contemptuous of
Keir Hardie, who seemed to them to be crude, emotional and
unintellectual. The Trades Union Congress in 1903 passed a resolution unanimously in protest at 'the Government's insult to Labour in
the selection of the members of the Royal Commission . . .' and
recommended that no affiliated organisation should give evidence
to it.[1] During the course of the debate, J. Wignall, one of the leaders
of the Dock Workers, said that he did not think that Sidney Webb
ought to be included in the Commission, as he had already passed
judgment against the trade unions, having stated that they should not
have the legal privilege of immunity from actions for damages.[2]

During 1904 and 1905 the Parliamentary Committee continued its
campaign against the Taff Vale Judgment. Mass meetings, sponsored
by the Parliamentary Committee, were held in all the large towns in
support of the Trade Disputes Bill. Legal decisions based on the
obnoxious precedents, which cost the trade unions heavy damages,
occurred frequently, and were a constant reminder to the organised
workers of the need for new legislation.[3] In his presidential address
to the 1904 Congress, Richard Bell, secretary to the A.S.R.S., compared the tenderness which the Government showed towards the
liquor trade, when it rushed through a Licensing Act to compensate
displaced licence holders, with its refusal to give any parliamentary
time for the consideration of the Trade Disputes Bill, which was
strongly supported both inside and outside the House. Balfour was
clearly not going to do anything to relieve the trade unions from the
grip of the courts. His attitude was that the question was merely an
abstract one of the state of the law, and hence primarily a problem to
be settled by lawyers rather than by the Government. Having been
forced to appoint a Royal Commission he was content to wait for its
report, and made no attempt to induce it to speed up its deliberations,
which proceeded at a leisurely pace. In any case the Conservatives
were not anxious to have a report before the next general election, which they knew could not be very far away. During the 1905
session of Parliament the Government allowed the Parliamentary

[1] *T.U.C. Annual Report*, 1903.
[2] See Webb, S. and B., *Industrial Democracy*, Ed. 1902 Preface.
[3] In 1904 the South Wales Miners were mulcted of over £57,000, and the Yorkshire Miners' Federation had to pay out an even larger sum. Cf. Presidential
Address—*T.U.C. Annual Report*, 1904.

Committee's Bill to go through to the committee stage, where it was wrecked deliberately by amendments moved by the Solicitor-General.

Among the most consistent supporters of the Parliamentary Committee's Bill in the House of Commons were the Irish Nationalist members. In exchange for their support, they asked the Parliamentary Committee to include in the Bill words which would cover the conspiracy laws as they affected Irish agricultural organisations. The Committee was at first reluctant to agree in case this might prejudice the Bill's chances of being carried, but they eventually decided to recommend to Congress that the Committee should be authorised to negotiate with the Irish leader, John Redmond, with a view of seeing whether his request could be met. However, before action could be taken, Balfour handed in his resignation, and Sir Henry Campbell-Bannerman became Prime Minister, at the head of a Liberal Government which lasted only until Parliament was dissolved a few weeks later.

Education, Protection and South Africa

Although the Taff Vale question was the main item on the agenda of the Trades Union Congress for half a dozen years, it was not the only one to arouse the passions of the delegates. The Education Act of 1902, which did violence to the beliefs of the Nonconformists, stirred up strong emotions in the working class. The Parliamentary Committee vigorously attacked the Bill, and organised a special conference of protest against its provisions at the Exeter Hall in London. The main grounds on which the trade unions were opposed to the Bill were reiterated by W. C. Steadman, in his presidential address to the 1902 Congress.

> The Bill [said Steadman] abolishes School Boards and places the schools under the Municipal and Borough Councils, with power to nominate a given number to form a Schools Committee, they in turn having the power to co-opt other members—this in itself being a blow to democratic representation, an interference with the right of citizenship and public control stunted and arrested.[1]

He went on to say that the Bill gave no answer to the question of how secondary education was to be brought within the reach of working-class children. What the T.U.C. desired to see was one educational authority directly elected for all educational purposes without any sectarian bias. The opposition of the trade unions to the Bill was perhaps short-sighted, for it embodied notable improvements in the educational system, but the feeling was strong that the liquidation of

[1] *T.U.C. Annual Report*, 1902.

the school boards would mean less democratic education. The special conference convened by the Parliamentary Committee instructed it to take steps to secure the defeat of all candidates at the next election who would not support the educational policy of the T.U.C.

When Chamberlain hinted at his conversion to protection in the summer of 1903 the trade unions were at once suspicious that the Government was going to abandon free trade. They no longer trusted the 'great radical', because of his failure to carry out his promises with regard to old age pensions, and his policy of imperialism at the Colonial Office, but little did they realise, when Congress met that year, that Chamberlain had already informed Balfour of his intention of resigning so as to be free to campaign for imperial preference. At the 1903 Congress the president devoted a substantial part of his address to Chamberlain's speeches on the need for preferential tariffs, and precedence was given to a resolution: 'That this Congress strongly condemns the suggested change by Mr. Chamberlain on our present fiscal policy as most mischievous and dangerous to the best interests of the people of the country. . . .'[1] Within less than a week of the conclusion of Congress Chamberlain had resigned, and protection had become a major political issue. During the following year the Parliamentary Committee distributed over 50,000 leaflets to trade unionists in order to combat Chamberlain's fiscal reform movement, and it organised meetings and deputations in opposition. At the 1905 Congress, held only three months before the general election, it was decided, by 1,253,000 to 26,000,

> That in the opinion of this Congress any departure from the principles of Free Trade would be detrimental to the interests of the working classes, on whom the burdens of Protection would press most heavily and injurious(ly) . . . that Protective duties by increasing the cost of the people's necessaries are unjust in incidence and economically unsound, subsidising capital at the expense of labour; and that as a system of Preference or Retaliation by creating cause for dispute with other countries, would be a hindrance to international progress and peace.[2]

Chamberlain was again the subject of attack when it was thought that he intended to permit the importation of Chinese labour into South Africa. In fact, this was doing Chamberlain an injustice, for he was well aware of the opposition to this policy, and he had counselled caution; when the issue came to a head he was no longer a member of the Government.[3] During the next two years the

---

[1] *T.U.C. Annual Report*, 1903.   [2] *Ibid.*, 1905.

[3] 'It is impossible to say what Chamberlain would have done had he still been in office when the Labour crisis came to a head in the spring of 1904. We may conjecture, however, that on purely political grounds, he would still have delayed

immigration into South Africa of large numbers of indentured Chinese labourers for work in the mines of the Rand aroused a tremendous outcry when it was learned in Britain that they were unable to bring their wives and were lodged in compounds that savoured of slave camps. It was not simply humanitarian motives that led the trade unions to make this vigorous protest, although they were incensed at the treatment of labour as merely a commodity by the capitalists of South Africa. They strongly condemned 'the introduction of cheap Chinese labour . . . in view of the fact of the vast expenditure of blood and treasure; and that many thousands of British workmen, many of whom fought this country's battles in South Africa are today out of employment. . . .'[1]

The unions considered, that since Britain had won the war, South Africa ought to be a white man's country, and that permitting the mine owners to import Chinese labour was depriving British workers of opportunities of employment in this new country. Chamberlain had twitted his opponents with the remark that they were marching to the polling booths to the tune of Chin, Chin, Chinaman! 'Let the workers take up the challenge, and prove at the polls that that was no false rallying cry', said Mr. J. Sexton moving the resolution on Chinese labour at Congress in 1904.[2] The delegates to the Trades Union Congress saw nothing contradictory in denouncing the South African War—albeit by a narrow majority—as one 'of the most remarkable and unjust wars of modern times' whilst at the same time condemning the Government for permitting South African mine owners to defraud white workers of their full share in the fruits of successful imperialism.

Alien Immigration

The trade unions were hardly more consistent in their demands for the prohibition of poor immigrants into Britain.

In the slump years of the eighties and nineties, attention had been drawn by the trade unions to the influx of impoverished workers—mainly from Eastern Europe; their fear being that competition from this supply of cheap labour would lead to a lowering of wage standards. The Conservative Government set up a select committee to examine the question in 1886, but the trade unions forgot the matter as trade improved, only to remember it again when unemployment

giving his assent to the import of Chinese coolies.' Amery, Julian, *Life of Joseph Chamberlain*, vol. IV, p. 335. See also, Mrs. Asquith, *Autobiography*, vol. II, p. 65, quoted by Halévy, *History of the English People*, vol. III, *Epilogue*, p. 128. Pelican Ed.

[1] *T.U.C. Annual Report*, 1904.   [2] *Ibid.*,

returned in 1892. At the Trades Union Congress of that year a resolution was passed calling for the prevention of 'foreign pauper labour' from entering Britain; and a similar resolution was again carried in 1894. The idea of prohibiting the entry of foreign immigrants, and refugees at that, as many of them were, was anathema to Liberals, though not to Conservatives, whose philosophy placed patriotic nationalism at the forefront of their creed. In 1896 the Conservative Government announced its intention of making immigration less easy, and two years later a Bill was debated in the House of Lords, but as employment was again almost full and the outcry had ceased, legislation was not proceeded with. The end of the South African War brought with it rising unemployment, and the Government decided to appoint a Royal Commission on Alien Immigration in 1902. The Commission reported in the following year, and the Government eventually introduced a Bill to give effect to its recommendations, but this failed to receive the approval of Parliament. A second measure was subsequently introduced and carried into law. The Aliens Act of 1905 empowered immigration officers to classify as undesirable any alien who could not prove that he was able to secure a job or had other means of supporting himself in a desirable manner. Aliens suffering from any infirmity which might mean that, at some time, they might be a charge to poor relief, were to be banned altogether; and the Home Secretary was given power to expel any foreigner from the country who was, in his opinion, suffering from poverty, living in insanitary conditions or was guilty of a crime. This Act was vigorously denounced by James Sexton in his presidential address to the 1905 Congress. He said,

> the Government and its false prophets are anticipating that this appeal to stupid, blind prejudice will have its effect at the General Election in their favour. It is claimed that the Bill will relieve the sweated workpeople by prohibiting the introduction of cheap labour from other countries. The political dishonesty of the measure needs no other argument than the fact that while the promoters profess to shut out undesirables from the United Kingdom in order to help the British workman here, they rushed a measure through to enable the mineowner to introduce the most undesirable kind of labour into South Africa. . . .[1]

Most trade unionists agreed with Sexton that the Conservatives were politically dishonest on this question, especially when, in the next

[1] *T.U.C. Annual Report*, 1905. See also resolution carried by a special Conference of Trade Unions, Socialist and Co-operative Organisations on unemployment—25 January 1905. *Parliamentary Debates*, 2 May 1905, 1445–775. Keir Hardie opposed the Aliens Bill on the grounds that immigrants do not contribute *per se* to pauperism or increased crime. The Bill was a step towards protection and for that reason Labour members were against it.

session, the Government permitted a Bill, sponsored by the Parliamentary Committee, to prevent the importation of foreign 'blacklegs' during a strike or lockout to pass the Commons without opposition, subsequently allowing it to be rejected by the Conservative-controlled House of Lords.[1]

However, concerned with two enormous problems of sweating and unemployment, the trade unions were not disposed to accept Sexton's advice to oppose the Aliens Act; they preferred to put practical expediency before idealism and wanted, if anything, to see it strengthened.

Since the Aliens Act appealed to the protective instinct of the trade unions its passing was a shrewd move by the Conservatives, but politically they gained nothing by it. Although the Act itself was devoid of specific racial discrimination in its terms of reference, it was calculated to give official support to the wave of popular anti-semitic feeling that was passing over the country. Anti-semitism was stimulated by the South African War, largely because those in opposition saw the conflict as due to the machinations of finance capitalists, many of whom were Jewish. John Ward, leader of the Navvies' Union, and a typical representative of the British labourer, rather insular and narrow-minded, suspicious of anything foreign and yielding to none in patriotism, speaking at the Trades Union Congress in 1900, said 'that practically £100,000,000 of the taxpayers' money had been spent in trying to secure the goldfields of South Africa for cosmopolitan Jews, most of whom had no patriotism and no country'.[2] 'Sweating' was another factor which contributed to anti-semitism, for it was at its worst in the clothing trades, located in the East End of London, where thousands of Jewish refugees from Russia and Poland had settled. It is difficult to gauge how strong was anti-semitism in the trade union movement at this time, but the organised workers were bitterly opposed to sweating and inclined to blame the racial characteristics of both Jewish masters and workers for the shocking conditions of employment. However, for a number of years a Jewish Tailors' Union had been affiliated to the T.U.C. and Congress had supported its demands for Jewish-speaking factory inspectors. At the Trades Union Congress of 1902 and in the following years resolutions were moved and carried unanimously, calling upon the Government to reduce the naturalisation fee and simplify the procedure. This may seem inconsistent with the demand for the restriction of immigration, but the main interest of the British worker was to prevent his position from being undermined by the

[1] *Parliamentary Debates*, 17 May 1906, pp. 157–739. Hardie, Crooks and Henderson protested at the action of the Lords.
[2] *T.U.C. Annual Report*, 1900.

influx of cheap labour; once the labour was here, the trade unions wanted for their own protection to ensure that it enjoyed the same standards of living, and possessed the same rights as their own members.

In another sense the trade unions were inconsistent, for the Aliens Act was a violation of the Liberal principles on which free trade rested, and which were being supported ardently by them against the protectionism of Chamberlain. The trade unions were not prepared to extend the principles of protection, which they claimed for themselves by supporting the Aliens Bill, to industry and agriculture, since to do this, they felt, would be to the advantage of farmers and industrialists at their members' expense.[1] The language of the trade unions was often that of Cobdenite liberalism, but their practice was more often determined by opportunistic advantage to their members.

T.U.C. Adopt Policy to Reduce Unemployment

Unemployment, which was as low as 2 per cent in 1900, reached 6 per cent in 1904. Hitherto, when unemployment increased, it had usually been accompanied by a fall in prices; this time, however, prices actually rose as unemployment increased.[2] As wages were stationary, real wages began to fall after the turn of the century, reversing a trend that had continued with minor set-backs for nearly a hundred years. Two resolutions were passed by the Trades Union Congress of 1904, drawing attention to the growing distress from unemployment. One of them instructed the Parliamentary Committee

> to approach the government with the object of laying before them the necessity of establishing a special department of the Board of Trade, whose work it shall be to deal with recurring periods of depression and distress by co-ordinating the efforts of local authorities and acting in conjunction with such authorities; and further by introducing such legislation as would empower both local and central authorities to deal adequately with the problem.[3]

An attempt to persuade Balfour to call a special autumn session of Parliament to take urgent action to deal with the growing distress from unemployment failed; the Parliamentary Committee therefore decided to call a conference with the Management Committee of the G.F.T.U. and the Labour Members of Parliament, to draft a report for presentation to the Government. The Conference came to the conclusion that the main causes of unemployment were:

[1] Cf. Halévy, *History of the English People*, vol. III, *Epilogue*, p. 120. Pelican Ed.
[2] Layton and Crowther, *The Study of Prices*.   [3] *T.U.C. Annual Report*, 1904.

... the absence of organisation in industry, intensified by the increased production of labour saving appliances unaccompanied by an adequate reduction of hours of labour or a sufficient increase in remuneration.

The displacement of men by women and young persons through the introduction of automatic machinery.

The absence particularly in Government works of any attempt to regulate the distribution of work so as to maintain employment at an even level, thereby causing alternate periods of rush and stagnation.

The fact that the financial resources of the country are being constantly drained in avoidable wars and extravagant expenditure.[1]

The report went on to say that the existing methods of dealing with the problem of unemployment were inadequate, and suggested the following remedial proposals: (a) that the Government be urged to regulate the distribution of work under its jurisdiction; (b) that this principle be urged by the Government upon all public bodies and recommended to private firms; (c) that the practice of working overtime be generally discountenanced; (d) that local bodies similar to those under Mr. Long's recent scheme for London, with the addition of a considerable proportion of trade union representatives, be permanently established in all localities throughout the country.[2]

The Government should create more employment, the report stated, by seeing that works of public utility were carried out with the least possible delay, and it gave as examples, the extension of the port and docks of London, coast protection and reafforestation. Public bodies might be formed, it was suggested, with power to acquire land on which the unemployed could be settled, with a view to the workers and their families eventually becoming self-supporting through a system of co-operative farming.

The idea of the authors of the report was that the public bodies set up to organise the public works and farms should obtain their labour through the trade unions, and, in exceptional circumstances, from the board of guardians. The report stated that

Trade unions, by reasons of their existing practical machinery by which workmen are advised as to places where employment can be obtained; their system of aid to unemployed members travelling in search of employment; their recognised agents in every part of the

[1] *T.U.C. Special Report on Unemployment*, 1905.
[2] In the winter of 1904, Walter Long, President of the Local Government Board. attempted to alleviate the growing distress by setting up voluntary committees in London, consisting of representatives of the local authorities, boards of guardians, and social workers, with a central committee to co-ordinate their activities. These committees were not to be merely relief agencies, but were to try and stimulate schemes of employment for men not coming under the Poor Law. They had to rely entirely on private charity, for the Government was not prepared to supply funds to relieve unemployment.

Kingdom; and their financial responsibility for unemployment benefit alone which now amounts to £600,000 per year, together with their knowledge of the character, suitability and antecedents of their members, should be the recognised agency to deal with workers described by Mr. Long as, 'Those who are respectable men temporarily distressed owing to inability to obtain employment.' The report suggested that the 'ordinary applicants for Poor Law Relief,' who were apparently not respectable, should still be the responsibility of the Poor Law Guardians.[1]

While the report emphasised the State's responsibility to take action that would reduce the number of unemployed, it made no real break with the past. In proposing schemes of land settlement and co-operative farming it was harking back to the panacea which had been revived by radicals, at times of crisis, again and again since the days of Robert Owen. The report said nothing at all about the financing of these schemes, but hinted that the solution was to be found in the nationalisation of the land. The aim of its authors was to reduce the supply of labour seeking jobs in the industrial areas, in the belief that the ordinary process of supply and demand would then prevent the cutting of wages. Additional support was to be given to this policy by an all-round reduction in hours, which would spread the available jobs over a greater number of heads. It was suggested that the voluntary employment committees already established in London should be extended over the country, and made permanent bodies, but the report made no recommendation that the State should endow them with funds. The grievance of the trade unions was that these committees were mainly composed of people who regarded unemployed workers as a species of criminal, seeing it as largely their own fault that they were without jobs. The principal desire of the trade unions was that they themselves should be officially recognised as the proper agencies for the placing of unemployed workers in jobs; this would, if jobs were available, have given them greater control over the labour market and added to their strength. The philosophy of the report, but for the section on public works, was in keeping more with Liberal economic thinking and utilitarian doctrines of social policy than with any advanced notions of State collectivism.

After the report had been adopted a deputation presented it to the Prime Minister. Mr. Balfour refused to discuss the question of reafforestation and farm colonies as real remedies. He agreed that some more permanent machinery was desirable, but he did not think it was the duty of the State to provide employment, as he said this would do more harm than good. 'Now we all know, and nobody

[1] *T.U.C. Special Report on Unemployment*, 1905.

better than the representatives of the Trade Unions, that in every
great community, and certainly in our community, there is a residuum
. . . which cannot truly be counted among the number of those who
can be effectively helped, because they and their character are the
cause of the distress in which they find themselves,' stated Balfour.[1]
The trade unions had, in fact, accepted this premise in their report,
but they were also concerned about the respectable working men
and while Balfour agreed that there was a problem, he added that
there was little the Government could do about it.

Increasing unemployment and distress from poverty, the agitation
of the trade unions and the growing unpopularity of the Govern-
ment, however, convinced Balfour of the need to do something.
Walter Long drew up a Bill which was based on the extension of his
London scheme of voluntary employment committees throughout
the country, on a permanent basis, as the trade unions had asked.
The Bill was actually introduced by Gerald Balfour, who succeeded
Long at the Local Government Board following a reshuffle of the
Government in March 1905. It gave the Government power to set
up committees, similar to those in London, in all the large towns, and
permitted subventions from the local rates to cover a small proportion of their expenditure. These local committees were to be controlled by a central co-ordinating committee, which was to be
responsible for the setting up of labour exchanges and employment
registers.[2] There were, however, a number of clauses in the Bill which
the trade unions found obnoxious. The Bill was considered by a joint
conference of the committees of the three Labour organisations,
T.U.C., G.F.T.U. and L.R.C., which issued a statement marked by
a considerable shift from the mild proposals of the report issued only
a short time before. The joint conference noted that

> the recognition of responsibility of the public authorities to provide
> work for the unemployed, and the removal of disfranchisement as a
> consequence of such public relief are principles upon which to base any
> attempt to deal with Unemployment. [The statement continued.] But
> we declare that (1) Unless the Bill is made to apply all over the country,
> (2) Unless the Exchequer finds most of the cost, (3) Unless the Com-
> mittees and the areas which they cover are so arranged that the Bill will
> not empty the country unemployed into London and the County
> Boroughs; and (4) Unless all limitations upon rates of wages paid which
> are a serious menace to Trade Unions are removed, the Bill cannot be
> accepted by organised Labour in the country and ought to be rejected
> by the votes of every friend of Labour in the House of Commons.[3]

[1] *T.U.C. Special Report on Deputation to the Prime Minister*, 1905.
[2] The Conservative Government had passed an Act in 1902 giving the recently
established metropolitan boroughs power to set up labour exchanges.
[3] *Report of the Parliamentary Committee*, 1905.

To a deputation from the Joint Conference, which placed these views before him, Gerald Balfour replied that it was impossible to allow the amount earned on relief works to be equal to the payment for a week of 'ordinary' work. However, the Government were willing to pay the trade union rate for the district, but would limit the days of work given to any one man in order to keep his weekly earnings less than if he were employed normally. As for demands for Exchequer assistance, Balfour told them that this showed a misunderstanding of the purpose of the Bill, which was simply to deal with a temporary problem of distress.

The president of the Local Government Board could not rid himself of the ingrained conviction that unemployment was mainly the fault of the unemployed, and, therefore, that anything the Government might do should carry with it some penalty as a deterrent to others. This negative reply and the withdrawal of rate aid to men working on the land, led the three national committees to decide to oppose the Bill. It had a few supporters from the Labour ranks, the most conspicuous of them being John Burns, who still considered himself to be the unofficial spokesman of the London unemployed. He thought that the Bill was worth having as a recognition of the principle that the State had a responsibility for providing employment. In this Burns was right, for though the Conservatives had only taken a small step forward in putting this Act through, to prevent themselves having to take a big stride later, they could not stop the march towards more and more State responsibility. Again the Conservatives had given way to pressure, in a bid to retrieve some of the support they had lost, and again it was a case of too little and too late, as far as the working-class vote was concerned.

The Government Attacked as Anti-Union Employer

The trade unions had another powerful grievance against the Government. By this time the State employed a large number of workers, and its record as an employer was pretty bad. By the Fair Wages resolution passed in 1891, and a resolution passed in 1893, calling on the Government to see that the State was a model employer, the House of Commons had committed the Government to setting an example to private industry. The Government recognised the trade unions and treated with them, but did little or nothing to insist on the Government departments responsible for the employment of labour honouring their obligations. Every year resolutions were carried at the Trades Union Congress instructing the Parliamentary Committee to press Government departments to pay trade union rates to their employees. The deputations of the Parliamentary

Committee to the ministers concerned were either fobbed off with bland replies and little done to improve matters, or else they were pointedly ignored. Under the Conservative administration, the Post Office, Admiralty and War Office were notorious for their refusal to admit the right of trade unions to bargain on behalf of members employed in establishments coming under their control. The Parliamentary Committee, at the request of the Association of Postal Service Employees and Postmen's Federation, wrote to the Postmaster-General, Lord Londonderry, asking him to receive a delegation to discuss the grievances of the Post Office workers, including the planting of industrial spies among them, refusal to allow them to come under the Workmen's Compensation Act, and other questions. His Lordship merely acknowledged receipt of the letter and refused even to reply. The Secretary for War, Mr. Broderick replied to a similar request, with regard to 'sweating' at Woolwich Arsenal, that he would receive any communication from the workmen themselves but he would not receive a deputation from outside bodies.[1] When Keir Hardie and Richard Bell protested in the House of Commons at the attitude of the Government, Lord Londonderry told them to mind their own business. Naturally when this was the attitude of the political heads of the departments the civil servants took their cue from it. At the 1903 Congress a resolution of 'protest against the refusal of heads of the various departments to grant interviews to the accredited representatives of the men' who worked in the State-owned army clothing establishments was carried. The attitude of the Government not only incensed the unions directly concerned, but outraged the whole movement, when great private employers like the Railway Companies and Lord Penrhyn could justify their refusal to recognise the trade unions by pointing to the practices of the Government.

Closer Relations between the T.U.C., the G.F.T.U. and the Labour Party

The refusal of the Conservative Government to remedy the many grievances of the workers, and the failure of the Liberals to give convincing proof that they would pursue a policy of vigorous social reform if returned to power, impelled the trade unions to seek more resolutely for their own political salvation. By 1903 many of the unions which had looked upon the formation of the Labour Representation Committee with deep suspicion had become affiliated.[2]

[1] *T.U.C. Annual Report*, 1902.
[2] The bulk of the miners remained outside the L.R.C., but such events as the bitter disputes at Denaby and Hemsworth, in 1902 and 1905, were gradually turning them away from their traditional support of the Liberals to more radical political doctrines.

Increasingly voices were raised within the ranks of the Labour movement demanding closer unity between its various sections. At the 1902 Congress a resolution was carried calling upon the Parliamentary Committee to establish a joint headquarters with the General Federation of Trade Unions and the Labour Representation Committee, but this proposal came to naught because of the suspicions entertained in each of the three organisations against the others. Although the T.U.C. had hived off the Labour Representation Committee as a separate organisation, the exact relationship of the L.R.C. with its parent was not made clear until 1904. A number of resolutions were down on the agenda that year relating to the Labour Representation Committee, but Richard Bell, the president, upheld the ruling of the General Purposes Committee that any resolution 'to endorse or amend the constitution of an independent and outside body is not in order'.[1] A resolution confirming this ruling was put to the delegates and carried.

From the year of its foundation, reports from the Labour Representation Committee on its progress had been presented annually to Congress; fraternal delegates, however, were present for the first time in 1904, in the persons of J. Ramsay MacDonald and Arthur Henderson. In his speech to Congress on behalf of the delegation, Ramsay MacDonald said, 'The Labour Representation Committee is neither sister nor brother to Congress, but its child. We come, therefore, to offer our filial respects.' In spite of MacDonald's insistence that the child was cast in the image of its parent, a note of anxiety over its behaviour was raised by W. B. Hornidge, secretary of the Boot and Shoe Operatives, when in seconding a vote of thanks he said that he hoped that this lusty child of Congress would not turn out to be a disobedient one.

The three Labour organisations first came together to co-ordinate their efforts to obtain a new Trade Union Act to over-throw the Taff Vale decision; thereafter they met jointly from time to time on a number of different subjects. As a result of resolutions urging unity on the three organisations, in order to put forward a maximum effort to return Labour candidates at the general election which everyone knew could not be far off, a joint conference was held at Caxton Hall on 16 February 1905, out of which sprang a permanent co-ordinating committee. This was composed of three representatives from each of the three organisations, with the addition of three joint secretaries. The conference decided to call this standing committee the Joint Board.

[1] *T.U.C. Annual Report*, 1904. Bell was anxious to avoid a discussion on the constitution of the L.R.C. because he had supported a Liberal at a by-election, and it was known that an attack on his action was to be made from the floor of Congress.

The first meeting of the Joint Board was held in the offices of the Parliamentary Committee in Effingham House, Arundel Street, Strand, on Wednesday, 29 November 1905. D. C. Cummings, D. J. Shackleton, J. J. Stevenson and W. C. Steadman[1] represented the Parliamentary Committee; Keir Hardie, J. R. Macdonald and Arthur Henderson the L.R.C.; P. Curran, Allan Gee, John Ward and I. Mitchell the G.F.T.U. Cummings was appointed chairman and Mitchell, Steadman and MacDonald joint secretaries, and it was agreed that no statement would be issued unless signed by all three secretaries. The first resolution passed by the Joint Board was a protest at the absence of a trade unionist on the Royal Commission on the Poor Law, which Balfour had set up in an attempt to sidetrack the growing demand from the trade unions for a change in the Poor Law and in the way it was administered. As a result of this pressure F. Chandler, secretary of the Amalgamated Society of Carpenters and Joiners was appointed to the Commission.

At the 1905 Trades Union Congress a resolution was moved by J. Anderson of the Stevedores' Union calling upon the Parliamentary Committee to convene a conference of the three organisations in order to arrange for their amalgamation into one body. The opinion of the stevedores was that one organisation would be more effective and powerful than three. It was a different motive, however, which prompted F. Kennedy of the Builders' Labourers' Union to support the resolution. This delegate voiced the animus which still existed in the trade unions against having socialists on the Labour Representation Committee; he wanted the amalgamation in order to put the L.R.C. under the complete control of the trade unions. After listening to a number of cautious and sensible speeches pointing out that any such attempt at forced unity would be dangerous and impracticable, the delegates rejected the resolution by a substantial majority.

The majority of the delegates were satisfied with the agreement reached at the Caxton Hall Conference, which they endorsed. The essence of this agreement was that all candidates approved by the Parliamentary Committee and the L.R.C. would receive the full support of both organisations, and that the L.R.C. would not be considered disloyal if it refused to support a Labour candidate adopted on any other party platform. However, the L.R.C. had to make it clear that their national constitution did not require the abstention of any Labour elector where a Labour candidate was not running. The agreement was necessary in this form because there were a large number of unions, including the miners, still unaffiliated with the L.R.C. who were bent on supporting the Lib-Lab candidates.

[1] Steadman had been elected secretary of the Parliamentary Committee in 1904. See p. 196.

During 1905 the Parliamentary Committee urged the trades councils in the large industrial centres to organise an afternoon conference, to be followed by a large public meeting, at which the main speaker would be a member of the Committee, in order to bring before the public the policy of the Trades Union Congress. As the election drew near it was decided to issue a manifesto, embodying the principal resolutions passed by Congress, and pointing out that changes in the law would be secured only if wage earners voted for candidates who pledged themselves to support this programme. Over a million copies of this leaflet were distributed during the election, and it had an important influence on the future. The ten points for which the Parliamentary Committee asked support were:

1. The principles embodied in the T.U.C. Trades Disputes Bill.
2. A Workmen's Compensation Act to make payments from the date of the accident.
3. A Truck Amendment Act to prevent all deductions from wages.
4. A new Unemployed Act to provide work at trade union rates.
5. Abolition of Chinese Labour in South Africa.
6. State pensions at 60 years of age.
7. An extension of the Housing of Working Classes Act.
8. Adult Suffrage.
9. Payment of Returning Officers' Fees by the Exchequer.
10. Establishment of an Eight-Hour Day.[1]

The L.R.C., the I.L.P., the S.D.F. and the Miners' Federation all put out their own manifestoes. That of the L.R.C. followed fairly closely the lines of the Parliamentary Committee's manifesto, except that it made reference to protection, which it opposed, but did not mention electoral reform at all.

The Parliamentary Committee endorsed 51 Labour candidates, 15 of whom were not supported by the L.R.C., mainly because they were representatives of the Miners' Federation. A number of Lib-Lab candidates, most of whom had no longer any direct responsibility to the trade unions, including Thomas Burt, John Burns, W. R. Cremer, Charles Fenwick and Henry Broadhurst, were not endorsed either by the Parliamentary Committee or the L.R.C., but relied on their personal following and the official support of the Liberals.

The election was fought mainly on the issue of protection, with Home Rule for Ireland and a Trade Disputes Bill to reverse the Taff Vale judgment as important secondary questions. The result of the poll was staggering, for the Conservatives were not merely defeated, but were utterly routed. In this resounding victory for free trade and the Liberal-Labour platform, the Liberals secured a clear majority over all the other parties, and, with Labour, had a majority of 271

[1] *Report of the Parliamentary Committee*, 1906.

over the Conservatives and their supporters. The Labour Representation Committee was astounded to find that 29 of its candidates had been successful, making with the 25 Lib-Lab victories, 54 Labour members in the new Parliament.[1]

The Labour Representation Committee had fought the election as an independent organisation, although there was a semi-secret official alliance with the national leaders of the Liberal Party, and in a large number of the constituencies in which Labour candidates were successful no Liberal candidate appeared.[2] The programme of the Labour candidates had been moderate, and not very dissimilar from that of many Liberals, and there had been complete accord on the basic issue of protection or free trade. In return, most Liberal candidates pledged themselves to support a Trade Disputes Bill on the lines of the one demanded by the Parliamentary Committee of the Trades Union Congress. Nevertheless this situation did not prevent the Labour Representation Committee from proclaiming on the morrow of the election that henceforth it would no longer be known as a Representation Committee, but would be a fully fledged Labour Party, with its own officers and whips.

Up to 1885 Thomas Burt, Alexander Macdonald and Henry Broadhurst were the only members of the Parliamentary Committee to have been elected to Parliament during their terms of office; from that time onwards until the election of 1900 there were one or more members of the Committee with seats in the House of Commons. The defeat of Sam Woods and W. C. Steadman by Conservatives in the 'Khaki Election' of that year left the Committee without a member of Parliament in its ranks, and it was not until Richard Bell was re-elected to the Committee in 1902 that this direct representation was restored. Bell was joined by D. J. Shackleton in 1904, both men having been elected to Parliament under the auspices of the Labour Representation Committee. Though Bell left the L.R.C. in 1904, to join the Liberals, he retained his seat on the Parliamentary Committee, since Congress was not disposed to discriminate in favour of supporters of the L.R.C.

The 1906 election brought a dramatic change in the number of members of the Parliamentary Committee who also had seats in the House of Commons. Out of a Committee of thirteen, including the secretary, nine were members of Parliament. These were D. J. Shackleton, secretary of the Northern Counties Amalgamated

[1] See Cole, G. D. H., *British Working Class Politics, 1832–1914*, p. 179.

[2] Had the local Liberal associations been willing, on a larger scale, to adopt working-men candidates it is possible that the Labour Party would not have come into being. It was the failure of many local Liberal associations to make politically minded working men feel that it was their party, as much as any other factor, which led to the formation of the L.R.C.

Association of Weavers; A. H. Gill, secretary of the Amalgamated Cotton Spinners; G. N. Barnes, secretary of the Amalgamated Society of Engineers; Richard Bell, secretary of the Amalgamated Society of Railway Servants; C. W. Bowerman, secretary of the London Society of Compositors; Alex Wilkie, secretary of the Associated Society of Shipwrights; Will Thorne, secretary of the Gasworkers and General Labourers; James Haslam, secretary of the Derbyshire Miners; and W. C. Steadman, secretary of the Parliamentary Committee. The non-members of Parliament who were on the Committee were W. J. Davis, secretary of the Brassworkers; F. Chandler, secretary of the Carpenters and Joiners; and D. C. Cummings, secretary of the Boilermakers and Iron Shipbuilders. Gill, Shackleton, Thorne, Barnes, Bowerman and Wilkie were elected as candidates of the L.R.C. while Steadman, Bell and Haslam had stood as Lib-Lab candidates endorsed by the T.U.C., but not by the L.R.C.

With nine of its members sitting in the House of Commons the strength of the Committee as a pressure group was considerably increased, for they could keep a close watch on the activities of the Government in the House of Commons and could act quickly as a group when necessary. It also meant that the Committee could exercise a good deal of influence over the parliamentary tactics of the much strengthened Labour Party. The position of the Parliamentary Committee was that of being almost a party within a party; this raised questions of co-ordination, and it also encouraged the Committee to continue to engage in political activities rather than confine itself to industrial problems and leave parliamentary policy and tactics to the Labour Party. Another effect was to bring the Lib-Lab and Labour Party members together and help to heal the breach between them, and, perhaps, equally important, from the point of view of parliamentary tactics, to act as a link between the Liberal Party and the Labour Party.

Improving the Administration of the T.U.C.

The activities of the Parliamentary Committee had steadily increased during the nineties, and had gone on increasing after the turn of the century—as the expanding size of the Committee's annual reports bears witness. In the year 1904–5 the Parliamentary Committee met thirty-five times. In Broadhurst's day the Committee met less frequently, and very often decisions were taken by the secretary in consultation with those members who were available on the spot in London. Neither Fenwick, nor his successor, Woods, exercised the same personal domination over the Committee as Broadhurst; and the growth in the status of the Committee, as the pace of social legislation gathered speed, made necessary more frequent meetings, which provincial members would have missed with reluctance. The amount of work undertaken by the Committee during the last year of Conservative rule was substantial. It promoted Bills in Parliament to amend the law relating to trade disputes; workmen's compensation; shop clubs; the safe working of steam engines and boilers; compulsory weighing where workers were paid per ton; traffic regulation; Saturday and Sunday holidays for textile workers. Pushing these Bills through Parliament entailed members of the Committee attending the House of Commons to lobby Members of Parliament for their assistance; the holding of meetings and conferences, drafting reports, and sending out circulars requesting M.P.s to be present to vote in the divisions. The Committee was also active in support of a number of other Bills introduced by Liberal members. During the year deputations from the Committee waited on the Prime Minister, Postmaster-General, President of the Board of Trade, Home Secretary, First Lord of the Admiralty and the Secretary of State for War, to discuss a wide variety of questions on which Congress had passed resolutions. These included unemployment, on which the Committee had drafted a special report; fair wages; civil rights of postal servants; factory safety; Truck Acts; weights and measures; workmen's compensation; conditions of work in the Royal Dockyards; and piece-work in use at the Woolwich Royal Arsenal.

In addition to this Parliamentary work of lobbying members and putting pressure on ministers, the Committee sent representatives to a number of meetings and conferences; arbitrated in a dispute between the Gasworkers' and General Labourers' Union and the Blastfurnacemen's Federation; and assisted a number of unions which were endeavouring to secure better conditions for their members. All these activities entailed a great deal of correspondence, skilled drafting and organising. In the drafting of Bills the secretary was assisted by the Standing Counsel of the Committee, Mr. Edmund Browne, a barrister who had advised the Committee for a number of years and had agreed to accept the post, when it was officially created in 1900, for the modest honorarium of £50 per year. The only other assistance enjoyed by the secretary apart from the voluntary work of members of the Committee and the chairman, was a clerk, who received a salary of £150 per year. Up to 1902 the secretary had been paid a salary of £300 per year, out of which he had to pay for his own clerical assistance. At the 1902 Congress it was decided to pay the secretary £250 per year, free of income tax, and to provide separately for a clerical assistant. This change roused a good deal of discussion, and there were criticisms from those who felt that the secretary ought not to be paid such a high salary. Whenever the question of salaries for their own employees has been discussed it has always been astonishing how many trade unionists have been prepared to cast away the principle of the rate for the job—to which they tenaciously cling for themselves—and it is so even at the present day. It was further suggested that the secretary should devote his full time to his job, but this proposal was defeated after Sam Woods had told the delegates that he could handle all the work of the Committee easily enough. He pointed out that the factor that really held up greater efficiency was the scarcity of funds; the amount of work that could be done was governed by the money available to spend. After another lengthy argument Congress decided to increase the affiliation fee from £1 per 1,000 members to £1 10s. 0d., which increased the income of the Parliamentary Committee from £1,348 in 1902 to £1,948 in 1903. One of the first decisions on the use of the higher income was to move from Buckingham Street, Strand, to more commodious offices in Victoria Street; these premises were only occupied until 1905 when it was decided to return to the Strand to larger headquarters at Effingham House, Arundel Street. Here the Committee remained until 1911, when another move was necessary because it had outgrown the facilities available at this address. When in 1903 the new offices were taken in Victoria Street, the Committee decided to improve the efficiency of the secretary by providing him with a new typewriter, a telephone and a telegraphic address.

During 1904 Sam Woods was taken ill and had to resign his post as secretary to the Committee, which he had held for ten years. W. C. Steadman, of the Barge Builders' Union, member of the L.C.C., and a member of the Parliamentary Committee since 1899, was appointed by his colleagues as secretary until the next Congress. At the election Steadman, a dry-humoured cockney, one of the most popular and respected of trade union leaders, was opposed by Albert Stanley, a leader of the Miners' Federation. Steadman was confirmed in office, but by a very narrow majority; 770,000 votes were cast in his favour and 752,000 for the miners' candidate. This result was a testimony to the regard with which Steadman was held, for his own union, with only 400 members had merely the minimum figure of 1,000 votes with which to back him, whereas Stanley could count on 330,000.

When Woods retired, the Parliamentary Committee decided to recommend to Congress that, owing to the increased amount of work devolving upon the office, the new secretary should be required to devote his whole time to this work. This suggestion, which had been first made in 1902, was now acted upon by Congress and incorporated into its constitution. Steadman, in thanking Congress for appointing him as secretary, assured the delegates that he would give the whole of his time to the work of the Committee—except for parliamentary duties which would arise if he was elected to Parliament. It was the view of the Parliamentary Committee and Congress that the secretary should be a member of Parliament, as this would be of advantage in pushing the legislative policy of the T.U.C. and a proviso was included in the new standing order that whole-time secretarial work did not exclude parliamentary duties. But Steadman did not quite live up to his promise to concentrate exclusively on the work of the T.U.C., for he remained secretary of the Barge Builders until 1908; however, this does not seem to have taken up too much of his time, for no adverse comments were made about it at Congress.

Up to 1904 the secretary had been elected annually together with the members of the Parliamentary Committee; a further change in the standing orders that year put the holder of the office of secretary on the basis of permanent employment 'so long as his work and conduct gave satisfaction to the Parliamentary Committee and the representatives attending Congress', thus bringing to an end a procedure which had existed since the foundation of Congress. Not that the election had meant a great deal, for, although it had often been contested, Charles Fenwick was the only holder of the office who had been defeated, and after the acute divisions in Congress during the early nineties had faded away it had become the practice for the secretary to be returned unopposed.

From the very first the influence of the Parliamentary Committee over Congress had been considerable; it was very great during the time Broadhurst was secretary, then diminished under the onslaught of the new unionists, to reappear gradually from 1895. At the instance of the Parliamentary Committee the standing orders of Congress were revised in 1900.

The scope of the Committee's functions was not increased, but the redrafted standing order on the duties of the Committee gave it greater authority over Congress. The Committee proposed that standing order number eleven should read as follows:

The duties of the Parliamentary Committee shall be (1) To watch all legislative measures directly affecting the question of labour. (2) To initiate such legislative action as Congress may direct. (3) To prepare the programme for the Congress *from resolutions forwarded by the respective societies, and be empowered to rearrange and place only such propositions which are generally accepted as coming within the objects and aims of Trade Unionism.* (4) To examine and decide as to the validity of delegates' credentials. (5) The Parliamentary Committee shall meet at least seven days before the meeting of Congress for the purpose of classifying resolutions and amendments, and shall ballot for order of procedure of the same, *also for the position of delegates' seats in Congress Hall.*[1]

[1] *T.U.C. Annual Report*, 1900.

The London Society of Compositors' delegates took exception to the addition (in italics) to the standing orders, on the grounds that it would give the Parliamentary Committee too much power, and asked for it to be withdrawn. Another delegate suggested that it was aimed at preventing socialist resolutions from appearing. When it was put to the vote, the new standing order was carried by 572,000 to 394,000. Earlier, a resolution had been moved to secure a greater turnover of membership of the Parliamentary Committee, by making two-thirds of the Committee each year ineligible for re-election for a period of two years. The mover complained of the small unions being dominated by the large ones, namely the coal, cotton and gas workers. He stated that the Parliamentary Committee had become a closed corporation and that there was trafficking in votes. These strictures had some foundation in fact, for coal, cotton and gas accounted for about a quarter of the votes at Congress and their representatives were almost always on the Committee. It had become very difficult for the representative of a small society to get on to the Parliamentary Committee since the introduction of the card vote in 1895, and when one was successful, such as W. C. Steadman, it was because of personal popularity with the larger societies.[1] It was admitted that the larger unions bartered their votes, but the proposal was heavily defeated by them. However, it was Utopian to imagine that the large societies would acquiesce in a change which might have had the result of depriving their leaders of their seats on the Parliamentary Committee, and of replacing them with less powerful and less experienced figures.[2] The Parliamentary Committee again roused the anger of the small unions by proposing that in future the chairman of the Parliamentary Committee for the past year should be the president of Congress, instead of a delegate from the town where Congress was being held. The smaller unions secured more support on this issue, which was one of long-standing dispute. Perhaps if the delegates had not been treated to an immensely long and boring lecture by Mr. Pickles, the president of that year, on

[1] The *Clarion* conducted a vigorous campaign against the block vote and the domination of Congress by the large unions for several years. P. J. King compared the election of the Parliamentary Committee to the election of a candidate at Woodstock, before the Reform Act of 1832. It was, he claimed, as impossible to secure election to the Parliamentary Committee, without the support of Mr. David Holmes (Cotton Operatives) and Mr. Sam Woods (Miners), as it was to win the seat at Woodstock without the patronage of the Duke of Marlborough. *Clarion*, 10 September 1898. A year later the *Clarion* returned to the subject, and admitted that the bartering of votes was 'a taint from which even the advanced wing are not by any means free'. *Clarion*, 6 September 1898.

[2] The domination of the Parliamentary Committee by the large unions was one of the reasons why the small unions favoured the establishment of the Labour Representation Committee.

the anthropological theories of Darwin, Huxley and Spencer; a speech which was described as more suitable for a learned society than for the T.U.C., this proposal would not have gone through. The effect of the change was to tend to strengthen the control of the Parliamentary Committee over Congress, and enable it to give a lead to the delegates at the beginning of the week of their deliberations.

The divisions in Congress ran many ways, and were by no means solely confined to disputes between the large and small unions. Sectional interests were inevitable in so large and diverse a movement, and its leaders recognised that it was futile to ignore them. Very often unions were in disagreement with a policy which had been adopted, but most of them were too well aware of the value of Congress to abandon it light-heartedly, and few unions followed the example of the A.S.E. when they disagreed with its policy or a decision went against them.[1] A case in point was that of prohibiting child labour. The cotton delegates opposed for a number of years the resolution supported by the miners and most of the rest of Congress, 'in favour of the abolition of the employment of children under the age of fifteen years', because part-time employment of children under the school leaving age existed on a considerable scale in Lancashire, and the cotton men argued that this juvenile labour was essential to the well-being of the industry. They did not, however, leave the T.U.C. when defeated by the votes of other unions. The foundation of Ruskin Hall, later Ruskin College, affords another example of the division of Congress on different lines. The support which the Parliamentary Committee had given to the promoters of Ruskin was attacked mainly on the grounds that the bona fides of the institution were dubious, and that the trade union movement could not afford the cost of such a college. The real reason underlying this criticism was a parochial one, and came largely from members of the London Trades Council, who were jealous of the College being set up at Oxford, and afraid of the politics it might teach. The London Trades Council carried out its own educational courses, and felt that it had a proprietary right in this field.

These sectional divisions might have been a menace to the unity of the Trades Union Congress had the Parliamentary Committee attempted to adopt and enforce a centralised policy at the expense of the autonomy of the individual unions. Fortunately for the movement, it did not try to interfere, and by leaving the unions to carry out their own policy it greatly reduced the danger of serious conflict.

[1] See Chapter IV, p. 169.

CHAPTER VI

PRESSURE FOR SOCIAL REFORM

The report of the Royal Commission on Trade Disputes was published on the 15 January 1906, when the general election was already in progress. The Commission had completed its work some time before, but the Conservative Government had indicated privately that the report should be held back in order that its findings should not be used politically during the election.[1] The Majority Report, signed by Lord Dunedin, Sidney Webb and Arthur Cohen, recommended a change in the law on a point vital to the trade unions. Prior to the Taff Vale decision, which made the trade unions liable for damages as a result of acts committed by their members, it had been assumed by lawyers and laymen alike that trade unions were not legal entities, except in so far as they were recognised by statute, and that, therefore, they could not be sued as corporate bodies for committing a civil wrong. The Commission refused to recommend a return to that situation, on the grounds that to do so would be to perpetuate an outrageous perversion. Instead it was proposed that trade unions should be declared legal associations by statute, but that they should only be liable for the actions of their members if these had been expressly authorised by an executive committee. In addition, it was proposed to give the trade unions the power to enter into agreements with employers, or with their own members, which would be legally binding contracts enforceable through the courts. Strikes, whether primary or secondary, from whatever motive they were instigated, should be declared legal, unless criminal or in breach of contract, and it should be made lawful to persuade an individual to strike, but not to break a contract, stated the report. It also advised that the watching and besetting clause of the 1875 Act, which was loosely phrased, should be repealed, and in its place a clause substituted which would only prohibit actions if they were carried out in such a manner 'as to cause a reasonable apprehension in the mind of any person that violence will be used to him or his family, or damage be done to his property'.[2] In addition it was advocated that an individual should not be liable for doing any act not in itself an actionable tort on the ground only that it was an interference with another person's trade, business or employment. Lastly, it was

[1] Webb, B., *Our Partnership*, p. 267.
[2] *Report of the Royal Commission on Trade Disputes and Trade Combinations.*

suggested that the benefit funds of a trade union, if separated from the general fund, should be immune from any action resulting in a grant of damages against the union.

The two other members of the Commission were not disposed to grant so much protection to the trade unions, and made recommendations of their own to increase union liabilities. Sidney Webb added a rider to the report to the effect that while he fully concurred with its recommendations he could not agree with its underlying assumption that conflict in industry was inevitable or strikes a necessity, and he drew attention to the compulsory arbitration laws in force in the antipodes, suggesting that similar legislation covering all classes of labour and conditions of work might be considered as a logical step forward in this country.[1]

The Trade Disputes Act

Soon after the Report of the Royal Commission had been published, the Parliamentary Committee met to consider the situation, and passed a resolution 'That the Committee in no way recognises the report of the Royal Commission on Trade Disputes . . .'[2] This was followed by an intense lobbying of the newly elected Members of Parliament, whose response confirmed the Parliamentary Committee in its determination to push its own Trade Disputes Bill, and not to rely on any measure which the Government might bring forth. On the 22 March the Government announced that it would introduce both a Workmen's Compensation Bill and a Trade Disputes Bill. The latter was tabled on the 28 March, and followed closely the recommendations in the Report of the Royal Commission. On the vital point of whether an action would lie against a trade union, if any of its members committed a tortious act during a trade dispute, the Bill proposed to exclude this possibility unless such an act had been carried out or sanctioned by the legally recognised executive committee of the union. The Attorney-General, introducing the Bill to the House of Commons, insisted that to return to the position in which the trade unions were free from all liability would confer on them a privilege that was unjustifiable, and would encourage irresponsible activities to which the trade unions would not really wish to be committed. The Attorney-General quoted from speeches made by Richard Bell and Thomas Burt in 1903, at the Trades Union Congress, to the effect that the trade unions had no desire to be placed in a privileged position under the law.[3] It is possible that had the

---

[1] Ibid.
[2] T.U.C. Annual Report, 1906.
[3] House of Commons Official Report, 28 March 1906.

Conservative Government introduced legislation on the lines of this
Bill in 1903, the trade unions would have been satisfied, but by 1906
opinions had hardened and they would accept nothing short of total
immunity. The bitter resentment at the treatment meted out for years
by the law courts had made it difficult for the trade unions to accept
a Bill which seemed to leave their fate in the hands of the judges.
They preferred to be outside the law, where they would be completely immune from legal proceedings.

On the day after the introduction of the Government's Bill, the
Parliamentary Committee had a meeting with forty-four of the
Labour members of Parliament, and it was decided to press the Committee's Trade Disputes Bill, which was due to come up for its
second reading on the next day, to a division. This policy was adhered
to, and, in the course of an acrimonious debate, the Government's
Bill came under severe attack. The Prime Minister, realising that
feeling was running high and that most of his supporters, including
the Attorney-General, had pledged their word during the election, to vote for the Parliamentary Committee's Bill, intervened
dramatically to say that the Government would be prepared to
accept the principle of complete immunity, which would be incorporated in the Government's measure, if it were carried by the
House. This sudden reversal of policy staggered the members of all
parties, but when the vote was taken the Parliamentary Committee's
Bill was carried by a majority of 350—a majority large enough to put
the issue beyond doubt. The next time the Government's Bill came
before the House it embodied the principle of the T.U.C. measure
and, thereafter, went through its remaining stages with ease. The trade
unions secured a further concession when the Government agreed to
accept an amendment which safeguarded the trade unions from legal
proceedings, even when a strike involved a breach of contract. The
House of Lords, with the exception of the former Lord Chancellor,
Lord Halsbury, who, describing the measure, said, 'anything more
outrageously unjust, anything more tyrannical, I can hardly con-
ceive',[1] were busy wrecking other Liberal measures, and thought
it prudent not to stir up opposition to themselves on this issue,
since its support in the Commons had been overwhelming, and the
Conservatives had, under Balfour's leadership, refused to vote
against the Bill on its third reading. The lawyers of both parties
were horrified at the thought of having this legal monstrosity
thrust upon them, but political expediency triumphed, since neither
party was anxious to be saddled with the onus of deliberately
denying to the trade unions protection for their funds. A distinguished historian has written, 'Its enactment was a victory not of

[1] House of Lords, 4 December 1906, *Parliamentary Debates*, vol. CLXVI.

the Liberals over the Conservatives, but of the proletariat over the bourgeoisie.'[1]

The Liberal Government makes Concessions to the T.U.C.

In addition to the Trade Disputes Act the Liberal Government, in its first year of power under Henry Campbell-Bannerman, passed a Workmen's Compensation Act, the second point on the T.U.C.'s election programme. This was a sweeping measure, which for the first time included 'any person who has entered into or works under a contract of service or apprenticeship with an employer, whether by way of manual labour, clerical work, or otherwise, and whether the contract is expressed or implied, is oral or in writing'.[2] Policemen, casual labourers and outworkers were excluded from its provisions, but the Act brought an additional six million workers under the protection of compensation for injury at work. It was not entirely satisfactory to the trade unions, for the rate of compensation was restricted to 50 per cent of the injured worker's weekly earnings, and payment did not commence until the injured worker had been absent from work at least a week. The trade unions endeavoured to persuade the Government to reduce the waiting period to three days, and were successful in obtaining a concession that, if a person was prevented by an accident from working for a fortnight, payment for the injury would be made retrospectively from the day of the accident. Industrial diseases were, for the first time, brought within the scope of workmen's compensation; a worker affected through his work with any of six diseases enumerated in the schedule would henceforth be entitled to claim in the same way as if he had suffered an accident. This provision was extremely important, and a great step forward, for industrial diseases such as anthrax and lead poisoning claimed an annual toll of workers engaged in certain industries running into considerable numbers. Under pressure from the Parliamentary Committee and the Labour members, the Home Secretary agreed to include powers in the Bill to extend the schedule, and set up a committee to advise him on its extension; this resulted in the addition, in the following year, of eighteen more industrial diseases. The Act covered most of the provisions set out in the Parliamentary Committee's Workmen's Compensation Bill, which had been pressed on the Conservative Government for a number of years without result. The passing of the new Act did not, however, guarantee that a workman would be paid compensation, even if he were entitled to it, for

[1] E. Halévy, *A History of the English People, 1905–1915*, vol. II, p. 97.

[2] *Workmen's Compensation Act, 1906*. Persons earning more than £250 per year in non-manual employment were excluded from the provisions of the Act.

no provision had been made to ensure that employers would insure against the contingency of having to pay compensation to their employees. The Committee sent a deputation to the Home Secretary and urged him to include a compulsory insurance clause, but the maximum concession the Government was prepared to make was a promise, given during the debates on the Bill, that the matter would be looked into. It took the trade unions a number of years of agitation before the Government was persuaded of the need to adopt this suggestion.

The Government also accepted, during its first year of office, a Bill sponsored by the Labour Party to enable local authorities to provide meals for needy school children.[1] The Education (Provision of Meals) Act was merely a permissive measure with a severely limited application to children suffering from acute under-feeding, and it was mainly designed to supplement the work of local charity committees. Restricted as the measure was to small subventions from the rates, it was, in principle, a recognition that the community, which insists on its members having a minimum of education, has also a duty to see that they have as far as possible healthy bodies to permit them to take advantage of it. 'The prevention of physical deterioration', as the trade unions, rather pompously, referred to the provision of school meals, had been pioneered by Fred Jowett and his I.L.P. friends on the Bradford City Council. Jowett, not satisfied with this measure, fought to extend its application and eventually succeeded in obtaining an amending Act which enabled local authorities to feed necessitous school children during their holidays, as well as in term time.[2]

With R. B. Haldane at the War Office, Lord Tweedmouth at the Admiralty and Sydney Buxton at the Post Office, the relations between the trade unions and these Government departments showed a notable improvement under the Liberal administration. The employment practices of these departments were still by no means to the satisfaction of the trade unions, but the new ministers did not treat union representatives with the aristocratic indifference that had been usual with their Conservative predecessors.

The enforcement of the 'fair wages clause' depended on the vigilance of the trade unions, but they were up against very great difficulties in carrying out their task, as they had no information as to whether a firm had obtained a Government contract or not. In 1902 the Parliamentary Committee had been instructed by Congress to press the Government to publish in the *Labour Gazette* the names of all the firms undertaking Government contracts. The Government

[1] *T.U.C. Annual Report*, 1907.
[2] Brockway, F., *Socialism over Sixty Years*, p. 78.

refused, and no progress was made until after the defeat of the Conservatives. Following deputations from the Parliamentary Committee, after the Liberal Government had taken office, the War Minister and the First Lord of the Admiralty agreed to supply the trade unions with information concerning contracts, and a working arrangement was arrived at for the investigation of alleged breaches of the 'fair wages clause' in service department contracts. The procedure was for any trade union with a complaint against a contractor to communicate with the secretary of the Parliamentary Committee, who would then put the matter before the department concerned. There it would be investigated by a departmental committee and a report submitted to the Parliamentary Committee. The Postmaster-General agreed to fall in with these arrangements, and the Home Office agreed to inform the Parliamentary Committee of any draft regulations it proposed to make under the Factory and Workshop Act.

The 1906 Congress passed a resolution that to prevent sweating and evasion of the 'fair wages clause' on printing and binding contracts for H.M. Stationery Office, this work ought to be carried out by the Government itself in its own workshops under trade union wages and conditions. This view was put to the Treasury by a deputation from the Parliamentary Committee and resulted in the appointment of a departmental committee to consider whether the Government should execute its printing in its own establishment. The Parliamentary Committee, invited to give evidence, appointed C. W. Bowerman, M.P., one of its members, and a representative of the London Society of Compositors, as its official spokesman. Largely as a result of this inquiry the Government accepted the case of the trade unions and created a State printing department.

The Parliamentary Committee Presses the Government on Social Reform

All this was an auspicious start for the trade union movement to the tenure of office of the Liberal Government, but after the legislative advances of the first year the pace of reform slackened. Apart from several minor amending Acts, including one which brought laundries within the scope of the Factory and Workshop Act of 1901; some improvement in the law protecting female employees, and a Small Holdings and Allotments Act to assist the settlement of small farmers as tenants of the county councils, there was nothing in the Government's programme to allay the economic discontent which had started to grow. The Parliamentary Committee expressed its satisfaction at the progress so far achieved when it presented its report to Congress in 1907, but was by no means content. It stated,

We have for the time being settled our legal position and workmen's compensation. We urge our members to take up the following social and industrial reforms:

1. Miners' legal eight-hour day, and a reduction of hours in all trades;
2. Old-age pensions.
3. Unemployed.
4. Compulsory State insurance.
5. Land nationalisation.
6. Amendment of Poor Laws.
7. Legal restriction of systematic overtime; and
8. Housing of the working classes.[1]

Here was a clear policy of social reform, round which the Labour movement could find the unity it did not yet possess. The strategy was put clearly by Alderman Ben Turner, speaking as fraternal delegate of the Labour Representation Committee, to the annual conference of the General Federation of Trade Unions, when he said,

The danger is, if we do not deceive ourselves, that the Labour Party may be split up in the fight by the question of the House of Lords with the Liberal Party, and anti-Home Rule and Protection with the Conservatives. But we must force the attention of public opinion to the issues of social reform, old age pensions, unemployment, and questions of that character. In that way we shall achieve our destiny of making human history more humane and sensible from the working-class point of view.[2]

Much was to be achieved along the lines of social reform stressed by Ben Turner, but the dangers of division in the Labour movement did not subside; they loomed far larger at the end of a remarkable quinquennium of Liberal Government than at the beginning.

There were a number of signs in 1907 that the stock of the Government had slumped with working-class electors, and that that of the Labour Party had gone up. The defeat of the Government candidate by Pete Curran, one of the leaders of the Gasworkers' Union, by a handsome majority, at the Jarrow by-election in the summer of 1907, was an indication that the rank and file workers were not satisfied with mere snippets of social reform. A few weeks later, the election of Victor Grayson, a revolutionary socialist, at Colne Valley, confirmed this trend of opinion. Another indication was the rapid expansion of membership and activities of the socialist organisations, Fabian Society, I.L.P. and S.D.F. which occurred at this time.

What seems to have happened is that the reforms of the Liberal

[1] *T.U.C. Annual Report*, 1907.   [2] *G.F.T.U. Annual Report*, 1907.

Government in its first year of office had been credited by the leaders of the rank and file—who were immensely jubilant and optimistic—to independent Labour representation and so they wanted more of it. Some of them were in no mood to tolerate the existence of those Labour leaders who refused to join the Labour Party, and they tried to prevent the Parliamentary Committee from working to promote unity among the Labour members in the House of Commons. At the 1906 Congress James Sexton had moved a resolution, which had been carried, calling upon the Parliamentary Committee to convene a conference which would bring the two groups together 'with the object of securing perfect political unity of action in the country and the House of Commons on strict independent lines'. The Parliamentary Committee, having both Labour and Lib-Lab members, was in a good position to act as an intermediary, but it was not in a position to report much success from its efforts to the 1907 Congress. Negotiations had broken down because the Lib-Lab trade unionists refused to agree to members of the Labour Party, who had been elected as socialists and not as trade unionists, taking part in the joint policy-making meeting which had been proposed by the Parliamentary Committee. A number of delegates were extremely critical of the Lib-Labs who had supported the Liberal candidate, defeated by Pete Curran for the Labour Party, at the Jarrow by-election; and the proposal was made that the Parliamentary Committee should give up its attempt to bring about a working arrangement between the two groups. This was defeated after William Brace, Enoch Edwards and William Abrahams, three of the leaders of the Miners' Federation, who were all Lib-Labs, had made conciliatory speeches in which they disowned the intervention against Pete Curran and held out the hope that a concordat would be arrived at which would settle the differences between them.

A further indication of the trend away from a close connection with the Liberals was the change in the standing orders made later in the week at the 1907 Congress. An amendment was moved by the delegate of the Amalgamated Stevedores, so as to make in future any candidate not prepared to sign the constitution of the Labour Party ineligible to hold the post of secretary. After W. C. Steadman, who had been elected to Parliament as a Lib-Lab, had assured Congress that he was now a wholehearted supporter of the Labour Party—though he was not yet a member—the amendment was carried unanimously. The president, A. H. Gill, apparently felt that Steadman's position was sufficiently ambiguous to give rise to criticism, for he intervened at this stage to emphasise to Congress that the amendment just passed did not apply to the present secretary but 'only to any future candidate'.

The main cause of the growing discontent was economic, aggravated by a sense of frustration at the failure of the Government to live up to the high level of expec ation which had been generated by the result of the election. The Government had come into office on the crest of a prosperity wave that was then beginning to recede. In 1906 the percentage of unemployed was 3·6; by 1908 it had more than doubled to reach almost 8 per cent and, moreover, the retail price level was moving up sharply. Money wages had risen rapidly in the prosperous year of 1906, but with the onset of the depression they began to fall again, so that real wages in 1908 were very much below the level they had reached when the Liberal Government took office.[1]

The most sensitive index of discontent was that of industrial unrest. Though the number of man-days lost was less than in the year before, the number of disputes recorded in 1907 was over a hundred more than in 1906, whilst in 1908 the number of man-days lost through disputes was more than five times as great as the average of the previous two years.[2] The year 1907 began with a strike of music-hall artists and employees, which had a flavour of the sensational and caught the interest of the public. It focused the attention of the working class on its basic conditions of employment, and reminded them that the Trade Disputes Act had set the trade unions free to engage in militant industrial action. The strike was settled through the intervention of the Board of Trade conciliation department, and resulted in substantial gains to the employees of the entertainment industry. Before the end of the year a much more serious strike threatened.

Trade unionism had existed on the railways since the 1870s, but the railway companies had absolutely refused to recognise any of the men's organisations, contending that to do so would be fatal to the military type of discipline that was essential to the efficient and safe conduct of this public service. That the rate of accidents on the railways was high it was impossible for anyone to deny, but that this was due in part to the fantastically long hours and wretchedly poor wages for the responsibility the work entailed, the employers refused to see.[3] Instead they imposed discipline that was stupid and brutal, and opposed any improvement in working conditions, primarily because they could not bear the thought that the 'lower orders' had any right to challenge that which the employers deemed was good for

[1] Layton and Crowther, *The Study of Prices.*

[2] Board of Trade (Labour Department), *Reports on Strikes and Lockouts 1906, 1907, 1908, 1909, 1910.*

[3] Cf. McKillop, Norman, *The Lighted Flame,* pp. 79 *et seq*; Kenney, Rowland, *Men and Rails,* p. 78.

them. Early in 1907 the railway unions published a national programme which included reductions in hours and increases in wages,
and invited the companies to enter into negotiations, but the employers remained intransigent.[1] With the assistance of two Cambridge
economists, Mr. Layton and Mr. Liddle, the Amalgamated Society
of Railway Servants published a volume containing 136 pages of
statistics on the conditions of employment on the railways. In March,
the House of Commons passed a resolution which declared that the
hours worked on the railways were excessive, and that fresh legislation ought to be introduced if the existing laws were not strong
enough to secure a reduction. The directors of the companies replied
to this campaign with a general attack on the trade union movement,
and refused to make any concessions to the railway unions. Having
exhausted every avenue of peaceable approach to the railway
companies, and having met with only the most crass obstruction, the
unions decided to ballot their members on whether to call a general
railway strike. As the ballot was in progress the Parliamentary
Committee of the T.U.C., which had met to consider the dispute on
the 16 October, issued a statement on behalf of the whole trade union
movement supporting the railwaymen and placing the blame for the
impasse on the shoulders of the railway directors. The Committee
also sent a delegation to a conference of representatives from all the
railway unions, which succeeded, at least, in securing temporary
unity between them. The result of the ballot, when announced at the
end of October, showed an overwhelming majority in favour of a
strike; almost 80,000 having voted for strike action and fewer than
9,000 against.[2] At this stage, Lloyd George, probably at the suggestion of the chairman of the Parliamentary Committee, who had
seen him privately shortly before, personally intervened and invited
both sides to meet him. Although the employers obstinately refused
to meet the representatives of the men, an agreement was reached
through the President of the Board of Trade and his conciliators to
set up a system of conciliation boards to deal with the grievances of
the workers. The unions were not recognised, but they were persuaded to accept a system whereby the men were represented on the
boards by representatives chosen from the workers in the employ of
the railway companies. A strike was averted and the prestige of
Lloyd George considerably enhanced, but the scheme proved to be
too complicated to be successful, and, as it evaded the basic issue of
recognition, proved to be only a temporary solution to the em-
bittered state of industrial relations on the railways. The pattern of

[1] Alcock, G. W., *Fifty Years of Railway Trade Unionism*; Watney, C. and
Little, J. A., *Industrial Warfare, the Aims and Claims of Capital and Labour*.
[2] Alcock, G. W., *Fifty Years of Railway Trade Unionism*, p. 378.

the machinery established had, however, a lasting influence and the present-day procedure on the railways can be traced back to the 1907 settlement.

Following his successful intervention in the railway dispute Lloyd George began to entertain the belief that he had a genius for settling industrial strife, and soon after he personally intervened in a strike of the Oldham cotton spinners, and again, a few months later, in a strike of Tyneside engineers. In each case the settlement was a compromise with a slight concession wrung from the employers, and the struggle temporarily died down.

John Burns fails to satisfy the T.U.C.

With the return of the Liberal Government in 1906 the Parliamentary Committee had abandoned its previous uncompromising opposition to the Unemployed Workmen's Act passed by the Conservatives, and made attempts to secure an improvement in its operation. This change of attitude was in part due to the low level of unemployment that year. John Burns had drifted away from the increasingly collectivist trends in the Labour movement to hold views hardly dissimilar from those of the orthodox Liberal, but his appointment as a Cabinet Minister, and President of the Local Government Board, roused hopes of a more sympathetic and vigorous treatment of the unemployed problem, of which he had peculiar knowledge, and for which, now, special responsibility. Under pressure from the Parliamentary Committee, and the Labour members, especially Keir Hardie, the Government decided to make an Exchequer grant of £200,000 towards the relief of unemployment. With the Trade Disputes Bill not yet passed, the Parliamentary Committee was not disposed to be too critical of the Government, and stated in its report to the 1906 Congress, 'We frankly admit that this sum is totally inadequate from the point of view of the magnitude of the problem, but we must not forget that this is the first time a Government has realised its responsibilities towards solving the unemployed problem by a grant from national funds.'[1]

The attitude of John Burns towards the problem of unemployment was hardly what the trade unions might have expected. In many ways he soon proved to be a less sympathetic and competent minister than some of his Tory predecessors. His permanent officials had played on his vanity and he adopted the posture of a strong man standing firm against the sentimental pleading of his erstwhile comrades.[2] Speaking

[1] *Report of the Parliamentary Committee*, 1906.
[2] Mrs. Webb, who previously had held a higher opinion of John Burns than of any of the other working-class leaders, wrote in her diary on the 30 October

in reply to an Amendment to the Address, on the 20 February 1907, which was moved by Will Thorne, regretting that no mention had been made in the King's Speech of measures to deal with the menace of unemployment, Burns lectured the working class on its feckless expenditure on drink, and suggested if the money so spent was used on buying better homes the problem would solve itself. No wonder Walter Long, himself an ex-President of the Local Government Board, could ask what would have happened to him had he enunciated such doctrines.

Burns's refusal to take any serious steps to tackle the unemployment problem led the Joint Board to draft its own Unemployed Workmen Bill. This followed fairly closely the recommendations made to the Conservative Government in the special report drawn up by the Parliamentary Committee and the G.F.T.U. in 1905.[1] The Bill secured a second reading early in 1908, and was supported by a number of Liberals as well as by the members of the Labour Party.[2] The main proposal of the Bill was the settlement of the unemployed on the land in farm colonies, and this came in for severe criticism from Maddison and Vivian, two of the Lib-Lab members of Parliament, as well as from John Burns in his reply for the Government. Burns said the measures advocated by the Labour Party were already being carried out at the Hollesley Bay Colony and elsewhere. The Government had made an annual net loss of £20,000 and the Bill would involve local authorities with a similar responsibility. He argued that the Government was doing everything possible, and urged the rejection of the Bill, and the House accepted this advice; 116 votes were cast in favour and 265 against.[3] Burns was undoubtedly right in opposing farm colonies as a panacea for unemployment. Those that existed were a failure, and this was not surprising, considering that most of the men who found themselves in the colonies had not been used to heavy labouring, and were in a

1907, 'John Burns has become a monstrosity. He is, of course, a respectable hard-working man, who wants, when he is not blinded by vanity and malice against those who have abused him, to see straight. But this faculty of seeing facts as they are is being over-grown by a sort of fatty complacency with the world as it is: an enormous personal vanity, feeding on the deference and flattery yielded to patronage and power. He talks incessantly, and never listens to anyone except the officials to whom he *must* listen, in order to accomplish the routine work of his office. Hence, he is completely in their hands, and is becoming the most hidebound of departmental chiefs, gulled by an obstructive fact or reactionary argument, taken in by the most naïve commonplaces of middle-class administrative routine.' Webb, B., *Our Partnership*, p. 393.

[1] See Chapter V, p. 185.

[2] A special joint conference was held immediately prior to the Annual Labour Party Conference on 17 January 1908, to win support for the Bill.

[3] *House of Commons Reports*, vol. CLXXXVI, 13 March 1908.

deplorable physical and psychological condition. Nor was the trade union movement entirely opposed to the views held by Burns. At the 1908 Trades Union Congress a resolution was moved repudiating the opinions of Burns, Maddison and Vivian, but this was carried only by the narrow majority of 25,000—826,000 voting for the resolution and 801,000 against.[1] Not all those who voted against the resolution concurred with all Burns's statements, but many of the delegates were still anti-Labour Party, and resented criticism of the Lib-Labs. Where Burns showed himself to be in complete opposition to the Labour Party, and to the bulk of trade unionists, was in the belief which he now held that unemployment was largely a moral and not an economic problem, and in a Benthamite attitude towards its cure. When Beatrice Webb was explaining her Minority Poor Law Report to him, he stated, 'I should prefer to make the police the authority for vagrants and able-bodied men. . . .'[2] This was the authentic voice of the old Poor Law, and reminiscent of its most harsh and oppressive administrators, whom the trade unions had fought throughout the nineteenth century.

As a cure for unemployment the trade unions continued to press for a reduction in the hours of work. Realising that a general eight-hours provision was unlikely to be enacted, the Trades Union Congress supported the efforts of individual unions to bring about shorter hours in particular industries, and it instructed the Parliamentary Committee to press for legislation to reduce the hours of shop assistants, bakehouse workers, textile workers and miners. Most of these measures had become hardy annuals, and rarely got further than an airing in the House of Commons if some Labour sympathiser was lucky enough to win a place in the ballot for time to move the Bill. With the advent of the Liberal Government and the increase in the number of Labour supporters in the House hopes of greater success were raised.

Miners Win Eight-Hour Day

For years the Trades Union Congress had supported the demand of the Miners' Federation for a Mines Regulation Act which would limit work below ground to a maximum of eight hours per day. The Northumberland and Durham miners had steadfastly opposed the imposition of a legal limitation of work to eight hours out of fear that, with their system of working, which was different from that of the other coalfields, this would result for them in an increase rather than a decrease in the number of hours worked by adult miners. This division in the ranks of the miners had been one of the main

[1] *T.U.C. Annual Report*, 1908.   [2] Webb, B., *Our Partnership*, p. 411.

weaknesses in the trade union campaign to obtain an Eight Hours Act for the mines, but the legal attack on the trade unions and the rising cost of living, coupled with reductions in wages, gradually changed opinion in the north-eastern coalfields in favour of the Federation's policy.[1]

The Liberal Government was in a quandary. It was reluctant to concede the case of the trade unions, for fear that this would lead to more radical demands, but it was equally afraid of the consequences of doing nothing, which might lead to a coal strike and drive the Lib-Lab miners' representatives into the Labour Party. When the Miners' Eight Hours Bill came up for a second reading in May 1906, the Home Secretary announced that the Government would set up a Royal Commission to examine working conditions in the mines and a departmental committee to inquire into the economic effect of an eight-hour day. After a delay of over a year, during which time the committee discovered nothing fresh about the problem, and criticism of the Government grew, a Bill was introduced by the Home Secretary on the 1 August 1907; but the Government was in no hurry to push the measure through and the debates dragged on until the autumn of 1908, when the Bill was finally carried. The Eight Hours Act did not give the miners all they desired, though it was felt in trade union circles that an important principle had been established. Nor did it save the miners for the Liberal Party, for the pressure which had been required to get the Bill through, and the removal of the bone of contention between the two sections of the miners by the passing of the Act, brought about greater unity between them and the Labour Party, which they formally joined in 1909.

As far as the other Bills to reduce the hours of work were concerned, the Liberal Government showed itself to be little more interested than its Conservative predecessor. Nor, for that matter, were the trade unions always agreed on the measure to be promoted. In the case of the abolition of half-time employment of school children, this proposal, which was carried annually by Congress and sponsored as a Bill by the Parliamentary Committee, was strongly opposed by the representatives of the cotton trade unions, who argued in more or less the same terms as Nassau Senior had used in the early nineteenth century in defence of child labour, that the half-time employment of school children was an economic necessity for the industry.

Sectional advantage secured through the legislature was not confined to demands for shorter hours in particular industries; the Engines and Boilers (persons in charge) Bill which legitimately sought to protect the workers from accidents resulting from having

[1] See Webb, S. and B., *The History of Trade Unionism*. Webb, S., *Story of the Durham Miners*.

unqualified persons in charge of steam boilers, was also designed to protect the interest of the boilermen by making it a tightly controlled profession. The licensing of carmen, the employment of two drivers on an electric train, the prevention of competition from army and navy bands, were motivated primarily with the idea of creating greater security of employment.

The Parliamentary Committee launches Pensions Campaign

Soon after the Liberal Government took office the Parliamentary Committee sent a deputation to interview the Prime Minister and the Chancellor of the Exchequer on the question of old age pensions. Whilst not committing themselves they gave the deputation to understand that this was one of the reforms the Government desired to introduce, but nothing further was heard about it for a whole year. Meanwhile, in January 1907, the Parliamentary Committee decided to start a campaign, in the country and in the lobbies of the House, for old age pensions. Since no mention of old age pensions was made in the King's Speech at the commencement of the new session, George Barnes moved an amendment regretting this omission. The Chancellor of the Exchequer, replying for the Government, promised to make a statement on the Government's intentions at the time of the Budget; again the Government tried to delay, promising to introduce a measure 'if we are allowed to have our way'—a rather ironical remark considering the size of its majority—before the end of the next session. The Labour members and the trade unions were extremely dissatisfied with the Budget, and with the failure of the Government to revise drastically, in a progressive direction, the nation's fiscal policy, so as to permit the payment of old age pensions. In July 1907, a Blue Book was published on old age pensions; but this 'was mainly a re-publication of schemes unsatisfactory to the Trade Unionists of this country' stated the Parliamentary Committee.[1] At the Trades Union Congress of 1907 a resolution was carried deploring the Government's procrastination, and demanding a budget in the following year that would permit the State to commence payment of pensions of not less than five shillings per week to all persons of sixty years and upwards. Immediately Congress was over the Parliamentary Committee initiated a nation-wide agitation, holding big meetings in all the main industrial centres, which impressed the Government and convinced it that further delay was not possible. The long-promised scheme was presented to the House of Commons in the summer of 1908, by Lloyd George, who had been made Chancellor of the Exchequer in Asquith's Government,

[1] *T.U.C. Annual Report*, 1907.

formed after the death of Campbell-Bannerman earlier that year. The measure should have been presented by John Burns, but the President of the Local Government Board had so damned a private member's Bill to establish old age pensions, which had been before the House in the summer of 1907, that it can hardly have been a surprise to him when Lloyd George was given the task of piloting the Bill through; Burns cannot have been pleased at being supplanted by the Chancellor, for whom, with Churchill, he had a great distrust.[1]

With the aid of the closure the Bill was rapidly pushed through Parliament so as to come into force on the 1 January 1909. It failed to come up to the expectations of the trade unions, since it contained more niggardly restrictions than the New Zealand model on which it was based, but the T.U.C. recognised, as in the case of the Mines Eight Hours Act, that an important new principle of social welfare had been conceded, which could be built upon in the future.[2]

The Establishment of Trade Boards

With the passing of the Old Age Pensions and Miners' Eight Hours legislation, two measures long advocated by the T.U.C., and both of immense social significance, had been achieved, but socially significant principles cut little ice with the mass of rank and file workers, who were barely touched by these reforms. Unemployment, 'sweating' and falling real wages were the social facts of life that were understood by the great majority. The knowledge that even in good times many thousands of workers were living in acute poverty led to a growing support for the idea of a legal minimum wage. In 1906 the Trades Union Congress had passed a resolution, without much consideration, in support of a minimum wage of 30s. for Government workers in London; though it had led to a certain amount of sectional dispute and sharp debate, this demand was extended some years later to include every worker. Meanwhile the 1907 Congress instructed the Parliamentary Committee to support the Sweated Industries Bill, which had been moved that year by Arthur Henderson. The principal features of this Bill were that (1) wages boards should be established in districts on the application of trades councils, or six employers or employees, and after an inquiry by the Home Secretary; (2) the boards to consist of half employers and half employees, with the chairman chosen either by the board or nominated by the Home Secretary; (3) the board to fix a minimum wage; (4) any person paying or offering less than the minimum to be liable

[1] Cf. Halévy, *History of the English People, 1905–1915*, vol. II, p. 275; Kent, William, *John Burns—Labour's Lost Leader*, pp. 184, 200.
[2] *Report of the Parliamentary Committee*, 1908.

to a fine on conviction. When this Bill was reintroduced in 1908 it was passed by the House of Commons, and then remitted to a select committee on home work set up by the Government. During the second reading debate, the Home Secretary, Herbert Gladstone, stated that the Government would consider the report of the committee but could not promise any new legislation, and in any case it could not accept the principle of a legal minimum wage; but the Government soon found it expedient to withdraw from the position to which it had been committed.

The Sweated Industries Bill, sponsored by the Labour Party and supported by the Trades Union Congress, followed fairly closely the lines of a Bill which Sir Charles Dilke had introduced in Parliament annually, since 1900, to secure the establishment of wages boards with power to put wages on a fixed legal basis. The source of inspiration for Dilke, and for the Labour movement, was Australia, where the labour legislation then in force was much admired by many social reformers and leaders of the trade unions. The support of the T.U.C. for the wages boards was important because there was a division of opinion in the Labour Party as to the best method of eliminating sweating. Ramsay MacDonald and his wife, who played a leading role in the Women's Industrial Council, were in favour of licensing the individual workers who wished to do work at home—a system then in force in parts of the United States—and were not enamoured of the Australian system. Mrs. MacDonald gave evidence before the select committee in support of the licensing system, but after considering the evidence the committee reported in favour of setting up wages boards, which should be empowered to fix minimum time and piece rates.[1]

The Parliamentary Committee played little part in persuading the Government to change its mind and put the Trade Boards Act on the Statute Book, as the Government did after the select committee had reported. The main pressure came from Mary Macarthur,[2] Susan Lawrence, Gertrude Tuckwell and the Women's Trade Union

[1] *Report of the Select Committee on Home Work.*

[2] Mary Macarthur was born in Glasgow in 1880, the daughter of the owner of a large draper's shop. Her father was a Conservative and a leading figure in the Primrose League. After finishing her education in Germany Mary Macarthur entered her father's business as his book-keeper. In February 1901 she attended a meeting of shop assistants which had been called by the organiser of the Shop Assistants' Union with the object of persuading them to form a branch of the union. Miss Macarthur had been asked to go to the meeting by a local Conservative newspaper and to write an article poking fun at it. Instead she came away converted to trade unionism, and soon afterwards became chairman of the Ayr branch of the Shop Assistants' Union.

In 1902 she was elected president of the Scottish National District Council of the union, and in 1903 she came to London and was appointed secretary of the

League, with the support of Sir Charles and Lady Dilke. The Government's Bill was introduced by Winston Churchill, who had been made President of the Board of Trade in Asquith's first Cabinet; it was similar to the one which had been supported by the Labour members, and followed closely the recommendations of the select committee. The Parliamentary Committee, in its report to Congress in 1909, merely reported that the Trade Boards Bill had been presented, and that it provided for the establishment of trade boards in the ready-made tailoring, cardboard box-making, machine-made lace and net finishing, and ready-made blouse industries. The boards would be empowered to fix and enforce a minimum wage, to act as centres of information and organisation, to nourish the interest of the workers, and foster a healthy state of industry in the trades in which the boards operated. Nor did the delegates to Congress betray any great interest in the new measure, although they did pass a resolution, moved by Mary Macarthur, regretting the restriction of the Bill to only four industries. The reason for the lukewarm attitude of the Parliamentary Committee and the Trades Union Congress was that they were more concerned about unemployment and sickness insurance, and the Labour Exchanges Bill. The Trade Boards Bill did not affect the great majority of trade unions; it was a measure mainly of value to the women trade unionists who certainly ought to have this protection, the men felt, but the men themselves at this time were more interested in other matters.

Labour Exchanges

Shortly after the 1908 Trades Union Congress had concluded, the Parliamentary Committee learnt that the Government was considering

Women's Trade Union League. In 1906 she founded the National Federation of Women Workers on the lines of a general Labour union and ran it side by side with the W.T.U.L. A year later she launched a penny weekly paper for women trade unionists, the *Woman Worker* which reached a circulation of 20,000 per week. During the next few years Mary Macarthur played a great part in the fight to obtain protection and better conditions for female labour, which was often intolerably exploited. In 1909 she was chosen as one of the Labour delegates to the first I.L.O. Conference held in Washington, where she played a notable part in persuading the Conference to adopt a Maternity and Childbirth Convention for the protection of mothers throughout the world. She returned from America a sick person, but found the energy to negotiate the amalgamation of the National Federation of Women Workers with the National Union of General and Municipal Workers, and to make preparations for the Women's Trade Union League to become the women's section of the newly-founded General Council of the Trades Union Congress. On the 1 January 1921, this remarkable woman, who had left a secure and easy-going middle-class home for the hurly-burly life of a trade union organiser died, worn out, barely two years after the death of her husband, W. C. Anderson, one of the leaders of the I.L.P.

the introduction of legislation to establish a national system of labour exchanges and unemployment and sickness insurance, which would probably be modelled on the scheme in operation in Germany. The Committee at once decided to send a delegation to Germany to investigate the way in which these schemes worked there, and to find out how they were viewed by the German trade unions. When the delegation returned, it reported to a national delegate conference of trade union representatives, called by the Parliamentary Committee, that it had been favourably impressed by what it had seen and heard from the trade unions in Germany. The conference approved the establishment of labour exchanges 'provided the management boards contain an equal proportion of employers and representatives from Trade Unions'.[1] It was, however, less enthusiastic about the introduction of compulsory unemployment and sickness insurance. Soon after this conference, Winston Churchill introduced a Bill in the House of Commons to establish labour exchanges. The Parliamentary Committee welcomed the Bill, but was extremely worried about the way in which the exchanges might be conducted, fearing they might be used to supply blacklegs in times of disputes, or to send workers to jobs where the wages and working conditions were below those recognised by the trade unions. Churchill ensured a smooth passage for the Bill, so far as the Parliamentary Committee was concerned, by taking the Committee into his confidence and consulting with it during the time the Bill was before the Houses of Parliament. He also introduced a new stage in the relationship between the trade union movement and members of the Government, when he asked the Parliamentary Committee to establish a sub-committee which could be consulted by him whenever he needed advice on matters arising out of the administration of the Act, affecting trade unionists.

William Beveridge, then a young economist who had just published a book on the cure of unemployment by means of a system of labour exchanges,[2] was appointed by Churchill to organise the whole scheme. What pleased the trade union movement most of all was the appointment, by the President of the Board of Trade, of a committee consisting of an employer, a representative of the trade unions and a civil service commissioner, to make the appointments of all but the most important officials who would be employed in running the new labour exchanges. The trade unionist chosen to fill this post, which was an honorary and temporary one, was D. J. Shackleton, the president of the Trades Union Congress for that year. His

[1] *Report of Special Conference*, 19 March 1909. *The Quarterly Report*, June 1909.
[2] Beveridge, W. H., *Unemployment: A Problem of Industry*, 1909.

selection was due not only to his personal capacities, but also to the position he held in the trade union movement, for it was meant to be a public recognition of the important regard which the minister had for the co-operation of the T.U.C. in the successful working of the Act.[1]

Great hopes were placed in the labour exchanges by the Liberal progressives. It was assumed by them that the main cause of unemployment was imperfection in the labour market, and they thought that it was sound Liberal doctrine for the State to be given power to intervene to clear away the obstacles that were blocking the channels of supply and demand. The trade unions agreed with the Liberals in this view, but went some way further. The T.U.C. had been demanding the establishment of a system of labour exchanges for several years, but it did not believe that this alone was the solution to the problem of unemployment. In the evidence submitted by the Parliamentary Committee to the Royal Commission on the Poor Law, emphasis was placed on over-production as the main cause of unemployment, and it was suggested that workers ought to be encouraged to belong to unions, rather than deterred from joining, 'as a means of increasing their wages and thereby increasing their effective demand for commodities'.[2] Members of the Parliamentary Committee of the T.U.C. were not professional economists, and their analysis was based on common sense unsupported by an elegant theoretical argument, but it was nearer the truth of the matter than its critics at the time, and for many years after, realised.[3]

The Attitude of the T.U.C. to the Report of the Royal Commission on the Poor Law

The Royal Commission on the Poor Law had been appointed by Balfour on the day of his resignation in 1905, and had ever since been gathering and sifting evidence. When the Liberal Government rejected the Labour movement's Unemployed Workmen Bill, it asked the Labour members to wait until the Royal Commission had published its report, promising that some action would then be taken. The Commission reported early in 1909, but its conclusions were not unanimous. The report signed by the majority of the Commission's members recommended little beyond the transference of the duties

[1] Up to 31 August 1910, 700 persons had been appointed. Out of 190 division officers, managers and assistant managers, 56 were trade union officials. Out of 272 correspondence and registration clerks 12 were trade union officials, 95 were clerical workers and 56 other workers. Letter from G. R. Askwith of Labour Department, Board of Trade to C. W. Bowerman—quoted in the *Report of the Parliamentary Committee*, 1910.

[2] T.U.C. evidence to the Royal Commission on the Poor Law.

[3] Cf. Keynes, J. M., *General Theory of Employment, Interest and Money*, p. 14.

carried out by the boards of guardians to committees elected by county councils. The Minority Report, of which the main authors were the Webbs, went much further, and gathered together most of the ideas which had been advocated by the Labour movement, in the Trades Union Congress, Fabian Society and the Labour Party, for a good many years, to make a powerful case against the existing system of alleviating social misery mainly through private charity, with public relief administered in such a way as to deter all but the most desperate cases from seeking aid.

The Parliamentary Committee told Congress that its representative on the Poor Law Commission, F. W. Chandler,[1] could not concur with the Majority Report. The Committee summarised the Minority Report as follows: 'The Minority Report demands not only the abolition of the workhouses and the Boards of Guardians, but also the sweeping away, once and for all, of the whole notion of the Poor Law relief and the stigma of pauperism. It is proposed that the care of the several sections of the non-able-bodied poor should simply be merged in the municipal services already dealing with children, the sick, and pensions for the aged, under the control of the directly elected Town or County Councils. With regard to the unemployed, the Minority Report lay stress on the complete failure of local authorities to grapple with the evil; and it argues that, whether with regard to vagrancy or to the stagnant pools of unemployed men in particular centres, local authorities can never succeed in really solving the problem. The Minority Report demands, accordingly, the appointment of a Minister for Labour who should be charged to deal systematically with the whole question in all its ramifications. The Minority Report recommends a national system of Labour Exchanges as the beginning of all reform; but it does not support a Government insurance scheme for out-of-work pay, recommending as an alternative an annual grant from Parliament to enable Trade Unions to extend their out-of-work benefits in their own way. For the minimising of unemployment, the report suggests a whole series of measures, such as the regularisation of the national demand for labour by concentration of Government work in lean years, the drastic curtailment of boy labour, a reduction of hours, the development of afforestation and land reclamation, etc. All these things will, however, be of little avail to the man who is actually unemployed, and for him and his family if work cannot be found; and if he is not provided for by insurance the Minority Report demands full and honourable maintenance with whatever physical or technical training he may be found to be capable of.'[2]

[1] General secretary, Amalgamated Society of Carpenters and Joiners.
[2] *Report of the Parliamentary Committee*, 1909.

The Parliamentary Committee cautiously concluded this summary with the statement that, 'Whatever may be thought of some of these proposals, the Minority Report as a whole, elaborately worked out as it is into practical schemes, with all necessary details, has been acclaimed as a most important contribution to the problem.'[1]

Congress that year paid no attention to the Minority Report as such; many of the recommendations in it were settled T.U.C. policy, and came up for discussion as resolutions, but no attempt was made to commit Congress to the support of the Minority Report. Nor did the Parliamentary Committee take any part in the campaign which the Webbs launched to secure support for the Minority Report, though its chairman, D. J. Shackleton, associated himself with it.[2]

Relations between the Parliamentary Committee and the Government were closer in 1909 than they had been at any time since the passing of the Trade Disputes Act. This was mainly the doing of Winston Churchill and Lloyd George, who were vying with one another to capture popular support. The Committee and Congress were enthusiastic over Lloyd George's radical Budget of 1909; Shackleton, in his presidential address, described it as 'the greatest financial reform of modern times'. After eulogising on its proposals and speculating on the avenues of reform which the budget opened up, Shackleton concluded 'We hail with pleasure the Chancellor of the Exchequer's efforts to place the burden of the national expenditure on the shoulders of those who derive most benefit from it.'[3]

Unemployment remained at a high level in 1909 and unrest and agitation against the failure of the Government to remedy the situation continued in the industrial areas.[4] The leaders of the trade unions and the Labour Party were fiercely denounced by those socialists, including Grayson and Blatchford, who felt that their attitude was too subservient towards the Liberal Government. As a result of the clamour, Asquith had agreed that the Government's grant to the central unemployed fund should be doubled and had promised further legislation. However, the Labour Party's Unemployed Workmen Bill, retitled 'Right to Work Bill', was rejected by a large majority when introduced in 1909. John Burns, hostile to the

[1] Ibid.

[2] The Parliamentary Committee had already decided to suggest the policy of national unemployment insurance on a tripartite basis, employer, worker and State, which the Minority Report rejected as detrimental to the trade union movement.

[3] T.U.C. Annual Report, 1909.

[4] In 1908 the cause of the vast majority of strikes and lockouts was attributed to wage disputes; in 1909 wages directly only accounted for a small proportion of the stoppages, demands for changes in hours of work were the principal cause of strikes and lockouts.

Minority Report of the Poor Law Commission, alternately indulged in verbose and flamboyant speeches, or sulked in rancorous silence at the spectacle of Churchill and Lloyd George stealing his limelight, but he did nothing for the unemployed. The Government's promised legislation, the Labour Exchange Bill, welcomed by the Parliamentary Committee, gave little satisfaction to the unemployed rank and file, and in the summer of 1909, under pressure from some of its constituent unions, the Parliamentary Committee wrote to Asquith suggesting that the Prime Minister should take immediate steps to promote 'large and comprehensive schemes of work of public utility' so as to provide large numbers of people with employment, and thereby minimise the distress as far as possible.[1] At the same time the Committee sent a copy of this mild appeal to every affiliated union and suggested that each should write to the Prime Minister in support of this request. The Prime Minister's reply was a model of complacency, saying no more than all that could be done was to hope that trade would soon improve. The reluctance of the Parliamentary Committee, and, for that matter, most of the delegates to Congress, to criticise the Government, stands out clearly at this time, for no comment on the reply was made by the Committee, and it was ignored by the delegates when they met a month later.

Trade did begin to improve in 1909, as Asquith had hoped it would, and in 1910, unemployment was only half as great as in the year before. The discontent which had manifested itself during 1908 and 1909 did not subside, however; in fact the return of prosperity acted as a stimulus to the lower-paid workers to seek better economic conditions through direct industrial action. No one took much heed of the warning that had been given during the years of industrial slump; both trade union leaders and politicians believed that dissatisfaction would evaporate as trade improved, but many of the workers were growing restive at the failure of the political parties to resolve their quarrels and check the steep rise in the cost of living. The eyes of the nation were riveted on the spectacular political struggle between Lloyd George and the House of Lords, which had thrown out his Budget, and the politicians had little time to concentrate on the grievances of the working class. The Labour Party was anxiously calculating its political prospects, and had lost the initiative on social reform to Lloyd George, for, without the support of the Liberals, the Labour Party could achieve little; on the other hand it could not enjoy the fruits of opposition to the Government, since, without a victory for the Liberals over the Peers, there was little hope of any great advance in social reform in the immediate future. The leaders of the trade union movement felt the weight of their growing

[1] *Report of the Parliamentary Committee*, 1909.

importance and responsibility, and were more or less satisfied with the steady stream of social improvements. The Parliamentary Committee could legitimately point with pride and triumph to the Statute Book, but the members of the unions averted their eyes and demanded better wages, lower prices, shorter hours and more secure jobs. These were the very things which the enlightened social legislation of the incipient Welfare State could not provide; and the gap between the leaders, who made statesmanlike speeches, and the rank and file members, who wanted tangible results, grew wider.

The overwhelmingly Tory House of Lords, fearful of the threat to privilege contained in the Budget of 1909, and goaded into fury by the brilliantly malicious attacks made on it by Lloyd George, tossed out the Budget in November of that year, thus making an election early in the New Year inevitable. On the 6 December the Parliamentary Committee of the T.U.C. issued an election manifesto which praised the merits of the Budget, and called for the abolition of the House of Lords. It also demanded further social legislation on the lines urged by resolutions passed at the Trades Union Congress during the past few years. In addition it stressed the need for radical electoral reform, including the payment of members by the State.[1]

The Osborne Judgment

The Labour movement, in the midst of the election campaign, found itself faced with a situation against which it had believed it was safeguarded by the law. On the 21 December 1909, the Law Lords delivered their judgment upholding a decision of the Court of Appeal which would, in future, prevent the trade unions from spending their funds on political activities, as they had been doing for the past fifty years or more. Thus the lifeblood of the Labour Party, its funds, provided by trade unions, was cut off at a period of crucial political importance.

In 1908 the secretary of the Walthamstow Branch of the Amalgamated Society of Railway Servants, W. V. Osborne, had brought an action to test his contention that the executive committee of the A.S.R.S. had no power to compel members to subscribe for parliamentary representation, and that not only was the rule permitting this *ultra vires*, but it had, in any case, been adopted unconstitutionally. In 1902, the A.S.R.S. had, at its annual general meeting, adopted a rule empowering the executive committee to levy members one shilling per year to cover the cost of parliamentary representation. An amendment moved in 1904 to make it compulsory that

[1] *Commons v. Lords: Which Shall Prevail?* Manifesto issued by the Parliamentary Committee, December 1909.

candidates should sign the constitution of the Labour Party as a condition of their support by the Society, was defeated, but there was a good deal of controversy about both this proposal and the whole question of parliamentary representation. In order to be certain that the rule was legally valid the executive of the A.S.R.S. had consulted Sir Robert Reid, K.C. (Lord Chancellor at the time of the Osborne Judgment) and Sir Edward Clarke, K.C., both of whom gave it as their opinion that the Society could support parliamentary representatives and levy members for this purpose. However, they told the Society that the rule had not been properly framed, according to the constitution of the union, and was, therefore invalid. It was then decided to put the rule before the 1905 annual general meeting in order to have it correctly adopted; this was done and the rule was incorporated in the constitution of the union. An amendment insisting on parliamentary candidates pledging themselves to the constitution of the Labour Party and accepting its whip was defeated, but the subject came up again in 1906 when it was carried and became part of the rule.

Osborne's action was heard in July 1908, before Mr. Justice Neville, who delivered judgment in favour of the Society with costs against the plaintiff. This decision was in line with the views which had been expressed by the two eminent counsel to the union; it was also in accord with the decision in the case brought by a miner named Steele, with the support of the Conservatives, against his union making a political levy. As the rules of the South Wales Miners' Federation provided for such a levy this action had been dismissed. Osborne, no doubt, on good advice, and with financial support obtained from somewhere,[1] appealed against the decision, and with success, for the Court of Appeal reversed the judgment of Mr. Justice Neville. The rule was declared invalid and an injunction was granted restraining the Society from levying its members for the purposes mentioned in the rule; in addition the Society was ordered to pay the costs of the action and of the appeal. The Society thereupon lodged an appeal with the House of Lords, which heard the case in July and gave its decision in December 1909. The essence of the Lords judgment, which upheld the Court of Appeal, was that trade unions were bodies created by legislation and that, as such, they could only act in accordance with the provisions Parliament had specifically laid down to govern the activities of trade unions. The Lords found these provisions in the Statute of 1876, which did not mention political activities or the use of trade union funds to sub-

---

[1] Cf. Webb, S. and B., *The History of Trade Unionism*, p. 608; Alcock, G. W., *Fifty Years of Railway Trade Unionism*; Osborne, W., *My Case: The Cause and Effects of the Osborne Judgment*.

sidise political candidates; therefore, as their Lordships did not find political activities a necessary part of the activities sanctioned by the statute, they deemed they could not lawfully be carried out by a trade union.

The potential consequences of the Osborne Judgment were extremely far-reaching, for it appeared to confine the activities of trade unions to the functions mentioned in the Act of 1876. The fact that Parliament had no intention of limiting the activities of trade unions to that which had been included in the defining clause of the statute at the time that it was passed, did not weigh with the Law Lords because of the general principle followed by the English courts that the wording of a statute must be rigidly interpreted. This does not, of course, prevent the courts from making interpretations that in fact constitute new law, often different from that which Parliament intended to introduce. In view of the long history of political activities engaged in by trade unions, and the close relations which had developed between the Parliamentary Committee of the T.U.C. and members of the House of Commons, it is difficult to exonerate the Judges concerned from the charge that they allowed themselves to be unduly influenced by political prejudice and by dislike for the privileged position enjoyed by the trade unions under the 1906 Trade Disputes Act. Whatever the influences that had guided the logic of the Judicial Bench, political activities had been made illegal, and inferentially so, perhaps, were affiliations to trades councils, and to the T.U.C.

Although the Osborne Case had been before the courts for well over a year, the decision of the House of Lords took the trade unions by surprise. It was only after a number of injunctions had been granted restraining them from using their funds for political purposes that the seriousness of the situation dawned upon the unions. There was a section of the membership which greeted the Osborne decision with satisfaction because it wanted the trade unions to cease supporting the Labour Party, but the majority of union leaders, whatever their political opinions were, considered that the courts had gone too far. It was not until August 1910 that the three organisations clearly stated their attitude towards the decision; on the 22nd of that month the Joint Board passed three resolutions calling for new legislation and urged affiliated organisations to co-operate actively in a campaign in support of this aim. At the Trades Union Congress, held in September, a lengthy debate on the Osborne decision took place. Powerful speeches were made by William Brace, one of the leaders of the Miners' Federation, who was by no means a socialist, by J. R. Clynes, and by many others, warning the Government that the trade unions would not rest until their right to spend their funds as they pleased had been restored. Two speeches were made in favour of the Osborne decision; one by a delegate from the Operative Bricklayers, and the other by a delegate from the A.S.R.S. who was a friend of Osborne. Both speeches were confused and woolly pleas that the trade unions should have nothing to do with politics. D. J. Shackleton, replying to the debate on behalf of the Parliamentary Committee, blamed the lack of unity on the question as the factor responsible for the failure of the Government to introduce amending legislation. Referring to some of the speeches that had been made by prominent trade unionists, he stated that to have their attention drawn to them when interviewing the Prime Minister was rather embarrassing to him and his colleagues.[1]

Criticism of the Parliamentary Committee and of the Labour members of Parliament, which was voiced in a constant stream of interruptions, came not only from those who supported the Osborne decision, but also from those who were opposed, on syndicalist grounds, to the trade unions having anything to do with Parliament. The Labour Party was under fire for being too subservient to the Liberals, and there was some impatience with the explanation that Arthur Henderson, speaking as fraternal delegate from the Labour Party, gave of its difficulties.

The first election of 1910 had resulted in the wiping out of the huge Liberal majority; it was replaced by a dependency on the votes of the Irish Nationalists and the Labour Party. The number of Labour members had been reduced; but for the first time there was a united Labour Party in the House. Lib-Labism had come to an end, for Burt, Wilson and Fenwick were no longer identified with the official trade union movement, although they were still associated with the Northumberland and Durham Miners' Union.

The irony of the situation was that the election had left the Labour Party in the House in a most difficult position; it was almost as much tied to the Liberals as in 1906. The leaders of the Labour Party and the Parliamentary Committee realised that the only course they could pursue was to persuade the Government to put through legislation to remedy the Osborne Judgment. They had no desire to see in power a Tory administration from which they could expect even less sympathy, and they also had good hopes that the Government would introduce legislation when the House of Lords issue was settled.[2] The resolution supported by the Parliamentary Committee at the 1910 T.U.C., calling for legislation to reverse the Osborne decision, was carried by the large majority of 1,717,000 to 13,000, but the rank and file, disappointed at the results achieved by the Parliamentary

[1] *T.U.C. Annual Report*, 1910.
[2] Cf. Speech of D. J. Shackleton, T.U.C., 1910.

Labour Party, soon showed that it was ready to accept a less sophisticated answer to its needs. The moment was propitious for the advocates of a more primitive approach to politics, and for the next few years the sane and rational progress of social reform was interrupted by tumultuous industrial strife until in turn this upsurge of frustrated human sentiment was sublimated by the demands of an even mightier conflict.

The Parliamentary Committee and Inter-Union Disputes

The membership of unions affiliated to the Trades Union Congress declined by over 70,000 between 1908 and 1909. This drop in numbers was mainly accounted for by unemployment, which caused out-of-work members to allow their union subscriptions to lapse. Affiliated membership of the T.U.C. had risen substantially since 1905 in spite of this, and in spite of the fickleness of the Amalgamated Society of Engineers, which had disaffiliated in 1899, rejoined in 1905, and then, dissatisfied with the policy of the Parliamentary Committee, had again decided to withdraw in 1907. In 1905, 218 unions with a total membership of 1,501,000 were affiliated to the T.U.C.; in 1909 the figures were 219 unions with a membership of 1,750,000.

In 1906 the size of the Parliamentary Committee was increased from thirteen to sixteen members, and it was agreed to base the election of its members on trade groups in future. Congress was to be divided into twelve industrial sections, from each of which, except the twelfth group, Congress was to elect one representative to the Parliamentary Committee. From the 'Miscellaneous Trades' section five members were to be elected, each from a different trade within that group. 'Canvassing and bartering of votes for any position or purpose shall be strictly forbidden' [1] the amending standing order stated; and it also introduced a three years' disqualification for the individual and society proved to have contravened this injunction. Ever since the change-over in 1895 to the use of the 'block' vote, complaints had been made of the bartering and selling of votes, but threats and admonitions had achieved little and the practice continued as strong as ever. Everyone agreed that it was a bad practice and ought to be stopped, but no one had been willing voluntarily to discard the influence which a number of votes could wield in the jockeying for power which went on behind the scenes of every Congress.

The adoption of the penalty clause had given satisfaction to the smaller unions, but it proved to be little more than window-dressing, and the practice of vote 'swapping' went on as before.

[1] *T.U.C. Standing Orders*, 1906.

Having agreed to increase the size of the Parliamentary Committee, Congress went on to amend the standing orders to allow the Committee, as formerly, to place three resolutions on the agenda; but an attempt to restore the pre-1900 position whereby the president of Congress was elected by the delegates was defeated. An attempt was also defeated to secure the deletion of standing order number twenty. Under this rule any society engaged in a dispute that considered that members of another society had assisted to defeat those on strike, could report the circumstances to the Parliamentary Committee, which could then take any steps it felt the situation warranted. The Committee was only empowered to interfere in an inter-union dispute if definite charges of blacklegging were made. The amendment rose out of a refusal by the Parliamentary Committee to give a decision in the case of a dispute between the Coachmakers' Society and the Carpenters' and Joiners' Union, which had been reported to it. D. J. Shackleton told the 1906 Congress that had the case been one in which blacklegging had been involved it would have come under the standing order, but the Parliamentary Committee had no power to interfere in a question which was purely one of demarcation. As a result of the refusal of the Parliamentary Committee to intervene in this dispute, the standing orders were amended in 1907, so as to permit the Parliamentary Committee to act as arbitrator in any dispute between two unions when one complained to the Committee that the policy of the other was calculated to injure the members of the complaining union. In the following year the Committee reported to Congress that it had been called upon to intervene in many cases of dispute, which, in its judgment, ought not to have been submitted to it, and which could have been better dealt with by the federations of the trades concerned. Unions had refused to accept the arbitration of the Parliamentary Committee, and to pay the costs of the inquiry as the standing order laid down. The Committee, therefore, proposed that Congress should revert to the position where the duties of the Committee were confined to definite charges of blacklegging. In the course of the debate many delegates spoke in favour of the Committee having a wider scope of authority than this, but the revision was carried through. Experience had soon shown that many unions were not ready for a stronger control at the centre of the trade union movement, and that if the Parliamentary Committee's award did not go in their favour they would simply refuse to accept it.

The Parliamentary Committee was not the only body before which inter-union disputes were placed, for the Joint Board gradually assumed an authority to deal with organisational problems of this kind. The Conference of General Labour Unions was the first organisation to request the support of the Joint Board; early in 1907 it asked the Board not to recognise any new unions which might be set up to cater for general labourers, and to condemn the policy of the Municipal Employees' Association for confining its organisation to workers employed by public authorities, thus dividing them from their fellow labourers in private industry. After investigating these charges the Joint Board recommended that the Municipal Employees' Association should amend its rules so as to bring them into line with the 'principles of trade unionism', and the Association agreed to do this.[1] When, in practice, the Municipal Employees' Association continued to organise as before, the Joint Board had no power to make it behave differently.

In addition to inter-union disputes the Joint Board concerned itself with the question of overlapping agendas at the conferences of the three organisations, about which it was able to do nothing. The creation of a central headquarters in London at which all three organisations would be located was another matter to which the Board gave its attention, but failed to come to any satisfactory conclusion. The Parliamentary Committee asked the Joint Board to consider the question of starting a daily Labour paper. Every year since 1903, resolutions had been carried at Congress instructing the Parliamentary Committee to take steps to start one, and, following the adoption by the 1904 Congress of a scheme sponsored by the London Printing Trades' Societies, a draft was circulated to the unions, but the number of favourable replies was so small that the Committee did not proceed with the scheme. The demand for a national journal was raised again in 1906, when a resolution was carried asking the Parliamentary Committee to consult with the other two Labour organisations on the possibility of publishing a newspaper. The Joint Board appointed a sub-committee consisting of Arthur Henderson, C. W. Bowerman and Ramsay MacDonald to draw up a report. When the sub-committee presented its findings it stated that a daily paper was impracticable, but that a weekly paper would be a possibility if £40,000 could be raised, and the sub-committee felt that this could be done. The advocates of a daily newspaper were not satisfied with this report, and at the next Congress moved that the Parliamentary Committee should call a national conference of trade unions to consider the whole question. This conference was eventually held in the Caxton Hall, in February 1908. The London Society of Compositors had, before the conference, submitted to the Parliamentary Committee a carefully prepared scheme to found a paper to be called the *Morning Herald* which the Parliamentary Committee after consideration decided to adopt and remit to the conference. After a lengthy discussion the conference,

[1] *Report of the Joint Board*, 1907.

which was attended by 108 delegates, representing 62 unions affiliated to the T.U.C., endorsed the scheme and instructed the Parliamentary Committee to put it before the Joint Board for the approval of the whole Labour movement. The Joint Board, after consulting the Registrar of Friendly Societies on the legality of trade unions holding shares in a newspaper, and finding that it would be in order if the trade unions adopted a rule to cover this purpose, asked each union to say how much it would be prepared to subscribe towards the £100,000 capital which was deemed necessary to start the paper. No union except the London Society of Compositors made any definite offer to put money into the paper, and the Parliamentary Committee decided that the wisest course was to let the matter drop. The lack of enthusiasm on the part of the Committee aroused strong criticism at the 1909 Congress from the representatives of the London Society of Compositors. The Committee defended its attitude, which was supported by the Joint Board, on the grounds 'that considering the depression in trade and the claims already being made on the unions it would be courting disaster to ask them to contribute towards the establishment of a daily newspaper'.[1] The delegates supported this view; overwhelmingly defeating a resolution moved by T. E. Naylor, of the London Society of Compositors, instructing the Committee to proceed at once with the formation of a company to establish a daily Labour newspaper. Had the Parliamentary Committee had more courage and gone ahead with the scheme it might, with a newspaper to voice its point of view, have had greater influence over the situation that was to develop in the near future.

At the 1908 Congress a resolution calling on the Parliamentary Committee to issue a quarterly report containing an account of the work of the Committee was carried by accident. The cotton unions and the miners were opposed to the demand for more information on what the Committee was doing in between annual congresses because of the expense that this would entail; they claimed that the unions obtained all the information which they needed from the annual reports. This narrow and conservative attitude would have prevailed, but for the fact that the votes of the miners—over 500,000 —were disallowed when the vote was taken because they had not shown their voting card. They were unable to comply with the rules as the card was held by the leader of their delegation, who was absent from the room when the roll was called; a hazard that is inseparable from the block voting system. The incident gave rise to some satisfaction among those who were opposed to the use of this method, and the president took the opportunity to deliver a little homily to

[1] Statement by the president in reply to criticism. *T.U.C. Annual Report*, 1909.

the delegates on the unwisdom of permitting one man to carry all the votes. In the event the Parliamentary Committee published its first quarterly report at the beginning of 1909, and thereafter it soon established itself as a useful medium for keeping the unions informed on the activities of the Committee. Events were to demonstrate that no development was more important than the building of effective lines of communication between the leadership and the broad mass of the trade union movement, which was beginning to listen to siren voices and turn to direct industrial action as a solution to its problems.

CHAPTER VII

UNSETTLED YEARS

The year 1910 commenced with a strike. On the 1 January, the Coal Mines Regulation Act, which limited the hours of work underground to eight per day, came into operation in the north-eastern coalfields. As the miners of Durham and Northumberland had feared, with the passing of the Act the colliery owners insisted, on the grounds of economy, that it was essential to bring to an end the old system of working. The traditional two-shift cycle was increased to three per day and this disrupted the family life of the miners. The leaders of the coalfields realised that they had little choice but to agree to the change and gave their assent to the introduction of the extra shift, but some of the men refused to work under the new system and repudiated their leaders. They remained out on strike for over four months, obstinately paying no attention to pleas that they should return to work.

This unofficial strike of miners, whose allegiance to their leaders had been incredibly staunch in the past, was symptomatic of a change in the attitude of the rank and file trade unionists that had started with the depression in 1907. The strike wave which began in 1908, and which had died down in 1909, now suddenly welled up again to bring the Edwardian era to a close on a crescendo of industrial unrest. The tempo continued to mount, so that the first few years of the new reign were marked by social turbulence unmatched since the days of the Chartists. Strikes seemed to break out spontaneously on the flimsiest of pretexts. Men were ready to down tools in defiance of union rules and official advice, and, if their leaders were unwilling to undertake aggressive action, they were pushed into it.[1]

There were others besides the workers who were ready to sweep aside the law and traditional codes of behaviour; the House of Lords, the Suffragettes and the army in Ireland, were all prompted to act in the same spirit of anger and unreasonableness. It was as if the nation had suddenly caught a disease which frustrated every section of the community, and made it irritable and less inclined to listen to those who counselled reason and moderation.[2]

Unemployment was one of the factors stimulating industrial

[1] Cf. Tillett, Ben, *Memories and Reflections*; Snowden, Philip, quoted in *Labour Leader*, 15 September 1911; MacDonald, J. R., *The Social Unrest*.
[2] Cf. Dangerfield, George, *The Strange Death of Liberal England*.

unrest, but hardly the main one, for industrial activity picked up sharply in 1910, and continued to improve over the next four years. Unemployment among trade unionists, which had been as high as 8 per cent in 1908 and 1909 fell by more than half in 1910, and continued to fall until it was only 2 per cent in 1913. Real wages, however, were in 1910 substantially below what they had been in 1900, and they did not begin to climb up until 1914. Prices rose steadily from 1896 to 1907, and, then, after the recession, from 1910 to 1913. Wages did not, however, keep pace with the rise in prices, so that the victories won through militant strike action were not enough to do more than offset the increase in the cost of living.[1] The movements of prices and wages during this period and the considerable fall in the share of the national income going to wage earners[2] after a long period of rising prosperity must obviously be reckoned as an important cause of the unrest that occurred.[3]

Rising prices always cause an acute feeling of injustice among lower paid workers, especially when they see the well-off unaffected. The extravagant opulence of the very wealthy, then being depicted in the newly created popular Press, contributed towards confirming the workers in their belief that they were being excluded from sharing in the general benefits of prosperity. The feeling was strong that the employers were making enough profits to pay better wages; and the workers were not to be fobbed off with arguments about foreign competition and higher import prices, for signs of a trade boom were too evident for that story, true as it was, to have any force.

Strikes among the miners in the Midlands, the woollen workers of Bradford, the employees of the North Eastern Railway, and also in the Welsh coalfields, were all to some extent revolts against union discipline. J. Haslam, M.P., leader of the Derbyshire Miners, and president of the Trades Union Congress in 1910, referred, in his presidential address that year, to the unrest in the trade union world; he called upon trade union members not to put collective bargaining in jeopardy by ill-considered actions. However, no sooner was

[1] Phelps Brown, E. H., and Hopkins, S. V., 'The Course of Wage Rates in Five Countries, 1860–1939', *Oxford Economic Papers*, June 1950.
[2] Phelps Brown, E. H., and Hart, P. E., 'The Share of Wages in the National Income', *The Economic Journal*, June 1952.
[3] Askwith, Lord, *Industrial Problems and Disputes*, p. 175:

'What is to be said about these disputes? My own strong opinion is that they were economic. Trade had been improving, but employers thought too much of making up for some lean years in the past, and of making money, without sufficient regard to the importance of considering the position of their workpeople at a time of improvement of trade. Prices had been rising but no sufficient increase of wages and certainly no general increase, had followed the rise.'

Congress over than a strike started, in South Wales, against attempts by the owners of the Cambrian collieries to work a difficult seam at what the mineworkers regarded as starvation wages. Efforts, made by the executive committee of the South Wales Miners' Federation, to arrive at a settlement, were scornfully rejected by the men, who would accept no compromise with their demand for a rate of 2s. 6d. per ton. The strike spread, and by November the whole of the Rhondda and adjacent valleys were in the grip of the dispute.

The executive committee of the S.W.M.F. issued a stern warning to the men out on strike and ordered them back to work. Most of them went back, except for the miners of the Rhondda Valley, who refused to go back until they had obtained a minimum daily wage of 8s. for skilled and 5s. for unskilled workers. The situation was exacerbated by the gratuitous provocation of the mine-owners who had made reductions of pay and imported blacklegs under the protection of the police. Feeling in the valleys mounted, as the miners grew increasingly hostile towards the colliery owners, who replied to the demands of the men by asking for soldiers to be sent to maintain order. The state of tension and imminent possibility of violent disturbances led Mr. Churchill, who was then Home Secretary, to decide to make a show of force. The fears of the Home Secretary were well founded, but the sending of a squadron of cavalry did not improve matters, since it appeared to be merely acceding to panic requests. Before an uneasy calm was restored pitched battles were fought between angry, bitter men and the police. The Rhondda Miners refused to return to work; they stubbornly insisted on having their grievances remedied and demanded that the Miners' Federation of Great Britain should call a general strike. This the Federation refused to do, though it did make a grant of £3,000 per week until May 1911; it then withdrew the grant because of the refusal of the men to make any compromise. With the drying up of their funds the men were finally starved into submission in the following August.[1]

Tom Mann and the Syndicalist Revolt

Prominent in the Rhondda during the dispute had been Tom Mann. He had gone down to South Wales in November with his new philosophy of syndicalism, and found much support among the younger miners who were dissatisfied with an old-fashioned leadership which sought improvements for the workers through conciliation boards and arbitration committees. The executive committee of the South Wales Miners had for a long time been under fire for its manner of handling the colliery owners; the traditional methods of

[1] Edwards, Ness, *History of the South Wales Miners*.

wage settlement were considered feeble by the younger men, who wanted a more militant policy to be pursued. Thus the ground was already well prepared for Tom Mann's intervention, and his gospel fell upon ears eager to listen.

Tom Mann had been out of the country for over eight years. In 1902 he had left Britain to visit Australia and New Zealand to examine the much-vaunted social and economic progress made there. Since the dock strike of 1889, which the Australian Labour movement had helped to win with its magnificent contribution of £30,000, the British trade unions had had a profound respect for the Labour movement in the antipodes, and were extremely interested in the social legislation which had been put into operation there. At the Trades Union Congress, Australia and New Zealand were often quoted as examples worthy of emulation in Britain. A Labour Party had been formed in Australia as early as 1891, and from that year the citizens of this young country had been electing its members to the colonial assemblies. Four years after the Commonwealth of Australia had been brought into existence in 1900, a Federal Ministry was formed by the Labour leader, J. C. Watson. A second Labour Government held office for a short period in 1908, but in 1910, the year that Tom Mann returned to England, the Labour Party was returned to power and remained in office to govern Australia for over three years.[1]

Tom Mann was unimpressed by the social legislation of Australia and New Zealand, which he thought had conferred no great benefits on the workers of those countries. In fact, he acquired a deep distrust of all State action during his sojourn in Australia, and became a convert to syndicalism. Returning to Britain by way of South Africa, he arrived home in May 1910, and was met on the landing-stage by a large reception party organised by Guy Bowman, the translator of Gustave Hervé's anti-militarist book, *My Country Right or Wrong*, and a fervid supporter of the French anarcho-syndicalists. According to Bowman, Tom Mann's first words on landing were, 'Let us go and see the men of direct action', whereupon they immediately went to France to learn of the methods used by the French syndicalists to foment and organise strikes.[2]

On his return from France, Tom Mann began to propagate his syndicalist ideas through a series of monthly pamphlets issued under the title of the *Industrial Syndicalist*, which he edited and Bowman published; the first number appeared in July 1910. An indefatigable speaker, Tom Mann stumped the country, and soon gathered to his banner a nucleus of devoted supporters in the main industrial centres.

[1] Fitzpatrick, Brian, *A Short History of the Australian Labour Movement*.
[2] Mann, Tom, *From Single Tax to Syndicalism*—preface by G. Bowman.

Mann was by no means the first to preach syndicalist doctrines; James Connolly had been doing so for a number of years, and a good deal had been heard of the Industrial Workers of the World, which had been formed in Chicago in 1905. Passionate support for the I.W.W. was one of the factors involved in the revolt against the teaching at Ruskin College, in 1909.[1] Tom Mann had been influenced by the I.W.W. when in Australia, where it had become quite a powerful force, but he differed from it in so far as he rejected the notion of building a revolutionary class-conscious organisation outside the existing trade union movement. Mann wrote in the first issue of the *Industrial Syndicalist*, 'I have given close attention to the arguments submitted by those who adopt this view and I consider them insufficient. I know it will be a formidable task to get the existing unions to

[1] Ruskin College was founded in 1899, as a result of efforts made by two Americans, Walter Vrooman and Charles Beard, with the support of individual members of the University of Oxford, the local Trades Council, Trades Union Congress and a number of trade unions. Although the T.U.C., London Trades Council, Amalgamated Society of Engineers and the Co-operative Union were represented on the Council of Ruskin Hall, a suspicion grew that the class-conscious idealism of the students was being perverted by the teaching given at the college, and by their contact with the university.

Dissatisfaction with the education policy of the college was stimulated by Dennis Hird, the rather vain and eccentric principal, who was more interested in propagating a hotch-potch of atheism, biology and Marxism, which he called sociology, than in developing the more genuine fields of educational discipline, The dispute over the content of the teaching policy sanctioned by the governing council culminated in the dismissal of Hird. This was followed by a strike of the students, who refused to attend any lectures but those delivered by the principal. The outcome of this situation was the withdrawal of a body of students with Dennis Hird, who, with the encouragement of the Miners' Federation, established a rival institution, which later became the Central Labour College. Apart from Hird's personality, the crux of the matter lay in the rising impatience of the younger trade unionists with the existing state of society, and the cautious policy pursued by the trade union leaders. At a meeting organised during Congress week in 1909, in support of Ruskin Hall, C. W. Bowerman, one of the T.U.C. representatives of the governing council, and David Shackleton, firmly insisted that the college should provide education and not be a propaganda agency.

Shortly after the 1909 Congress a conference of all the working-class organisations that supported Ruskin was held in Oxford, and a new governing council was elected, consisting of two representatives from the T.U.C., and the G.F.T.U., the Co-operative Union and the Working Men's Club and Institute Union, with one representative of every working-class organisation that paid for a student to go to the college. In addition three academic advisors were appointed without votes. The clash of principle, however, over the policy and functions of Ruskin continued, and in 1913, the Parliamentary Committee had to withdraw a resolution to raise funds for the college, which it had sponsored at the Trades Union Congress of that year, owing to the opposition of the miners and of other unions which supported the Central Labour College. See *The Story of Ruskin College, 1899–1949*; Sanderson Furness, *Memories of Sixty Years*; *Trades Union Congress Annual Reports*, 1900, 1901, 1902, 1903, 1913; *The Times*, 9 September 1909.

unite wholeheartedly and share courageously in the class war. But I believe that it can be done.'[1]

The essence of Tom Mann's beliefs was that the existing trade unions were moribund. They were unable to act in a militant fashion because they had accepted the philosophy of liberal-capitalism, and their organisation, based on the craft divisions of industry, was not fitted for the struggle with the capitalist owners who had improved on the example of the workers and organised themselves on industrial lines. He advocated the creation of industrial trade unions, linked together in national federations, under the central direction of the General Federation of Trade Unions, which should then be affiliated to an international federation of trade unions. He urged the abandonment of collective agreements, which, he alleged, sapped the vigour of the trade unions because they bound them to the employers, thus destroying the unions' freedom to attack. Trade unions had no right to sacrifice their independence in this way, he argued; all collective agreements should therefore be denounced and employers assaulted at every opportunity by means of the strike. For tactical reasons, Tom Mann did not suggest the dissolution of the Labour Party, but he did not believe that the workers could abolish capitalism by constitutional political means; this objective could only be achieved by the use of direct industrial action. The workers ought, therefore, to concentrate on preparing for the revolutionary strike, and not waste their time working for reforms through a parliamentary system which only corrupted their representatives. This line of reasoning evoked a surprising response in view of the substantial social reforms achieved through Parliament in the past few years.

In November 1910, Tom Mann and his followers organised a conference on industrial syndicalism at the Coal Exchange, Manchester. There were present representatives from over seventy trade union branches, and sixteen trades councils, mainly from the Manchester area. The chairman of the conference was A. A. Purcell, then an organiser in the furnishing trades and later to become prominent in the councils of the T.U.C. Conspicuous among the delegates was James Larkin,[2] a disciple of James Connolly, and one of the leaders of the Irish Transport and General Workers' Union. The chairman opened the proceedings by reading a letter of support for

---

[1] *Industrial Syndicalist*, vol. I, No. 1, July 1910.

[2] James Larkin was born in Liverpool of Irish parents and claimed descent from the Fenian of the same name, executed in Manchester for the murder of a police sergeant in 1867. In 1906 Larkin organised the dock labourers of Belfast, in 1909 he became an organiser for the National Union of Dock Workers, and soon afterwards leader of the Irish Transport and General Workers' Union. He established a reputation during the turbulent years from 1910 to 1914 as one of the greatest mass orators ever known in the Labour movement.

the conference from Tom Mann's old colleague, Ben Tillett. But many of the delegates had little understanding of syndicalism, and some had no desire to transform trade union structure into the pattern demanded by Mann. What they wanted from the leaders of the unions was the pursuit of a more militant policy, and a number of delegates suggested that this could be achieved without any radical change in trade union structure and tactics. The majority, however, decided to support Tom Mann's proposal to set up an Industrial Syndicalist League to propagate the gospel of 'direct action' and industrial unionism.[1]

Tom Mann could congratulate himself on his share in the outbreak of industrial unrest in South Wales, but events in the following year gave him a greater opportunity of exercising his ability as an agitator.

One of the first things Tom Mann had done on his return to England had been, through Ben Tillett, to encourage the formation of a National Transport Workers' Federation. In August 1910, Tillett wrote to all the transport unions proposing that a conference be held to discuss the formation of such a federation. Soon afterwards a preliminary conference was held in London, and this was followed by a second conference in November 1910. This was presided over by Harry Gosling, secretary of the Lightermen's Union, deputy chairman of the London County Council, and a member of the Port of London Authority. Gosling was an earnest, conscientious trade union leader, a good fighter and careful organiser, but no syndicalist. Other well-known figures who were present and supported the establishment of a Federation were Will Thorne, of the National Union of Gasworkers and General Labourers, J. N. Bell, of the National Amalgamated Union of Labour, J. Havelock Wilson, of the National Sailors' and Firemen's Union, James Sexton, of the National Union of Dock Labourers and J. Cotter of the Ships' Stewards' Union. None of them was a syndicalist, but they all wanted to see stronger trade union organisation. The outcome of the conference was the formation of the National Transport Workers' Federation, with Harry Gosling as president, and James Anderson of the Stevedores' Union as secretary. The first task which the Federation set itself was to improve the organisation of the trade unions in and around the ports throughout the country.

Meanwhile Tom Mann had been in close touch with Havelock Wilson in promoting an organising drive among seamen. Wilson was determined to secure recognition for his union from the Shipowners' Federation, which for twenty years had treated it with contempt. The union asked the Shipowners' Federation if it would enter into negotiations with a view to remedying the grievances of the sailors,

[1] *Industrial Syndicalist*, vol. I, No. 6, December 1910.

only to receive replies that were couched in terms both arrogant and threatening. Wilson thereupon decided to call a national strike of seamen in June 1911, the month of King George's coronation, when the traffic entering the ports of the United Kingdom would be at its highest. The strike started with the men coaling the new liner *Olympic*, which was about to sail to bring back visitors from the United States for the coronation, refusing to go on with their work until they secured an improvement in their working conditions. The *Olympic* having been prevented from sailing on its maiden voyage, the Seamen's Union called out its members in every port on the 14 June. With the seamen out on strike, the dockers and the other waterside trades began to come out in sympathy, instinctively realising that this was an opportunity for them to secure better conditions. In a few days, with the turn-round of ships being brought to a halt in ports all over the country, the Shipowners' Federation realised that it was beaten and its members began to negotiate with the union, making considerable concessions to the men. But the capitulation of the shipowners did not settle the trouble in the ports, for the dockers and other waterside workers refused to go back until they, too, had secured some gains.

No sooner had strikes at the ports of Hull, Manchester and Liverpool been settled, through the intervention of the Labour Department's conciliation officers, than the workers in the Port of London came out on strike. The newly-formed National Transport Workers' Federation immediately seized its opportunity and took command of the situation, ordering that no section of the workers should return until an agreement had been reached which covered them all.[1] With work in the port entirely at a standstill the Government intervened, and negotiations between the Port Employers and the unions were opened. These ended in a resounding victory for the Transport Workers' Federation, for not only were increased wages and better working conditions won, but the employers were compelled to recognise the trade unions. This success gave a fillip to the arguments of those who were urging closer unity among the unions and the more careful co-ordination of strike action.[2]

During the time that the dispute in the Port of London was in progress Tom Mann, who had organised the strike committee in Liverpool, had transferred his attention to the railwaymen, who had

[1] It was during the course of this stoppage that Ben Tillett is said to have led a large and excited meeting in a fervent invocation to the Almighty to 'strike Lord Devonport dead'. Lord Devonport, the chairman of the Port of London Authority, was regarded by the workers at the port as the quintessential manifestation of the bloated capitalist mordantly portrayed by Will Dyson in his famous cartoons.

[2] Tillett, Ben, *History of the London Transport Workers' Strike*, 1911.

plenty of grievances to be worked upon. The men employed in the goods department of the Lancashire and Yorkshire Railway were the first to come out on strike, but they were rapidly followed by railwaymen in other areas. The executives of the railwaymen's unions, faced with this large-scale unofficial strike, hurriedly met together; they decided to give the men official support and called for a national stoppage of work on the railways, unless the railway companies agreed to meet them in negotiations. At that time the railway companies still refused to recognise trade unionism, and the main complaint of the unions was that the companies had failed to honour the 1907 Conciliation Boards agreement. The Government, faced with the prospect of a complete breakdown in rail transport, again intervened, after the railway companies had refused to meet the unions. The companies believed that they could keep the railways running with the aid of blackleg labour. The leaders of the unions were summoned to the Board of Trade for a conference with members of the Government, and were informed by the Prime Minister, after hearing their complaints, that he was prepared to set up a Royal Commission to investigate the facts. In making this offer Asquith appeared to threaten the use of force against the strikers unless there was an immediate resumption of work, and unless the unions called off their ultimatum. The union leaders refused to be browbeaten and gave a blunt refusal to this offer, which they were convinced was an attempt to shelve the issue, whereupon Asquith left the room, muttering as he went, it is said, the injudicious words, 'Then the blood be on your own head.'[1] The union leaders immediately sent off two thousand telegrams calling out their members all over the country; soon the railways had been brought to an almost complete stop. The Government was by now thoroughly alarmed, and Mr. Churchill busied himself with dispatching troops to keep order, which, up to this act of provocation, had not been disturbed.[2] On the 19 August 1911, Lloyd George personally intervened and persuaded the railway companies that in the light of the international situation, which was tense over the Moroccan crisis, they should meet the men and settle the dispute. Under this pressure the companies reluctantly agreed, and the strike was terminated while a Royal Commission investigated the complaints of the unions, but it was not until some time afterwards that a settlement was arrived at. Though assurances had been given, the companies tried to wriggle out of their obligations, and were finally only persuaded to meet the unions by a resolution calling on them to do so passed by the House of Commons in November; even then they evaded the question of

[1] Askwith, Lord, *Industrial Problems and Disputes*, p. 164.
[2] *Parliamentary Reports, House of Commons*, 22 August 1911.

recognition. The attitude of the railway companies was not dictated simply by economic circumstances; it was expressive of an ingrained sense of social superiority which led the owners to believe that workers were an inferior kind of being, and should accept orders without question. In their hatred of the trade unions the directors of the railway companies were moved by a class consciousness as extreme as that which motivated the syndicalists. There can be no doubt that this kind of attitude, manifest by the owners and managers of industry, towards wage earners, exacerbated long-suffered resentment, and had much to do with the stimulation of the current wave of industrial unrest. The outlook of these great employers of labour was in strange contrast to the national recognition given to the trade union movement, when, in 1911, the T.U.C. was invited to send representatives to the coronation ceremony of George V in Westminster Abbey.

Demand for Greater Centralisation of Authority

When the Trades Union Congress assembled at Newcastle-on-Tyne in September 1911, it was in an atmosphere of elation at the recent victories of the workers. The Parliamentary Committee, in its report to Congress, found the cause of the strikes to be 'in the employers refusing to meet the accredited representatives of the men, the economic conditions prevailing and the unorganised condition of many workers'.[1] It laid the blame for the outbreaks of violence on 'the needless display of force by the police and military', but went on to say that while appreciating the gains made and the growing signs of unity, the permanent success of the workers could only be assured by thorough discipline. This cautious approbation of the strike policy was swept aside by the delegates when they enthusiastically passed a resolution congratulating the transport workers on their successful strikes, and resolved, 'that no effort shall be spared by the forces of organised labour to arouse and maintain the discontent of underpaid workers with their conditions, and to quicken and assist their determination to use all possible means to win for themselves a living wage'.[2] They then went on to express their indignation at a Bill which had been tabled in the House of Commons by Will Crooks, Arthur Henderson, George Barnes and Charles Fenwick, which was designed to prevent strikes by making them illegal unless thirty days' notice had been given in advance. This Bill, which had not been officially authorised, either by the T.U.C. or the Labour Party, though it probably had the support of many of the leaders of the Labour movement, was evidence of the divergence of views which

[1] *T.U.C. Annual Report*, 1911.   [2] *Ibid.*

had developed during the past few years between different sections
of the movement.

Feeling was great among the delegates at the shooting down of
workers demonstrating during the strikes that summer, and the
militant section seized the opportunity to attack the Parliamentary
Committee, and, by implication, the political wing of the movement,
for inviting representatives of Government departments to observe
the proceedings of Congress, when the Government had deliberately
used military force to overawe men on strike. Replying to the strictures made by John Bromley of the Associated Society of Locomotive
Engineers and Firemen, and Robert Smillie, the rising star of the
Miners' Federation, C. W. Bowerman—who later in the week was
elected to the post of secretary, W. C. Steadman having died, after a
long illness, a few weeks before Congress—pointed out that invitations had been issued since the formation of the Labour Department
in 1892. Four of the observers present were ex-trade union leaders;
these were D. J. Shackleton, who had just been appointed Labour
Advisor to the Home Office, C. J. Drummond, Isaac Mitchell, and
D. Cummings, who were employed in the Labour Department of the
Board of Trade. Although careful not to attack these individuals
personally, the militant section was hostile to trade union leaders
accepting employment with the Government, believing that this
merely provided a cloak to shelter the nefarious activities of their
employers. Much of the emotional heat which had been generated
was dissipated by the calm words of William Brace, one of the old
Lib-Lab school of miners, who counselled the delegates to reject the
advice of his colleague Smillie, on the grounds that the trade unions
always sought to have close contact with Government departments,
and that this in no way committed the T.U.C. to the support of the
policy of any Government. The majority for the Parliamentary
Committee against the motion of censure was substantial. Having
failed in their purpose, the minority ostentatiously walked out of
Congress when the official resolution, condemning the use of troops,
and calling for an inquiry into the shooting incidents was put to the
vote immediately afterwards. It was considered by the militants to
be too weak in its wording, as it simply denounced the policy of the
Home Secretary, Mr. Churchill, and failed to indict the Government
as a whole.

It could not be gainsaid that the upsurge of militancy in the ranks
of the workers had brought some results, and there were widespread
demands for changes in the organisation of the Labour movement
so as to bring about closer unity. Tom Mann and his followers were
not the only ones who sought to make sweeping changes in the
structure of the movement; a number of proposals were being

canvassed, none of them new and none of them likely to be adopted without a considerable change in the attitude of the average trade unionist.

At the 1910 Congress the Dock, Wharf, Riverside and General Workers' Union had sponsored a resolution instructing the Parliamentary Committee to inquire from the unions affiliated to the T.U.C. whether they would be willing to support the establishment of a National Federation or Confederation of Unions, and agree to the termination of all industrial agreements on the same day each year. The resolution was carried by a huge majority, but the Parliamentary Committee reported to the 1911 Congress that only fourteen unions had deemed the circular that had been sent out worthy of a reply, and that of these few only one was definitely in favour. Some unions had pointed to the existence of the General Federation of Trade Unions, and suggested that if every union affiliated to it there would be no need to set up an additional body. As, however, most of the larger unions were not prepared to do that, there was little chance that they would hand over their autonomy to any other all-embracing federal organisation.

Tom Ring, a Sheffield syndicalist and delegate from the Cabinet Makers, had skilfully moved a further resolution at the 1910 Congress, advocating industrial unionism and calling upon the Parliamentary Committee to ascertain the views of the unions with a view to promoting a general scheme of amalgamation to be placed before the 1911 Congress. Many speeches were made against the resolution by the representatives of the small craft unions, but it was carried by the huge majority of 1,175,000 to 256,000. The response to the questionnaire on the subject did not match the fervour displayed at Congress, since only 17 unions bothered to reply, and only 10 of them were in favour. Despite this depressing result the 1911 Congress buoyantly passed a resolution calling on the Parliamentary Committee to take steps to bring about the amalgamation of trade unions organising the same type of worker. As a consequence of this resolution the Committee was asked to call a conference of the unions in the building trade. The initiative from inside the building industry had come from a number of industrial unionists, led by George Hicks and J. V. Wills, who had secured a great deal of influence in the Operative Bricklayers' Society. The conference, at which 21 unions were represented, decided in favour of the principle of amalgamation. However, when the question was put to a ballot of the members, the opposition to the proposals was great enough to prevent the necessary majorities from being secured, and the proposals fell through.[1]

[1] Postgate, R. W., *The Builders' History*, p. 408.

Another idea, which was supported for widely different reasons, was the unification of the T.U.C., Labour Party and G.F.T.U. A resolution asking for the amalgamation of the three bodies was debated at the 1910 Trades Union Congress, and rejected narrowly by 779,000 to 750,000. The same resolution, however, was carried at the Labour Party Conference, with the result that the matter was placed in the hands of the Joint Board. At a special conference it was agreed that there was a need for closer unity, but only the Labour Party put forward specific proposals. These were: the amalgamation of the three bodies; the building of a central headquarters for the entire movement; and the setting up of a sub-committee to consider giving effect to them. A sub-committee appointed by the Joint Board to consider the findings of this conference recommended, however, that no further steps be taken for the time being. The question was again discussed at the T.U.C. in 1911, when this time it was suggested that only the T.U.C. and the Labour Party should be united into one central organisation. The G.F.T.U. was left out because that organisation had made it clear that it was unwilling to enter into such a scheme. The leading spirit in this demand for unification was John Hill, the secretary of the Boilermakers' Society. His union had been supporting ideas of centralisation since the early 1870s, and now it drew up an elaborate scheme, which was remitted to the Parliamentary Committee and the executive of the Labour Party for consideration. No further steps, however, were taken by either national committee, and the Joint Board let the matter drop on the grounds of opposition from the G.F.T.U. At the 1912 Trades Union Congress the Boilermakers raised the question again, but in an atmosphere much less propitious to the support of its scheme, and the delegates overwhelmingly defeated it.

The demand for the unification of the Labour movement had been supported for different reasons. Some like John Hill, wanted it because they felt that the Labour Party and the G.F.T.U. ought to be committees under the control of the Trades Union Congress; others, like Will Thorne and J. R. Clynes, felt that one organisation would be more efficient and effective politically. The idea was opposed on the realistic grounds that each organisation had a distinct job to do and should be left to get on with it. It was also opposed by some syndicalists out of fear that it would strengthen the position of the politicians, and the *Labour Leader* thought that the resolution had only been carried in 1911 because the delegates were convinced that the T.U.C. was 'played out', and that in future the industrial functions of the Labour movement would be carried out by the G.F.T.U.[1] The fate of these endeavours amply demonstrated that it was one

[1] *Labour Leader*, 15 September 1911.

thing to pass a resolution in the heady atmosphere of Congress, but quite another when the delegates returned home, and had to face the practical job of persuading the men they represented that their union should abridge its autonomy. Doubts that were apt to disappear when listening to passionate oratory, soon crept back when Congress was over, and attention was focused on everyday problems.

The principle of centralisation was discussed at the annual meeting of the G.F.T.U. in 1911. The leaders of the Federation urged its members to give it greater control over disputes because the Federation was constantly being dragged at the heels of some little society involved in a dispute, and simply had to pay out benefits.[1] As the Federation had no power to decide which strike would be worth fighting, its value as a militant organisation was much reduced. None of its member organisations were, however, prepared to sacrifice their interests for the benefit of some grandiose plan of attack on the employers. The G.F.T.U. fulfilled its purpose, so far as most of its members were concerned, by providing a certain insurance that they would be able to pay out strike benefit if they became involved in a dispute. A strike or lockout might seem petty from the point of view of a grand strategy, but to the members of the union concerned it was of primary importance.

A much more sensible but modest suggestion, which did not have the dubious merit of being sensational or revolutionary in its purpose, was turned down without discussion at the Trades Union Congress in 1911. It was proposed that the Parliamentary Committee should establish an information bureau which would have the task of collecting material relating to wages and working conditions for the use of the affiliated organisations. When the mover of this resolution sat down, J. M. Jack, secretary of the Scottish Iron-moulders, an old-fashioned, narrow-minded craft unionist, rose and said, 'Mr. Baker has lectured us very well, but the resolution leads nowhere. Therefore, I move the previous question.'[2] This was immediately carried—the resolution having no appeal either to the conservative craft unionists or to those who wanted to make fundamental changes.

Conflict at Congress

The divisions in the Labour movement at this time were exposed by almost every issue, and a conflict flared up over the Government's National Insurance Bill.[3] The Parliamentary Committee had been

---

[1] *G.F.T.U. Annual Report*, 1911.   [2] *T.U.C. Annual Report*, 1911.
[3] The atmosphere of 1911 seemed to rouse the delegates to anger and irritation. Twice during the 1911 Congress tempers flared and terrible rows occurred. Ben

in favour of a system of national insurance since the prospect of legislation to introduce the system into this country had first been mooted in 1908. Since that time the political situation had changed considerably, and there was now a strong body of opinion in the Labour movement that regarded a scheme of contributory insurance with antipathy. The three national committees of the T.U.C., Labour Party and G.F.T.U., met in conference to consider the Bill; they approved its main provisions, but the militant socialists and trade unionists violently denounced this decision. The readiness to hurl abuse at the leaders of the movement to which they insist they give their loyalty has always been a curious feature of the behaviour of the socialist wing of the Labour movement.

The National Insurance legislation was welcomed by the Parliamentary Committee and the Management Committee of the G.F.T.U. because it promised to give the trade unions with little to offer by way of friendly benefits an opportunity to consolidate their hold on their members through the part that might be played by the unions in the administration of the scheme. Even for trade unions that already paid substantial benefits it offered additional security for their members, and the prospect of some financial gain in acting as agents for the payment of national insurance benefits. The Parliamentary Committee saw a practical opportunity here of creating greater unity between the unions, and suggested that they should group together to administer the scheme. The socialists were against the Bill because they wanted social security made available on a non-contributory basis, and paid for out of taxes on the high-income groups. The Fabians were against the Bill because it was a substitute

Tillett, a rather truculent character, in the course of an argument with another delegate outside the hall, considered himself insulted and emphasised his point of view with a blow that landed on his opponent's jaw. When he rose to speak in the debate shortly afterwards he had to face a hostile demonstration, and the Standing Orders Committee was called upon to make an inquiry into the incident. On the following day another disorderly scene occurred. It began when Will Thorne moved a resolution that called for 'a national system of education under full popular control, free and *secular*. . . .' The Roman Catholic delegates objected to the anti-religious sentiments expressed by Thorne, and there were a number of interventions. As soon as James Sexton rose to put the point of view of the Catholic minority an excited delegate jumped to his feet to protest, 'and then there was' according to the official report, 'a general rising and a babel of angry shouts. Taunts were flung at Mr. Sexton from the gallery and other parts of the hall, and at one time an ugly rush was made up the central pathway towards the would-be speaker, who shook his fist and shouted in protest at the refusal of Congress to hear him speak. Several of Mr. Sexton's friends tried to persuade him to submit to the President's ruling and resume his seat, but he fiercely declared that he would rather be carried out than give way. For ten minutes the storm raged, the bell of the President all the time adding to the general din. At last Mr. Sexton sat down, and the storm subsided as quickly as it had risen.'

for the comprehensive scheme put forward by the Webbs in the Minority Report of the Poor Law Commission.[1] In addition the Bill was fiercely attacked by Chesterton, Belloc and others in the *Labour Leader*, as an attempt to batten down the workers, deprive them of their independence and make them servile subjects of the State.

The issue between the two main points of view was raised squarely at the 1911 Trades Union Congress when J. C. Gordon, a representative of the Sheetmetal Workers, moved a resolution that 'It is the opinion of this Congress that no scheme of national insurance against sickness, disablement or unemployment can be satisfactory which is not wholly non-contributory and the funds provided by Parliament.'[2] This resolution was only narrowly defeated by 594,000 to 325,000 with many abstentions. Immediately afterwards a resolution moved by Mary Macarthur, 'That any scheme of State insurance must in the opinion of this Congress place the whole burden of insuring all workers whatever their age, whose wages are less than 15*s*. per week, upon the State and the employer',[3] was carried by a narrow majority. The Parliamentary Committee had come near to having its policy of support for the Bill rejected; had the trade unions decided to oppose the legislation it would have been a considerable triumph for the militant section of the delegates.

The new militant spirit of the workers influenced the debates but, as in the 1890s, the weight of tradition, vested interest and the common sense of the delegates proved too great to be easily pushed aside. Strong sentiments were expressed, but no revolutionary policy was adopted, and no new faith embraced. Syndicalism was not mentioned, and Tom Mann and his activities were ignored. Most delegates agreed that the militancy had brought beneficial results and many demanded more of it, but those who expected the Parliamentary Committee to seize the opportunity to redefine the social aims of the trade union movement, and boldly support revolutionary tactics to achieve them were once again disappointed.

The 1911 Congress provided another conspicuous example of how the large block vote of the Miners could affect the decision of the delegates. A resolution had been moved by the National Union of Clerks, with the strong support of the militant section of Congress, calling for an inquiry into the administration of labour exchanges.

---

[1] Cf. The speech by Beatrice Webb to the 1913 Labour Party Conference: 'The Fabian Society while there was yet time opposed the contributory principle but the tide was too strong against them. The Liberal Government had introduced the contributory principle, the Conservatives had accepted it, and the Labour Party had accepted it as a dark horse which would bolt into the stable of the trade unions. The Fabian Society feared it would bolt into the stable of the Insurance Companies.'

[2] *T.U.C. Annual Report*, 1911.   [3] *Ibid.*

After a number of wild statements had been made by its supporters, and answered by the more responsible leaders, the resolution was put to the vote and defeated by 823,000 to 547,000. It was announced shortly afterwards that the Miners had inadvertently cast their votes against the resolution instead of for it, which would have made the result, for the resolution, 1,097,000 against 273,000.[1]

Attempts by Government to Reduce Industrial Unrest

In the first month of 1912 the country was again in the throes of industrial unrest; 160,000 weavers were locked out in Lancashire, and a serious strike involved the dockers on the Clyde. The most serious storm centre, however, was in the coalfields. The 'abnormal place' problem—where the nature of the coal seam made it difficult for the miner to earn a reasonable wage—which had been the cause of the Cambrian dispute in South Wales at the end of 1910, had continued to agitate the miners. Several abortive meetings between the officials of the miners' unions and the colliery owners had been held to consider the miners' claim for a minimum wage. Dissatisfied with the negative results of these negotiations, the Miners' Federation took a ballot of all the coalfields in December 1911, which resulted in an overwhelming majority in favour of a national strike.

After further inconclusive negotiations the Government intervened and tried to secure a settlement of the dispute by supporting the claims of the miners to a minimum wage, though it insisted on the minimum being settled locally, if not by agreement, then by arbitration. The miners refused to accept these proposals unless the owners would agree to a minimum wage of 5*s*. per shift for adult miners and 2*s*. for boys. The owners, who had not even agreed to the Government's proposals, refused this demand, whereupon the miners, who had already given notice that they intended to strike, terminated work on the 28 February. On 1 March over a million men were on strike. This was the largest single stoppage that had ever occurred in Britain, and the first time that the miners in all the coalfields had acted together in a dispute.

The Government, having completely failed to get the men to agree on a settlement of the dispute, introduced, in desperation, a Minimum Wage Bill. This was based on the proposals which had been put forward by the Prime Minister at the earlier stage. It did not meet the demands of the miners, which were for a national minimum, and the Labour members tried to get the 'five and two' claim of the Federation inserted, but the Government resisted this amendment,

[1] *T.U.C. Annual Report*, 1911.

and the Bill, having been rushed through Parliament, became law by the end of March, without it. What the Minimum Wage Act did was to guarantee to miners working in 'abnormal places' a minimum wage that was fixed by a District Wage Board, on the basis of a recognised standard wage determined by ordinary collective bargaining. The owners accepted the terms of the Act when it became law, but it was rejected by the miners when put to a ballot vote; however, the majority was considered by the miners' leaders as too narrow to justify continuing the strike, and they ordered a resumption of work.[1]

Not long after the miners had reluctantly returned to work the country was again in the grip of strike fever. In May, a dispute arose on the Thames over the employment of non-union workers. It began with the Society of Watermen, Lightermen and Bargemen calling out their members on strike. This union was a member of the National Transport Workers' Federation, and its general secretary, Harry Gosling, was the president. The Federation, which had been smarting under the behaviour of the employers in the Port of London, who had seized every opportunity of escaping from the agreement reached after the big strike of 1911, swiftly called a general strike of all the workers in the Port of London and on the Medway. Again the Government stepped in, and a special inquiry into the grievances of the workers was undertaken by Sir Edward Clarke, K.C. Finally, the Government proposed that the various trades should come to an agreement, which should be cemented by money guarantees to be forfeited in case of a breach of the agreement by either side—a system that had been adopted in the boot and shoe industry after the 1895 lockout, and had worked well. The employers, however, refused to have anything to do with this idea, since they were bent on smashing the power of the Federation, before which they had been compelled to retreat in the previous year.

The Federation, realising that it was not going to have an easy victory this time, tried to extend the strike by calling on the workers in every port throughout the country to rally to the aid of the London strikers. The response to this call proved poor. It revealed that the strength of the Federation was not as great as its militant supporters had fooled themselves into believing. The strikers knew they were defeated when the Federation failed to achieve a national stoppage, but continued to deny it for two more weeks against increasing odds, until, on 27 June, the executive of the Federation ordered the men to return to work. The effect of this severe defeat was to bring home

---

[1] For a full account of this strike see Watney, C., and Little, J. A., *Industrial Warfare and its Aims*; Dangerfield, George, *The Strange Death of Liberal England*.

to many trade unionists the limitations of the strike weapon, but it did not shake the confidence of the militants, who continued to preach bigger strikes as the one certain road to success.[1]

Following the great railway strike of 1911 the Government, at a loss to know how to cope with industrial unrest on the scale it was then experiencing, decided to adopt an idea of its Chief Industrial Commissioner, Mr. George Askwith (later Lord Askwith) on whom had fallen the principal burden of conciliating the opposing sides in the great disputes of those years. This was to set up an Industrial Council composed of representatives from both sides of industry to help him in his work. The trade union representatives, all of them able, cautious, responsible individuals, were Thomas Burt, M.P., T. Ashton, general secretary of the Lancashire and Cheshire Miners' Federation, C. W. Bowerman, secretary of the T.U.C., F. Chandler, general secretary of the Amalgamated Society of Carpenters and Joiners, J. R. Clynes, M.P., Harry Gosling, secretary of the Watermen and Lightermen, Arthur Henderson, M.P., J. Hodge, M.P., W. Mosses, general secretary of the Pattern Makers' Society, W. Mullin, of the Card Room Operatives, E. L. Poulton, secretary of the Boot and Shoe Operatives, J. E. Williams, secretary of the Amalgamated Society of Railway Servants and Alexander Wilkie, M.P.

The Industrial Council was mainly a fact-finding body, and possessed no powers to intervene in a dispute unless invited by the protagonists, or, in special circumstances, by the Board of Trade. It was hoped by the Government that the trade unions and the employers would, before coming to grips in a strike or lockout, seek the advice of the Industrial Council, but this hope was vain, for both sides, when involved in a dispute, were intensely suspicious of the new body and were afraid of weakening their position. Those industries which had no representative on the Council considered themselves to be at a disadvantage, whilst others opposed it from a political point of view. When the Council failed to settle a strike in the Bristol Channel ports, and the cotton industry refused to have anything to do with it, the Government lost interest in its activities. In his autobiography, Lord Askwith pointed out the difficulty of a large body undertaking the work of industrial conciliation; 'Settlement of labour disputes requires selection of an exact moment for action, complete and speedy grasp of the real causes of the dispute and the technicalities of the points at issue, speed and experience in judging the characters, sayings, and real views of the individuals on

[1] MacDonald, J. R., "The Truth about the Transport Dispute", *Labour Leader*, 27 June 1912. This is an extremely forthright criticism of the militant policy and its weaknesses as revealed by the Transport strike.

either side, both in and out of the conference room. Committees are singularly inapt bodies for these purposes.'[1]

The most important accomplishment of the Industrial Council was an investigation into the best method of securing the fulfilment of industrial agreements, and whether they should be enforced throughout a trade or district. The Council, after holding thirty-eight meetings and examining ninety-two witnesses came to the conclusion that 'the evidence of a considerable majority of the witnesses is to the effect that agreements have, viewed generally, been fulfilled by both parties'.[2] On the second point the Council stated, 'an agreement entered into between associations of employers and of workmen, representing a substantial body of those in the trade or district should on application of the parties to the agreement, be made applicable to the whole of the trade or district concerned'.[3] Since 1940 the National Arbitration Tribunal, and thereafter the Industrial Disputes Tribunal, have been empowered to compel employers to observe recognised terms and conditions of employment. The Liberal Government, half a century ago was not, however, prepared to accept this policy. The report of the Council was ignored, and its labours went largely unnoticed by anybody. When the strike wave seemed to be over the Government 'quietly dropped it, without referring any more questions to its judgment, or maintaining its existence for possible emergencies'.[4]

Syndicalism Rejected by the T.U.C.

Although a number of prominent trade union leaders were members of the Industrial Council, it attracted no great interest from the trade unions, and was strongly criticised by the militant section of the movement. Will Thorne, who was president of the T.U.C. in 1911–12, refused to become a member, on the grounds that the Council was a device to prevent strikes, and so diminish the militancy of the workers.[5] However, the failure of the Transport Workers' Federation strike exposed the limitations of the tactics of the militants, and by the time the 1912 Congress arrived, there was a considerable change in the atmosphere. The prolonged and bitter national strike of the miners had brought the word 'syndicalism' into the news. The syndicalists had a strong hold on the miners of South Wales, and the appearance in 1912 of a pamphlet entitled *The Miners' Next Step*

[1] Askwith, Lord, *Industrial Problems and Disputes*, p. 180.
[2] *Industrial Council. Report on Enquiry into Industrial Agreements*, p. 4.
[3] *Ibid.* p. 17.
[4] Askwith, Lord, *Industrial Problems and Disputes*, p. 181.
[5] Letter from Thorne, Will, *Labour Leader*, 20 October 1911.

created something of a sensation. This pamphlet set out succinctly a policy for the miners based on the ideas which had been advocated by Tom Mann and his followers since 1910. It proposed that the miners' unions should reorganise themselves on industrial lines with a strong centralised direction of policy, the object of which would be to bring the industry to a standstill, with strike after strike, until the system of private ownership collapsed. Then the miners would take over the paralysed industry and reorganise it on the basis of workers' control. The ultimate aim of the authors was to see their lead followed by the trade unions in other industries. The final stage would be with:

> The co-ordination of all industries on a central Production Board, who, with a statistical department to ascertain the needs of the people, will issue its demands on the different departments of industry, leaving to the men themselves to determine under what conditions and how, the work should be done. This would mean real democracy in real life. . . . Any other form of democracy is a delusion and a snare.

The object of the syndicalists' attack was not only orthodox trade unionism, but also the whole concept of 'State' socialism brought about by political means. This policy invoked a sharp reaction from the socialists, who, while quite willing to support militant action both inside and outside Parliament, and the reorganisation of the trade union structure by means of amalgamations and federations, were not prepared to endorse any such indiscriminate and irresponsible programme of strike action as the one proposed. The orthodox trade union leaders were even more caustic in their criticisms of the syndicalists. Among the well-known leaders of the trade unions there were no avowed syndicalists, for the element of unreason and appeal to primitive instinct, which was a marked feature of syndicalism, generally had no attraction for the bureaucratic instincts of the established trade union leader. The danger to the unions, whose power and influence had been so laboriously built up and sustained, and the threat to their own security of office and authority, which lurked in the adoption of a policy based on revolution and violence was too obvious to be whole-heartedly accepted by any but the romantic fanatics of the Labour movement.

The Parliamentary Committee, in its annual report to the Trades Union Congress of 1912, referred to the coal strike and the Transport Federation's debacle, but made no significant comment on the strike problem or syndicalism. This was supplied by Keir Hardie in an interview given to the American socialist newspaper *Call*, and published in Britain during Congress week. Asked about syndicalism, Hardie replied, 'We have no such thing in Great Britain . . . the effect of the transport workers' strike of this year has been disastrous, and has shown more than anything else could have done the futility of trying to fight the capitalists by what are known as syndicalist methods.'[1]

Despite the publicity which the syndicalists received during the year, the waning enthusiasm for militant action was apparent at the Congress. On the opening day of the 1912 gathering, a resolution moved by J. V. Wills, a well-known advocate of militant industrial unionism, to reaffirm the principle of industrial unionism and instruct the Parliamentary Committee to inaugurate an educational campaign in support of the amalgamation of unions on industrial lines, was amended so that the part which committed the T.U.C. to supporting industrial unionism was deleted.

> The mistake our friends are making [said the delegate of the National Union of Dock Labourers, moving the amendment] is in assuming that at any time the workers of the country ought to be prepared to 'down tools' whenever someone makes a call. No more dangerous policy could be imagined than that . . . And more than that. This resolution is based on the assumption that a great national strike is bound to be successful. I venture to say that if we had had a national transport strike in recent months, we should have been beaten and smashed and sent back to work, and the organisation work of twenty years would have been lost.[2]

The amendment was carried by 1,123,000 votes to 573,000.

This resolution did not raise the question of syndicalism squarely, for there were many delegates who were not in favour of swallowing syndicalist doctrines whole, but who were in sympathy with industrial unionism and a militant policy. Support for the syndicalists was tested more fully in a resolution later in the week reaffirming the continued support of Congress for independent working-class political action, and the centralisation of social and industrial questions in the hands of the Government and local authorities. In this debate Noah Ablett, one of the authors of *The Miners' Next Step*, a delegate of the South Wales Miners, put the case for the syndicalists in a clear, hard-hitting speech. J. V. Wills criticised the Parliamentary Committee for subtly phrasing the resolution so as to avoid a direct condemnation of syndicalism and thus confusing the issue. There was some justification for this complaint, but nevertheless the delegates were well aware that they were voting for or against syndicalism. After many of the leading figures in Congress had spoken against syndicalism the debate was finally closed, and the voting revealed that the resolution had been carried by the huge majority of 1,693,000 votes to 48,000.[3] Syndicalism was dead; it had

---

[1] *Daily Herald*, September 1912.　　[2] *T.U.C. Annual Report*, 1912.　　[3] *Ibid.*

perhaps never been more than half-alive, but this was by no means
the end of the demand for industrial unionism, or of the belief that a
militant strike policy produced effective results.

The Militants found a Newspaper

During the year the militant section of the trade union movement
had obtained a new forum for their views with the publication of the
Daily Herald, which had commenced in April 1912. This venture in
Labour journalism had its origins in the scheme, referred to in the
previous chapter, which had been proposed by the London Society
of Compositors and discussed by the Trades Union Congress and
the Joint Board in 1907. The factor which precipitated the appearance
of the paper was the fight waged by the London printing trades
against the Master Printers' Association in 1911 for the forty-eight
hour week. During the stoppage the London Society of Compositors
published a four-page strike sheet to explain its case. The strike paper
appeared daily for four months until the printers gained their claims,
and its success during this time stimulated a demand for its continuance as a daily newspaper covering all aspects of the Labour movement. When the printers' struggle was drawing to its close the
publishers of the paper sought wider support for its maintenance.
Several conferences of trade union representatives were held, and
eventually a scheme, reminiscent of George Potter's when founding
the *Beehive*, was launched to raise capital by the issue of five shilling
shares. The moving spirits behind the founding of the *Daily Herald*
were H. W. Hobart and T. E. Naylor of the London Society of
Compositors, both of whom, at this time, were very close to the
syndicalists in their outlook. They were strongly supported by the
other militant members of the trade union movement, and received
encouragement from C. W. Bowerman, the secretary of the Trades
Union Congress.

Meanwhile, Ramsay MacDonald, G. H. Roberts, Clifford Allen
and other leaders of the Labour Party and the I.L.P., alarmed at the
prospect of the militant section of the Labour movement having a
daily newspaper to propagate its opinions, took steps to found a rival
newspaper that would represent the official point of view. The promoters of the *Daily Herald* approached the Parliamentary Committee
first and secured permission for one of their number to address the
delegates at the 1911 Trades Union Congress on their proposed
scheme. Soon afterwards the Labour Party Committee applied to the
Parliamentary Committee for similar permission. The Parliamentary
Committee at this stage had given no official support to either
scheme, and it suggested to Congress that representatives of both

groups should be heard. T. E. Naylor addressed the delegates on the proposed *Daily Herald*, which he said would 'represent the Trade Union Movement as such and take up an absolutely independent line in politics'. He was followed by G. H. Roberts, who outlined a more impressive and costly scheme for a newspaper to be printed in Manchester, which would be the official organ of the Labour Party. No discussion on either speech was permitted.

In the course of the following year the Parliamentary Committee accepted an invitation to be represented on the board of directors of the *Daily Herald*, but remained aloof from the Labour Party scheme. The reason for this curious behaviour was that C. W. Bowerman was sympathetic to the *Daily Herald*, having been a leading official of the London Society of Compositors for many years, and one of the originators of the abortive plan to launch a daily paper named the *Morning Herald* only a few years before.[1] Bowerman and W. Matkin, secretary of the General Union of Carpenters and Joiners, had joined the board of directors of the *Daily Herald* as representatives of the Parliamentary Committee. In addition to Bowerman's personal inclinations, a number of members of the Parliamentary Committee were sceptical of the possibility of maintaining two daily Labour newspapers, and were inclined to give the *Daily Herald* support since it was actually in existence from early in 1912, whereas the official Labour Party paper was still in the process of gestation.

The failure of the Parliamentary Committee to support the Labour Party paper led to a good deal of ill-feeling, and a rather tart correspondence took place between Bowerman and Clifford Allen, secretary of the company set up to publish the official paper. At the 1912 Trades Union Congress the Parliamentary Committee were extremely uncomfortable at finding themselves in a position where they had to defend their support of a newspaper that was advocating extreme policies, and criticising the official leadership of the Labour movement. Bowerman explained that the sole reason why the Parliamentary Committee had not appointed representatives to the board of the *Daily Citizen*, the name chosen for the official paper, was that no invitation had been received; but this excuse sounded too obviously disingenuous to be convincing. Some strong words about the attitude of the Parliamentary Committee had been uttered at the Labour Party Conference, earlier in the year, and Ramsay Mac-Donald, who was fraternal delegate from the Labour Party said to the delegates at the Trades Union Congress 'I am not afraid to say to you that the *Daily Citizen* is going to be the official organ of the Labour Party. You are not going to have your Labour Party

[1] Cf. Chapter VI, p. 229.

criticised, inspired, and interpreted to the great masses of Labour by any sectional production.' Facing a barrage of criticism, the Parliamentary Committee protested its neutrality between the two newspapers, insisted that they were fully prepared to support the *Daily Citizen* as soon as it appeared, and urged every trade union to give it support. The fact, however, that the *Daily Herald* had been on sale since the previous April, and that it was not yet certain when the *Daily Citizen* would appear, somewhat diminished the strength of the attack on the Parliamentary Committee.[1]

During the next year a national conference, presided over by the chairman of the Parliamentary Committee, W. J. Davis, in support of the *Daily Citizen*, was held, and as a result £70,000 was raised. By the 1913 Trades Union Congress the Parliamentary Committee had abandoned support of the *Daily Herald*, which, already short of funds, had found it necessary to reduce its size from a large page newspaper to one only half as big. With the change in format came a bigger change in style and content. The *Herald* had started by giving a wide coverage to general news of interest to Labour readers, but it became more and more a propaganda journal, concentrating on articles by syndicalists, guild socialists, distributist individualists and militant socialists, usually written in a virulent tone.[2] The *Daily Citizen*, when it appeared in 1913, was orthodox in its format, resembling the other national dailies, and orthodox in its politics, supporting the trade unions in their day to day struggles and the policies of the Labour Party, but containing little that was intellectually stimulating.

The Trade Union Act of 1913

The outburst of strike activity and the advocacy of militant revolutionary tactics, which were in part a consequence of the weakness of the Labour Party, had distracted attention from the need to secure legislation to reverse the effects of the Osborne Judgment. The introduction of State salaries for members of

[1] The *Daily Herald* came out for the first time during the week that the *Titanic* was sunk in collision with an iceberg, with an appalling loss of life. For weeks it ran a great campaign denouncing the saving of first-class passengers at the expense of women and children travelling steerage, for whom there were not enough lifeboats, and of whom many were drowned. The sustained pressure of the *Herald* was undoubtedly the factor mainly responsible for forcing an inquiry into the disaster.

[2] The *Daily Herald* had a succession of editors until George Lansbury took over the responsibility in 1913. It was largely due to his personality that the *Herald* survived; it was aptly called 'the miracle of Fleet Street'. Cf. Lansbury, George, *My Life*, p. 172; Postgate, Raymond, *The Life of George Lansbury*.

Parliament, in 1911, of which the Labour movement had long been in favour, was a concession to the Labour Party, prompted by the difficult situation in which it had been placed. No doubt Asquith had in mind the hope that this innovation would satisfy the more moderate trade union leaders, and at least would enable him to avoid freeing the trade unions entirely from the political restrictions imposed upon them. The 1911 Trades Union Congress made it quite clear that the trade union movement was not going to sell its freedom to engage in political activities for a salary of £400 per year paid to its representatives in Parliament, as some newspapers suggested was the case.[1]

The Liberal government, as a result of continued pressure, introduced a Trade Union Bill to the House in the same session; the Bill gave the trade unions certain limited rights to spend their funds on political objects, but did not restore the pre-Osborne situation. As a result the Trades Union Congress voted unanimously in favour of a resolution instructing the Parliamentary Committee to oppose the Bill strenuously, and the same resolution was again carried in 1912. The Government made little effort to push the Bill through until 1913, when, in spite of its clear instruction to resist its passage, the Parliamentary Committee supported the Labour members in their efforts to improve the Bill by amendments; the Committee later called a special conference of trade union representatives which endorsed this action.[2] One factor which induced this change of policy was the fear that had been aroused in trade union circles by the anti-union activities of the employers and of the Conservatives. The employers had communicated with the Prime Minister, asking for severe legal restrictions on the trade unions, and Lord Robert Cecil had introduced a Bill into the House of Lords which would have crippled the trade unions had it passed. The Bill sought to restore the Taff Vale decision; to again make trade unions liable for damages for procuring breaches of contract; and to restrict picketing to two persons, each of whom would have to wear a badge and not be permitted to use 'peaceful persuasion', which henceforth would become an offence.[3] Moreover, attempts were made by the Conservatives on the committee stage of the Trade Union Bill to introduce these same hated proposals into it by amendments. In its annual report for 1912 the G.F.T.U. stated that 'During the year the enemies of the Trade Union movement have never ceased their efforts to increase the legal disabilities under which the unions suffer. Chambers of Commerce, benches of magistrates and employers'

[1] *Sheffield Daily Telegraph*, 4 September 1911.
[2] *The Times*, 4 January 1913.
[3] *Trade Disputes Law (Amendment) Bill*, Parliamentary Papers, 1912–13, vol. v.

associations have pressed continuously for legislation having this
end in view.'[1] Many of those who previously would have accepted
nothing less than a full restoration of freedom to undertake political
activities were now prepared to put up with the limitations which the
Government's Bill imposed, for it at least gave the trade union
movement the chance to use its financial resources to fight the
Conservatives in the political field.

The Trade Union Act of 1913, when finally passed, permitted
unions to engage in political activities providing that they first took a
ballot of their members and secured a majority in favour of establishing such activities as an object of the union, set up a separate
political fund and allowed members to 'contract out' from paying
contributions to it without incurring any disability or disadvantage
from so doing. At the 1913 Trades Union Congress a resolution was
moved by W. E. Harvey, one of the leaders of the M.F.G.B., calling
on all trade unionists to vote in favour of political activities in the
ballots that would soon be held under the Act. T. E. Naylor, John
Bromley and James Stokes, a member of the Glass Blowers' Union,
assailed the Parliamentary Committee and the Labour members for
accepting the Act. Stokes said that he was a socialist, but he did not
believe there were many socialists in the trade union movement.

> That is rather a bold thing to say, perhaps, but I do know, with respect
> to the great number of men who are organised in the mining, cotton and
> engineering industries, that when we ask for a straight Labour vote, as
> we have done in recent Parliamentary by-elections we do not get it.
> When it comes to a vote which would be a straight one for direct political
> representation of the kind the Socialists advocate we never get it. It is the
> Liberal expression of opinion that comes from the Trades Union
> Congress.[2]

There was much truth in these observations, and this was admitted
by J. R. Clynes, who put the official point of view of the Labour
Party and Parliamentary Committee. He stated

> There is the foolish impression that this Bill was offered to us by the
> Liberal government. The reverse is the case. This Act represents the most
> we could extract from them. They would have been glad if we had
> rejected it. So would the Tories have been glad also. It was the utmost
> measure of freedom we were able to secure.[3] [Clynes went on to say]
> It would appear to the Syndicalist that the Labour Party is lacking in
> its duty if it is not a Syndicalist Party; the Suffragists again think we
> must put forward the women's claim to the vote; and there is another
> section of the community which thinks we ought above all to demand
> the land for the people. To the Socialists and all the extremists, we are

[1] *G.F.T.U. Annual Report*, 1912   [2] *T.U.C. Annual Report*, 1913.   [3] *Ibid.*

of no use unless we specially represent them. But to all these people we have but one answer to give. We say, 'Whatever you are pleased to call us, we are the Labour Party.' We are seeking to combine all the differences into one harmonious whole, bringing the Liberal, the Tory and others along with us, and making the best of our opportunities.[1]

This was the authentic voice of the British Labour movement, moderating the extremes, ready to compromise, refusing to be bound by theories and, in the tradition of British political institutions, not troubled by inconsistency as to principle, but prepared to make a virtue out of necessity if that satisfied practical needs and ameliorated conflicting social pressures. In 1913 socialism and syndicalism had already profoundly influenced the British Labour movement, but both doctrines were in the process of being absorbed and blended with Liberal and Conservative strains already deeply ingrained in the trade union movement, to produce a distinctive philosophy and policy in harmony with the aspirations of the working class which desired something of all these creeds.

Further Attempts to Achieve Closer Unity

The advocates of amalgamation and industrial unionism had a notable success in 1913, with the culmination of a long series of negotiations in the formation of the National Union of Railwaymen out of three of the unions concerned with the organisation of manual workers on the railways. In spite of the failure which had attended the negotiations taking place in a number of other industries to reduce the number of competing unions, the achievement of the railwaymen encouraged the supporters of industrial unionism and closer unity to increase their efforts. In fact, however, it was only a partial success, as the Associated Society of Locomotive Engineers and Firemen, and the Railway Clerks' Association remained aloof.

Another attempt was made at the 1913 Congress to widen the scope of the work of the T.U.C. in the interest of more effective organisation, but the proposal met with defeat. It had been suggested by the National Labourers' Union that the standing orders should be amended to permit Congress to establish an industrial committee, which would have the duties of conducting a statistical department, investigating and suggesting schemes to cut out overlapping unions, to inquire into wages and working conditions, and to assist organisation by carrying on propaganda, especially among agricultural and women workers. This resolution met with opposition from most sections of Congress. It was damned by the venerable

[1] *Ibid.*

president, W. J. Davis—quite improperly from the chair—before the debate began, with a sarcastic reference to the cost of carrying it out. It was opposed by the craft unions and by the large unions, which had no desire to see the T.U.C. exercise such far-reaching authority over their organisations; and it was not approved by the members of the Parliamentary Committee, who did not relish the prospect of a rival committee. Though much lip-service was paid to the need for a greater degree of centralisation, when it came to the actual business of giving the 'platform' more power, some excuse for avoiding it was usually found. Even attempts to reduce the number of resolutions on the agenda at Congress met with strong opposition, in spite of the fact that only half the resolutions were dealt with each year. At the previous Congress a resolution had been moved to exclude from the agenda any resolution which had been carried at three successive Congresses, for a period of three years. This sensible proposal was urgently needed, for many of the items which came up for discussion, year after year, were of a purely sectional character, and other items of a more general interest were often squeezed out for lack of time, or, what was perhaps worse, disposed of without adequate consideration. However, delegate after delegate rose to say more or less that the main value of the Trades Union Congress for the smaller trade unions was its use as a platform from which some national publicity might be gained and sympathy elicited for their particular griev-ances. Intense suspicion was displayed during the debate that the resolution was a trick through which the large organisations would be able to monopolise the subjects discussed at Congress, to the disad-vantage of the smaller unions. In spite of the opposition of the small craft unions, the miners, for reasons of their own, decided to cast their vote against the resolution, which they described as reactionary. The resolution was easily defeated, and Congress continued to spend a great deal of its time listening to the same arguments year after year, proving that 'dicky straps, skid pans and brakes' ought to be enforced by statute, and that taxi-cabs ought to have free access to Hyde Park.

During 1912 overtures for closer unity in the Labour movement came from an unexpected quarter. The Co-operative Union proposed to the Parliamentary Committee, and to the executive committee of the Labour Party, that a joint conference should be held between representatives of the three organisations to consider how best they could help one another. For many years the relations between the Co-operative movement and the trade union movement had been coloured by the constant state of warfare between Co-operative societies and the trade unions which organised their employees. The joint committee of the Co-operative Union and the Parliamentary

Committee, which had been in existence for twenty years, had done excellent work in the settlement of disputes between trade unions and the Co-operative societies, but its terms of reference did not permit the Committee to consider matters of a wider interest.[1] At the invitation of the Co-operative Union the conference was held in Manchester on the 8 February 1913. After an exploratory discussion the conference was adjourned until the 30 May. When it met again the Parliamentary Committee submitted the following proposals:

1. That we recommend the co-operative movement to deduct from dividends the entrance fee, so that a larger number of poorly paid labourers may be enabled to secure the advantages of the movement.

2. That when any meetings are being convened by any of the three bodies for propaganda work, each should notify the other and ask for support.

3. That in the case of any strike any union may approach the local co-operative society to issue food tickets on union assets, assuming that such assets are invested, thereby obviating the necessity of realising at once, which would probably involve the union in a serious loss.

4. That provided an Advisory Committee be appointed, it shall have movable meetings with a view of utilising such meetings for propaganda for each section concerned.

5. That we recommend that increased facilities in banking should be provided through the various stores in the country, so that cheques presented by Trades Unions could be presented at a later time than that now allowed by ordinary banks.[2]

The delegates from the Co-operative Union were unable to commit themselves to any of these proposals until they had been submitted to the Co-operative Congress. There was no further meeting between the three organisations before the outbreak of the war, for the Co-operative Congress turned down the resolution on the question of 'co-operation with other forces', primarily on the grounds that it would be unwise for the Co-operative movement to become embroiled in political activities. The ideas contained in the proposals of the T.U.C. continued to excite interest, however, and in the next few years were much discussed in trade union circles.

The refusal of the Parliamentary Committee to go further than associate itself with such modest proposals for strengthening the trade union movement as those recounted above, incited some of its militant critics to denounce it for failing to give a more vigorous lead. Others, who thought the T.U.C. and its Parliamentary Committee had outlived their usefulness, feared the possibility of their taking on a new lease of life, and remaining a stumbling-block to a wholesale revision of the structure of the trade union movement. Among

[1] See Chapter V.   [2] *T.U.C. Annual Report*, 1913.

the latter were G. D. H. Cole and William Mellor, both ardent supporters of 'greater unionism' and syndicalist in outlook. In 1913 they wrote,

There are at present three bodies professing to co-ordinate the Labour Movement. The Labour Party is purely political, the General Federation purely industrial, and the T.U.C. a highly academic body—a debating society rather than a legislative assembly. Its Parliamentary Committee formed mainly to carry on the work that is now done by the Labour Party has of late shown a desire to launch out on the industrial side, and to encroach on the sphere of the General Federation. The existence of such an ill-defined body is a source of weakness to the Labour Movement and the Parliamentary Committee must hand over its work and powers to other bodies more fitted for the task. All the unions must come into the General Federation. These are the only lines upon which the fusion of the two bodies can produce satisfactory results. We should then approximate to the position of Germany; the Labour Party corresponding to the Social Democratic Party, and the reformed General Federation to the central organisation of the German Trade Unions. In fact industrial solidarity cannot be realised without central direction. The work of organising the unorganised must be paid for and controlled by the trade unions as a whole, through the General Federation. Its demonstrations in the great centres are already doing a little, but it is hampered for lack of funds and there has been in this country no sort of organised trade union propaganda. Germany is so well organised because its movement has spread from the centre outwards, and has been inspired by consistent policy and a deliberate aim. The trade union muddle here results from the entire absence of central direction. This centralisation must come, and the only way is by means of the General Federation.[1]

G. D. H. Cole and William Mellor were not the only ones to be impressed by the German Labour movement; it also impressed the Webbs, and the leaders of the T.U.C. were full of envy and admiration. The Parliamentary Committee of the T.U.C. published lengthy accounts of the organisation and policy of the German trade unions in the years before 1914. Ironically the first fraternal delegate from Germany was present at the Trades Union Congress of 1913, where he was received with the greatest enthusiasm, and tributes to German efficiency in achieving such a large membership were showered on him. The German trade union movement was the most bureaucratic in Europe,[2] but the militant critics of the trade union leaders in Britain were probably ignorant of this fact when they advocated that the German trade union movement should be emulated here.

[1] Cole, G. D. H., and Mellor, William, *The Greater Unionism*.
[2] Michels, Robert, *Political Parties*, Ed. 1949, The Free Press, Illinois.

Opposition to the General Federation of Trade Unions

The Cole and Mellor scheme for the reorganisation of the British Labour movement had little hope of success, for apart from the fact that it emanated from a quarter that was suspect to a great many trade unionists, there was a growing feeling among members of the Parliamentary Committee that the activities of the G.F.T.U. constituted a threat to the supremacy of the T.U.C. as the national representative authority of the trade union movement. This change in attitude on the part of the Parliamentary Committee was, perhaps, seen most clearly in the sphere of international trade union affairs. Up to 1899, the Parliamentary Committee had, from time to time, dabbled, often rather distastefully, in the international Labour movement. After the formation of the G.F.T.U. in 1899, the Parliamentary Committee left representation of the British trade union movement abroad to the G.F.T.U., although it continued to exchange fraternal delegates with the American Federation of Labour, an arrangement which it had commenced in 1894. In 1913 the Parliamentary Committee began to change its policy, but it was not until after the end of the First World War that the G.F.T.U. ceased entirely to represent the British trade union movement at international trade union gatherings.

A loose international trade union organisation had been founded in 1901, largely through the efforts of the G.F.T.U., and the Scandinavian and German trade union movements, which was known as the International Conference of Trade Union Secretaries. Its title was changed and the organisation put on to a more formal basis at a conference held in Zürich in 1913, to which the Parliamentary Committee as well as the G.F.T.U. sent a representative.[1] A further manifestation of the growing interest of the Parliamentary Committee in international trade unionism was seen in the presence of fraternal delegates, at the 1913 Trades Union Congress, from the Canadian Congress of Labour, the French Confédération Général du Travail, and the German Trade Union Federation, as well as from the American Federation of Labour. Moreover, the Parliamentary Committee reciprocated these visits by sending fraternal delegates in return.

The continued propaganda for a more positive central direction of the trade union movement was one of the factors which induced this new attitude on the part of the Parliamentary Committee, but it was also influenced by the hostility of some of the larger unions towards

[1] Price, John, *The International Labour Movement*, Royal Institute of International Affairs, p. 19; Sassenbach, J., *Twenty-Five Years of International Trade Unionism*, I.F.T.U., Amsterdam, 1926.

the G.F.T.U. The Miners' Federation of Great Britain, in particular, was opposed to the General Federation of Trade Unions. This hostility came to a head in 1913 when a dispute broke out between the two organisations. In January of that year the National Amalgamated Union of Labour charged the M.F.G.B. with 'poaching' members and of 'blacklegging' by placing members of the M.F.G.B. in jobs that were vacant because the members of the Labourers' union were on strike—one of the most heinous crimes in the trade union calendar. The N.A.U.L., an affiliate of the G.F.T.U., reported these charges to the Management Committee of that organisation and requested its help. The Management Committee, having received this request, set up a sub-committee, as it was entitled to do under its constitution, then presented its report to the M.F.G.B. and asked that body for its comments. The Miners' Federation, which had refused to give the sub-committee any assistance when it was making its inquiries, refused to accept the report or the right of the G.F.T.U. to intervene in any way, whereupon the G.F.T.U. submitted the whole matter to the Joint Board. The Joint Board summoned the M.F.G.B. to give its answer to the charges, but the Miners' Federation refused to accept the jurisdiction of the Joint Board. The Parliamentary Committee, as a section of the Joint Board, followed its normal practice, and published the minutes of the Joint Board, including an account of this dispute, in its annual report in 1913. After the report had been presented to Congress, Robert Smillie, on behalf of the M.F.G.B., moved the deletion of these references, asserting that the Joint Board had never been officially recognised by the T.U.C., a contention that was obviously nonsensical to all but the miners' delegates. In the debate which followed, the Miners' Federation was sharply criticised for attempting to crush the smaller union by undemocratic tactics, and it was pointed out that the T.U.C. had been accepting the reports of the Joint Board since 1906, and that the M.F.G.B. had never questioned this procedure before. On a show of hands, the resolution for the deletion of the minutes relating to the work of the Joint Board was lost by 134 to 284.

From this time onwards the Miners' Federation displayed a bitter hatred of the General Federation of Trade Unions, and refused to be associated with the work of the Joint Board while the G.F.T.U. was part of that body. The basis of this intense dislike of the G.F.T.U. was the realisation by the miners, who were strong supporters of industrial unionism, that the G.F.T.U. not only assisted the small unions financially through its strike insurance fund, but that it was powerful enough to deter the large unions from indulging in unrestrained predatory activities, and that it had also become a centre of craft union conservatism. Moreover, the M.F.G.B., which was approaching the G.F.T.U. in size and strength, was jealous of the status of the latter body in the national councils of the Labour movement. Towards the end of 1913 the M.F.G.B. suggested to the Parliamentary Committee that the Joint Board should be reconstituted so as to be composed in future of the Parliamentary Committee and the Labour Party executive only. The Parliamentary Committee asked the miners to send a deputation to meet them and discuss the whole question. This suggestion was accepted, and the meeting with the Parliamentary Committee took place on the 3 September 1914. The miners' representatives suggested that the presence of the G.F.T.U. on the Joint Board was an anomaly and stated they 'felt that the Trades Union Congress Parliamentary Committee represented the British Trade Union movement, and that the Labour Party represented the political side of the Labour movement, and that a joint committee should exist which could be called together in a time of crisis, in order to decide on a common action'.[1]

Pressure from the Miners' Federation, and other large unions, eventually persuaded the Parliamentary Committee to seek a change in the constitution of the Joint Board. The failure of the G.F.T.U. to induce all of its member unions to pay their share of the levy which had been imposed on all unions to fight the Osborne Case, provided a convenient excuse to raise the question of the competence of the General Federation to be a part of the Joint Board. After a special meeting of the Joint Board, held early in 1915 to discuss its reconstitution, it was agreed

> That the composition of the Joint Board remain as at present, that its functions be confined to consultative and advisory purposes, and that new machinery be set up for the purpose of settling disputes, to be composed of Trade Union representatives only, and that a Sub-Committee be appointed to indicate in what way the constitution should be altered.[2]

The Dublin Transport Strike and its Consequences

The attention of delegates to the 1913 Trades Union Congress was distracted from their normal conduct of business by events taking place in Dublin, where James Larkin and his Irish Transport and General Workers' Union were locked in combat with the employers, led by W. M. Murphy, the formidable owner of the Dublin tramways. Larkin, who was an agitator of genius, had used the lightning strike and secondary boycott with great effect, but had suddenly found himself confronted by the Dublin employers, determined to smash his

---

[1] *Report of the Parliamentary Committee*, 1914.
[2] *Minutes of the Joint Board*, 6 May 1915.

union and put an end to these tactics. The strike had been precipitated by Murphy threatening to dismiss every member of the
Transport Workers' Union in his employ, giving Larkin little choice
but to accept the challenge and call out his members on strike,
or to suffer a severe blow to his prestige.

As the Trades Union Congress opened at Manchester, on 3 September, the newspapers were filled with the story of a violent police
charge which had resulted in bloodshed among assembled strikers
waiting in O'Connell Street to hear Larkin speak. The delegates to
Congress were already in a frame of mind to be easily aroused by
such news. Only a few weeks before, the indignation of the British
Labour movement had been intense at the news of the suppression of
a general strike on the Rand by the police shooting down the strikers.
At the outset of Congress the president read a telegram received
from the Dublin Trades Council appealing for the help of the T.U.C.
The anger of the delegates was soon running at fever pitch, and it was
decided to send a delegation immediately to Dublin to intercede
with the authorities to prevent the repetition of brutal behaviour
by the police, and to try to settle the strike through mediation. For
the first time in these stormy years of industrial unrest the Trades
Union Congress found itself involved directly in a major dispute.

The delegation from the T.U.C. eventually reported failure in its
attempt to bring about a settlement, but the T.U.C. Parliamentary
Committee could not easily extricate itself from an awkward situation, in which it was now committed to supporting the irresponsible
policy of Mr. Larkin. Continuing its efforts to bring the strike to an
end, the Committee launched an appeal for funds to help the strikers
and their families, and over £60,000 were soon subscribed. Meanwhile, in conjunction with the Co-operative Wholesale Society, the
Committee chartered a ship and sent it to Dublin loaded with food
for the starving strikers. Having failed to settle the issue, the Parliamentary Committee handed its responsibility over to the Joint Board,
in December 1913.[1] Repeated delegations to Dublin and several
conferences arranged by the Joint Board came to naught, and eventually the Board had also to report its failure. The strike simmered on
well into 1914, but gradually petered out as the men drifted back to
work.

Although the Parliamentary Committee had been pushed into
supporting this strike by the emotion of the delegates at Congress, it
had acted vigorously and with well-defined purpose. Its interference
did not, however, inspire any thanks from Larkin, who seized the
opportunity to come to Britain and stimulate a number of senseless
sympathetic strikes which rapidly fizzled out, whilst at the same time

[1] *T.U.C. Annual Report*, 1913.

he poured scorn and invective on the Parliamentary Committee, denouncing its members as cowards and traitors to the working class because they would not order a general strike in support of his union.

The Dublin strike raised the issue of union recognition, and a special conference called by the Parliamentary Committee on the 9 December 1913, pledged itself to maintain its support for the strikers 'to uphold the right of combination', and called on all unions to refuse to handle goods coming from or going to the firms which refused to recognise the Irish Transport and General Workers' Union. This policy did not go far enough for the leaders of the Dublin union, nor did it satisfy the militant trade unionists in Britain, but it was as far as most British trade unions were prepared to go. The success of the T.U.C. and the Joint Board in organising support for the Dublin strikers kindled belief in the possibilities of sympathetic strike action on a grand scale. But the miners and the railwaymen had little confidence in the ability or the desire of the smaller unions to sustain a common front if called upon to take part in a general strike; moreover the Miners' Federation was determined to have nothing to do with a national strike if the G.F.T.U. was concerned in it. They had, in fact, refused to be associated with the Joint Board for this reason when it was given the task of organising aid for the strikers on the Rand and in Dublin. At the special T.U.C. conference in December, Robert Smillie proposed that the miners, railwaymen and transport workers should enter into a formal alliance for the purpose of undertaking common action when any one of them should be involved in a dispute. This idea, which had been vaguely discussed during the past two or three years, was not adopted by the conference, but it received much support from the militant trade unionists, and was taken up by the three bodies immediately afterwards.

Following conversations between the leaders of these unions a delegate conference was held which set up a sub-committee to prepare a draft scheme. This was completed by June 1914, and submitted to the three organisations for their ratification. The draft proposals were to establish a joint advisory council which was to have the authority to formulate common demands and negotiate agreements which would all terminate on the same date, so that if any one of them could not secure these demands the others would not enter into separate agreements, but all would strike together in sympathy. The formulation of this scheme was extremely loose, but if the three organisations could find it possible to act in concert on this basis, it promised to be the most formidable concentration of industrial strength ever achieved by the trade union movement. Between them, the three industries employed over two million workers, and all of them were highly organised; however, before the scheme could be officially adopted Britain found herself at war, and the whole situation was radically changed.

One effect of the Dublin strike was to recrystallise the antagonism between the orthodox trade unionists and the advocates of militant strike action at any cost. Flagging support for syndicalist ideas was whipped up by excited meetings, and by bellicose articles in the *Daily Herald* and elsewhere, in support of the Dublin strikers. The Irish workers were depicted as being in the vanguard of a mighty struggle between capital and labour that might at any moment burst into open battle all over Britain. It was partly out of the fear that unless the trade union executives themselves took the lead they would be supplanted from below by unofficial leaders more in touch with the sentiments of the rank and file, that the official leaders of the miners, railwaymen and transport workers formed the Triple Alliance. Men like Robert Smillie, J. H. Thomas and J. Havelock Wilson were no more prepared to tolerate unofficial movements inside their own organisations than were the most conservative leaders of the craft unions, but they had to take account of the sentiments of their members. Nor were they all revolutionaries, in the sense that they sought to overthrow the existing structure of society by means of a general strike. Though Smillie was moving that way, the leaders of the other unions did not look so far ahead or think in the philosophic terms of the handful of genuine syndicalists who wanted consciously to bring about a general strike for revolutionary reasons. Nevertheless, the fact of setting up the Triple Alliance, in conjunction with the atmosphere created by the Dublin strike, did much to nurture a belief that one day the general strike would come, and that, when it did arrive, the power of the employing class would be broken. It was widely suggested by the militant propagandists that the workers of Dublin only went down to defeat because of the failure of the British trade union movement to follow the lead that had been given to it. The solidarity and fervour aroused were used to exemplify what might be achieved if next time there were greater unity of action, and the news of the formation of the Triple Alliance was received with elation by the militants. The general strike myth, which was revived in these years, took deep root and was not dissipated until it was tried many years later.

In the summer of 1914, all the signs pointed to the trade union movement soon becoming involved again in a gigantic clash with the employers.[1] Unemployment was rising and with it the temperature

[1] Askwith, Lord, *Industrial Problems and Disputes*, p. 349. 'Within a comparatively short time there may be movements in this country coming to a head of which recent events have been a small foreshadowing.'

of discontent. 'Wait till autumn', was the current phrase;[1] wait until the Triple Alliance was ready to make its demands and back them up by a co-ordinated stoppage of work in three vital industries. The Parliamentary Committee, throughout the stormy years through which it had passed, had maintained its traditional role of providing cautious, responsible and constructive leadership to the trade union movement. Its position had remained practically unshaken despite the powerful intellectual attack made on it by the militant advocates of a syndicalist form of society. The Triple Alliance was, however, the most powerful threat to the supremacy of the Parliamentary Committee yet to appear, and supporters of the Committee must have been as alarmed at the prospect ahead as the Government, which was feverishly making preparations to meet the threatened clash.[2] The Triple Alliance had the power to dominate Congress, and the Parliamentary Committee was in danger of finding itself relegated to playing a subordinate role. This challenge to the Parliamentary Committee never came, for before Congress could meet the nation was at war, and the trade unions had new problems to face.

[1] *Ibid.*, p. 356.
[2] Childs, Major-General Sir Wyndham, *Episodes and Reflections*, pp. 95, 96.

CHAPTER VIII

THE IMPACT OF WAR

The outbreak of war in Europe took the trade union movement by surprise, as it surprised almost every one in the country. The Labour Press had paid little attention to the serious tension between Austria and Serbia, and it was not until hostilities between these two countries had actually begun that there was any realisation of the danger that Britain might be involved. Right up to the moment, on 4 August, when Britain entered the war, it was believed that this calamity could be avoided.

The reluctance of the Labour movement to face up to the imminence of war was in part due to the hope and trust which all sections of it placed in the capacity of the German Social Democrats and trade unionists to deter their Government from joining in the conflict. It was a bitter disappointment when the most powerful Labour movement on the Continent, after a few feeble protests, gave its support to the military adventure embarked upon by the Kaiser and his ministers. German delegates, who had boasted of the strength and unity of their movement, had much impressed British Labour leaders, and convinced them that it would be a bulwark of peace.

The attention of the British Labour movement had been distracted from the portentous developments in Eastern Europe by the Ulster rebellion and the suppression, by force of arms, of gun-running in Southern Ireland, which was looked upon as iniquitous, in view of the Government's toleration of Carson's armed volunteers. The atmosphere at home was clouded by industrial strife and laden with the threat of further storms. Union after union had been engaged, during the summer of 1914, in industrial disputes, and the Triple Alliance was busily preparing for its first great clash with the employers, which was expected to come when the railway unions moved for a fresh agreement with the railway companies later in the year.

The reaction of the entire Labour movement to the news of the outbreak of war between Austria and Serbia was that Britain should not be dragged into a European conflict, but should remain neutral and play the part of peacemaker. From 1911 there had been a suspicion that Britain was pledged to the support of France and Russia should those two countries find themselves engaged in hostilities, but the Foreign Secretary, Sir Edward Grey, and the

Prime Minister, had both told the House of Commons, in categorical terms, that Britain was not under any such obligation. The Labour movement was strongly opposed to the foreign policy of the Government, because it was anti-German and involved the support of autocratic Czarist Russia.[1] Despite the truculent attitude of the Kaiser in the years prior to 1914, faith in the pacific intentions of Germany remained strong in the Labour movement; a few, notably Robert Blatchford, warned that this was a mistake, but these warnings went unheeded. Hatred of the Russian Government was intense, and year after year the Trades Union Congress had protested at the brutal suppression of the trade unions by the Czar. In 1906 a fund had been set up by Congress to assist Russian workers and peasants in their struggle for freedom; and as recently as 1912 the president of the T.U.C. had formally moved a resolution, expressing the sympathy of the British trade unions with the struggle of the workers in Russia, which had been carried unanimously by Congress. The British Labour movement was against any alliance with a Government which it regarded as the most barbarous in Europe, and was outraged at the thought that Britain might be committed by a secret agreement that was directed against Germany, with its mighty Labour movement.

On 2 August, as destiny was rapidly deciding that there was to be no escape for Britain from the war that was spreading across Europe, great crowds of workers gathered in Trafalgar Square and in the main towns and cities, to hear leaders of the Labour movement urge them to stand together against militarism for peace. At this stage it was still believed that 'The Government of Britain should rigidly decline to engage in war, but should confine itself to efforts to bring about peace as speedily as possible.'[2] On the following Monday afternoon Sir Edward Grey gave a moving and sombre account of the international situation to the House of Commons, informing it, and the country that, unless Germany halted its intentions, Britain was inexorably committed to come to the aid of the other Entente powers. Ramsay MacDonald and Keir Hardie both opposed the decision of the Government, but by the following morning they no longer represented the views of the mass of the Labour movement. The unprovoked violation of Belgium by the German armies was a fact before which criticism of Grey's foreign policy no longer appeared significant. That was of the past; the task now was to stop the aggressor.

On the 5 August, the day after war was declared, representatives of the Parliamentary Committee were present at a hastily summoned conference held in the House of Commons. This conference had

[1] See the resolution carried at the Labour Party Conference in 1912.
[2] Resolution passed at the Trafalgar Square meeting on 2 August 1914.

been called over the weekend by Bowerman and Henderson, with the object of framing a policy to try to arrest the swift onrush towards war. When the representatives of the various sections of the Labour movement which had been invited to this conference met, war was already a fact. The conference thereupon decided to establish a 'War Emergency Workers' National Committee'—representative of the whole Labour movement—which would have the responsibility of shielding the workers from the economic impact of the war.[1] It was generally believed that the national economy would be dislocated, and that this would give rise to serious unemployment, and consequently bring severe hardship to many thousands of workers who would be suddenly deprived of their jobs.

On the 7 August the Labour Party issued a statement in support of the conclusions of the House of Commons conference, and on the same day Ramsay MacDonald resigned from his position as leader of the Party; Arthur Henderson, the trade unionist politician, was elected in his place. Although the Labour Party statement was rather equivocal in its attitude towards the Government, MacDonald's resignation clarified the Party's position, for Henderson saw clearly that the Labour movement must contribute its share to the winning of the war. The I.L.P. as a whole was firmly in support of MacDonald and Hardie in their opposition to Britain's participation in the war, but the trade unions and the great mass of workers ranged themselves solidly behind Henderson. Up to this stage the Parliamentary Committee of the T.U.C. had made no pronouncement on the war situation, but it was already known that many of its members were in support of the Government's action. The Committee did not, in fact, meet until the 12 August; it was then decided to postpone the annual meeting of Congress due to open on the 7 September. No statement of the attitude of the Committee towards the war was issued, but it was agreed to prepare a manifesto for consideration at the next meeting of the Committee, which was arranged for the 2 September.

The readiness of the Parliamentary Committee to make the maximum contribution to the winning of the war became apparent when, on the 24 August, the Joint Board met and agreed to urge every union to make an immediate effort to terminate all existing trade disputes; it recommended that for the duration of the war everything should be done to arrive at an amicable settlement of disputes without resorting to a stoppage of work. There were those who were highly critical of the Parliamentary Committee for calling an industrial truce without asking for concessions from the employers

[1] See Cole, G. D. H., *Labour in Wartime*, for an account of the work done by this Committee.

and the Government, but this view did not deter the leaders of the unions from loyally following the course called for by the Parliamentary Committee and the Joint Board.[1]

After three weeks of war it looked as if the worst fears of the trade unions would be justified, for something of a panic seized the business community, contracts were cancelled and men were laid off in large numbers. This sudden increase in unemployment threw a severe strain on those trade unions which paid unemployment benefits, and they feared that their funds would be rapidly depleted. The Joint Board requested the Government to alleviate this situation by granting a subsidy to the unions paying unemployment benefit. If such help were granted, it was recommended to the unions, by the Joint Board, that they should exempt members who joined the armed forces from contributions, thus maintaining their membership; in addition it urged the unions to make liberal donations to the national relief fund which had been established by the Prince of Wales. A deputation from the Joint Board waited upon the Prime Minister with these proposals, but the Government was reluctant to accept them; however, after six weeks' delay a modified version of the Joint Board's proposals was introduced. The financial help offered by the Government was, unfortunately for the unions, so hedged in by restrictions that only a few organisations were able or willing to take advantage of it. The scheme, in fact, came too late, for business was already returning to normal, and, as the demand for labour in the war industries began to grow, unemployment began to disappear. In May of the following year, only six months after the subsidy scheme commenced, the Board of Trade announced that it would pay no more grants after the end of the month.

By the beginning of September the opinion of the Parliamentary Committee had crystallised and the day after its meeting on the 2 September, the Committee issued its first manifesto on the war situation. This document expressed the Committee's approval of the decision of the Labour Party to lend its support to the national recruiting campaign that had been launched by the Government. It went on to hint that unless voluntary recruiting was successful, the trade union movement would be faced with the prospect of having to accept conscription, to which it had long been absolutely opposed. The manifesto concluded by asserting that if men had a duty to the State, at such time as this, the State owed a duty to those who were prepared to make sacrifices in its defence, and called upon the

---

[1] 'At the beginning of August there were 100 disputes known to the Department to be in existence. At the end of the month there were twenty.' . . . 'Disputes melted away as fast as the hours of the day and often of the night.' Askwith, Lord, *Industrial Problems and Disputes*, p. 357.

Government to take a liberal and generous view of its responsibilities in looking after the dependants of its soldier citizens.[1]

The Trade Union Attitude to Production in Wartime

By the end of the year the light-hearted excitement which marked the first few weeks of hostilities had completely disappeared, and the grim realities of war had begun to impress the Government and the people. Certain commodities were becoming scarce, and the prices of essentials were rising rapidly. As complaints from the rank and file about the increasing cost of living poured in, the Labour movement began to demand that the Government should control the price of food, fuel and house rents. In addition there was much anger at the way in which national relief funds—to which the trade unions had made substantial grants—were being handled. These funds were dispensed through local committees, which were often controlled by professional charity mongers who resisted the appointment of trade union representatives, although this right had been granted. Their attitude, which was often callous and class-conscious towards the recipients of relief, aroused the wrath of the workers.

As the winter months slipped by it became increasingly obvious that the supply of labour to the essential industries was a major problem. The cutting of contracts had led to unemployment in the civilian industries, especially in cotton, which the Treasury was persuaded to subsidise in order to save the industry from collapse, while orders from the War departments piled up demands for such goods as khaki and munitions, and created a shortage of labour in these industries. An optimistic belief that the war would be of short duration deterred changes in normal practice. Following peacetime routine, there was no co-ordination between Government departments; each one pursued its own policy, and the result was mounting confusion in industry. Lack of a national industrial policy, failure to inform the public clearly of the tasks it had to perform, disasters at the front and the growing social impact of the war, combined to produce a mood of frustration in the ranks of the workers.[2] Alarmed by the deterioration of morale and the increasing need for munitions

[1] *T.U.C. Annual Report*, 1915.

[2] 'Men did not realise the coming long periods of difficulty; the necessity was not explained to them, or so far as it was explained to leaders, those leaders were pledged not to divulge the position, lest it should help the enemy. The rank and file did not and could not know, except by instinct. The whole fabric of effort rested upon spirit and faith, and with the reaction from first efforts, the winter months, the lack of information, the lack of imagination or understanding of the necessity of a long pull and a pull all together, and many disintegrating influences, faith began to fail, wrangles began, and once beginning, gained force.' Askwith, Lord, *Industrial Problems and Disputes*, p. 364.

of war, the Government appointed a Committee of Production, early in the new year, under the chairmanship of the Chief Industrial Commissioner, Sir George Askwith. The job of the Committee was to discover how labour could be better utilised in the engineering and shipbuilding works engaged on Government contracts. After consultations with the employers and the trade unions the Committee recommended that no piece-rates should be cut, and that the abandonment of trade practices during the emergency should not prejudice their restoration when the war was over; it also suggested that in the event of a dispute, instead of a stoppage of work, the matter should be referred to an impartial tribunal. The Government accepted the reports of the Committee and empowered it to deal with disputes arising under these recommendations; thus the Committee became a kind of national arbitration tribunal.

Meanwhile, as the Committee was making its reports, strikes broke out among the shipbuilding and engineering workers on the Clyde. These strikes were ostensibly over a question of differentials, but their causes lay deeper. They expressed the discontent which workers all over the country were feeling at the failure of the Government to deal vigorously with the social and economic problems arising from the war. They were also in revolt against the leadership of the unions. There was a growing feeling among many sections of the workers, fostered by anti-war militants, that the leaders of the trade unions had rushed precipitously into an industrial truce without taking steps to ensure that their members' interests were not sacrificed. Prices and profits were soaring, and certain sections of the workers were growing impatient with the efforts of the union leaders to correct abuses which became more blatantly obvious every day. The influence of the I.L.P. was extremely strong on the Clyde, and its anti-war policy had many enthusiastic canvassers, who found the engineering and shipbuilding workers receptive to the view that it was the search by capitalists for profits that had begotten the war.[1] With the official trade union leadership bound to a no-strike policy, these workers turned to their leaders in the workshops, who were of a different temper, and readily followed their advice to down tools. The Clyde dispute was eventually settled, but the unofficial committee which had conducted the strike developed into a 'shop stewards' movement' which came to have an important influence on the trade unions in the engineering and allied industries.[2]

[1] The fourth report of the Committee on Production which dealt with profits and suggested Government control of armament and shipbuilding firms, was kept secret by the Government. Askwith, Lord, p. 3.

[2] Cole, G. D. H., *Trade Unionism and Munitions*; and *Workshop Organisation*; Carnegie Series—History of the Great War.

The Government was anxious to increase the flow of munitions by persuading the trade unions to put aside their restrictive practices and, instead of resorting to strike action, to accept arbitration, as the Committee on Production had recommended. The leaders of the unions, sensitive to the mood of the rank and file, realised that if they attempted to put the recommendations of the Committee of Production—which they practically all supported—into practice, they would further undermine their authority over their members. The Parliamentary Committee of the T.U.C. was in close contact with members of the Cabinet, and it was apparently on the initiative of the trade union leaders that the Government decided to call a special conference of trade union representatives to discuss the putting into effect of the proposals of the Committee on Production.[1] The union leaders knew it would be far easier to carry the rank and file with them, if the Government put its demands to the unions for their consideration, thus leaving them free agents to bargain and not to carry the onus of responsibility for suggesting the abandonment, however temporary, of cherished trade union practices.

The Parliamentary Committee and thirty-six unions were represented at the conference which was held at the Treasury, on the 17 March, and lasted three days.[2] The proceedings were opened by a lengthy statement from Lloyd George, then Chancellor of the Exchequer, setting out the objectives of the Government. At the end of the conference an agreement was reached with all the unions, except the miners, who had withdrawn on the first day, and the Amalgamated Society of Engineers, which refused to sign the Agreement until additional guarantees had been given. The substance of the Treasury Agreement was that unions would not engage in strike action for the duration of the war, and that disputes, in all cases of failure to reach a settlement, would be referred to arbitration. An advisory committee of trade union representatives would be appointed by the Government in order to facilitate the carrying out of the Agreement. The unions signing the Agreement undertook to recommend to their members that trade customs should be relaxed, in order to permit an acceleration of output, on the following conditions: that all contractors engaged on war work would be required by the Government to observe certain safeguards; that the Government would ensure that any departures from traditional practices would be for the duration

[1] Hurwitz, S. J., *State Intervention in Great Britain*. p. 274. 'The confidential official history of the Ministry of Munitions discloses that the Treasury Agreement of March 1915, which resulted in the Treasury Agreement of the same month, was called by the Government at the instance of the trade unions.'

[2] For a discussion of the attitude of the Miners' Federation see Cole, G. D. H., *Labour in the Coalmining Industry*, Ch. II.

of the war only, and would not prejudice the restoration of those practices at the end of the war; that a record should be kept on all such changes by every establishment and be open to Government inspection; and, where unskilled or female labour was introduced, that it should not adversely affect the wage of the skilled worker. After a further meeting with the Government, the Amalgamated Society of Engineers decided to accept the Treasury Agreement, on receiving a promise that the unions would only be asked to suspend trade practices in establishments producing war supplies, and, in addition, that controls would be introduced to limit the profits of firms engaged on war production.

The Munitions of War Act

The Treasury Agreement was acclaimed on all sides; some saw it as 'opening up a great new chapter in the history of Labour in its relations with the State'. Others praised or attacked the Agreement as a check to the power of the trade unions, according to their standpoint. The Agreement was certainly evidence of the importance now attached to the trade union movement by the Government; but whatever promise it contained it was not fated to operate for long, for a few months later the Government decided to establish a system of compulsory arbitration. It could hardly be said that the Treasury Agreement had been a failure, for insufficient time had been allowed to elapse to test its value.

Responsibility for the Agreement not being properly carried out lay mainly with the Government, and primarily with Lloyd George. For months prior to the Treasury Agreement attacks had been made on the alleged behaviour of the workers; they were accused of retarding the supply of munitions through persistent bad time-keeping, drunkenness and intransigently refusing to abandon their trade practices.[1] There was nothing new in these charges; they had always been made by that section of the community which wanted a scapegoat for its own sins, but when the same theme was taken up by the Chancellor of the Exchequer it was a serious blow to those who, by signing the Treasury Agreement, were seeking to lead the trade unions along the path of loyal co-operation with the Government.[2]

The National Labour Advisory Council, over which Arthur Henderson presided, had been established to secure close liaison between the unions and the Government, and this body carefully investigated the allegations, only to find them completely unproven. When the National Labour Advisory Council urged the Government

[1] Cf. *The Times* during first few months of 1915.
[2] *House of Commons Debates*, 29 April 1915, vol. LXXI.

to enforce the provisions of the Agreement which applied to employers, and establish local machinery to put it into operation, nothing was done. The reason for Lloyd George's tactics soon became apparent; he was at that time concerned in bringing about changes in the Cabinet that would place him in control of the supply of munitions. In May 1915, Arthur Henderson was invited to become a member of the Cabinet, and junior positions were offered to G. H. Roberts and William Brace. With much misgiving, the Labour Party agreed to be represented in the first Coalition Government; a decision that was supported by the Parliamentary Committee, and later endorsed by the Trades Union Congress. At the same time a Ministry of Munitions was created which was given to Lloyd George. Soon afterwards trade union representatives were summoned to another conference at the Treasury, where they were informed that the Government had decided to take powers to settle industrial disputes by compulsion. From the sequence of events it is probable that Lloyd George had this result in mind when he negotiated the Treasury Agreement with the trade unions; he no doubt shrewdly realised that once he had obtained the voluntary agreement of the unions for the policy adopted at the Treasury meetings, it would be difficult for them to oppose the Government's action in taking powers to see that the objects of the Agreement were achieved; the more so since the Labour Party was now represented in the Government.

The Minister of Munitions, careful not to strain the loyalty of the trade unions too far, asked the National Labour Advisory Council to draft the Bill; a clever move, for it committed the Labour Party to the Bill before it came to the House of Commons. Although there was a good deal of private fear expressed at the powers to be taken by the Government, the gravity of the war situation, and the astuteness of Lloyd George had placed the trade union leaders in a position from which there was no drawing back. Only the miners and the cotton operatives expressed opposition to the Bill and, except for the efforts of one or two members of the I.L.P., no attempt was made during the passage of the Bill through Parliament to strengthen the rights of the trade unions under it. Arthur Henderson and the trade union leaders responsible for the Bill were, on the whole, satisfied that in the circumstances the measure was a reasonable one to ask the trade unions to accept, for as a *quid pro quo* the employers would not be allowed to act as they pleased. The real problem lay ahead; would the legislation be administered fairly as between capital and labour?

The main features of the Munitions of War Act were that strikes and lockouts were prohibited, unless twenty-one days' notice had been given to the Board of Trade, and unless in that period the

Board of Trade had not referred the dispute to the arbitration machinery for settlement; for this purpose the Committee on Production, Sir George Askwith's arbitration tribunal, was maintained in being. The part of the Act which aroused most fear was the section which permitted the minister to apply its provisions of compulsory arbitration to any dispute in any industry, whether engaged on direct war production or not, simply by means of a proclamation by the King. The miners realised at once that this provision was directed mainly at them, and shortly afterwards they showed their contempt for it.[1] Part Two of the Act gave the minister power to schedule any establishment, in which munitions work was carried on, as 'controlled'. In a 'controlled' establishment the level of profits was fixed by a decision of the minister; at the same time no change could be made in the level of wages, salaries or emoluments, without the consent of the minister; restrictive practices were to be given up and no workman was to be permitted to leave his employment, if he worked in a 'controlled' establishment, without first obtaining a certificate of leave.

By the end of the summer the trade union movement was by no means satisfied with the way in which the Munitions Act was being administered, and criticism of the minister was officially voiced by J. A. Seddon, in his presidential address to the Trades Union Congress, in September 1915. These strictures drew a telegram from Lloyd George, denying that he had failed to keep his promises to the trade unions, whereupon it was decided to invite the Minister of Munitions to address Congress in person. The invitation was promptly accepted, and, for the second time in his career, Lloyd George attended a gathering of the T.U.C.[2] Exercising all his oratorical skill, subtly flattering the delegates, and making a clever sally against Ramsay MacDonald, which was highly appreciated by many of his audience, Lloyd George claimed that the Government had done everything which the trade unions had asked. In return he asked them for co-operation, and urged them to put an end to their restrictive practices, citing an alleged instance of obstruction at a Coventry munitions works. The minister left Congress to a tumult of enthusiastic cheers, but by the next day the spell of the 'Welsh Wizard' had worn off, and the Parliamentary Committee was pressed to investigate his charges. These were later proved to have very little substance in them.

It was undoubtedly true that there was a good deal of opposition

---

[1] The miners of South Wales stopped work in July to enforce a claim for higher wages and the Munitions Act was invoked against them, but they remained steadfast, and despite the minister's personal intervention he was rapidly forced to concede their demands.

[2] He had addressed the T.U.C. in 1902 on the Penrhyn dispute.

to the breaking down of traditional workshop practices, but the reason for that was lack of confidence in the promised protection of the workers' interests; wild charges only served to stimulate more suspicion, which a few concrete actions on the part of the Government might have prevented.

The two main debates at the 1915 Congress were concerned with support for the war, and the question of conscription. After a lengthy discussion, in which Fred Bramley—a future secretary of the T.U.C. —was one of the very few to express any international sentiments that looked beyond the militant win-the-war patriotism uttered by most delegates, the resolution in support of the war effort was carried with only seven dissentients. There were no dissentient voices at all raised against the resolution on conscription, which was passed unanimously. It was a curious resolution, which did not bind the Parliamentary Committee to oppose conscription if it was introduced by the Government; it condemned the Press for advocating compulsory military service, and affirmed the belief of the trade unions that the voluntary system could supply all the men required for the forces if properly organised. When Clynes and Will Thorne tried to get the Parliamentary Committee to make some definite pronouncement on what its attitude would be if the Government should decide to introduce conscription, the question was evaded. Robert Smillie, who was opposed to the war, called on the trade unions to prevent conscription from being carried out if it was introduced, but other speakers were less forthright in their opposition; they condemned the principle of conscription, but contented themselves with demanding that the trade union movement should be taken into closer consultation with the Government before it ceased to rely on the voluntary system of recruitment.

Although Congress emphatically affirmed the determination of the trade union movement to support the war effort, most of the resolutions on the agenda were of the business-as-usual variety. The delegates were looking backwards, rather than forward to the post-war situation. An exception was an important addendum to a resolution on 'Women and War Service' which instructed the Parliamentary Committee to co-operate with the Labour Party in introducing a Bill into the House of Commons 'to nullify all emergency legislation curtailing individual liberty during the war to the effect that all such measures shall be void at the close of the war'.

Congress was thrown into internal controversy when the miners brought forward a resolution asking for the larger societies to be given an additional representative on the Parliamentary Committee. This raised the long-standing conflict between the large and small unions, and the issue of industrial unionism, which was now bound up with it. After a debate, in which all the usual arguments were put and several resolutions and amendments had been discussed, the delegates finally carried a resolution which permitted societies with a membership of over 500,000 to have an extra representative on the Parliamentary Committee, if elected by Congress; the resolution also proposed that Congress should return to the system of electing each member of the Parliamentary Committee by the vote of the whole Congress. A number of unions had pressed for many years before the war that members of the Committee should be elected by the groups from which they were nominated, instead of by the whole Congress, and this had been carried in 1913. The aim of the sponsors of this change had been to prevent the bartering of votes between the large societies, but it had only succeeded in turning many of the groups into pocket boroughs of the large unions which were included in them. Even in the case of the Mineworkers, now with 600,000 members, it could not be absolutely certain of the election of any of its nominees when election was on the basis of the whole Congress, but on the group system its nominees were assured of election.

The Trade Unions begin to Look to the End of the War

During the year following the 1915 Congress a change began to appear in the attitude of the trade union movement towards the war. This was brought about by a growing dissatisfaction with the conduct of the war effort and the prospect of hostilities continuing indefinitely. The determination to win was firm, but lengthening casualty lists, long hours of work and social hardship; above all the introduction of conscription for unmarried men, in January 1916, produced a growing volume of interest in peace and post-war reconstruction. When the Government announced that the recruiting scheme, carried on under the aegis of Lord Derby, in which the trade unions had participated, had failed to secure the men required, and that they intended to pass a Conscription Act, the Parliamentary Committee took no action, but the Labour Party held an emergency conference which called upon the Parliamentary Party to oppose the Bill. This led Arthur Henderson and his two Labour colleagues to hand in their resignations to the Prime Minister. The fear of the Labour Party was that military conscription would be extended to married men; that it might lead to industrial conscription, and that this might be carried on as a permanent policy when the war was over. Asquith met the executive members of the Labour Party and gave them assurances on these points, whereupon it was agreed that the resignations should be withdrawn.[1] At the National Conference of the Labour Party two

[1] Cole, G. D. H., *A History of the Labour Party from 1914.*

weeks later, the decision to participate in the Government was endorsed by a large majority while, at the same time, conscription was
condemned, but a resolution instructing the Party to agitate for the
repeal of the Conscription Act was defeated. Thus the Labour movement swallowed its opposition with a face-saving protest. Though
divided over the need to introduce military conscription, the Labour
movement was completely unanimous on the necessity of its immediate abolition at the end of the war. The 1916 Congress made no
reference to the attitude of the Parliamentary Committee over the
introduction of conscription, but it clearly instructed the Committee
'to lose no opportunity after the war to press for the repeal of all
Acts of Parliament imposing economic, industrial and military
compulsion upon the mankind of the nation, and to re-establish
individual liberty, with the right voluntarily to refrain from organised
destruction'.[1]

Early in 1916 the Parliamentary Committee had received a communication from the American Federation of Labour, which suggested that an international labour conference of delegates from
Allied, enemy and non-belligerent countries should be held at the
same time and place as any conference that might be held to settle
peace terms at the end of the war. Although misgivings had been
voiced about the need for conscription, feeling was still very strong
among the delegates that the war should be prosecuted with the
utmost energy, and when the idea was broached at the 1916 Congress
that trade unions from the enemy countries should be invited to send
representatives to an international conference to discuss with Allied
trade unionists what the attitude of the working class should be
towards the peace proposals, it aroused the strongest dissension.
Will Thorne opened the attack on the recommendation of the
Parliamentary Committee, which was in favour of co-operating with
the A.F. of L. in an international conference of the kind suggested.
Tom Shaw, one of the leaders of the Lancashire Weavers, supported
by Ernest Bevin, moved that this section of the report should be
referred back, and more concrete proposals submitted for the consideration of Congress. However, when it was proposed by one of the
delegates of the Miners' Federation that the reference should be
deleted altogether, the degree of anti-German feeling was sufficient
for the delegates to carry it by a majority of over 700,000.[2]

The anti-war attitude of the I.L.P. and the continued participation
of its leaders in the councils of the Labour Party led a number of
right-wing trade union leaders to try to persuade Congress to secure
control of the political wing of the Labour movement, by bringing it
under the authority of the Parliamentary Committee, and thus making

[1] *T.U.C. Annual Report*, 1916.   [2] *Ibid.*

it directly responsible to the T.U.C. This resolution was defeated, as was another which called upon the Parliamentary Committee to exclude representation from the Labour Party at special conferences that were arranged, from time to time, by the T.U.C. to deal with matters of urgent importance.

In spite of the fact that the policy of the I.L.P. was supported by only a small minority of the Labour movement, and aroused the anger of many, the fundamental unity of the movement was maintained throughout the war and leaders of the I.L.P. remained in intimate association with the pro-war leaders of the Labour Party and trade unions. The avoidance of any split with the I.L.P. was to be of great significance to the Labour movement in the post-war years. Much of the credit for the tolerance that was exercised at this critical time must go to Arthur Henderson,[1] and men like Tom Shaw, who although an old-fashioned trade unionist, and in whole-hearted disagreement with the I.L.P., nevertheless made a powerful plea to the delegates at Congress not to pass a resolution which would formally divorce the minority from the rest of the Labour movement, and drive men like MacDonald, Snowden, Smillie, Anderson and Jowett into the wilderness.[2]

Far less tolerance was shown on another important issue which came before the 1916 Congress. This was a resolution moved by Robert Smillie for the Miners' Federation, which called for the reconstitution of the Joint Board. This was the culmination of the campaign which the miners had been waging against the General Federation of Trade Unions.[3] The burden of Smillie's speech was that the miners were not opposed to the work the Federation was doing, but that they disagreed with the principle of duplicated membership. This argument was patently dishonest, and not the real reason for the miners' attack on the G.F.T.U., as some delegates pointed out, but the situation had now reached the stage where argument on the floor of Congress meant little, as the National Union of Railwaymen, which was against the G.F.T.U. for the same reasons as the miners, had privately agreed to support the miners' resolution and together these two huge organisations accounted for nearly one million votes. With the addition of the votes of a number of other unions, the resolution was carried, and in the month following Congress the Joint Board was reconstituted without the G.F.T.U. There was little change in the new constitution; its main functions continued to be the determination of the bona fides of any trade union applying to either the T.U.C., or the Labour Party, for

[1] Hamilton, Mary Agnes, *Arthur Henderson—A Biography*, p. 97.
[2] *T.U.C. Annual Report*, 1916.
[3] See Chapter VII, p. 264.

affiliation, the settlement of inter-union disputes, and joint action agreed to by the two organisations.

The miners' victory, though it was a triumph for the advocates of industrial unionism, finally eliminated any prospect of the G.F.T.U. playing the role that had been advocated for it by Cole and his associates before the war. It also helped to push the leaders of the G.F.T.U. into a position in which they became hostile critics of the policies subsequently adopted by the Parliamentary Committee.

The most memorable feature of the 1916 Congress was the presidential address delivered by Harry Gosling, which was outstanding in its quality. Having dealt with the immediate problems, Gosling looked ahead and urged the Government to make plans so as to be ready to meet the problem of unemployment, which he felt would recur when the nation returned to peace. He continued:

> But we hope for something better than a mere avoidance of unemployment and strikes. We are tired of war in the industrial field. The British workman cannot quietly submit to an autocratic government of the conditions of his own life. He will not take 'Prussianism' lying down, even in the dock, the factory, or the mine. Would it not be possible for the employers of this country, on the conclusion of peace, when we have rid ourselves of the restrictive legislation to which we have submitted for war purposes, to agree to put their businesses on a new footing by admitting the workmen to some participation, not in profits but in control?
>
> We workmen do not ask that we should be admitted to any share in what is essentially the employers' own business—that is in those matters which do not concern us directly in the industry or employment in which we may be engaged. We do not seek to sit on the board of directors, or to interfere with the buying of materials, or with the selling of the product. But in the daily management of the employment in which we spend our working lives, in the atmosphere and under the conditions in which we have to work, in the hours of beginning and ending work, in the conditions of remuneration, and even in the manner and practices of the foreman with whom we have to be in contact, in all these matters we feel that we, as workmen, have a right to a voice—even to an equal voice —with the management itself. Believe me, we shall never get any lasting industrial peace except on the lines of democracy.[1]

These views were expressions of the practical wisdom that had characterised the traditional trade union leadership; while they were far removed from the more extreme theories that were still much in the air, they had been influenced by the legitimate criticism directed by the syndicalists and guild socialists at the employer-employee

[1] *T.U.C. Annual Report*, 1916.

relationship. The trade unions had achieved considerable political influence in the State and the war had further raised their status, but the position of the trade unions at the place of work, with the exception of the skilled craftsmen's organisations, was by contrast, often relatively weak, and subject to constant attack. This situation had developed out of the pattern of trade union growth which had been built on a structure of organisation outside of the actual place of employment. It was not only Gosling who was thinking along these lines; the reports of the Whitley Committee, which was set up shortly after this Congress, show that others also accepted the need to improve industrial relations at the workplace.

Gosling went on to say,

> The Trades Union Congress is without question the largest and most influential body in reflecting the aims and aspirations of Labour, not only in Great Britain, but in the whole world. Those of us whose connection with the Congress as delegates goes back for twenty years or more know how the work has increased in volume and importance, and yet no real provision has been made to meet the increase. Whilst we have improved in our office accommodation the staff is practically the same; the affiliation fees which were fixed fourteen years ago are still in operation, and only amount to a payment of 1*d*. per annum for every three members affiliated. Fortunately we have one of the best men in the movement as our Secretary, to whom nothing but praise is due for the devoted way in which he serves us. He, together with his clerk, compose the whole of the staff employed in this great work.
>
> We see on all hands that the employers are hastening to put matters right as far as their own particular interests are concerned. The employers' interests in the near future will be protected by powerfully organised and well directed associations. This Congress will have to undertake still greater responsibilities. Its work will be even more important and far-reaching in character than anything it has yet attempted. The work of the Parliamentary Committee will be greater than ever. Its offices and its staff must be added to, and the affiliation fees—if they are not sufficient—must be increased. We must not be satisfied until organised Labour is as important in its greater and more national aspects as any Department of State, with its own block of offices and civil service, commodious and well appointed.[1]

At the conclusion of his speech Ernest Bevin rose to ask where these matters were referred to in the report of the Parliamentary Committee. Gosling replied that he thought a sub-committee of the Parliamentary Committee would be established, which would go into the question and present a report; this was duly done and the next Congress had concrete proposals placed before it.

[1] *Ibid.*

Lloyd George becomes Prime Minister

Before the plans for improving the efficiency of the Parliamentary Committee had been taken very far, the status of the Labour movement was considerably raised by political events. In August 1916, just before Congress assembled, Arthur Henderson had been permitted to resign his post of President of the Board of Education, where he had been in an anomalous position, as his main work had lain in the field of labour problems, to take the newly-created title of Labour Adviser to the Government. This change gave the trade unions some satisfaction, but they were not content with what amounted to a partial recognition of their demand for a fully fledged Ministry of Labour, for which they continued to press. Their efforts were rewarded sooner than they expected. In December 1916, the campaign cunningly waged by Lloyd George and his friends to oust Asquith from the premiership, was successful, and Lloyd George became Prime Minister.[1] In constructing his Government, Lloyd George offered Henderson a seat in the inner War Cabinet, in order to win the support of the Labour movement, and agreed to establish State control over the mines and shipping, and to introduce a better system of food distribution; these were all demands which the trade unions had made repeatedly, but which up to this point had been resisted as unnecessary. In addition, a Ministry of Labour would be established, with a Labour man at its head. These terms were too attractive to be easily turned down, and the decision to accept them was endorsed by a very large majority at the Labour Party Conference held in January 1917. John Hodge, M.P., secretary of the Steel Smelters, was made Minister of Labour, and Sir David Shackleton appointed Permanent Secretary; G. N. Barnes, one of the leaders of the Amalgamated Society of Engineers, was given the post of Minister of Pensions. Lloyd George had the hope that this would give the engineering workers greater confidence in the Government. G. H. Roberts and William Brace were retained in junior posts, and James Parker joined them. When the Ministry of Food was established soon afterwards, J. R. Clynes, who, up to this stage, had been against

[1] The Parliamentary Committee issued the following statement sharply criticising the crisis engineered by Lloyd George:

'That we express our profound regret that certain statesmen of the country led and influenced by a Press campaign, have in the hour of the nation's crisis, entirely failed to observe the loyalty and self-sacrifice they have repeatedly urged upon the workers during the war. Further, we express the earnest hope that the present unseemly quarrel amongst some of those entrusted with great responsibilities shall immediately cease, and so set a better example to the workers, who, we trust, in spite of the wrecking tactics adopted, will continue to give of their best in the national interest.' December 1916.

joining the Coalition, but had now changed his mind, was given the post of Parliamentary Secretary, and later became Food Controller.

The creation of the new Government revived the nation at a point when war weariness was beginning to creep over it, but the increased representation of the Labour movement, and the adoption of policies which it had been recommending, did not still the growing criticism in the Labour ranks of the 'fight to a finish' attitude of Lloyd George.[1] Despite the firm refusal of the British Government to have anything to do with the offer of President Wilson to act as mediator between the warring nations, the proposals of the American President encouraged hopes of a negotiated peace. The number of strikes had risen sharply in 1916, and when in the spring of 1917 a further drive was launched to comb out the war factories for able-bodied men, and the dilution of labour on a wider scale was undertaken, a spate of serious strikes organised by the shop stewards' movement resulted. The Government was seriously alarmed by these strikes, and appointed Commissions of Inquiry. The Commissioners, under the chairmanship of G. N. Barnes, found that the loyalty of the workers was not wanting, and that they had a whole string of justifiable grievances which had contributed to their fatigue and irritation. Apart from the extremely long hours, and the breaking down of traditional customs, which caused them to be anxious about the future, it was found that the fear of enlistment had been used to compel workers to accept conditions of employment which they resented; that the cost of living had risen faster than wages and that the rank and file had lost confidence in the leadership of the unions.[2] One of the results of the Commissions of Inquiry was the abolition of the hated leaving certificate, which tied men to their jobs in munitions factories and, it was thought, had been exploited by employers to keep wages down.

The Parliamentary Committee secured a number of important concessions from the new Government during its first months of existence, but they were not of the kind to rouse the militant members of the rank and file to great enthusiasm. Soon after the appointment of the Minister of Labour the Parliamentary Committee interviewed him to propose that the Committee on Production should be reconstituted so that it could deal more rapidly with the disputes submitted to it for arbitration, and this request was granted. The Minister of

---

[1] The war, to many at home, now seemed futile. The armies of the hostile powers were in the relentless grip of the fantastic Flanders mud; neither side seemed capable of making a decisive move; all they appeared to accomplish was the sacrifice each day of thousands of young men.

[2] *Commission of Enquiry into Industrial Unrest*, Cmd. 8662, 8663, 8664, 8665, 8667, 8669, 1917.

Labour introduced a Bill to render the amalgamation of two trade unions less difficult by making it a statutory requirement for only 50 per cent of the members to vote, and a majority of 20 per cent to be in favour, instead of the consent of two-thirds of the members being required. This failed to give the trade unions what they wanted, which was a simple majority, but was a concession to demands for an easing of the law governing amalgamation, for which the T.U.C. had been pressing for some years. A third success achieved by the Parliamentary Committee was an amendment to the Workmen's Compensation Act of 1906, which increased by 25 per cent the grant payable to totally incapacitated workers.

The T.U.C. and the Whitley Report

In the summer of 1917 the sub-committee on Relations between Employers and Employed, of the Committee on Reconstruction, published its first report. This Committee, better known under the name of its chairman, J. H. Whitley, Speaker of the House of Commons, had been appointed by the Government in 1916, at the moment when the Labour movement was just beginning to discuss post-war problems. Industrial unrest had been growing and the Government wanted an antidote to the shop stewards' movement; since the Government was pledged to end the controls it had imposed on labour as soon as the wartime emergency came to an end, it was obvious that, once hostilities had ceased, the trade unions would be under immense pressure to abandon the restraint which they had exercised from the beginning of the war. Harry Gosling had made it clear, in his presidential address to the 1916 Congress, that far-sighted trade union leaders had no wish to return to the old conditions of industrial warfare, if this could be avoided without sacrifice of legitimate trade union interests. The bulk of the union leaders were, therefore, no less concerned than the Government to find a way of curbing the power of the unofficial shop stewards' movement.

The Whitley Committee included among its members two trade unionists, J. R. Clynes and Robert Smillie, and in addition Susan Lawrence and J. J. Mallon, who were both closely connected with the Labour movement, and the economist J. A. Hobson, who was also sympathetic. The first report of the Whitley Committee was concerned with the establishment of Joint Industrial Councils as a means of improving the machinery of collective bargaining in those industries where it hardly existed. It was submitted by the Minister of Labour to the Parliamentary Committee so that the Government could have the benefit of trade union comment on the report before it decided on its own attitude. In the Committee's reply to the

minister, agreement with the general terms of the Whitley report
was expressed, but the Parliamentary Committee thought the matter
far too important to give any hurried consideration to it. The
Labour movement was now much more concerned with post-war
problems than it had been when the Committee was established;
furthermore the temper of the trade union movement had become
more critical of the Government. The Parliamentary Committee was
well aware of the suspicion with which a large section of the trade
union movement regarded the Whitley Committee, notwithstanding
the Labour representation on it; it therefore circulated a copy of the
report and the minister's accompanying letter, to all affiliated
organisations and asked them to submit their views.

The Parliamentary Committee made no recommendation to the
1917 Congress, but simply left the report to a free discussion of the
delegates. The result was extremely unsatisfactory, and it was obvious
that the Parliamentary Committee had not at this stage made up its
mind on the policy it desired to see Congress pursue. The general
workers' unions were strongly in favour of the Whitley report,
which they thought would help them to bring the employers to the
bargaining table, but in spite of the fact that Smillie had been a
member of the Committee, and spoke in favour of the report, the
miners expressed extreme hostility towards it on the grounds that the
assumption that permanently good relations could be established
between employers and employed was 'absolutely subversive to the
aspirations of the workers and the proper development of the Trade
Union movement'.[1] Eventually it was agreed to accept a suggestion,
made by Ernest Bevin, that the report should be referred to a sub-
committee of the Parliamentary Committee for further consideration.

In all, the Whitley Committee issued five reports and recommended, in addition to the formation of Joint Industrial Councils,
the establishment of Joint Works' Committees, the statutory regulation of wages in industries where trade unionism had not been
established, the extension of powers for Trade Boards, a permanent
court of arbitration, and increased authority for the Minister of
Labour to hold inquiries into trade disputes. The Whitley scheme,
as a whole, was an impressive attempt to create a coherent system
of arrangements through which the relations between employers and
workers could be conducted on a voluntary basis. It conceded the
claim of the workers for a greater share in the running of industry,
but its basic ideas were cast in the traditional pattern of State intervention in industrial relations in Britain; that voluntary machinery
should be promoted and assisted, with legal compulsion only
sparingly used. The implementation of the recommendations was

[1] *T.U.C. Annual Report*, 1917. See speech by Frank Hodges.

left in the main to the voluntary acceptance of both sides of industry, except in the case of the unorganised industries, where, in lieu of effective trade unions it was proposed to continue the principle of State protection through Trade Boards.

The Whitley Committee's proposals excited a good deal of discussion. They were not satisfactory to the advanced 'guild socialists', nor to militants of the shop stewards' movement, who rightly saw in them a challenge to their own demands for more fundamental social and economic changes in the capitalist system; nor were they regarded with enthusiasm by the old-fashioned craft unionists, who looked upon State intervention in the conduct of industrial relations as dangerous to the independence of the unions. In its report to the 1918 Congress the Parliamentary Committee stated, 'your Committee desire to impress upon officials and members of the unions the desirability of a frank acceptance of the principles embodied in the Whitley Report, and the setting up in each industry of Joint Industrial Councils, thereby averting future serious disputes and consequent trade dislocation'. No detailed examination of the Whitley scheme, as requested by the 1917 Congress, was presented, and the only resolution concerning the Whitley report was one tabled by the Fawcett Association,[1] which called upon the Government to apply the principles of the Whitley report to all Government departments. It is clear that the Parliamentary Committee was not anxious for a debate on the Whitley report, for this resolution was left until the very end when delegates were rushing off to catch their trains. Although the resolution was carried by quite a substantial majority it was necessary for the secretary of the Parliamentary Committee to intervene to inform the delegates that Congress had accepted the principles of the report the year before, and that to follow the advice of the delegates from the Amalgamated Society of Engineers, Locomotive Engineers, Carpenters and Shipwrights, to reject the resolution, would be to condemn the action of the Parliamentary Committee. The thing that carried the resolution, however, was the argument advanced by the delegates of the civil service unions; it was all very well, they said, for the miners, engineers and railwaymen to refuse to have anything to do with the Whitley report, but the situation in the State services was very different and the recommendations of the Whitley report, if applied, might be of great value to them. No one referred to the fact that the Parliamentary Committee had specifically refused to commit itself in favour of the Whitley report at the previous year's Congress, or that the Committee had failed to carry out its undertaking to examine and report

[1] An organisation of post office employees subsequently amalgamated in the Union of Post Office Workers.

on the scheme, yet the secretary now informed a depleted Congress that the report had been accepted in 1917. The lack of authority of the Parliamentary Committee over the affiliated unions, the disunity that was growing more apparent owing to the social upheaval brought about by the war, and the disagreements inside the trade union movement as to the policy that ought to be adopted, no doubt led the Parliamentary Committee to pursue this manœuvre, and avoid a debate on an awkward issue.

The Impact of the Russian Revolution

An event which undoubtedly quickened the temper of the militant wing, and profoundly influenced the policy of the whole Labour movement was the Russian Revolution in March 1917. Immediately the news was received the Labour Party arranged to send a delegation to convey the good wishes of the British Labour movement. Included among the delegates was Will Thorne, who was a member of the Parliamentary Committee, and he was asked to express on behalf of the Trades Union Congress 'the satisfaction and admiration of the. manner in which the momentous change had been brought about, coupled with the hope and expectation that the whole of the Labour forces of Russia will act unitedly in the support of the new Government'.[1] He was also requested to ask the Russian trade union movement to send a fraternal delegate to the next Trades Union Congress. Following the report of Will Thorne and his companion, James O'Grady, which stated that there was no trade union centre as yet in existence, a further invitation was sent through Arthur Henderson, who was visiting Russia, to report on the situation there for the War Cabinet, inviting the President of the Council of Workmen's and Soldiers' Delegates to appoint a fraternal delegate to represent the Russian Labour movement. The Committee also offered to send two members of the Parliamentary Committee to Russia to help in the task of building up the trade union movement, but this offer was not taken up.

In May it had become known that the Russian Government was strongly in favour of holding the International Socialist Conference, which the European leaders of the Socialist International had proposed should be held in Stockholm, for the purpose of securing agreement on the war aims of the socialist and Labour movements. The Labour Party Executive was divided on whether it should accept the invitation and decided to wait until more information was available. Arthur Henderson returned from Russia convinced that the

[1] *T.U.C. Annual Report*, 1917.

conference ought to be held, and that the British Labour movement should send a delegation; otherwise, he thought, there was a grave danger that the Russians would become allies of the German socialists, who were expected to be present. On the 25 July 1917, two days after Henderson's return from Russia, the Parliamentary Committee, which was aware of Henderson's report, passed a resolution to the effect that the Committee ought 'to take its proper place in convening and participating in all international Labour gatherings', and it decided to be represented at a national conference to be called by the Labour Party to consider whether the invitation to send a delegation to Stockholm should be accepted.[1] The Committee further decided that if the national conference agreed to be represented at Stockholm, the Committee would send eight delegates, subject to the approval of Congress. When the national conference was held, the decision to be represented at Stockholm was carried by a large majority, but an additional resolution was moved by the miners, and carried overwhelmingly, that representation should be confined to the T.U.C. and the Labour Party. This decision created a serious problem because the sponsors of the Stockholm Conference had more in common with the I.L.P., which was now debarred, than with the T.U.C., and had insisted that each national delegation should include representatives of the minority point of view. Faced with an awkward situation, the conference decided to adjourn for ten days in order to try and find a way of resolving this difficulty. However, before it reassembled two events had occurred which entirely changed the situation. On the morrow of the conference Arthur Henderson resigned from the War Cabinet, feeling that he could no longer act as secretary of the Labour Party, and at the same time be a member of the Government when it had suddenly changed from support of Labour representation at the Stockholm Conference to outright hostility to the idea.[2] Lloyd George seized the opportunity to discredit Henderson by the release of a dubious story that the Russians were no longer in favour of holding the conference, and he let it be known that the Government would not issue passports to any delegation the Labour Party might choose to send to Stockholm.[3]

When the conference reassembled on the 21 August, a strong protest was made at the Government's refusal to issue passports, but the doubt and confusion which had been raised, and the bitterness which

[1] *Report of the Parliamentary Committee*, 1917.

[2] When Henderson departed for Russia, Lloyd George had been in favour of the Labour Party sending representatives to Stockholm to counteract the influence of the Germans on the Russians, but he changed his mind during Henderson's absence.

[3] Hamilton, M. A., *Arthur Henderson—A Biography*, Ch. VII; *War Memoirs of David Lloyd George*, vol. IV., Ch. LVIII.

the proposal to participate in the conference had caused in the Labour movement, had made a large number of delegates change their minds about the wisdom of sending a delegation; the vote reflected this shift in opinion since the previous decision was only confirmed by a narrow majority of 3,000, and the delegates still refused to agree to representation of the I.L.P. minority.

The Parliamentary Committee accepted an invitation to take part in the Inter-Allied Conference of Labour and Socialist Organisations, which was held in London on the 28 August, to draw up a united policy to be presented at the Stockholm Conference. Delegates from Belgium, France, Italy, Portugal, Greece, South Africa and Russia were present, and the conference set up two Commissions to prepare reports, one on the Stockholm Conference and the other on war aims. The first Commission was unanimous in condemning the British Government for refusing to issue passports, but although a majority was in favour of attending the Stockholm Conference, there was a large minority against. It was the second Commission, however, which finally finished the chances of the Stockholm Conference, for it was quite unable to come to any agreement on what should be the war aims of the Allied socialists. It was obvious that agreement could not be reached, and the Parliamentary Committee came to the conclusion that in these circumstances it would be futile to send any delegation to Stockholm.

When the Parliamentary Committee reported these events to the 1917 Congress, J. Havelock Wilson, who had become notorious for his extreme anti-German views, moved to refer the report back on the grounds that the T.U.C. should have nothing to do with any conference that included Germans and socialists. The Committee had suggested that in the light of events it should be empowered by the Congress to do everything possible to secure agreement between the working classes of the Allied nations, and that it should assist in the arrangements for any international Labour and socialist conference that might be held, subject only to the condition that voting at such a conference should be confined to the majority movement, or else on the basis of membership of each organisation. What the Committee was determined to avoid was that minority groups, such as the I.L.P., should have any chance of securing control of the national movement through the fact that a number of important leaders of the Labour Party were members of the I.L.P. This was not, however, sufficiently uncompromising for Havelock Wilson, whose hatred for the Germans approached mania. He was no less violently opposed to any suggestion that the Labour movement should formulate its peace aims or contemplate the formation of an international organisation, when the war was over, to preserve the peace. Such ideas were to him rank treason; products of the pacifist mentality of the I.L.P. His one object was to make the Germans pay for the wrongs they had done, and he scorned the sentimentality of those who distinguished between good and bad Germans. In the long, confused and bitter debate which followed he used every trick of sentiment to play on the emotions of the delegates; retailing, what were, no doubt, genuine atrocity stories, to persuade the delegates to reject the recommendations of the Parliamentary Committee. Wilson, now becoming a frail old man with a tremulous voice, visibly moved Congress as he broke down telling of the sufferings of his seamen, but the attitude of the delegates had shifted so much since the previous year that when the vote was taken the reference back of the report was defeated by over 2,250,000 votes.

The result was a triumph for Arthur Henderson, who attended this Congress as fraternal delegate from the Labour Party, barely a month after he had resigned from the Cabinet. He had been given a tremendous welcome, and his speech to Congress was listened to with the closest attention. Not a good speaker, with little flair for the memorable phrase, and inclined to be ponderous and involved, he yet had, like Ernest Bevin, that indescribable capacity for identifying himself with the members of his audience; as it were, of thinking out loud with them, and giving them the feeling that they had worked out for themselves the policy he wanted them to accept.

Henderson said that the Labour Party welcomed the decision of the Congress to extend its international work,[1] and went on to develop the theme that some kind of international organisation would be essential after the war. He condemned those who thought only in terms of destroying the enemy.

> Is it too much to say that this great world conflict, which has entailed such tremendous sacrifices in blood, treasure and effort, could only be finally successful—and I emphasise that word 'finally' for I am afraid that some people mistake the military victory for the final and complete success—could only be finally successful when autocratic government has been completely and for ever destroyed? May I say—though the position may not commend itself to all of you—that this is the great reason why I would rather consult with the German minority before peace than I would with the representatives of a discredited autocratic government when a military victory has been secured.

Most of the remainder of Henderson's speech was concerned with justifying his attitude towards the Stockholm Conference, and making clear the international issues which lay before Congress.

[1] *T.U.C. Annual Report*, 1917.

The Parliamentary Committee Extends its Work

The decision of the Parliamentary Committee, endorsed by Congress, to extend its work in the international field was of considerable significance, since it was evidence of the much closer accord that now existed between the leaders of the majority of the unions and the leaders of the Labour Party. There was, however, an articulate minority in the unions, and in the Labour Party, which did not look upon this development with favour. It meant that the T.U.C. would participate directly in future Labour and socialist conferences to the exclusion of the G.F.T.U.; it also meant that the influence of the I.L.P. would be considerably weakened. The harmony of views that had now been reached by the majority of leaders opened the way for changes in the constitution and policy of the Labour Party; in 1918 fundamental revisions were agreed upon which made the Party a more effective political instrument.

The Parliamentary Committee took steps, at the 1917 Congress, to improve its own organisation so as to equip itself to deal more effectively with problems arising at home and abroad. It followed the lead given by Harry Gosling the year before, when, in his presidential address, he had made an eloquent statement of the need for the Trades Union Congress to modernise its organisation and methods. The resolution, prepared by the Parliamentary Committee for submission to Congress, incorporated a number of proposals that had been before the delegates in the past and rejected; but the Committee was now confident that the delegates were ready to admit the need for an advance and it proposed:

> That in view of the growing need for the Trade Union movement, both national and international, the Parliamentary Committee be authorised to set up machinery to develop the work of the Trades Union Congress.
>
> To render help to Trade Unions in such organising matters as may be approved by the Parliamentary Committee, such help to include speakers at meetings, leaflets, etc.
>
> To establish a Trade Union Information Bureau.
>
> To arrange for the exchange of correspondence and journals with the Trade Union movement throughout the world, and to codify and classify them for the use of the Trade Union movement in this country.
>
> To appoint an Assistant Secretary, whose duties it shall be to take charge of the office in the absence of the Secretary, and to assist the Secretary generally.
>
> To appoint an Advisory Assistant, amongst whose duties it shall be to examine Trade Union agreements, Bills and Acts of Parliament, and advise constituent societies thereon. Both officers shall be under the control of the Secretary.

To substitute for the present quarterly circular a monthly circular to Trade Unions, and to take such steps as are necessary to ensure effective Press notices.

To provide such office accommodation and employ such clerical staff as may be necessary to carry out the above objects.

To levy affiliated societies for the money necessary up to a maximum of 10s. per 1,000 affiliated members.[1]

The Committee had gauged the situation correctly, the ground having been well prepared so that no criticisms were made from the floor of Congress and the resolution went through with general assent after two or three short speeches had been made in favour of it. Having secured the necessary support, the Parliamentary Committee were able to go ahead. They appointed Fred Bramley,[2] a well-known socialist, as assistant secretary, and secured more commodious office premises in Eccleston Square. An international trades union review was published, and in the following summer steps were taken to establish an international trades union bureau.

In July 1918, the Parliamentary Committee convened a special conference of trade unions which were affiliated to the international federations, 'with the object of considering the desirability of making the Parliamentary Committee the British centre for dealing with international Trade Union matters'. It was agreed that the Parliamentary Committee should establish an international, statistical, and information bureau for the purpose of collecting, filing and distributing general information for the use of unions affiliated to Congress; and should seek to develop at once a close relationship between the British trade union movement and the trade union movements of Allied and neutral countries, the colonies and the United States of America.

Relations between the T.U.C., G.F.T.U. and A.F. of L.

Though it had been obvious before the 1917 Trades Union Congress that the Parliamentary Committee was intent on taking the place of the G.F.T.U. as the representative body of the British trade unions in international affairs, the General Federation considered that this sphere of activities was its prerogative and it continued to act on that assumption.

[1] *T.U.C. Annual Report*, 1917.

[2] Fred Bramley was born in 1874. He was an excellent speaker and as a *Clarion* 'Vanner' he had made a reputation early in his career. Bramley had joined the National Amalgamated Furnishing Trades Association as an apprentice, and later he became an organiser for this union. His appointment was clear evidence of the bridge that had by this time, been established between the majority of trade unionists and the socialist movement.

The G.F.T.U. had been hostile to the proposal made in March 1917, by the Swiss trade unions, that a conference of the members of the International Federation of Trade Unions should be held in Berne; later it was equally opposed to the proposal that an international Labour and socialist conference should be held in Stockholm. It was decided by the G.F.T.U. to send a cable to the American Federation of Labour urging it not to support these conferences, but to send representatives instead to a conference which the G.F.T.U. proposed to hold in the week following the next Trades Union Congress. Gompers, on behalf of the A.F. of L., accepted the invitation of the G.F.T.U. and nominated the fraternal delegates to the T.U.C. as its representatives.

The differences between the G.F.T.U. and the T.U.C. had now become acute. There was a case for the T.U.C. taking over the function of representing the unions in international affairs simply on the grounds that it was a far more representative organisation. The division between the two bodies was not, however, so much on those grounds as on ideology and policy. The leaders of the G.F.T.U. still adhered to close sympathy with the Liberal Government and they had joined Havelock Wilson in his campaign of hate against the 'Hun'. They were absolutely opposed, not only to the extreme socialists and pacifists who were in favour of 'peace at any price', but were also bitterly hostile to the more moderate position of the official leaders of the Labour Party and the T.U.C. In the eyes of the G.F.T.U. all discussion of peace aims, post-war reconstruction and the formation of a new international Labour organisation which would include the representatives of the German working class, after the war had been won, was tantamount to taking part in a treasonable activity.

The G.F.T.U. found allies for its point of view in the French, who held, perhaps more understandably, similar opinions about the Germans, and, from the time that America came into the war, in the A.F. of L. Up to 1917, it had been the policy of the A.F. of L. to maintain relations with both the German and British trade union movements, so as to try and bring them together in an international conference to discuss the terms of peace immediately the war ended. This policy of the A.F. of L. had been firmly rejected by the G.F.T.U. and the T.U.C. in 1916; since then the G.F.T.U., together with the A.F. of L., had travelled in an opposite direction from the T.U.C. The position occupied by the A.F. of L. at this stage, as put by one of its delegates, John Golden, at the 1917 Trades Union Congress, was not quite as uncompromising as that of the G.F.T.U. He said, 'There must be a reckoning; and we believe in our American way, that there is only one thing to do, and that is to defeat the German first, and then try to talk to him afterwards.'[1] It was clear, however, that the A.F. of L. held the view that the G.F.T.U. was more representative of British opinion than the T.U.C.

The fact that there were two national trade union organisations in Britain, both concerning the same unions, did tend to confuse overseas trade union movements, which were not aware of the exact status of the two bodies. The leaders of the G.F.T.U. encouraged the belief that their organisation was the truly representative body. W. A. Appleton, secretary of the G.F.T.U., addressing the conference, told the delegates, 'That there is no other body affiliated to the International Secretariat but the G.F.T.U.' This statement was strictly accurate, but calculated to mislead foreign delegates, especially since the T.U.C., in the week before had made plain their intention of henceforth taking responsibility for international affairs.

In the event the G.F.T.U. Conference achieved nothing except to exacerbate relations between the two groups. In addition to those from the A.F. of L., delegates were present from the Canadian Trades and Labour Congress, who had also attended the Trades Union Congress, the C.G.T. and the Serbian trade union movement; there were also representatives from the International Metal Workers' Federation. Several British unions sent delegates, including the textile workers and the Sailors' and Firemen's Union. J. T. Brownlie, secretary of the Amalgamated Society of Engineers—who at this time were not affiliated to Congress, was present. The Conference provided an opportunity for some captious propaganda against the T.U.C. and encouraged the G.F.T.U. to issue a circular, repudiating the decisions taken at the 1917 Trades Union Congress, to the trade union movements abroad.

The Management Committee of the G.F.T.U., still smarting under its elimination from the Joint Board, and now angry at the incursion of the Parliamentary Committee into the international field, which had been the preserve of the G.F.T.U. from its foundation up to the outbreak of the war, decided to sponsor a scheme of expansion of its own activities that ran almost exactly parallel to those which the 1917 Congress had instructed the Parliamentary Committee to undertake, and which would have made the G.F.T.U. a competing national trade union centre in home affairs. As soon as the action of the G.F.T.U. became known to the Parliamentary Committee, it issued a circular to all the affiliated unions setting out the proposals of the G.F.T.U., to show that they had been deliberately copied from those adopted by the T.U.C. It condemned the action of the G.F.T.U. as likely to lead to overlapping, and to a waste of money, time and

[1] *T.U.C. Annual Report*, 1917.

energy; and the unions affiliated to Congress were requested to refrain from giving any support to the G.F.T.U.

In the months following the 1917 Congress the Parliamentary Committee, in co-operation with the executive committee of the Labour Party, devoted a great deal of its time to the formulation of an international policy. A joint committee under the leadership of Henderson drew up a statement of the war aims of the Labour movement, which was endorsed by a special joint conference on 28 December 1917, for submission to another Allied Labour and Socialist Conference which was due to meet in London in the following February. The preparation of this statement had been encouraged by the declarations of President Wilson, setting forth the objectives of American policy and appealing over the heads of the German military leaders to the German people. Lloyd George, who was far from being in accord with Wilson's 'naïve' approach, was afraid of being pushed in that direction if the British Labour movement adopted the statement of war aims drafted by the two committees; he, therefore, decided to intervene and sent a letter to the conference warning it of dangerous consequences that might occur if the statement was accepted. In spite of this intervention, and of the opposition of the extreme anti-German section of the movement, the war aims memorandum was endorsed by 2,132,000 to 1,164,000 votes. It was a long and comprehensive statement at the heart of which was a demand for the creation of a League of Nations, a demand which Henderson, when moving the adoption of the statement, emphasised was supported by President Wilson.[1]

At the Allied Labour and Socialist Conference, presided over by J. W. Ogden, chairman of the Parliamentary Committee, which opened on 20 February 1918, the British declaration of war aims was adopted with only minor modifications. In spite of the fact that the famous Fourteen Points of President Wilson, which had been put out only a few weeks before, were in substantial agreement with the declaration of the British Labour movement, the A.F. of L., suspicious of the socialist influence at the conference, found it inconvenient to attend. Thus the ironic situation arose that just at the moment when President Wilson had given a new lead to the Allied powers, and was being supported most strongly by the majority section of organised Labour in Britain, the American trade union movement hesitated to co-operate with the T.U.C. and its associates.

The Parliamentary Committee was anxious to obtain the support of the American Federation of Labour for the declaration of war aims that had been adopted by the Allied Labour and Socialist

[1] *Report of Special Joint Conference*, 28 December 1917.

Conference, but Havelock Wilson, the G.F.T.U. leaders, and the Government, did their utmost to prevent this from happening.

Havelock Wilson, though he talked a great deal about democracy, was not prepared to accept the decision of the 1917 Congress, and he instructed the members of his union not to sail ships carrying delegates to conferences of which he disapproved. He prevented Camille Huysmans, secretary of the Socialist International, from crossing the Channel, and when the Parliamentary Committee decided to send a delegation to the United States to discuss international policy with the leaders of the A.F. of L., he announced that no members of his union would man any ship on which they proposed to travel. As a result the Parliamentary Committee asked Havelock Wilson to explain his conduct, but all they received was a disingenuous reply. It was not Wilson, however, who prevented the T.U.C. from sending its fraternal delegates to the A.F. of L. Convention in June 1918, but the Government, which refused to issue Margaret Bondfield with a passport. When the Trades Union Congress held its jubilee gathering at Derby in September 1918, a sharp protest was made against these attempts to thwart the decisions of Congress, and the work of the Parliamentary Committee. Many delegates who had voted against the policy adopted by the T.U.C. were nevertheless indignant at the Government's refusal to issue passports, and joined with the Parliamentary Committee in denouncing its interference in the work of Congress.

In the event, Samuel Gompers, president of the A.F. of L., decided to attend the 1918 Congress in person—this was his third visit as fraternal delegate—to find out for himself something about the situation in the British Labour movement. There were widespread rumours, fostered by the pro-Government Press, that Gompers was coming to put Arthur Henderson, and those members of the Parliamentary Committee who thought like him, in their place.

Undoubtedly the Americans were badly informed both by the British Press and the G.F.T.U. as to the truth about the Labour movement in Britain, and Gompers may have believed that Appleton and Havelock Wilson more truly represented the opinion of the trade union movement than the Parliamentary Committee and the Labour Party. If that was the case, then he was rapidly disillusioned, for Congress proceeded to pass, by a huge majority, a resolution which called upon the Central Powers to publish their war aims, and urged the British Government to establish peace negotiations immediately the enemy, either voluntarily or by compulsion, evacuated France and Belgium; the only delegates to speak against the resolution were Havelock Wilson and G. H. Roberts. Later, Wilson tried again to persuade Congress to accept a resolution that would have committed the trade union movement to the opinion that no negotiations should be entered into with the Germans until that nation had paid reparations in full for all its war crimes, but the previous question was moved and carried by an overwhelming majority.[1]

Before the American delegation arrived in Britain, the A.F. of L. had agreed to take part in another Allied Labour and Socialist Conference which was held soon after Congress was over. Opening on the 18 September, with G. H. Stuart-Bunning, the newly-elected chairman of the Parliamentary Committee presiding, this gathering was, perhaps, the most representative international Labour conference held during the war years, and was a triumph for the Parliamentary Committee and the Labour Party. Both the extreme right and the extreme left were decisively defeated. The left wing, led by Maxton of the I.L.P., and Jean Longuet, of the extreme section of the French Socialist Party, advanced a number of amendments that expressed the defeatist philosophy which has always characterised the socialist left wing. On the question of Germany, Longuet wanted the conference to say that it was ready to meet the German Labour movement unconditionally to bring the war to an immediate end, to which Henderson replied, 'British labour was not going to defend German Socialism and sacrifice world democracy. They declared on 14 February 1915, and at every conference that they had held since, that a victory for Germany would mean the destruction of democracy and the annihilation of liberty.'[2] On the other hand, when Gompers tried to commit the conference, with the support of the British right wing, to the position that it would 'meet in conference with those only of the Central Powers who are in open revolt against their autocratic governments', he was equally decisively rejected.

Although the A. F. of L. policy was not accepted, the conference cleared the air so far as relations with the T.U.C. were concerned, for the representatives of the Parliamentary Committee had shown conclusively that they were far removed from accepting the defeatist policy of the left wing. Although the A.F. of L. was not prepared to go as far as the British majority leaders, they did go a long way, and

---

[1] Havelock Wilson and his friends made a considerable effort to win the support of the delegates to Congress. A huge pro-Ally Labour Demonstration was staged on the Sunday before Congress opened, at which, Will Thorne, Jack Jones and Ben Tillett were the principal speakers. A champagne lunch was provided for the delegates in the British Seamen's Empire Tent that had been erected in the market place of Derby. The guests of honour at the luncheon were William Hughes, the boisterous Australian politician, well-known for his jingoistic opinions, Samuel Gompers and Havelock Wilson. Cigars were distributed freely to the large gathering after lunch, and a good time, at someone's expense, seems to have been had by all who attended this exuberant function.

[2] *The Times*, 21 September 1918.

at the end of the conference the difference between them was much less than that which separated them at the beginning of 1918. At the end of the conference the Americans, though refusing to vote for the final draft statement, agreed to appoint a representative on the international committee which was set up to organise an international Labour conference to be held, as the A.F. of L. had originally suggested, at the same time as the peace conference. This committee was also assigned the task of persuading the Allied Powers to agree to the inclusion of representatives of organised Labour in the official delegations to the peace conference.

The clash between the T.U.C. and the G.F.T.U. provided an important subject for consideration at the 1918 Congress. Fortunately, members of both the Parliamentary Committee and the Management Committee of the G.F.T.U. had realised that a public dispute at such a critical period could only result in dividing the trade union movement, so the counsel of the wiser members was accepted and a meeting of the two committees was arranged during Congress week. This did not, however, prevent the whole matter being raised and debated. Ben Cooper, a leading member of the G.F.T.U., complained of the ingratitude of the Parliamentary Committee and accused it of trying to restrict the Federation to the functions of a benefit paying society only. This, indeed, is what the Parliamentary Committee did desire, and eventually succeeded in obtaining. But at the 1918 Congress there was some feeling among delegates that the Management Committee of the General Federation had not been treated as generously as it deserved, and a glib speech by J. H. Thomas did not enhance the Parliamentary Committee's case, even though this was really quite a strong one. It was felt, with considerable justice, that the conflict between the G.F.T.U. and the Parliamentary Committee would never have come about had the Committee troubled about international affairs in years gone by, and the division between the two organisations might, even in the war years, have been mitigated had not one or two of the larger unions been bent on destroying the influence of the G.F.T.U. When the vote was taken, the reference back of that section of the report which dealt with relations with the G.F.T.U. was carried by 784,000 votes. That same evening the two national committees met together to discuss their differences, and when, later in the week, Harry Gosling moved a resolution asking Congress to endorse the action of the Parliamentary Committee in setting up an international department, he informed the delegates that better relations had been established with the G.F.T.U. and that a working arrangement would be announced soon. This resolution was seconded, as a gesture of goodwill, by Ben Cooper, who said that he recognised Congress as the right body to take charge of international work in the future, but that he was glad that the co-operation of the G.F.T.U. had been invited. Further discussions between the two organisations were held during the following year, and it was finally agreed that both organisations should be represented jointly on any delegation sent to an international Labour conference.

The Labour Party adopts New Aims and a New Constitution

The adoption by the Labour Party, in 1918, of a new constitution and statement of aims, raised issues of importance for the Trades Union Congress. The effect of the new constitution was to transform the Labour Party from a federation of national societies, with the minimum of central organisation, into a more unified national organisation with its own directly affiliated constituency organisations. In the past, the trade unions, through their voting strength and as the principal source of the Party's funds, had exercised a powerful influence over its policy, but organisation and propaganda had been principally undertaken by the affiliated socialist societies. The aim of Arthur Henderson and Sidney Webb, who were the main authors of the new constitution, was to build up a powerful political machine in the constituencies, which would provide the means for making a real challenge to the old parties. Membership was no longer to be confined to the members of the nationally affiliated organisations; in the future it would also be possible to join the party directly as an individual member of a constituency organisation. The trade unions were not, however, willing to give up their control of the political instrument which they had been primarily responsible for creating, and their special interest was recognised in the new constitution by giving them a preponderance of seats on the national executive committee, and so arranging the system of election that the trade unions would be able, through their voting strength, to determine its composition. Nothing less would have satisfied the trade unions, who, whilst recognising the value of the work done by the socialist organisations, would not permit them to obtain complete control over the policy of the Party.

The adoption of the new constitution and the Webbs' policy statement as the official doctrine of the Labour Party, led W. J. Davis, Havelock Wilson and J. B. Williams, secretary of the Musicians' Union, all members of the Parliamentary Committee, to attempt, as they had attempted before without success, to persuade the Trades Union Congress to abandon the Labour Party. This was a last desperate effort on the part of these three die-hard Lib-Labs to secure the exclusion of the socialists from the partnership which had existed between them and the trade unions since the foundation of the Labour Party. The opposition to the new constitution had been sufficiently strong to cause it to be referred back for further consideration when it was first presented to the Labour Party Conference in January 1918, but the concession of two more seats on the executive to the trade unions smoothed the way for the adoption of the constitution when the adjourned conference met one month later. Although it was perfectly clear that the trade unions would continue to have a dominating voice in the counsels of the Party under the new constitution, and though, in fact, the I.L.P. was seriously alarmed at the concessions made to the trade unions, this did not satisfy Davis, Wilson and Williams. A conference organised by these three was held in June 1918, to obtain support for their project, but little was forthcoming. At the Trades Union Congress held in the following September, W. J. Davis, who had never been in favour of a Labour Party independent of the control of the T.U.C. and who harked back to George Howell as the true guide whom the trade unions ought to follow, moved a resolution instructing the Parliamentary Committee to take the necessary steps to found a trade union 'Labour Party'. Davis and his seconder, E. Cathery, of the Sailors' and Firemen's Union, attacked the intellectuals in the Labour Party and denounced the broadening of the constitution which would allow middle-class socialists to flock in. However, an amendment which deprecated any movement designed to secure separate trade union political representation was carried with nearly four million votes in favour and only half a million against. There were, however, a larger number of delegates who, while not wishing to destroy the Labour Party, were apprehensive of the influence exercised by the I.L.P. and the socialist societies. When George Isaacs, delegate of the Operative Printers, moved another amendment, which instructed the Parliamentary Committee to take steps to safeguard and maintain bona fide trade union political action by the formation of the trade unions affiliated to the Labour Party into a political federation which would meet separately and formulate its own political policy, as did the I.L.P. and the British Socialist Party, this suggestion mustered more than twice as many votes as were given in support of a separate trade union party, but was defeated by a majority of two million.[1]

Distrust of middle-class socialist intellectuals was not exactly new, or confined to those who voted with the minority on these resolutions; but it was realised by many of the trade union leaders that the enthusiasm and organising ability of the I.L.P. was an asset which was indispensable to the Labour Party.

With the adoption of the new constitution, the aim of the Labour

[1] *T.U.C. Annual Report*, 1918.

Party was stated to be 'To secure for the producers by hand and by brain the full fruits of their industry, and the most equitable distribution thereof that may be possible, upon the basis of the common ownership of the means of production and the best obtainable system of popular administration and control of each industry and service.' This was the first time that the objective of the Party had definitely been laid down as the creation of a socialist system of society.[1] Although the Trades Union Congress had often carried resolutions calling for the nationalisation of this or that industry, it would have been impossible before the war to persuade a majority of unions that State socialism was a desirable objective. Even then, in 1918, the word socialism did not appear in the new constitution, and the definition of the kind of economic organisation of society which the constitution stated was the aim of the Party, carefully phrased as it was, raised criticism. At the 1918 Congress a delegate of the Liverpool Dockers' Union stated,

> I am a non-Socialist, and I venture to say that the majority whom I represent are also non-Socialists. While the Labour Party was carried out in the way it was formed for that was all right. It was formed on a working arrangement between Socialists and non-Socialists. At the last meeting of the Labour Party Conference, however, the constitution was changed, and I am in the position now, whether I like it or not, of being bound by the Socialist side of the constitution. I am not a rabid Socialist, but I have worked by the side of Socialists for many years as far as I could go, and would it not have been better for the old party to have kept upon the old lines, so as not to have outraged any man's consciences? In the position I am now laying before Congress I do not by any means stand alone.[2]

The truth of the matter was that a large number of trade unionists were still much nearer to the Liberal Party, in social and economic outlook, than they were to any full-blooded system of State socialism. However, the war had effected a considerable change in attitude, and it was equally not *laissez-faire* to which the trade unions wished to return. There was an overwhelming demand for a society in which a much greater degree of social justice prevailed, but there were several trends of thought in the Labour movement as to how this could best be achieved. All were agreed that a root and branch reform of the educational system was necessary, and a comprehensive policy on education was adopted unanimously by the Trades Union Congress.[3] However, when it came to the control of industry, there was not the same degree of unanimity, as the debates on nationalisation at the 1918 Congress indicated. At this Congress, resolutions

---

[1] See Cole, G. D. H., *A History of the Labour Party from 1914*, pp. 54 *et seq.*
[2] *T.U.C. Annual Report*, 1918.   [3] See Appendix 5.

calling for the nationalisation of canals and waterways, mines and minerals, railways, insurance, and the distribution of milk, were carried. In the case of the resolutions on canals and waterways and mines and minerals, the movers agreed to accept an amendment from Will Thorne, to substitute for nationalisation, socialisation, which Thorne said, meant that the industries would not only be nationally owned, but also democratically controlled; the mover of the resolution on the nationalisation of the railways refused to accept a similar amendment on the grounds that it did not indicate what was meant and was therefore impracticable. The delegate from the National Union of Licensed Vehicle Workers condemned nationalisation altogether, on the grounds that it would be the employers who would benefit and not the workers, for whom it would be a disaster. Under the influence of the guild socialists a strong body of opinion had developed, especially among some of the younger trade unionists and in certain unions like the Post Office Workers, National Union of Railwaymen and the Miners, that nationalisation of itself was not enough, that State socialism might be more tyrannical and bureaucratic than capitalist private ownership, and that, therefore, the control of industry should be vested in the workers. The doctrine of workers' control was also being vigorously pushed by the shop stewards' movement, and this made many trade union leaders suspicious of it. Whilst they were in favour of measures to raise the status of the workers and make industry more democratic, the cautious, empirical approach to socialism in the new constitution appealed to the majority of trade union leaders precisely because it did not commit them to a sweeping ideology of the kind advocated by any of the extreme minority groups.

In June 1918, a Labour Party Conference expanded the objectives of the new constitution when it adopted the reconstruction policy statement, *Labour and the New Social Order*. This was a thoroughgoing, comprehensive programme of social reform, but it was not a revolutionary programme by comparison with the demands of syndicalist and Marxian socialists for the abolition of the capitalist system. It took for granted that the existing political, economic and social structure of society would be changed through the process of traditional democratic procedures, of education, agitation and parliamentary legislation. Its significance lay in charting the way ahead for the orderly development of a complex industrial community like Britain, peopled by men and women with a strong sense of social responsibility and a deep attachment to their firmly established ways of life and social institutions. The novelty and the impact made by this programme were not due to the startling originality of any of its proposals, for most of them had been endorsed by the

Trades Union Congress, and some had been persistently canvassed by the Fabian Society and other sections of the Labour movement for the past two decades. It was due, rather, to the fact that they were drawn together and presented in general, though clear and precise, terms, at a time when the war had made the mind of the public receptive.

In summary, the programme demanded the replacement of competitive capitalism by planned co-operation in production and distribution, the elimination of inefficiency and waste and an increase in the production of useful goods and services. In accord with the repeated demands of the trade unions, it was urged that the Government should take steps to prevent a reduction of wages in the post-war period, should set an example by being a model employer, should insist on the full observance of the Fair Wages Clause, and should further the improvement of protective legislation to secure better conditions of health, education, leisure and subsistence. Demobilisation should be carefully planned so that jobs at trade union rates could be found for all ex-service men, and the trade union conditions abrogated during the war should be at once restored. To prevent post-war unemployment and to ensure that 'aggregate total demand for labour shall be maintained year in and year out' it was proposed that a ten years' investment programme of public works should be put in hand.

Then followed demands for the emancipation of women, restoration of personal liberty, political reform, including complete adult suffrage and the reform of the House of Lords, Home Rule for Ireland, constitutional devolution from Westminster for Scotland and Wales, and the reform of local government.

The programme further demanded that a national housing programme should be undertaken, the education system vastly improved, the Poor Law abolished, and greater control imposed on the liquor trade. Railways, canals, electricity, coal and mines, and life assurance should be nationalised, and the land brought under national control so as to bring a good life to rural areas. Finally, it was stated that the system of controls over industry built up during the war should be maintained; accumulated wealth should be conscripted on a graduated scale; and direct taxation on land, income and death duties raised.

Closer Relations with the Co-operative Movement

Just as the war brought about a new relationship between the trade unions and the Labour Party, it also brought the Co-operative movement into closer contact with the industrial and political wings of the Labour movement. Attempts just before the war to arrive at a

mutual aid agreement between the Co-operative Union and the
T.U.C. had ended in failure because of the reluctance of the Co-
operative Congress to sanction closer co-operation with the trade
union movement. Discrimination against the Co-operative societies
when goods began to be in short supply, and the application of the
excess profits tax to the dividend funds of the societies changed this
attitude; it led the Co-operative Union to seek the aid of the Parliamentary Committee of the T.U.C. to get its grievances redressed by
the Government. The 1916 Trades Union Congress had passed a
resolution which invited the Co-operative Union to appoint a committee of six to meet a like number appointed by the Parliamentary
Committee 'to prepare plans for mutual assistance in developing the
productive, distributive and banking activities of the Co-operative
movement'.[1] This suggestion was subsequently endorsed by the
Co-operative Congress, and as a result a United Advisory Council
was established in July 1917, charged with the task of harmonising
the relations between the two movements. On the 24 August the
Advisory Council issued a statement of the objectives which it sought
to attain. These included the recognition by Co-operative societies
of trade union rates of wages and working conditions; the encouragement of Co-operative employees to become members of their appropriate trade union; the improvement of banking facilities to meet the
needs of the trade unions and agreement to examine whether it
would be possible for the Co-operative societies to distribute food
supplies during important trade disputes, through the issue of
coupons, or by loans from the C.W.S. bank on the security of trade
union assets. In return the trade unions would do everything possible
to encourage their members and families to become members of the
Co-operative movement; they would consider how far it might be
possible to utilise their surplus funds by investing them in the
Co-operative societies, and so to assist in the expansion of their
business. To promote these aims it was decided to organise a joint
propaganda campaign and to set up local advisory committees. At
the 1918 Congress progress was reported, and the attention of the
trade unions specially drawn to the banking facilities which the
directors of the C.W.S. Bank were ready to place at their service.

Another development undertaken by the Co-operative movement
was to set up, in 1917, its own National Representation Committee
to sponsor Co-operative candidates for Parliament. In January
1918, the national committees of the Co-operative Congress, T.U.C.
and Labour Party agreed to form a joint committee for the purpose
of promoting common political action, and of avoiding the danger
that the three organisations might come into conflict during an

[1] *T.U.C. Annual Report*, 1916.

election. A considerable section of the Co-operative movement did not relish close ties with the Labour Party, since it was thought that it would be better for business to stay politically neutral; and this attitude severely handicapped those who wanted to bring the movement into what they considered to be its proper place as the third element in a closely-knit triumvirate of working-class organisations. In the event the Co-operative movement decided to sponsor its own candidates, but to enter into an arrangement with the Labour Party to avoid conflict.

The T.U.C. at the End of the War

At the end of the war the whole Labour movement was incomparably better equipped to meet the future than at any time in its past history. It was true that during the war the trade union movement had made great sacrifices. It had accepted with misgiving the restrictions imposed on its freedom to bargain collectively, to strike, and to protect its members by traditional workshop practices. The Conscription and Defence of the Realm Acts, with their serious curtailment of personal liberty, were deeply repugnant to the trade union movement; they had been tolerated as an unfortunate, but necessary, aspect of the struggle to win the war. These sacrifices were made with the support of the majority of the members of the trade union movement in the firm conviction that everything possible should be done on the home front to ensure that the men in battle had all the supplies they needed.

Sacrifices were one side of the picture, but the other showed immense gains. The trade union movement had vastly increased its membership and its financial strength. In 1913, 207 trade unions were affiliated to the T.U.C. with a membership of 2,232,446, and at the Congress of that year 560 delegates were present; five years later, at the Jubilee Congress of 1918, the number of trade unions affiliated had increased to 262, and membership had risen to 4,532,985 who were represented at Congress by 881 delegates, which was easily a record number. Over the same period of time the annual income of the T.U.C. had more than doubled.

Impressive as the gains in membership were, equally impressive was the rise in the status of the trade union movement. The exigencies of the war had compelled the political leaders of the older parties to recognise that the full participation of organised Labour was an indispensable condition of maximum public support for the war effort. Doubtless the front benches of both Liberals and Conservatives would have preferred to avoid making concessions to the Labour movement, but in the circumstances they had no alternative. From the Cabinet downwards the representatives of the trade unions had played their part in the prosecution of the war effort. Trade unions had demanded and secured the right to be represented on the many committees established to administer the distribution of national relief funds, the Munitions and Pensions Acts, rationing and food control. At a higher level the Parliamentary Committee had been in constant consultation with members of the Cabinet and heads of Government departments on all manner of subjects affecting the members of the unions during the war. The association of the trade union movement with the carrying out of national social and industrial policies, though stimulated by the emergency, was simply a logical step along the road which the trade unions had been following since the foundation of the Trades Union Congress in 1868.

During the early period of the war, when the tide of emotional patriotism was running at the flood, the Parliamentary Committee gave almost uncritical support to the Government; the nearly united determination of the trade unions to defeat the enemy sustained it against the few voices of dissent. Though there were at times signs of faltering here and there, the Parliamentary Committee never wavered throughout the war in its adherence to the cause of Allied victory. The trade union movement soon realised, however, that it was faced with a war on two fronts. It was in accord with the Government that the might of German militarism had to be overthrown if liberty and democracy were to survive in Europe; but, if in lending its aid to achieve this end the trade union movement contributed to the entrenchment of those interests engaged in exploitation, profiteering and the maintenance of class-dominated government at home, then clearly a military triumph over Prussian autocracy would be a pyrrhic victory for the workers. When the Parliamentary Committee and the other trade union leaders agreed to the temporary abandonment of long-established trade practices they were well aware of the dangers involved, but unlike their left-wing critics, who preferred to accept defeat rather than co-operate with the forces of capitalism, they were prepared to take the risk, believing that they had the ability to meet the dual challenge. At the other extreme, the right wing saw only the need to crush the Germans, and were prepared to endorse Government policies without question. The hatred of the two extremes for one another was intense, and any policy supported by one side was certain to arouse the bitter opposition of the other, irrespective of its intrinsic merits.

Most of the men who composed the Parliamentary Committee during the war years were solid, sensible, middle-of-the-road trade union officials, who sought to do their duty by their members and by their country.[1] Of those who served on the Committee at this time, R. Smillie and Fred Bramley were somewhat to the left of centre, and W. J. Davis a good deal to the right. During the first two years of the war, the balance of political opinion, was, where it had usually been on the Parliamentary Committee, rather to the right of centre, but as the war went on it gradually shifted, until at the Armistice it was slightly to the left.

The Committee had been overwhelmingly in favour of Labour representatives joining the Government, but it never made the mistake of becoming an agency for rubber-stamping the policies with which their colleagues were associated as members of the Government. It remained constantly firm in its resolve to see the war through to final victory, but developed its own independent line of action—often to the discomfiture of the Labour members of the Government—which had an important influence on Cabinet policy making. From 1916 onwards the trade union movement had grown increasingly critical of the conduct of the war on the home front, and more and more concerned about the making of the peace that one day had to follow the end of hostilities. Distrust of the Government developed because the workers felt that it was not honouring its promises. With evidence all around them of profiteering, irritated by the attitude of officials, who, they felt, often took a mean advantage of the powers conferred upon them by emergency legislation, and with the knowledge that many employers were free to exploit the concessions made by the trade unions, the rank and file became restive and filled with a sense of grievance. After the Russian Revolution it was not only cranks and pacifists who discussed the problem of the making of peace; this became the dominating thought of all sections of the Labour movement. The refusal of Lloyd George to look beyond the military defeat of the enemy aroused suspicions that it was the policy of the Government to carry the war to the bitter end in order to smash Germany and her allies for the benefit of capitalist aggrandisement. When President Wilson made his famous speech in January 1917, in which he looked to 'a peace without victory', it was merely the voice of an idealistic neutral; but before the year was out this doctrine had become a guiding principle for the

---

[1] Among those who served on the Committee between 1914 and 1918 were: Harry Gosling, Watermen; J. W. Ogden, Weavers; J. H. Thomas, Railwaymen; Robert Smillie and A. Onions, Miners; John Hill, Boilermakers; W. Thorne, General Workers; J. H. Jenkins, Shipwrights; J. Sexton, Dock Labourers; E. Judson and W. Mullin, Cotton Spinners; W. Mosses, Patternmakers; W. J. Davis, Brassworkers; G. H. Stuart-Bunning, Postmen; R. B. Walker, Agricultural Workers; Fred Bramley, Furnishing Trades; F. Chandler, Carpenters; E. L. Poulton, Boot and Shoe Operatives: T. A. Flynn, Tailors; and J. B. Williams, Musicians.

Labour movement. It was the basis of the famous *Memorandum on War Aims*, which, although it was attacked in Britain as an irresponsible left-wing outrage against a patriotic Prime Minister, was not a statement of extreme socialist aims, but the embodiment of ideals which appealed to all liberal-minded men; indeed it was a magnificent statement of Liberal principles, having the hallmarks of the great heritage from which the Labour movement drew much of its moral inspiration.

The war brought about a transformation in the social and administrative structure of the State. The Government had mobilised the people for the armed services, and to produce the weapons of war; it had taken control of national industries such as railways, shipping, coal and iron mining; bought and distributed food and raw materials, and altered the social and domestic life of most families in the country. In the undertaking of this vast enterprise, *laissez-faire* had had to be put aside, and the machinery of government and administration completely reorganised. The war jolted men's thoughts out of traditional patterns, provided a convincing demonstration of the need for a new definition of the political aims of the Labour movement, and made possible the adoption of *Labour and the New Social Order*.

The Parliamentary Committee mirrored this trend, following the traditional line of trade union leadership, carefully judging every issue on its merits, slowly adjusting its policy to meet changing circumstances and preserving the essential unity of the movement. At no time during the war was the Committee stampeded by either right or left into adopting policies which would have decisively split the movement; it always sought to find formulae which would rally the maximum of support and avoid driving the extremes out into the wilderness.[1] At the International Labour and Socialist Conferences it successfully played the same role as in the British Labour movement, holding together the A.F. of L. and left-wing socialists, and finally hammering out a policy which secured the maximum agreement.

With the rapid extension of the activities of the State, and the rise in membership and status of the trade union movement, the employers decided to improve their organisation. In 1916 they created

[1] During the war a number of right-wing trade union leaders, including J. B. Williams and Havelock Wilson, had allied themselves with a 'jingo' movement which called itself the British Workers' League; this body was financed by the Government to denounce the internationalists in the Labour movement, but it failed to win much support, and, if anything, served to consolidate the moderate leadership of the T.U.C. An offshoot of the British Workers' League, the National Democratic Party, did, however, play a not insignificant part in the General Election of 1918. See Chapter IX, p. 315.

the Federation of British Industries, which took the place of the old Employers' Parliamentary Association. This development was one of the factors which, together with the major changes in social trends, persuaded the Trades Union Congress to overhaul its own administrative machinery, and so permit the Parliamentary Committee to speak authoritatively on behalf of its affiliated member unions. The steps taken in 1917 to improve the technical efficiency of the Committee were an acknowledgment that this need was understood, but even when these changes were taken into account, the Committee was far from being the general staff of the trade union movement, with power and authority to impose its policy on its members. As the national representative body of a voluntary organisation, the Parliamentary Committee could acquire authority no faster than its members were prepared to permit it to go. However, at the end of the war, with the prestige of the trade union movement at its highest point, a national committee that would be truly a general staff of organised Labour was rapidly beginning to be seen as a necessary development if the T.U.C. was to exercise its influence to the full in the post-war world.

CHAPTER IX

MEETING THE CHALLENGE OF THE FUTURE

Soon after the 1918 Trades Union Congress had terminated it became clear that the end of the war could not be far away. At the time of the Congress it was believed that the war might continue for years, but within a matter of weeks Austria and Germany were in the throes of revolution, the Kaiser had abdicated, and on 11 November an armistice was signed. On the 14 November, at a specially summoned conference of the Labour Party, it was decided by a substantial majority that the representatives of the Party should resign from the Government, so as to free the determination of future policy from the limitations imposed upon the Party as a minority member of a coalition dominated by Liberals and Conservatives. This decision was by no means unanimous, and there was a strong feeling, especially among the trade union leaders, that it was mistaken. However, the sudden release from the constraints imposed by the need to win the war enormously stimulated support for the advocates of militancy in both the political and industrial fields, and the yearning for vigorous action by the leaders of the rank and file was too strong to be denied. J. R. Clynes, who had been one of those who urged the Party not to leave the coalition, because of the influence it could then bring to bear upon the reconstruction programme, loyally accepted the Party's decision and resigned his post as Food Controller, but G. H. Roberts, G. N. Barnes, James Parker and G. J. Wardle refused to join their colleagues in opposition and remained in the Government.

Almost before the Labour Party had had time to gather its wits after this series of momentous events, Lloyd George, seizing his opportunity, had thrust upon it the task of fighting a general election. The Party managed to put 363 candidates into the field, but, although enthusiasm among the active workers ran high, the odds against them were too great, and over three hundred went down to defeat. The prestige of the Prime Minister as the victorious war leader was high and his 'Coupon' a great asset to the Coalition candidates. Although the Labour Party, with the T.U.C. in support, campaigned on a programme which included measures for extensive social reform, this was engulfed in a welter of slogans calculated to appeal to popular prejudices. 'Hang the Kaiser' and 'Make the Germans Pay' caught the mood of an exultant populace in the first flush of victory, with far greater effect than a programme which directed the electorate's thinking to the future. Political divisions in the ranks of the trade unions, which had fermented during the war, further handicapped the Labour Party. The group of extreme 'Jingo' trade unionists had founded an organisation with the title 'British Workers' League'—which had, during the war, received assistance and encouragement from members of the Government—for the purpose of denouncing those leaders of the Labour movement who were internationalist in their outlook. With the end of the war the British Workers' League became the National Democratic Party and managed to put twenty-eight candidates into the field, including J. A. Seddon, chairman of the Parliamentary Committee in 1915, J. R. Bell, Sailors' and Firemen's Union, E. Hallas, a national official of the Gas, Municipal and General Workers' Union, and a number of other trade unionists and ex-Liberals. Ten National Democratic Party candidates were elected, one of them defeating Ramsay MacDonald at Leicester and another F. W. Jowett at Bradford. In addition, the Labour members who had refused to leave the Coalition stood as 'Coupon' candidates. This split in the Labour movement confused the public mind, and the bitter attacks of the National Democratic Party candidates on the peace aims of the Labour Party helped to smear the whole Party with pacifism, and to make the public forget the part played by the Labour movement in winning the war.

The return of only 57 Labour members to Parliament was a severe defeat for the high hopes that had been entertained in the Labour Party. In the circumstances, however, especially as the Party's machine was still in the early stages of reorganisation, it was not a discreditable performance, and the disintegration of the Liberal Party placed Labour in the position of His Majesty's Opposition. The defeat of Arthur Henderson and the I.L.P. leaders, MacDonald, Snowden, Jowett and Anderson, left the Labour Party bereft of its most experienced Parliamentarians at a time when they were most desperately needed; this set-back to the political hopes of the Labour movement contributed to the swing towards industrial action which was to be a marked feature of the next few years.

Threat of Industrial Unrest

During 1917 and 1918 industrial unrest had been on the increase, and 1919 commenced with a serious outbreak of unofficial strikes. The end of the war released the pent-up feelings of the workers who, the election over, turned their attention to improving their lot.

The Wages Temporary Regulation Act, passed under pressure from the trade unions at the end of the war, gave the workers for the time being some protection from a sudden cut in wages, but its duration was limited and the rank and file wanted tangible improvements in their conditions of employment while the going was good. In January the shipyards and engineering shops of the Clyde and Belfast were suddenly brought to a standstill by an unofficial strike. This was aimed as much at the leaders of the men's union as at the employers. In November, eight days after the Armistice had been signed, the leaders of the Amalgamated Society of Engineers had negotiated an agreement with the employers for a 47-hour week, and this had been endorsed by a substantial majority after being put to a ballot vote of the members. There was, however, a considerable minority vote against acceptance; this had been heaviest in those districts where the shop stewards' movement was particularly strong. The shop stewards demanded a 40-hour week, and, arguing that this would be secured now or never, urged their followers to take matters into their own hands, and not to trust the leaders of the union. Encouraged by inflammatory speeches, the strikers demonstrated provocatively, to which the authorities replied with a display of force, the result being a serious clash between the strikers and the police. The Government, alarmed at the situation which had developed, drafted in troops to quell any further disorder. Since the union's executive vigorously opposed the action of the men, the strike collapsed, but not before it had convinced the leaders of the Amalgamated Society of Engineers that it would be wise to reopen negotiations with the employers for a 44-hour week. As soon as the strike was over the Parliamentary Committee issued a circular to all affiliated unions drawing the attention of members to the danger to the trade union movement when accredited representatives and endorsed agreements were repudiated.[1]

More serious than these unofficial stoppages was the threat of a national miners' strike, officially led, with perhaps the support of the other members of the Triple Alliance. This threat was made at the conference of the Miners' Federation, held at Southport, in January 1919. The miners were not simply concerned with demanding shorter hours and higher wages; they wanted the Government, instead of handing back the mines to their owners, to put into operation the miners' plan for national ownership, which would have given half the seats on the proposed governing body for the industry to the Miners' Federation.

On the 12 February, the Miners' Federation decided to conduct a strike ballot.[2] Two days later the Labour members of Parliament

[1] *Industrial Unrest and Unofficial Strikes*, 12 February 1919.
[2] *M.F.G.B. Annual Report*, 1919.

moved an amendment to the address urging the Government to take action to prevent labour unrest. By this time the Government had grown alive to the fact that the industrial situation was rapidly becoming critical. After conferences between members of the Cabinet and officials of the Ministry of Labour it was announced on the 17 February that the Government would call a National Joint Industrial Conference of representatives from the trade unions, employers and official joint industrial bodies, which would be held on the 27 February.[1] On the 21 February the Prime Minister met representatives of the Miners' Federation, and offered to set up a Royal Commission on the Mines, which would include the miners' president, Robert Smillie, and two other representatives; he also proposed to give them the right to nominate three other members of the Commission.[2] After a few hours' consideration of the proposal, the miners' representatives agreed to accept this offer, and held up their preparations for a strike on the Government's undertaking that it would carry out the recommendations of the Commission, which was charged to report on the wages and hours questions by the 20 March.[3] On the 25 February, the executive committees of the members of the Triple Alliance met and decided to postpone consideration of strike action until after the Royal Commission had reported.

The National Industrial Conference convened as planned on the 27 February; it was presided over by the Minister of Labour, Sir Robert Horne, who opened the proceedings with a lengthy statement on the need for better relations between capital and labour.[4] The employers proposed that a National Industrial Committee, consisting of twenty representatives from each side of industry, and representatives of the Ministry of Labour, should be established to make recommendations to the Government. This suggestion was supported by Arthur Henderson, who, however, criticised the assumption of the employers that the existing industrial unrest was merely a temporary phenomenon and proposed an amendment to the employers' resolution. The amendment was designed to ensure that the Committee would be empowered to discuss those matters which the unions considered to be of fundamental importance. It recommended that the National Industrial Committee should consider questions of wages and hours and general conditions of employment, unemployment and its future prevention, and the best methods of promoting co-operation between capital and labour. Speed was

[1] *The Times*, 17 February 1919.
[2] According to Mrs. Webb this was Sidney's idea. He had suggested this course to Lloyd George at a dinner party given by Haldane. He then put the same idea to Robert Smillie and persuaded him to suggest it to the Prime Minister. Beatrice Webb's *Diaries 1912–1924*, Ed. M. I. Cole, pp. 147 *et seq.*
[3] *The Times*, 22 February 1919.   [4] *Ibid.*, 28 February 1919.

considered essential, and it was urged that the Committee should present a report to the whole conference not later than the 5 April. Lloyd George supported Henderson's proposals, but his speech gives the impression that this was a tactical move; he was mainly concerned in getting over the crisis in industrial relations, and it may be doubted that he had any wish to see the Committee explore the deeper issues involved. After Henderson's amendment had been accepted by the conference, Ernest Bevin spoke strongly against it, declaring that the conference had been convened merely to side-track the struggle which the workers were making to improve their conditions. J. H. Thomas presented a memorandum to the conference on behalf of the Triple Alliance, but this was ignored, and the railwaymen, miners and transport workers refused to have anything to do with the Provisional Joint Committee which the conference set up. Suspicion of the motives of the Government and the employers was not confined to the Triple Alliance and the left wing of the Labour movement, but Henderson and most members of the Parliamentary Committee had no wish to see the country plunged into industrial strife, as was desired by some of the leaders of the Triple Alliance; it was realised that this was likely to end in disaster for both the trade unions and the Labour Party.

On the 27 March the reports of the sub-committees which had been set up by the Provisional Joint Committee were published.[1] The main proposals were the establishment of a legal maximum working week of 48 hours, minimum time rates of wages, the continuance of stabilised wage rates for a further six months, the introduction of measures for stabilising employment and the creation of a permanent National Industrial Council. When the conference reassembled on the 4 April, the Minister of Labour stated that the Government had hoped that the National Industrial Council would have been set up, and that the Prime Minister would have presented to its first meeting the intentions of the Government.[2] The Labour representatives were not, however, prepared to establish another committee until they had proof of the Government's sincerity. When, on the 1 May, Sir Robert Horne read a letter from Lloyd George to the Provisional Joint Committee, in which he stated, 'I fully accept in principle your recommendations as to the fixing of maximum hours and minimum rates' and promised legislation, it looked as if Henderson and the trade union leaders who had collaborated on the Provisional Joint Committee were to be justified in their action. The Parliamentary Committee was able to report to the delegates to the Trades Union Congress in September that the Government had tabled a Bill to limit hours of work to a maximum of 48 per week, with certain

[1] *The Times*, 27 March 1919.   [2] *Ibid.*, 5 April 1919.

exceptions, but events were to prove right those who suspected that the Government would change its mind once it had surmounted the crisis which it faced in the early months of 1919.[1]

Meanwhile, overshadowing the deliberations of the Industrial Conference, was the prospect of a national coal strike. On the 20 March the Sankey Commission published an interim report which conceded the miners' claim for higher wages and a seven-hour day. What, however, attracted most attention, was the statement in the interim report by Mr. Justice Sankey that 'Even upon the evidence already given, the present system of ownership and working in the coal industry stands condemned, and some other system must be substituted for it, either nationalisation or a method of unification by national purchase and/or by joint control.'[2] The report did state in a later paragraph that 'No sufficient evidence has as yet been tendered, and no sufficient criticism has yet been made to show whether nationalisation or a method of unification by national purchase and/or by joint control is best in the interests of the country and its export trade, the workers, and the owners.'[3] The Miners' Federation, its hopes aroused by the interim report, decided to postpone its threatened strike until after the Commission had published its final recommendations on the organisation of the industry, which the miners now confidently expected would be in favour of their policy of nationalisation. The miners' leaders, however, especially Smillie, the militant pacifist, had by no means abandoned their belief in the value of direct action on a national scale as the most effective means of achieving their ends.

Demand for Direct Action

On the 3 April 1919, the executive committee of the Labour Party and the Parliamentary Committee of the T.U.C. convened a special conference to define their attitude to the proposed Covenant of the League of Nations. At this meeting, the miners submitted a resolution which called on the Government to cease its intervention in Russia, lift the blockade against Germany, bring conscription to an immediate end, and release the conscientious objectors from prison;

[1] The 48-hours Bill was not considered satisfactory by the Labour representatives because of its escape clauses. The Government refused to make any further concessions and, in protest against this attitude, the Labour representatives in 1921 resigned from the National Industrial Conference, which had long been moribund, and the Government seized the opportunity to drop the measure.

[2] *Coal Industry Commission Act 1919*, Interim Report, Cmd. 84, paragraph ix. Signatories to the interim report were Mr. Justice Sankey, Mr. Arthur Balfour, Sir Arthur Duckham and Sir Thomas Royden.

[3] *Ibid.*, paragraph xiii.

it further called on the conference to take action to compel the Government to carry out these demands. G. H. Stuart-Bunning, chairman of the Parliamentary Committee, who was presiding over the conference, refused to accept the second part of the resolution because it implied taking industrial action, a course to which, he said, the political section of the Labour movement could not be committed. It was clear to most delegates that the miners were bent on provoking a general strike, but the chairman's ruling was accepted, and the conference went on to pass the first half of the resolution. The miners then brought their resolution before a meeting of the leaders of the Triple Alliance, who passed it with a rider calling on the Parliamentary Committee to summon a special national Congress to discuss the action that should be taken. On the 26 April the Parliamentary Committee received a deputation from the Triple Alliance, consisting of Robert Smillie, C. T. Cramp, president of the National Union of Railwaymen, and Robert Williams of the Transport Workers, all of them leading advocates of the general strike. After considering the request of the Triple Alliance the Parliamentary Committee decided to interview the Prime Minister before taking any action.[1]

Just at this time George Lansbury secured a copy of a confidential military circular, which had been sent to all commanding officers, asking them whether they considered their men could be relied upon to carry out orders if the Government used them to man industries brought to a standstill by strike action. The publication of this leaflet in the *Daily Herald*[2] aroused indignation throughout the Labour movement and strengthened the suspicion that the Government was only playing for time with the National Industrial Conference and the Coal Commission, and would not implement its promises unless compelled to do so.

The Parliamentary Committee was unable to see Lloyd George, as he was engaged at the Peace Conference in Paris, but an interview was granted instead with Bonar Law, on the 22 May. Bonar Law informed the Committee that it was the intention of the Government to withdraw conscripts from Russia and replace them with volunteers, and that it was not the aim of the British Government to impose a government on the Russians. He denied that the Government had violated its election pledges to end conscription, stated that it was only being maintained until Germany had signed the Peace Treaty, and informed the Committee that the blockade of Germany would be brought to an end at the same time. With regard to the conscientious objectors, the deputation had to admit that the trade union movement was divided on this issue, and agreed that it was one that

[1] *T.U.C. Annual Report*, 1919.   [2] *Daily Herald*, 13 May 1919.

would soon be dead. As to the secret military circular, he would give no undertaking, but promised to consider its withdrawal.[1] Bonar Law made it clear that if there was a general strike, 'either the outside movement must be fought, and beaten, or the outside movement must become the government of the country'.[2] He would not say what action the Government would take if a general strike occurred, but, to the members of the Parliamentary Committee, the implication was plain.[3] The Parliamentary Committee met again on the 28 May, and decided that in the circumstances that prevailed, Bonar Law's reply was satisfactory; they refused to take the action demanded of them by the Triple Alliance, but only by a narrow majority, the Committee being divided by seven votes to five.[4]

The refusal of the Parliamentary Committee to carry out the wish of the Triple Alliance was bitterly attacked in the left-wing Labour Press, and the National Union of Railwaymen passed a resolution strongly condemning the Committee. This was not the end of the matter, for the leaders of the Triple Alliance were resolved to carry the attack on the Parliamentary Committee to the annual Congress, but by the time Congress was held the atmosphere had cooled a little and the members of the Triple Alliance, except for the miners, were less certain of the wisdom of engaging in a national strike.

In the middle of June the awaited recommendations of the Sankey Commission were published, but there were four reports instead of one.[5] One report was signed by Sir John Sankey, another by the six Labour representatives, the third by five employers and the fourth by Sir Arthur Duckham. All four reports were in favour of public ownership of the coal itself, and Sir John Sankey and the Labour representatives' reports advocated the nationalisation of the industry. The employers' report naturally supported a continuance of

[1] The Labour members forced a debate in the House of Commons on the military circular on the 29 May. Replying to their strong protests at its issue Churchill stated that it would be outrageous to use troops in a minor strike, but that where the health and safety of large numbers were concerned it was the duty of the Government to take such steps as it considered necessary, and it was essential, therefore, to know what the troops were prepared to do. The fact that the Government found it necessary to obtain this information is an interesting comment on the morale of the armed forces, and on the state of tension which existed in the country at that time.

[2] The Times, 4 June 1919.

[3] In March Bonar Law had been prepared to crush a strike by the miners or railwaymen, by passing legislation to empower the Government to seize strike funds and arrest the union leaders. Cf. Blake, Robert, The Unknown Prime Minister, p. 413.

[4] A statement made by Robert Williams that was not contradicted, during a debate on the decision of the Parliamentary Committee at the 1919 Trades Union Congress.

[5] Coal Industry Commission Act 1919, Reports, Cmd. 210.

private ownership, but the Duckham report suggested a reorganisation of the industry under private ownership, which would permit
the appointment of miners' representatives on the boards of directors
of the colliery companies.

The miners, set on obtaining not only public ownership of the
mines, but also joint control of the industry, differed with the report
of the chairman, who recommended that the workers should only be
represented by a minority on the proposed National Mining Council.[1]
On the question of compensation the Labour members of the
Commission were divided; the M.F.G.B. members were opposed to
paying compensation to the royalty owners, but they were ready to
pay it to the owners of the collieries, while the other three Labour
representatives favoured paying compensation in both cases.

The miners were in a dilemma, but with some misgiving they
decided to accept the Sankey report at a national conference in July.
Up to this point the Government had made no announcement of its
intentions, and it delayed revealing the fact that it had decided to
reject Mr. Justice Sankey's report until 18 August, the day it tabled
a Bill to establish a statutory maximum working week of 48 hours,
as recommended by the Industrial Conference. Although Lloyd
George had promised to carry out the report of the Commission he
was able to justify not fulfilling his pledge on the grounds of the
divisions of opinion in the ranks of the Commission.[2] The Government was in a far stronger position to dare the miners to do their
worst than it had been in the early part of 1919, when coal stocks
were almost non-existent. During the year demobilisation had gone
ahead and millions of soldiers had returned to civilian life and had
settled in jobs. Prices were rising, but trade was booming, and the
temper of the rank and file was far from revolutionary at this stage;
however much some of the militant advocates of direct action might
have convinced themselves that this was a good moment to have a
showdown with the Government, others were more sceptical.

This was the situation faced by the miners after Lloyd George had
refused to accept Justice Sankey's report; proposing in its place a
modified form of the Duckham report. With this proposal the miners
would have nothing to do, since they were certain that if only they
could secure a sufficient demonstration of working-class force they
could achieve the nationalisation of the industry. After discussing

[1] *M.F.G.B. Annual Report*, 1919.

[2] Had the miners and their representatives signed the chairman's report they
would have been in a strong position. That they did not was mainly due to the
naïve optimism of Smillie, who was firmly convinced that capitalism would
collapse within five years, and that the mines would then be taken over by the
miners. It was, he argued, unnecessary to compromise on principle, when one
could remain true to one's faith in the certainty of success.

with the other two sections of the Triple Alliance, the question of strike action to compel the Government to carry out the Sankey report, the miners decided not to strike at once, but to refer the matter to the Trades Union Congress which was to meet soon afterwards.

Before the Congress was held there were rumours that the Triple Alliance unions would move a vote of censure on the Parliamentary Committee for failing to organise a national strike, and that efforts would be made to dislodge those members of the Committee who had voted against the Triple Alliance request for a special Congress. It was obvious that the president of Congress, G. H. Stuart-Bunning, took this threat of a challenge to the Committee seriously, for he devoted a major part of his presidential address to it.

To have called the Congress would inevitably have identified the Committee with the policy of a national strike on political matters, and from that aspect the Committee had to view the question, argued the President. He went on to say, 'Consider for a moment the exact position of affairs. This Congress has never yet fully accepted the policy of a national strike on industrial matters, which are its primary function. I do not think it has ever seriously discussed the national strike on a political issue, still less on several political issues, on some of which there were sharp divisions among our people.

'We were, therefore, asked to do something for which there was no precedent by executives who could not say definitely whether their own members were behind them, and we were asked to do this at a time when dark though the outlook was, there were bright spots in the sky. . . . The national strike might have been declared! What then? There were prominent men who sincerely believed that upon such a manifestation the Government would immediately reverse its policy. I cannot share that view, nor even understand how it was arrived at. The present Government is not renowned for courage, but driven to bay, as it would have been, it must have fought.

'If the Government fought it meant revolution. The project, therefore, resolves itself into a desperate gamble with the lives of men, women and children for the stakes. The Parliamentary Committee, therefore, might well hesitate to call a Congress.'[1]

The miners' representatives were not impressed by this line of argument, and as soon as the Parliamentary Committee's report was presented to Congress they seized the opportunity to move the reference back of that section which referred to the demand of the Triple Alliance for a special Congress. Robert Smillie, seeking to discredit the Parliamentary Committee, suggested that the Triple Alliance merely asked for a special Congress to consider action, and

[1] *T.U.C. Annual Report*, 1919.

not to decide whether a strike should take place. This was a disingenuous, if not downright dishonest criticism of the Parliamentary Committee, as J. R. Clynes demonstrated when he exhibited a strike ballot paper which the Triple Alliance had gone to the length of printing, but had not issued when the Parliamentary Committee refused to take the step of calling a special Congress. Although the weight of argument was on the side of the Parliamentary Committee there was among the delegates a feeling which had been assiduously fostered by the miners and the militant groups in the Labour movement, that the Parliamentary Committee had been weak in not putting stronger pressure on the Government; it was not, therefore, a great surprise when the reference back was carried by 2,586,000 votes to 1,876,000. The miners were elated with their success, but delivering a slap to the Parliamentary Committee was not committing Congress to the support of a policy of direct action on political issues, and it was Tom Shaw, M.P., one of the leaders of the cotton weavers, himself utterly opposed to the policy of the miners, who insisted on Congress facing the issue of principle.[1]

Shaw's resolution 'That this Congress declares against the principle of industrial action in purely political matters' was not debated until later in the week. Following the debate on the reference back, Arthur Henderson, speaking as fraternal delegate, had delivered a powerful plea to the Congress to consider seriously the consequences to the Labour Party if the trade unions adopted the policy of 'direct action'.[2] When the resolution was discussed, Frank Hodges of the miners and John Bromley, secretary of the Locomotive Engineers and Firemen, urged its rejection, but J. H. Thomas, secretary of the N.U.R., and one of the leaders of the Triple Alliance, made an ambiguous speech in which he said that 'direct action' might be necessary in certain circumstances, but left the impression that while it would be dangerous to vote for the resolution it would also be a mistake to vote against it. This was the feeling of a majority, though there were strong sections on both sides which would have

[1] *T.U.C. Annual Report*, 1919.
[2] 'I hear many people talking very glibly about "The Day" and they say that it is coming presently. . . . I have heard speeches today from responsible Trade Union leaders which would appear to indicate in some of their sentences, however much I would prefer to think otherwise, a withdrawal of confidence in the political and constitutional method. No greater calamity could come to Labour than that such a feeling should be displayed just at this momentous period in our history when the position is so promising. . . .

'I appeal to you . . . to give the political side of the movement such a trial as you have never given it before.'
From the speech of Arthur Henderson, fraternal delegate from the Labour Party to the Trades Union Congress, 1919. *Ibid.*

preferred a clear-cut decision; when the previous question was moved it was carried, although only by a narrow majority.

The miners had not secured the endorsement of Congress for their policy of 'direct action' but they had humbled the Parliamentary Committee, and obtained a good deal of publicity for their views; they also had the satisfaction of forcing the Parliamentary Committee to submit a resolution which embodied the main points of the Triple Alliance resolution. It called upon the Government to end conscription, and to cease intervention in Russia; when put to the vote this was carried almost without opposition. Moreover, the Parliamentary Committee, afraid that a resolution would be carried which called for 'direct action' if the Government refused to end conscription, proposed as an alternative to a definite instruction of this kind, that it should call a special Congress to discuss what action the movement should then take. By securing the acceptance of this resolution the Parliamentary Committee again slipped out of a tight corner, avoiding the danger of a split in the movement, and obtaining a further supply of its most precious asset, time. A similar compromise was arrived at when the miners moved their resolution asking Congress 'to co-operate with the M.F.G.B. to the fullest extent with a view to compelling the Government to adopt the scheme of national ownership and joint control recommended by the majority of the (Sankey) Commission in their report'. In the event of the Government continuing to refuse to implement its promise the Parliamentary Committee agreed to call a special Congress to decide the form of action to be taken to compel the Government to carry out the demands of the miners.

The Police Officers' Strike

The Parliamentary Committee survived a further attempt to censure its policy when the representatives of the Police and Prison Officers' Union moved the reference back to the section of the Committee's report which dealt with the strike of police early in August 1919.[1] The first strike of police officers had occurred in August 1918, and had been terminated when the Prime Minister had agreed that increases in pay should be granted. The police were also striking for the official recognition of their union, but Lloyd George told them that he would not concede recognition until the war was over. In fact the Prime Minister had no intention of recognising a bona fide trade union for policemen, but he was concerned to bring this dangerous rebellion to an end at once and to deal with its leaders later. There followed a series of negotiations with the Home Office,

[1] *The Times*, 1 August 1919.

which resulted in an agreement that a representative board would be established inside the force, separate from the union. As the Home Office had negotiated with the leaders of the union, it was naïvely assumed by them that the Government would continue to recognise the union, although no specific undertaking was given. In addition, the agreement, which the secretary of the union had signed, included a clause which stated

> that there will be no objection to a member of the force joining the National Union of Police and Prison Officers, so long as this union does not claim or attempt to interfere with the regulations and discipline of the Service, or to induce members of the force to withhold their services. but that in the event of a breach of this condition members of the force may be called upon to sever their connection with such union.

A further clause referring to the representative board stated that 'the organisation shall be entirely within the force and *shall be entirely independent of and unassociated with any outside body*'.[1] With the war over the Government was ready to take a firmer stand, and the representative board soon proved to be something different from what the union had imagined they were agreeing to set up, since the police chiefs made it clear to the men that they would not tolerate anything in the nature of collective bargaining.

In February 1919, the union applied to the T.U.C. for affiliation and this was accepted. This move gave the Government the excuse they wanted, and a Bill was introduced which proposed to establish a police federation 'entirely independent and unassociated with any body or person outside the police service'. Under the terms of the Bill no policeman would be allowed to join a trade union which had among its objects the control or influence of the pay, pensions or conditions of service of the police force. There was, however, a proviso which allowed a man who had been a member of a trade union before becoming a constable to retain his membership with the consent of the chief officer of the police.

The Parliamentary Committee, asked by the Police Officers' Union for help, saw the Home Secretary, who confronted them with the agreement signed by the secretary of the union, about which the Committee knew nothing, since it had not been informed of its existence by the union. The position was further complicated by the fact that the Parliamentary Labour Party had secured considerable support for a number of amendments to the Government's Bill; but when the union called out its members on strike, without warning the Party that it was considering this action, support for the amendments fell to twenty-six names. The Government at once took draconic

[1] My italics. *Report of the Parliamentary Committee*, 1919.

measures, and dismissed from the service thousands of police officers, who also lost their pension rights. The Parliamentary Committee tried to get the Home Secretary to reconsider his action, and reinstate the dismissed men, and warned the Government of the danger of serious repercussions. Faced, however, by the agreement not to associate with any outside body, signed by the union, the Committee was in a weak position, and was in no mood seriously to challenge the Government, which had indicated, by its actions, that it was not bluffing in its determination to crush any idea that might exist in the minds of policemen that they would be permitted to use the strike as a weapon to remedy their grievances.

Representatives of the Police Officers' Union attacked the Parliamentary Committee for having accepted the Home Office version of events which led up to the police strike, and they were supported by Walter Citrine, who accused the Parliamentary Committee of failing to give the union proper support for its demands. It was, however, Ernest Bevin[1] who toppled over the case of the union, when he told the delegates bluntly that the representatives of the policemen's union had got themselves into a mess, and then tried to repeat their success of the previous year by calling a strike; it was impossible for the Parliamentary Committee or the Labour members of Parliament to do anything now, and all that the trade union movement could do was to look after the men who had lost their jobs by raising a fund to help them. After James Sexton had made a withering attack on the tactics of the leaders of the Police Officers' Union, the reference back was withdrawn. Congress supported the recommendation of the Parliamentary Committee to raise a fund to help the men and their dependants, and passed a resolution which condemned the Police Act as a violation of trade union rights and called for a recognition of the union by the Government, and the reinstatement of the men dismissed. This, however, was little more than a gesture, as neither the Parliamentary Committee nor the majority of delegates was prepared to fight the Government on an issue which raised, even more clearly than the Triple Alliance resolution had done, the limits of trade union action in a democratic country.[2]

The Foundation of the International Labour Organisation

Having continued to display a great interest in international affairs, the Parliamentary Committee had a good deal of activity to report to Congress. In January 1919, the Parliamentary Committee

[1] This was not to be the last occasion on which Bevin and Citrine clashed during their long careers with the T.U.C.
[2] *T.U.C. Annual Report*, 1919.

had received an invitation from George Barnes, who was one of the
Government's representatives at the Paris Peace Conference, to send
at once a delegation of three members in order to confer with him
about a proposal to establish an international Labour organisation.
The Committee sent its chairman and secretary and R. Shirkie, a
representative of the miners, who was on the Committee. Arthur
Henderson and J. H. Thomas also went to Paris, but were invited
directly. When they arrived they were presented with a memorandum
which had been drawn up by Barnes and his assistants, H. B. Butler,
and Sir David Shackleton, which the British delegation proposed to
place before a Labour Commission about to be set up by the Peace
Conference.[1] The memorandum suggested the creation of a permanent international Labour office, and an international Labour conference to be held annually, constituted from representatives drawn
from Governments, employers' and Labour organisations, all of whom
would be able to vote independently of each other; decisions to be
taken by a two-thirds majority and to be then subject to ratification
by the Parliaments of the participating countries. The representatives of the Parliamentary Committee made several minor but important recommendations which were incorporated into the British
draft. The Labour Commission met soon afterwards, with Samuel
Gompers as its president, and after several weeks of discussion
adopted substantially the British draft proposals.

Immediately after the consultations in Paris, G. H. Stuart-Bunning,
J. H. Thomas and Robert Shirkie, who were joined by Margaret
Bondfield and T. Greenall, proceeded to Berne, where together with
delegates from the Labour Party, headed by Arthur Henderson, they
represented the British Labour movement at an International Labour
and Socialist Conference. It had been decided at the Allied Labour
Conference in 1918 to hold a conference to coincide with the meeting
of the Peace Conference, at which representatives of the Labour
movements from erstwhile enemy countries should be present. The
Berne Conference provided a forum for all the conflicting ideologies
in the European Labour movement; nevertheless, some progress
towards the reconstitution of a new International was made. In the
subsequent manœuvres after this conference, which eventually led
to the creation of the Labour and Socialist International, the Parliamentary Committee remained closely associated with the Labour
Party.

The Berne Conference was not mentioned in the Parliamentary
Committee's report to the 1919 Congress, and when asked the
reason for this omission the president of Congress replied that an
account had been published in the *Quarterly Report*, and it was

[1] Barnes, G. N., *From Workshop to Westminster*, Ch. XV.

purely an oversight that no mention had been made of it in the *Annual Report* of the Parliamentary Committee. The secretary of the G.F.T.U. had attacked the participation of the T.U.C. in the Berne Conference because the conference included socialists and representatives of Germany,[1] but no criticism of the Parliamentary Committee and no discussion of the Berne Conference occurred during the week of Congress. The restraint shown by the supporters of the G.F.T.U. in not attacking the Parliamentary Committee at Congress was probably due to the agreement which had been arrived at between the two national trade union organisations regarding British representation in the International Federation of Trade Unions.

The agreement reached between the Parliamentary Committee and the Management Committee of the G.F.T.U. provided that each organisation would be equally represented on any British delegation to international trade union conferences and that affiliation fees would be shared proportionately according to membership. The agreement had its first test when a joint delegation from the two organisations went to Amsterdam in July 1919, to attend a conference to recreate the International Federation of Trade Unions.[2] G. H. Stuart-Bunning, Will Thorne, J. B. Williams, J. Hill and T. Greenall represented the T.U.C., and W. A. Appleton, Ben Tillett, J. Asquith and James Crinion represented the G.F.T.U. The Parliamentary Committee reported to Congress that the joint delegation worked well;[3] W. A. Appleton, with the support of the T.U.C. delegates, had been elected president of the new International Federation, and J. B. Williams of the Parliamentary Committee was elected to the Management Committee.

This amity in relations between the two organisations was not, however, destined to last for long, for at the 1920 Congress a resolution was carried to exclude the G.F.T.U. from its partnership with the T.U.C. in representing the British trade union movement internationally. The resolution, moved by Robert Williams and seconded by John Bromley, proposed that the British trade union movement should be affiliated to the International Federation of Trade Unions only through the T.U.C., and that its Parliamentary Committee should refrain from co-operating with any other body.[4] The main point of attack was concentrated on W. A. Appleton and his newspaper, *The Democrat*. This journal had carried on a persistent criticism of the Triple Alliance and its policy of 'direct action', and had

---

[1] *The Democrat*, 10 April 1919. This paper had been founded in 1917 by W. A. Appleton.

[2] *Report of the Parliamentary Committee*, 1919.

[3] *T.U.C. Annual Report*, 1919.   [4] *Ibid.*, 1920.

denigrated especially the miners and their veteran leader, Robert Smillie. Though many trade unionists would have agreed with its strictures on the 'direct actionists', the paper was obviously out of tune with the sentiments of the majority of members; in the fondness that it showed for the Liberals and the respect that it paid to the middle classes *The Democrat* was reminiscent of the outlook of Henry Broadhurst. Since its influence was negligible, it could have been safely left to die a natural death, as it eventually did, but it provided the opportunity for the final act of revenge for which the miners had been waiting. With the passing of this resolution, the G.F.T.U. was at last reduced to the status of an insurance organisation.

No discussion took place on the International Federation of Trade Unions, but the amount of international work in which the Parliamentary Committee had been involved during the year previous to the 1919 Congress was cited by the president when replying to caustic criticism from H. H. Elvin, secretary of the Clerks' Union, who suggested that the Parliamentary Committee had failed to carry out the reform of its own organisation which it had been instructed to do in 1917.[1] Later in the week a rather vague resolution was carried without discussion, which instructed the Parliamentary Committee to take steps to prepare a scheme that would lead to the trade union movement speaking with a single voice in the future. This kind of resolution had been carried before and it aroused little interest, but events that were to occur soon after Congress was over brought a fresh urgency to the demand for organisational changes.

A resolution moved by Andrew Conley of the Garment Workers had a more lively reception, and pointed to the problem of giving the Parliamentary Committee greater authority over the affiliated organisations. It asked the Parliamentary Committee to take steps to secure the transference of all workers who were members of unions not primarily concerned with the clothing industry to the two unions which had been established to organise the workers in that industry. The resolution was naturally opposed by the General Workers' Union, but the feeling that the trade unions ought to put their house in order was sufficiently strong for the resolution to secure a bare majority.

As usual, much of the time of Congress was spent in discussing resolutions in favour of social reforms on which the majority of delegates were agreed. When the 1919 Congress adjourned it had carried resolutions in favour of the nationalisation of mines, railways, shipping, land and banking; an increase in old age pensions, sickness and maternity benefits and the abolition of the Poor Law. Perhaps

[1] See previous chapter.

the most exciting moment in a week which had provided few sensations was the announcement of the result of the Widnes by-election; Arthur Henderson had been elected, transforming a Coalition majority of 3,694 into a Labour majority of 987, and incidentally giving point to his plea to the delegates to eschew 'direct action' and give their support to the Labour Party.

The delegates had not specifically rejected the use of 'direct action' for political purposes, and in the next year it was used with notable success, but the failure of the miners to secure any representative on the Parliamentary Committee, and the re-election of almost all of the old Committee which had refused to take action on the Triple Alliance resolution did not suggest that strong support would be forthcoming from the Parliamentary Committee for a policy of large-scale strikes.

The Railway Strike and the Mediation Committee

Congress had only been over a matter of days when the rumblings of unrest on the railways mounted rapidly, and on the 26 September 1919, the country was faced with a national railway strike. The railways were still under the control which the Government had assumed over them during the war, and the trade unions, anxious to obtain better wages and working conditions, had been in prolonged negotiations with the Railway Executive Committee since the previous February. The Government had no intention of conceding the claims of the railwaymen, and made its preparations to deal with the possibility of a strike. There had been a division of opinion between the Associated Society of Locomotive Engineers and Firemen and the National Union of Railwaymen,[1] about the claims to be made for their members, and the Government appeared to think that it could play on these differences. On the 20 August it was announced that agreement had been reached on improved conditions of service for enginemen, but it soon became clear that the Government was not prepared to be as generous with the mass of other grades organised by the N.U.R. On the 21 September, J. H. Thomas issued a warning that the negotiations were rapidly approaching a state of crisis, but the Government refused to budge from its proposals, which in fact would have resulted in reductions in weekly wages of as much as 14s. per week for some grades.[2] In these circumstances the N.U.R. had little choice but to call its members out on strike, which it did on the 26 September. The Government had hoped that it would divide the two unions, and would be able to keep the transport system going

[1] McKillop, Norman, *The Lighted Flame*, p. 123.
[2] Rayner, R. M., *The Story of Trade Unionism*, pp. 198–9.

with the emergency arrangements which it had made to carry essential goods by road, together with the use of blacklegs, with whom, it was vainly assumed, the engine crews, having secured their own gains, would be prepared to work. In the light of past relations between these two unions the Government's hope could be understood, but it had forgotten that in John Bromley the locomotive engineers had one of the strongest supporters of militant trade unionism in the country, and he gave full support to the N.U.R.[1]

Despite a display of military force the workers remained orderly and stood firm, bringing the railways almost to a complete standstill, much to the surprise of the Government. Inspired by the slogan that the strike was an 'anarchist conspiracy' most of the Press indulged in a tremendous campaign of abuse against the strikers and their leaders. These attacks were manifestly stupid when applied to J. H. Thomas, who was far from being an adherent of the 'direct action' thesis; they served, however, to consolidate support of his leadership when he was under fire for not invoking the aid of the other members of the Triple Alliance. Thomas realised that the Government had made a strike inevitable, though he would have preferred a negotiated settlement, and had he not called the men out he would probably have lost control to more militant elements.[2] The N.U.R. was, in fact, ill-prepared for a national strike; its reserve funds were low, and no preparations had been made to meet a strike emergency, whereas the Government was ready to deal with a situation which it had deliberately done much to create.[3] The aim of the Government was to discredit the union in the eyes of the public. That it failed to achieve this result was largely due to the efforts of the Labour Research Department,[4] which saw to it that the case of the strikers was given wide and effective publicity.[5] In addition the Co-operative societies did what the trade unions had long wanted them to do; they printed special cheques and coupons which were used in lieu of money, and permitted the striking railwaymen to obtain food from Co-operative stores, thus staving off the danger of

[1] McKillop, Norman, *The Lighted Flame*, p. 132.

[2] Fuller, Basil, *The Life Story of J. H. Thomas*, p. 159.

[3] Rayner, R. M., *The Story of Trade Unionism*, p. 200.

[4] Cole, G. D. H., *A Short History of the British Working Class Movement*, p. 392. The Labour Research Department had been established in 1912 by the Webbs, mainly to assist the trade unions, but during the war it had been captured by the guild socialists under the leadership of G. D. H. Cole, and in 1917 had broken away from the Fabian Society to become an independent research bureau supported by trade union and Labour organisations.

[5] The compositors indicated that unless the case of the railwaymen was fairly stated and advertisements accepted from the union giving the workers' point of view they would refuse to print the newspapers. Their threat was successful in 1919, but when repeated in 1926 had unfortunate consequences.

the strike collapsing through lack of funds to sustain it. The factor which was, perhaps, most responsible for bringing the strike to a successful conclusion, was a meeting of unions affected by the strike at which a special committee was set up to mobilise support for the railwaymen. This conference was called by the Transport Workers' Federation, and was held on the 1 October, in the Caxton Hall, under the presidency of Harry Gosling.[1] Such moderates as J. R. Clynes, Arthur Henderson, C. W. Bowerman, and J. T. Brownlie of the A.S.E. were included in the Committee which, in fact, acted in a mediating capacity—becoming known as the Mediation Committee —and sought to bring the Cabinet and the leaders of the N.U.R. together. The Government finally saw that the trade union movement was in no mood to accept any reduction in wages and abandoned its attempt to destroy the N.U.R. after the strike had lasted nine days.[2]

This strike was significant in a number of ways. It indicated to the trade unions the need for the close co-operation of the whole Labour movement when one of their number became involved in a major dispute which had far-reaching repercussions on the fortunes of them all. It emphasised the importance of a skilled presentation of the trade union case by means of national publicity based on carefully assembled facts. As soon as the strike was over there was a demand for the creation of a permanent 'General Staff' for the trade union movement which would be able to undertake these duties. The Parliamentary Committee was assailed by its critics for failing to take charge of the strike and for merely functioning during the stoppage 'as a co-opted member of an unofficial committee chosen by a hastily summoned unofficial conference'.[3] The moral of the railway strike was driven home, and to give it further point the Mediation Committee decided to remain in being in case of future need for its assistance.

Proposals to Increase the Authority of the T.U.C.

Following the presentation of a report from the Mediation Committee, the Parliamentary Committee agreed to set up a Co-ordination Committee, to consider the establishment of new central machinery for the trade union movement. This Co-ordination Committee was constituted from six representatives of the Parliamentary

[1] *Annual Report of the National Transport Workers' Federation*, 1920. *The Times*, 2 October 1919.
[2] Cf. Webb, S. and B., *The History of Trade Unionism*, Ed. 1919, pp. 535 *et seq.* This is a fairly full account of the 1919 railway strike. See also Gleason, Arthur, *What the Workers Want*, p. 136.
[3] *The Guildsman*, November 1919.

Committee, four from the Mediation Committee and five from the trade union side of the National Provisional Joint Industrial Council.[1] These fifteen settled down to work and within a few weeks produced a report and recommendations which were presented to a special meeting of the Trades Union Congress in December.

The main reason for holding this special Congress was to consider what was to be done in face of the continued refusal of the Government to carry out the main report of the Sankey Commission; Lloyd George had offered, instead of nationalisation, to regroup the mines into more efficient units and, while maintaining private ownership, to give the miners representation on pit and district committees and on area and national boards. This scheme the miners scornfully rejected; they preferred to have the old system than an increase in 'capitalist trustification'. The decision as to what should be done by the T.U.C. to support the miners had, in fact, been taken before the Congress assembled; the leaders of the miners and the Parliamentary Committee had agreed to recommend to Congress that a national propaganda campaign should be held to bring public opinion round to support the miners' claims, more drastic measures for the time being to be postponed.

The special Congress opened on the 9 December with an address from J. H. Thomas, chairman of the Parliamentary Committee for the year, who presided over the gathering. Thomas urged the delegates to have faith in their political strength, and, by implication, to shun direct action to bring about the nationalisation of the mines. Political action 'was an instrument that for this purpose could be as powerful as was any industrial action, in as much as it was not so costly and certainly less inconvenient, to secure by the ballot box that for which men were prepared to strike'.[2] He was followed by Frank Hodges, the secretary of the M.F.G.B., who contented himself with a review of the interview with the Prime Minister, and stressed that the four executives of the Miners' Federation, T.U.C., Labour Party and Co-operative movement, were united in advocating the course of action proposed in the resolution. Those who expected a

[1] The Parliamentary Committee were represented by J. H. Thomas, Railwaymen; A. B. Swales, Amalgamated Society of Engineers; J. Hill, Boilermakers; H. Gosling, Lightermen; W. Thorne, National Union of General Workers; R. B. Walker, Agricultural Labourers. Mediation Committee: E. Bevin and R. Williams, Transport Workers; J. T. Brownlie, Amalgamated Society of Engineers; J. R. Clynes, National Union of General Workers. National Provisional Joint Industrial Council: A. Henderson; J. Hindle, Weavers' Association; W. Bradshaw, Building Trades; W. F. Purdy, Shipwrights; G. D. H. Cole, Labour Research Department.

[2] J. H. Thomas had been shocked to learn, after the settlement of the railway strike how much this action had cost the nation. Fuller, Basil, *The Life Story of J. H. Thomas*, p. 159.

militant speech from Hodges, calling for a general strike, were disappointed. Will Thorne then moved the resolution instructing the Parliamentary Committee to undertake the propaganda campaign in support of nationalisation, which was seconded enthusiastically by the veteran miners' M.P., William Brace, who had never been one of the 'direct action' group of miners' leaders; this was probably why he was chosen to second a resolution which was by no means to the liking of Hodges and Smillie. When Smillie spoke in the debate, he supported the resolution, but his disappointment could not be concealed. Personally he did not think that they would convert the House of Commons as then constituted, and he went on to aver that in his opinion there was nothing that would move the Government but industrial force.[1] He then made it plain that if the Government persisted in its attitude he would expect Congress, when it re-assembled at a later date, to take decisive action. With the miners' leaders taking this attitude the adoption of the resolution by the delegates was a foregone conclusion. For a time during the railway strike it looked as if the Labour movement was returning to its militant mood, but with plenty of employment and a settling down to normal standards of life, the tension relaxed once the strike was over so that when the special Congress met it was in a calm atmosphere. The considerable success of the Labour Party in the local government elections in November had also tended to weaken any appeal to direct action.

Why did Hodges and Smillie accept this propaganda campaign as a substitute for 'direct action' when they manifestly had no confidence in its success? The fact was that the miners had been isolated by the action of the railwaymen in September. J. H. Thomas was a shrewd, diplomatic negotiator, ready to use the strike as a weapon when necessary, but too good a judge of the trade union movement to have much faith in the indiscriminate use of 'direct action'. Robert Smillie was of a very different temperament; he was unsubtle, emotional and overflowing with moral fervour for the miners' cause. By leading the railwaymen to victory in their struggle with the Government in September 1919, without resorting to an appeal to the other partners in the Triple Alliance, and by accepting the good offices of the Mediation Committee, Thomas had placed the miners in a difficult position. Since the miners had not been asked to withdraw their labour in support during the railway strike, it was difficult for them to ask the railwaymen to come out again on strike. Moreover, the other partner in the Triple Alliance, the Transport Workers' Federation, had played the leading part in convening the Mediation Committee and was mainly responsible for persuading the Parliamentary

[1] *Report of the Special Trades Union Congress*, December 1919.

Committee to set up the Co-ordination Committee for the purpose of strengthening the authority of the central body. Thus the balance of power, which in the early months of 1919 had appeared to be shifting away from the Parliamentary Committee to the Triple Alliance, had now shifted back again. The miners had themselves contributed to this course of events when they accepted Thomas's advice and submitted their case to the T.U.C., on the grounds that a strike to achieve nationalisation of the mines was a matter which affected not only the miners but the whole of the organised workers. Hodges and Smillie had no confidence in the Parliamentary Committee, to which no representative of the miners had been elected that year, but having sought the help of the T.U.C., and having no prospect of support from the other two members of the Triple Alliance if they undertook drastic action to compel the Government to nationalise the mines, they had little choice but to accept the cautious policy of the Parliamentary Committee and hope that events would work in their favour.

The miners' leaders showed their distrust of the leadership of the Trades Union Congress when the report of the Co-ordination Committee was placed before the delegates the next day. The report stated:

> It appears to us that the body which is required should and must be developed out of the existing organisation of the Trades Union Congress and out of its closer co-operation with other sections of the working-class movement. At present, the Standing Orders do not permit the Parliamentary Committee to undertake the work which is required. Indeed, its functions, as they are now defined, are in great measure a survival from a previous period, when the chief duties of the Congress were political, and there existed no separate political organisations to express the policy and objects of Labour. We accordingly suggest that the whole functions and organisation of the Parliamentary Committee demand revision, with a view to developing out of it a real co-ordinating body for the industrial side of the whole Trade Union movement. It is also necessary to take into account the relation of the reorganised Central Industrial Committee to the other sections of the movement, and especially to the Labour Party and to the Co-operative Movement.

> If a better central organisation could be developed both on the industrial side, and by the closer joint working with the other wings of the working-class movement, a vast development of the very necessary work of publicity, information, and research would at once become possible. The research, publicity, and legal departments now working for the movement require co-ordination and extension equally with its industrial and political organisation. The research, publicity, and legal work now done by the Trades Union Congress, the Labour Party, and the Labour Research Department must be co-ordinated and greatly enlarged in close connection with the development of the executive machinery of the movement.

It is only possible for us, at the present stage, to put forward the general outline of the changes which, in our opinion, are necessary in order to make the organisation of Labour commensurate with its aspirations and demands. The greatness of our movement has outgrown the central administrative machinery which it has inherited from a past generation, and the time has come for an ambitious extension and co-ordination of our work. The detailed scheme required to carry out our proposals can only be presented after considerably more work has been spent upon its preparation than we have been able to spend in the brief time at our disposal; and we therefore ask the Congress, to sanction our continuance of the work which we have begun, with a view to the presentation of a full scheme on the lines suggested to a future Congress.[1]

It was then proposed that a resolution embodying the following points should be put to the Congress: that the standing orders should be revised so as to substitute for the Parliamentary Committee a General Council to be elected annually by Congress; to prepare a scheme for the composition of the General Council; to make arrangements to furnish the General Council with the necessary staff, officials and equipment to create an efficient trade union centre. Further, to avoid overlapping, the Parliamentary Committee should be instructed to consult with the Labour Party and the Co-operative movement with a view to devising a scheme to set up joint research, legal and publicity departments, for the benefit of all three movements.

The report of the Co-ordination Committee and the resolution were moved by Harry Gosling who, since 1916, had been a consistent advocate of extending the organisation of the T.U.C. on the lines now proposed by the Co-ordination Committee.[2] Gosling was strongly supported by Robert Williams and by Ernest Bevin. Williams, a militant advocate of 'direct action' spoke of the need for a general staff to direct the army of Labour in its class war with the employers. Bevin, who had never committed himself to outright support of 'direct action', and who stood midway between Thomas and Williams, wanted the reorganisation of the T.U.C. because he believed the future of trade unionism lay in big units of organisation. Bevin held the view that the greater the power of the trade union movement, the less need there would be to use that power to achieve its objectives. 'It is possible for the movement to organise without strikes, but in order to do so, and to save itself from waste, it must increase its collective bargaining power, and go on doing so.'[3]

John Bromley, the militant secretary of the Associated Society of

---

[1] *Report of the Co-ordination Committee to the 1919 Special T.U.C.*
[2] Gosling, H., *Up Stream and Down Stream*, pp. 132 *et seq.*
[3] *Daily Herald*, 8 October 1919.

Locomotive Engineers and Firemen, moved the reference back of the Co-ordination Committee's report. His case was that he was afraid the General Council elected annually by the Congress would merely be the Parliamentary Committee writ large. He was in favour of co-ordinating the activities of the trade union movement, but he wanted the new body to be a fighting organisation, and to get rid of bargaining and caucuses. He suggested that the General Council should be elected by the rank and file, and that its policy should be to seek to enlarge strikes, not 'merely pour oil on troubled waters'. Frank Hodges rose to second Bromley, and the first part of his speech was couched in exactly the same terms of criticism of the scheme as those used by the conservative opposition to the idea of a General Council, coming from some of the craft unions, who saw in it a threat to their autonomy. He said that there had not been sufficient time to consider the scheme; that the resolution committed the trade union movement in advance to the principle of co-ordination; and that no evidence had been brought forward to show that it was desirable.[1] He shared Bromley's suspicions that the General Council would act as cautiously as the Parliamentary Committee had done. If the Parliamentary Committee really wanted to act vigorously it could do so without any drastic alteration, and the miners would be ready to give it their complete backing. Hodges was afraid that the transport workers and the railwaymen would have no further interest in the Triple Alliance, and that the miners would find themselves isolated and in a minority, as indeed they were at that moment.

When the reference back was put to the vote it was defeated by 2,884,000 votes to 1,722,000. The substantial vote against the proposal to establish a General Council was composed of the 'direct actionists' and the 'conservatives' who opposed the idea for different reasons. The aims of the majority were equally divided; there was no agreed conception of the objects which the reorganisation of the T.U.C. was intended to serve; certainly the views of Arthur Henderson and J. H. Thomas were very different from those of Robert Williams. When the special Congress adjourned, the Co-ordination Committee was left with the task of reconciling these diverse points of view, and of producing an acceptable draft scheme of reorganisation.

Shortly after the special Congress the Parliamentary Committee was called upon to assist in settling a protracted dispute in which the unions in the foundry industry had been engaged since the previous

---

[1] This speech led the *New Statesman* to comment on 13 December 1919, 'the miners, most tenacious of any opinion which they do adopt, are among the various sections of the Trade Union Movement almost the slowest to take up any new idea'.

September. The dispute was complicated by the fact that a number of unions were involved, and it raised the delicate issues of inter-union policy and craft union prerogatives. After a series of meetings the Parliamentary Committee succeeded in bringing the employers and the unions together, but the strike was settled without the foundry workers securing the special advances for which they had struck. This was precisely the kind of mediating activity to which the militants were opposed. It led the *Clarion* to comment, however, 'The whole circumstances of the Moulders' strike attest the need for a central directing authority with large powers, including powers of imposing deterrent penalties on the mutineers. To talk of a General Strike in the actual conditions of trade union dissension and disunity is madness. There are not more than two or three unions united enough to carry a strike of their own industry to a successful issue— though several of them are quite strong enough to muddle the country into ruin by silly sectional strife.'[1]

Bevin Succeeds where Miners Fail

On the 11 March 1920, the adjourned Trades Union Congress reassembled, at the request of the miners, to decide what should be done next to compel the Government to nationalise the mines. The propaganda campaign which had been undertaken to obtain public support for the miners' case had been palpably a failure, and the issue appeared to be whether the movement should resort to direct action, or work politically for a Labour victory at the polls. The result of the debate was almost a foregone conclusion, for the miners themselves were deeply divided and interest in their demands had diminished considerably in the rest of the trade union movement. At the special conference which the miners held on the day before the T.U.C. met, it was decided to support 'direct action', but only by a vote of 524,000 to 364,000; this was not a large enough majority to carry conviction. It was also announced on the 10 March that the General Workers' Federation, with a membership of well over a million, had decided almost unanimously to vote against 'direct action', and on the same day it became known that the executive committee of the National Union of Railwaymen had decided to cast the 400,000 votes of the union against 'direct action'.[2]

Little wonder the miners were depressed when the Congress opened the next day. Frank Hodges, their brilliant secretary, made the best case that he could in favour of 'direct action', but he had to admit that the weight of argument lay with those who urged political action instead. Hodges was afraid that if there was no great movement for

[1] *Clarion*, 2 January 1920.   [2] *The Times*, 11 March 1920.

the nationalisation of the mines, the miners would be compelled to fight for better conditions simply on the question of wages, which would not arouse the same degree of sympathy in the Labour movement; he was well aware that, isolated, the miners had little hope of winning the new world they were so desperately anxious to achieve. The fervour of the miners' leaders, without Smillie, who was worn-out and ill, seemed to have cooled. J. H. Thomas, T. Shaw and J. R. Clynes all spoke effectively against 'direct action'; they laid great stress on the possibilities before the Labour Party, if intelligent use was made of the power given to them by the 'most democratic constitution in the world'. Thomas in particular emphasised the danger which lurked in defying the constitution; 'a general strike would lead to serious consequences such as none could foretell'. When the resolution in favour of a general strike was put it was defeated by a majority of almost three million, the votes in favour coming almost entirely from two unions, the miners and the engineers.[1]

It seemed as if 'direct action' had been decisively put aside, especially as the transport workers had just agreed to submit a wage claim to arbitration and Robert Williams had called upon the workers not to prejudice their case by strike action. Moreover, Ernest Bevin had demonstrated that the new machinery set up under the Industrial Courts Act could be used effectively by the trade unions if they carefully prepared their case. This tough leader of the dockers, uneducated, but gifted with a first-class brain and experienced in the rough and tumble of trade union life, had made mincemeat of the professional witnesses brought by the Port Employers to testify for them before the Shaw Commission of Inquiry into the dockers' claims. Here was the rising force in the trade union world, and it was Bevin who was soon to succeed, where the miners had conspicuously failed, in persuading the trade union movement to adopt 'direct action' as a means of compelling the Government to act as the trade unions desired.

Everything seemed fairly quiet in the spring and early summer of 1920; the dockers had won their case for a wage increase, and Bevin had become famous as 'The Dockers' K.C.', but he had also given an indication of the way in which his mind was moving. The Government, still involved in the war of intervention against Russia, was suddenly given a sharp reminder that Bevin was not only to be respected as a formidable advocate, but also as a powerful political

---

[1] Tom Mann had just been elected secretary of the new amalgamation of engineering unions which had taken the place of the old A.S.E. The constitution of the new union was so designed as to give the militant activists great influence and to prevent strong central leadership.

adversary. When a gang of dockers refused to load the steamship *Jolly George* with arms for Poland, Bevin gave them full union support, and again roused hopes among the militants that the Government's policy might be changed by resolute trade union action. The 'Hands off Russia' campaign which had been started by left-wing socialists was given a fresh stimulus to activity, but it was events in Ireland that precipitated the consideration once again of 'direct action' at another special Trades Union Congress.

The Congress, which was held on the 13 July, was called at the request of the Triple Alliance, following an incident when 700 members of the National Union of Railwaymen in Ireland had refused to handle munitions or carry soldiers and, as a consequence, had been suspended or dismissed from the service. It was clear that J. H. Thomas was not happy about the prospect of the T.U.C. being committed to a policy of 'direct action', and he would probably have preferred the Congress not to have taken place, but, pushed by the extremists in his own union, and under pressure from the leaders of the miners and other influential supporters of militancy, he was not in a position to resist their demand for some kind of official action. The resolution, framed by the railwaymen, that was moved at the Congress, condemned the Government for its policy in Ireland, and called for the withdrawal of British troops and the arrangement of a truce between the warring factions, but it cautiously refrained from proposing any action to be taken by the T.U.C. to enforce these demands. After a number of amendments had been defeated, this resolution was carried by the narrow majority of 200,000 votes, but then Frank Hodges immediately moved another resolution which called for a general down-tools policy if the Government did not comply with the demand for the withdrawal of all British troops engaged overseas, though only after the rank and file had been consulted by a ballot vote. This resolution was carried by a majority of just over one million, but after it had been passed delegates were still not clear what action was to be taken next, since the resolution merely asked for the support of the unions and did not instruct the Parliamentary Committee to do anything.[1]

Delegates had barely returned to their homes when rumours began to circulate that the Government was about to declare war against Russia and send troops to support Poland, whose armies were at that moment locked in battle with those of the Soviets. Tension mounted in the Labour movement, and with the inspiration of the *Jolly George* incident fresh in mind, the idea of calling a general strike to halt the policy of the Government rapidly took hold of even the more cautious leaders. On the 4 August, Henderson had called upon constituency

[1] *Report of Special Trades Union Congress*, 13 July 1920.

Labour parties to arrange demonstrations against the threat of war, which seemed imminent following a British note to Russia, and a special joint conference between the executive committees of the Labour Party, T.U.C., and representatives of the Parliamentary Labour Party was arranged for the 9 August to consider what further steps should be taken.

The conference, on the 9 August, passed a resolution which stated that a war against Soviet Russia would be 'an intolerable crime against humanity', and went on to warn the Government that if it persisted in its policy the whole industrial power of the organised workers would be used to defeat it. The most significant part of the resolution, however, was that which called upon all affiliated organisations to be ready to 'down tools' on instructions from a national conference 'and that a Council of Action be immediately constituted to take such steps as may be necessary to carry the above decisions into effect'.[1]

The Council of Action was then set up, consisting of five representatives from the Parliamentary Committee, Labour Party, and the Parliamentary Labour Party, and nine co-opted members. The most important fact was that for the first time, on the grave issue of the use of 'direct action' against the Government, there was unanimity between the 'constitutionalists' like J. H. Thomas and J. R. Clynes, and the 'direct actionists' like Frank Hodges and Robert Williams. The Council of Action at once appointed a delegation to interview Lloyd George on the following day. Although Bevin was not a member of any of the three main committees he was made leader of the delegation and acted as its spokesman at this interview. Bevin made no bones about the course which the Council of Action intended to take if the Government committed the country to war against Russia, but Lloyd George refused to give any undertaking that the Government would refrain from sending troops to Poland. The Council of Action thereupon urgently summoned a national conference of representatives from the local Councils of Action which had been hastily set up all over the country.

Over a thousand delegates assembled at the Central Hall, Westminster on Friday, 13 August, in an atmosphere that was tense and excited, to hear a report from their national leaders. This conference was one of those epoch-making events in the history of the British Labour movement when, as if by magic, all dissensions disappear, to reveal a massive solidarity. After the Right Honourable W. Adamson, chairman of the Parliamentary Labour Party, had opened the proceedings, Bevin was called upon to give a report of the negotiations in which the Council of Action had been engaged. In voice and

[1] *Report of the Parliamentary Committee*, 1920.

language, which, though powerful, may well have seemed to the sensitive ear rough and ungrammatical, he conveyed his message to the delegates in a manner they understood exactly. Until now they had been mainly concerned with wages, but the question they were called upon to decide that day was whether they were willing to take action to win world peace. If there were any who had doubts as to the wisdom of the course of action which Bevin had ponderously made clear he was determined to follow, there were none who voiced them after he had thumped home his opinions. J. R. Clynes, who previously had always opposed 'direct action', now felt that 'we must be saved from war by an effective League of Labour action working upon lines to make it impossible to send a ship, a gun, a man, to send material or money for this nefarious purpose'. Then J. H. Thomas moved a resolution to endorse the setting up of the Council of Action; he impressed the delegates with his declaration that he had always been in favour of using the ballot box instead of 'direct action', but that the seriousness of the situation demanded desperate remedies. He emphasised that it was not simply a matter of downing tools, but that if the policy was put into effect it meant a challenge to the whole constitution of the country.[1] Other speakers made it clear that if the Cabinet refused to give way the consequences might be the revolutionary overthrow of the Government. All the resolutions were carried unanimously; the main one instructed the Councils of Action to remain in being until they had secured a guarantee that the armed forces of Britain would not be used against the Soviet Union, and until the blockade had been withdrawn, and ordinary diplomatic and trading relations established. This resolution authorised the Council of Action to order the withdrawal of labour on any scale it might find necessary, and placed all officials of the Labour movement under the Council's instructions. To help implement the policy of the Council of Action the Parliamentary Committee was instructed to raise a special fund by means of a levy on every member of the affiliated trade unions.

In the event the Council of Action was not called upon to give the signal for a general strike; the Polish crisis subsided and war was averted. Whether the Government would have defied the Council of Action to do its worst, had Polish-Russian peace talks taken another course, it is impossible to say, but there is sufficient evidence to show that the Government was profoundly influenced by the attitude of organised Labour.[2]

The confirmed 'direct actionists' wanted the Council of Action to

[1] *The Council of Action, Report of the Special Conference on Labour and the Russian-Polish War*, Central Hall, Westminster, 13 August 1920.
[2] Crook, W. H., *The General Strike*, p. 267.

be kept in existence, but, with the primary objective achieved, it fell into a natural desuetude. Already when the Trades Union Congress assembled for its annual meeting, three weeks after the Council of Action had been established, the attention of the trade unions was beginning to turn to other matters. J. H. Thomas, in his presidential address to Congress, made it clear to the delegates that the Parliamentary Committee had no intention of permitting the Council of Action to remain in existence when its work was completed; it was not in their opinion desirable that it should usurp the authority of the other sections of the Labour movement.

The Miners Change their Tactics

As usual, one of the most important problems to come before Congress was that of the miners' claims. Having failed to compel or persuade the Government to nationalise the mines, the Miners' Federation had turned to demands for an increase in wages, as their secretary, Frank Hodges, had prophesied they would be compelled to do, to secure some redress for their grievances. Hodges was well aware that, isolated, the miners could not win their case, and having failed to obtain the full support of the trade union movement in their effort to compel the Government to carry out the report of Mr. Justice Sankey, they now, under his leadership, tried to enlist the aid of other workers and the general public, by coupling their demands for wage increases with demands for a reduction in the price of coal. The miners contended that there was a surplus profit in the industry, which, as it was still under the control of the Government, was going to the Exchequer, and that it was large enough to meet both these demands after the mine owners had been paid their guaranteed profits. Their proposals were turned down by the Government, but when Congress was in session discussion was still going on. The miners had submitted their case to the Triple Alliance during the week before Congress met, and it was endorsed as fair and reasonable by both the railwaymen and the transport workers. It was then suggested by the Parliamentary Committee that, as a coal strike would have serious repercussions for the whole trade union movement, Congress ought to make some statement as to its attitude. The miners, however, were reluctant to lose control of their claims to the Parliamentary Committee, remembering the fate of their campaign for nationalisation. It was, therefore, agreed that neither the miners nor the Parliamentary Committee would raise the question by resolution, but that if it was raised from the floor of Congress (and arrangements were made behind the scenes for this to happen) Standing orders would be suspended, and the miners would be permitted to make a statement of their case. This procedure was duly carried out, and Frank Hodges gave a lengthy and detailed account of the claim, at the end of which a resolution was carried without opposition, that Congress was of opinion 'that the claims are both reasonable and just, and should be conceded forthwith'.[1] That was all; no instructions were given to the Parliamentary Committee to take any action if they were not conceded.

The New Constitution Adopted

The miners again showed their distrust of the Trades Union Congress when the report of the Co-ordination Committee was presented. Since the special Congress in the previous December, the Co-ordination Committee had been working to get agreement on a draft to put before Congress. They had discussed alternative schemes for electing a General Council, which had been submitted in a memorandum drawn up by G. D. H. Cole. The first problem was whether it was better to have a large General Council or to maintain the size roughly the same or slightly larger than the existing Parliamentary Committee. The Committee had been elected on a group system since 1907. Cole retained this basis of representation, but reclassified the unions affiliated to Congress into a new series of occupational groups, of which there were to be either eleven or seventeen, and then allocated to each group a number of seats on the General Council according to whether it was decided to have a large or small Council. It was eventually agreed to have a large General Council, and Cole's scheme, which provided for seventeen industrial groupings, with the addition of a separate group for women workers, electing a Council of thirty-two was approved. Nominations were to come from the groups, but the election of members to the Council was to be by Congress as a whole. Cole further recommended that the General Council should establish five sub-committees, which were to be based on industrial groupings. It was also suggested that each group should elect its own chairman, and that full-time officials should be appointed to specialise on the work of the groups, which would be to establish the closest contact with the federations in those industries, and to collect and file information from the unions. What Cole was seeking to do was to turn the trade union movement from one that had 'just growed' into one that was neatly organised on an industrial pattern, by co-ordinating the activities of the existing unions at the industrial level, as well as nationally. This was the long-cherished objective of the industrial unionists and the resemblance to Cole and Mellor's plan put forward before the war was close.

[1] *T.U.C. Annual Report*, 1920.

It was recommended by the Co-ordination Committee that the functions of the General Council should be defined as follows:

(*a*) The General Council shall keep watch on all industrial movements, and shall attempt, where possible, to co-ordinate industrial action.

(*b*) It shall promote common action by the trade union movement on general questions, such as wages and hours of labour, and any other matter of general concern that may arise between trade unions and employers or between the Trade Union movement and the Government, and shall have power to assist any union which is attacked on any vital question of Trade Union principle.

(*c*) Where disputes arise, or threaten to arise, between Trade Unions it shall use its influence to promote a settlement.

(*d*) It shall assist Trade Unions in the work of organisation, and shall carry on propaganda with a view to strengthening the industrial side of the movement, and for the attainment of any or all of the above objects.

(*e*) It shall enter into relations with the Trade Union and Labour movements in other countries with a view to promoting common action and international solidarity.

In order to meet the cost of carrying out these duties it was proposed that the affiliation fee should be raised from 30*s*. per thousand members, to 1*d*. per member, which, on the basis of 6 million members, would produce an annual income of £25,000.[1]

When Harry Gosling moved the acceptance of this report, on behalf of the Parliamentary Committee, he said that there had been misgivings during the week among some unions that the report, if adopted, would interfere with their freedom and autonomy. The Parliamentary Committee, having considered this point, had agreed that the resolution should commence with the words, 'Subject to the necessary safeguards to secure the complete autonomy of the unions and federations affiliated to Congress.'[2] This was, of course, precisely what the drafters of the report were trying to change, for if the new General Council was to discharge effectively the functions which had been loaded on to it then inevitably it would find itself up against the problem of union autonomy.

J. R. Clynes seized on this contradiction and opposed the adoption of the report on the grounds that it did not co-ordinate anything. It was a curious speech for one who rarely failed to be absolutely lucid. Clynes's opposition was apparently based on the fear that the new constitution would give additional power to the Triple Alliance,

[1] *T.U.C. Annual Report*, 1920.   [2] *Ibid.*

and weight the industrial side of the Labour alliance against the political wing. His positive suggestion was that the scheme should be referred back, and a fresh scheme drafted that would incorporate the trade union and political sections of the Labour movement into one organisation; thus the political section would exercise some control over the industrial. The fusion of the industrial and political sections of the Labour movement had been canvassed in the past on the opposite grounds, with the object of placing the political wing under trade union control.

When Clynes sat down Ernest Bevin rose and delivered a scathing attack on his speech, accusing him of having put forward an alternative scheme in order to prevent anything from being done to co-ordinate the trade union movement. Bevin went on to say,

> It is true that the Co-ordination Committee has not attempted to lay down an actual final detailed plan as to how this new thing will work out. It would be a mistake if we did that. There is no finality in our conception of organisation. But we realise that there is great danger in trying to ride rough shod, and before we are allowed to create confidence by the existence of a body, to endeavour to ride rough shod over the national conservatism and fear of our movement.[1]

He then discussed the weaknesses of the Parliamentary Committee; its members were over-worked, they had to rely on outside assistance; it had an inadequate staff and its research was done by a voluntary body. 'It is a stigma on our movement that this thing goes on. . . . What I do want to do is to create a greatly improved equipment and efficiency, so that strikes will be less because of the power of our organisation.' Almost the same criticisms were to be made over a quarter of a century later.

Neither Smillie nor Hodges spoke in the debate; though the miners supported the adoption of the report, their point of view was put by C. T. Cramp, one of the leaders of the railwaymen who had been closely associated with them in their previous demands for 'direct action'. Cramp argued that the spirit which animated a movement, rather than its organisational form, determined its effectiveness. A body which was little more than an enlarged Parliamentary Committee might suffer from the same faults, and he preferred to rely on the rank and file throwing up an organisation such as the Council of Action, when this was required by circumstances. For these reasons, he said, he was not disposed to support the changes recommended. When the vote was taken the resolution was carried by 4,858,000 votes to 1,767,000. A week later Cramp expanded his views in an article in the *Clarion* in which he expressed the opinion that the

[1] *Ibid.*

reason for the overwhelming majority in favour of the changes 'was the desire of the unions, who have hitherto failed to gain direct representation upon the Parliamentary Committee, to see their own nominees serving upon the new body'.[1] There was undoubtedly some truth in this assertion, but it was far from the whole truth, for events over the past few years had provided convincing reasons for the changes, and, in fact, the need to set up the Council of Action had been the final spur.

The second section of the resolution passed by the special Congress in December 1919, which recommended the establishment of joint research, legal and publicity departments by the T.U.C., Labour Party and Co-operative Union, was still in the process of discussion, and Gosling informed Congress that a report would be submitted at a later date.

No miners' representatives had been elected on to the Parliamentary Committee the year before, and Robert Smillie, angry at their exclusion, was determined to prevent this from happening again. Smillie made a forceful denunciation of the system of bartering votes, which was almost openly carried on in violation of standing order number ten. Will Thorne stated frankly that if other delegates were not respecting the standing orders, neither would his union. This was a sentiment that did not meet with approval, but there was a reluctance to take action to prevent bartering. Smillie, however, moved that a committee of investigation should be set up to investigate the charges, and when this was agreed Bromley, Cramp, Williams, Hicks and Herbert Smith were elected, all of them associated with the militant section of the movement. Apart from moral indignation, it was Smillie's belief that the Parliamentary Committee would always remain in the hands of the 'conservatives', unless bartering was eliminated that led him to try and put a stop to a practice that had been in operation for very many years despite previous attempts to curb it.

As soon as Congress was over the committee met and took evidence from the secretary of the General Workers' Federation, Mr. James O'Grady, M.P., who candidly admitted to responsibility for systematic canvassing on behalf of certain individuals. The committee reported that the growth of federations had led to the possibility of arrangements being made by caucuses, but that if the information given to the committee was to be acted upon 'more than half of the membership of affiliated unions would be disqualified from having representation on the various elective bodies for at least three years'. It was, therefore, decided that nothing should be done about the past; and as the new method of electing the General Council

[1] *Clarion*, 17 September 1920.

would help to eliminate bartering, the committee recommended that the matter should be closed.[1]

The Triple Alliance Breaks Down

The miners, still struggling to secure their aims, had taken a strike ballot and were due to stop work on the 25 September. They hoped for the support of the other members of the Triple Alliance, but the railwaymen and the transport workers refused, after days of fruitless argument, to call out their members. Faced with the prospect of striking alone, the miners suspended their strike notice and reopened negotiations, with a new set of wage proposals; nothing was said this time about a reduction in the price of coal. Another strike ballot was held, and a national stoppage of coal production began on the 16 October. The strike was brought to a close on the 3 November, when a further ballot showed a growing proportion of the membership in favour of accepting an offer, granting a slight increase, that had been made for a temporary settlement, to last until the following March.[2]

This strike again revealed the weakness of the Triple Alliance, for although the railwaymen had reluctantly agreed to come out on the eve of the settlement, the lack of unity between the three organisations was obvious. There were differing points of view among the leaders as to the functions of the Alliance; the plan that each union would fight together, not for a common aim, but each for its own claims, was not really practicable, for the strategic moment that called for a strike was different for each industry, and could not be brought into harmony, as it had been believed when the Triple Alliance was founded. Moreover, the conditions under which a strike could be successfully prosecuted differed markedly from one industry to the other; in any case none of the three organisations was ready to allow its policy and tactics to be completely determined by the others. It was the end of the Triple Alliance, though this was not yet realised.

Although the Government could not produce coal with soldiers or blackleg labour, it could run the transport system and the public utilities in an emergency. This was a point which the miners always failed to see; they could openly threaten to strike and prepare almost at their leisure, but for other unions speed and surprise were essential factors. The Government realised this and made its preparations accordingly; especially to deal with a stoppage in the transport industries. The miners' strike in the autumn of 1920, however, provided the Government with an excuse to introduce an Emergency

[1] *Report of Committee of Inquiry into Bartering of Votes*, 15 October 1920.
[2] *M.F.G.B. Annual Report*, 1920.

Powers Act, which, after a 'state of emergency' had been declared, empowered the Government by Order in Council 'to make Regulations for securing the essentials of life to the community'. Although the Act gave the Government sweeping powers, it was not to be an offence to take part in a strike or peacefully to persuade others to do so. The Parliamentary Committee was alarmed by the Act, and took the professional advice of Sir John Simon and H. H. Asquith, who reassured them on a number of points, notably the liability of trade union funds. However, the fact that no concerted campaign was undertaken to try to secure the defeat of the Bill or to arouse public opinion against it, is a measure of the decline in militancy that had occurred by the end of 1920. During the miners' strike the Parliamentary Committee had called a meeting of trade union executive committees to discuss the situation caused by the stoppage, and also to consider the Emergency Powers Bill.[1] It passed a resolution condemning the Bill and decided that, if necessary, a special conference would be called; this step was not taken, and although a resolution calling for the repeal of the Act was carried at the 1921 Congress, it aroused little interest.

The powers given to the State under the Act of 1920 were used for the first time in April 1921. The Government, with an act of supreme public irresponsibility, had suddenly decided that it would bring to an end the Coal Mines Act of 1920, five months before this was due, knowing full well that the mine owners would at once seek to reduce wages, and that this would lead to a national coal strike. This is exactly what did happen, except that the owners did not wait until the men had decided to strike, since lockout notices were immediately posted throughout the coalfields. The miners were in an impossible position, and the Government and the owners knew this. Unemployment had grown in the past six months as post-war prosperity had given way to a major slump; more than a million and a quarter workers were without jobs at the end of March. For a time it looked as if the miners would be joined by their partners in the Triple Alliance, to whom they had appealed, but the fundamental weakness of the organisation was again revealed and the miners were left to fight alone.[2] Had fate played its hand differently the chapter of incidents which culminated in 'Black Friday', on 15 April 1921, the day on which the railwaymen and the transport workers withdrew their strike notices, might have led to a general strike. Had this happened it is almost certain the trade unions would have suffered

---

[1] *Report of Special Conference of Executives, 27 and 28 October 1920.*

[2] For detailed accounts see Cole, G. D. H., *A Short History of the British Working Class Movement, 1789–1947*; Crook, W. H., *The General Strike*; Hutt, A., *Post-War History of the British Working Class.*

defeat, as the miners were eventually defeated, for the strategic moment for a national stoppage had passed.[1] The fact was that the trade unions were not prepared for such a strike, and the result would have been as ignominious as was that of the general strike five years later. Something of a myth has grown up in left-wing circles that had it not been for the pusillanimous behaviour of J. H. Thomas, Ernest Bevin and others, a glorious victory would have been won for the workers, and the downward path of wages which the following few years brought would never have occurred. This is a view which utterly misinterprets the historical, social, political and economic facts of the period. The British trade union movement was not a revolutionary movement; if on rare occasions it had appeared to behave like one, for example when it established the Council of Action, it had been only too glad when the moment passed. The truth of the matter was that the movement was on the defensive, and at such times it had always instinctively acted with caution, showing much greater wisdom than some of its critics, who suffered from the delusion that economic and social problems were solved by shouting slogans and making threatening demonstrations.

Faced with failing markets, the employers began to cut their wage bills, unemployment mounted, and the earnings of those in jobs were sharply reduced. The Parliamentary Committee, in association with the Labour Party executive, held a joint conference on unemployment at the Kingsway Hall in January 1921, when resolutions were passed against wage cuts, and a call was made for a more extensive spending policy by the Government. But Government spending to combat a trade depression was regarded then, and for many years afterwards, in the offices of Whitehall and the City, as akin to financial lunacy.

Further Changes Proposed in Structure and Functions of the T.U.C.

Much of the time of the Parliamentary Committee was filled with settling inter-union disputes, but it was hoped that amalgamation, which was then going on apace, and the coming into being of the General Council, with its industrial sub-committees, would eliminate much of this. The Co-ordination Committee had again a long report to present to Congress when it met in September 1921. It was proposed that the work previously carried out by the Women's Trade Union League should in future be taken over by the T.U.C., and a special Women's Department established to which the staff, equipment, and duties of the League would be transferred. The Women's Department was to function in close co-operation with the Trade

[1] Cf. Orton, A. W., *Labour in Transition*, p. 244.

Boards Department, which Bevin had been most anxious to set up to look after the general interests of the three million workers covered by Trade Board Regulations.[1]

In view of the increase in committee work and the extension of departmental responsibility which the new organisation would entail, and also of the need to co-ordinate all these activities, it was recommended by the Committee that a full-time chairman of the General Council should be appointed by Congress. Before asking Harry Gosling to move a resolution to give effect to this recommendation of the Committee, the president of Congress, E. L. Poulton, general secretary of the Boot and Shoe Operatives, complained of the rumours which had been set in circulation concerning who was to be given this post, and the salary to be paid. He was unable, however, to dispel the suspicions aroused by the proposal to appoint a full-time chairman; nor was Harry Gosling, who made a cogent speech in favour of the suggestion, any more successful. As so often before, the conservatives and the militants joined together, for different reasons, to condemn the idea of appointing a full-time chairman. Tom Shaw, M.P., speaking for the Lancashire Weavers' Association, opposed the recommendation on the ground that it would lead to divided responsibility between the full-time chairman and the full-time general secretary. The miners and the railwaymen also opposed it, on the grounds that they wanted 'no tin gods' but the 'regular opportunity of putting in the man we feel should be placed there'.[1] The basic fear common to all those who were against the appointment of a full-time chairman was that it would strengthen the hand of the General Council against the unions, and also give the chairman a dominating position over the Council, and neither extreme was willing to take this risk. The question of personalities was also a major factor. Most trade union general secretaries tend to become 'prima donnas', and none of them relished the idea of one of their number becoming the supreme head of the trade union movement. It was significant that when Ben Tillett said that he was in favour of a full-time chairman, he wanted him to be a young man, and not one of the well-established older figures; however he cautioned Congress not to be in a hurry, and to wait and see how the General Council worked, before committing itself to appointing anyone to the post; his claim that the younger element in the trade unions was all in favour of a full-time chairman, was not, however, one that could be easily proved.

The resolution was not pushed to a division because it was realised that it would be defeated, and it was therefore withdrawn.

A scheme for co-ordinating the work of the T.U.C. and the

[1] *T.U.C. Annual Report*, 1921.

Labour Party, the Co-operative Union having withdrawn from the discussions, was accepted without discussion. It proposed the setting up of a National Joint Council composed of representatives of the General Council, the executive of the Labour Party and the Parliamentary Party. The duties of the National Joint Council were to be to:

(a) Consider all questions affecting the Labour movement as a whole, and make provision for taking immediate and united action on all questions of national emergency.

(b) Endeavour to secure a common policy and joint action, whether by legislation or otherwise, in all questions affecting the workers as producers, consumers, and citizens.

(c) Consult when necessary, a Joint Conference, consisting of the General Council of the Trades Union Congress and the Labour Party Executive, together with a number of Parliamentary Members, which with the Labour Party Executive will be equal in number to the numbers of the General Council of the Trades Union Congress.

(d) Present an annual report to the Trades Union Congress and the Labour Party Conference and the Parliamentary Party.[1]

The chairman of the General Council was to be the chairman of the National Joint Council, and the secretary of the Labour Party its secretary; expenditure by the National Joint Council was to be shared equally by the two organisations.

Under the control of the General Council and the executive committee of the Labour Party, common departments for research and information, international affairs, publicity and legal matters were to be set up and placed in charge of full-time paid officials. These departments were to be immediately responsible to joint sub-committees of the two organisations, and were to carry out work assigned to them by the T.U.C. and the Labour Party, either separately or jointly; they were also to be available to do special work for affiliated organisations. It was hoped 'by the creation and development of these joint departments to put an end to the overlapping of activity of departments under the control of the Labour Party and the General Council'[2] and to render a more efficient service to the Labour movement. There was still a possibility that the Co-operative movement would associate itself with this administrative centre, and discussions were still going on, but relations between the Co-operative movement and the trade unions which organised its employees, at that moment, were so far from harmonious that this prospect appeared distant.

Arthur Pugh, secretary of the Iron and Steel Trades' Confederation,

[1] *Final Report of the Co-ordination Committee, T.U.C. Annual Report*, 1921.
[2] *Ibid.*

raised again the basic issues underlying the attitudes of the unions towards the General Council and the role of the T.U.C., when he moved a resolution which called for the T.U.C. to be given power to obtain an equitable settlement of any major dispute before a stoppage of work occurred, and, failing such a settlement, power to co-ordinate the entire resources of the trade union movement to ensure a successful outcome. Further, the resolution proposed that the General Council should have the authority to use the power of the T.U.C. to help trade unions compel employers who refused to carry out collective agreements to come into line with other employers. The resolution was supported by the general workers, but was opposed by the same combination of unions as opposed the appointment of a full-time chairman, and, fundamentally, for the same reasons. Robert Smillie described this resolution as the most reactionary that had ever come before the Trades Union Congress; 'this is a motion proposing to draw the teeth of organised labour and take away its arms'.[1] C. T. Cramp, on behalf of the railwaymen, opposed the resolution because it would prevent aggressive action. John Hill, secretary of the Boilermakers' Union, criticised the resolution because he thought that under these conditions the autonomy and independence of the trade unions would atrophy. With these fears aroused, the resolution was defeated by a large majority.

The election of the first General Council proved to be an almost farcical event. When the scrutineers presented their report the miners' delegates complained that some of their votes had not been counted. Thereupon, the chairman of the scrutineers explained that some unions had voted for as many as five candidates when only two places were to be filled, and therefore the votes given to the additional candidates had been disallowed. J. H. Thomas immediately rose to his feet and objected to the scrutineers exceeding their instructions, as the Parliamentary Committee had previously decided that a union could divide its votes among as many candidates as it pleased, so long as it did not cast more votes than the aggregate to which it was entitled. It then transpired that the scrutineers had been confused by this instruction, and had asked the general secretary to clarify the position. He had advised them to conduct the election as in previous years; that is, to limit the votes cast to the number of candidates required for the places to be filled from each group. The scrutineers had endeavoured to inform delegates when they handed out the ballot papers that they would follow this procedure, but in the excitement of the occasion their instructions were improperly understood, with the result that some delegations

[1] T.U.C. Annual Report, 1921.

had voted one way and some another. The question now before Congress was what in the circumstances should be done? To make confusion more confounded many delegates had already left for home, unaware of the complication which had arisen; thus making it impossible to hold a fresh election there and then. A large number of delegates wanted to leave matters as they stood, since they were prepared to accept the result; however, others demanded a recount, and a number pressed for a fresh election, and suggested that the general secretary should send out new ballot papers by post. This last suggestion was eventually agreed upon by a narrow majority, and an end was put to the long and confused discussion, much to the relief of most concerned. Delegates left Congress for home knowing they had extricated themselves from a tangle, but feeling they had rather made fools of themselves over a disarmingly simple matter. The incident had revealed a weakness in the new constitution, for it contained no standing order to govern the way in which ballots should be cast, and an instruction was given that a new standing order covering this aspect of the elections to the General Council should be presented to the next Congress. In the event the re-taken election for the General Council provided exactly the same result as did the first, which was rather fortunate, since it left no ill-feeling to mar the inauguration of a new era in the life of the Trades Union Congress.

CHAPTER X

ACHIEVEMENT AND PROMISE

The Parliamentary Committee reported to Congress for the last time at Cardiff, in 1921; the recorded affiliated membership of the T.U.C. was then 6,417,910; a decrease of 87,000, on the peak figure of the year before. During the war over two million workers had joined the trade unions, and in the immediate post-war years their ranks were swollen by almost as many more. With this great increase of members had come a rise in the income of the T.U.C. from rather less than £4,000 in 1913 to almost £9,000 in 1918; but since prices had doubled during the war this income was not nearly large enough to finance its growing range of activities. The adoption of the new constitution was accompanied by an increase in affiliation fees which brought the annual income up to £37,000 in 1921, making it possible for the new General Council to appoint a larger staff and engage in a much wider field of activities. Even so, the income of the T.U.C. was not really very high for the work that was expected of the Council, but it would have been impossible to persuade the unions to increase their affiliation fees still further at this stage. Growing unemployment had led to only a slight reduction in affiliated membership during the year 1920–21, but in the year following, as unemployment reached levels worse than ever before recorded, membership was reduced by over a million and a quarter. Thus the General Council began its work under difficult and challenging circumstances, but with a wealth of experience and tradition behind it. How the Council faced its responsibilities will be told in another volume.

The growth in the status of the Trades Union Congress and its Parliamentary Committee had been achieved in a typically British way. It was not planned; it conformed to no explicit theory; it simply acquired its functions as it went along. As the State gradually abandoned *laissez-faire* and adopted collectivist ideas under the pressure of the trade union and other social reform movements, the activities and influence of the Parliamentary Committee developed concomitantly. Sometimes giving the lead, perhaps more often pushed by events, the Parliamentary Committee had interpreted the desires of the organised workers, as expressed through Congress, for a higher standard of life and a more positive role in the affairs of the State. In its half-century of existence it had become a powerful pressure group recognised by all parties and treated by all Governments as the authoritative spokesman of the opinions of organised Labour. Behind the Parliamentary Committee lay the growing power of the trade union movement; a political fact which could not be ignored by any party aspiring to govern Britain.

While the State, during the half-century for which the T.U.C. had existed had been primarily dominated by property interests, it had never been like the classic Marxist State, in which capitalists exercised untrammelled authority over a proletariat growing increasingly poverty-stricken. The rights of property, under the pressure of organised Labour, had gradually diminished and the lot of the workers had vastly improved. Owing to a unique compound of historical circumstances, which had produced an empirical approach to politics, deeply affecting the behaviour of all classes in the community, there had gradually emerged out of the individualism of the Industrial Revolution, and without a catastrophic clash of social forces, a social system which the Webbs called industrial democracy. Had the propertied classes not given way to the demands of Labour, conflict in society would surely have exploded into violence. Equally, had not the Parliamentary Committee of the T.U.C. recognised its responsibilities, even when pressed by events, and given a constructive leadership, the social progress achieved would have been impossible without more serious disturbances. The cautious attitude of the Parliamentary Committee, though open to criticism at certain times, was a vital factor in establishing its status as a responsible national institution, and went a long way to ensure that social reform was continued by a process of evolution.

Though the trade unions were looked upon by many influential and powerful persons as a threat to Liberal principles, it was more and more recognised that in a modern industrial democracy pressure groups were inevitable and indispensable; it was realised that no parliamentary system of government could operate effectively without the assistance of the collective views of those sections of the community who might be specifically affected by the legislation Parliament was compelled to pass. As some saw it the danger which confronted the community was that extra-parliamentary pressure might exceed the limits that made it tolerable as well as necessary. This was understood by generations of trade union leaders who sought to achieve their ends through the parliamentary system. The creation of the Labour Party ultimately served to deepen their respect for parliamentary institutions; it did not, however, prevent a shift in emphasis from industrial to political action and back again as circumstances changed. For a time, dissatisfaction with the results of political activity and the upsurge of militant syndicalism threatened to push the T.U.C. to the testing point. The danger was avoided because the revolutionary implications of a general strike were not in tune with the political hopes and aspirations of most of the leaders of the trade union movement, and because the war intervened to break the cycle of events that might have led to disaster. When, after the war, Bevin led his more cautious colleagues to challenge the State with a threat of a general strike, and succeeded in frightening the Government into reversing its policy, many of them were appalled at their own audacity. There were others, however, who had been nurtured in the bitter climate of industrial relations that poisoned life in the Celtic valleys. These men, who were dominated by a fanatical desire to smash the existing social, economic and political structure of society, and to replace it, after the cataclysm, with their own vision of a new Jerusalem, had no qualms about the consequences of the methods they wanted to use to achieve their ends. The course of events which brought the T.U.C. finally to the trial of the ardently-canvassed general strike will be told in the next volume.

Men like J. W. Ogden, W. Thorne, J. H. Thomas, J. R. Clynes, A. Pugh, and J. B. Williams had no desire to see the industrial unrest of pre-war days repeated. The difference between the pre-war and the immediate post-war years was that in the former the trade unions were taking aggressive action to improve their conditions, whereas in the latter the great strikes were defensive. There was common agreement among all trade unionists that standards had to be defended, if necessary by strikes, but the far-sighted members of the T.U.C. were taking steps to go ahead with a new constitution, albeit with caution, so as to permit the Parliamentary Committee, henceforth General Council, to exercise a greater and more intelligent influence on the industrial and economic affairs of the nation than ever before.

The new constitution of the T.U.C. acknowledged that the organisation had outgrown its old frame; it was more in keeping with the work which the trade union movement would be called upon to undertake. But, in a fundamental sense, it changed little. The Trades Union Congress remained what it had always been, a collection of autonomous trade unions, whose first concern was to protect their own members' interests. Although the new constitution gave the General Council authority to co-ordinate the activities of the unions affiliated to it over a wider field, so long as the unions clung to their autonomy its activity was circumscribed by the necessity to obtain their consent, unless, as hitherto, special circumstances impelled it to give them a lead. For this reason, the new constitution did not provide a sure guide to action for the General Council. However, its increased size of thirty-two members, as compared with the Parliamentary Committee of sixteen, improved the chances that the Council would be able to make more far-reaching decisions, if for no other reason than that the representatives of more unions would be participating in them. Nevertheless, no representative of a union on the General Council, even the senior officer, could be any more certain that his organisation would be prepared to carry out its policy, although he might support it, than he had been under the old constitution. The fact that each member of the General Council was well aware that he would have the task of carrying his own union with him, promised to lead naturally to caution and a reluctance to act without a clear mandate as in the case of the Parliamentary Committee in the past.

This situation was inevitable in a trade union movement in which the unions had grown up gradually to meet the particular needs of their members, and had acquired a spirit of independence in the course of their development. Although there was a class solidarity which transcended the sectional outlook of the individual unions, this had a limited influence; it had never been possible to ignore the fact that the interests of the members of one union were very often different from those of another. No amount of argument based on theories of class interest or organisation was sufficient to persuade members of trade unions to make a complete sacrifice of the independence of their own organisations. From 1874, as has been recounted, attempts had been made to turn the loosely organised trade union movement into a compact federation with great power at the centre, but they had always failed at the point at which autonomy had to be given up. Had the unions been dependent on the T.U.C. financially; if, for example, the major unions had found a real need for a central strike fund, as the promoters of the General Federation of Trade Unions had hoped would be the case, then a centralised organisation would probably have developed, but the fact was that the unions were able to stand on their own feet.

The Parliamentary Committee had gradually enlarged its authority, but it could never act decisively unless it was certain it had the support of the great majority of its affiliated organisations, since otherwise it risked the withdrawal of the dissatisfied unions from the T.U.C. The critics who denounced the Committee for alleged feeble leadership often seemed to ignore the crucial fact that the T.U.C. was a voluntary organisation. Others had castigated the members of the Parliamentary Committee for being bureaucratic and insensitive to the demands of the rank and file. To some extent this was true, and it remains the besetting sin of all large organisations, but when the militants inside and socialist intellectuals outside fiercely assailed the Parliamentary Committee for failing to carry out the policy which they proposed, they were often guilty of assuming that their policy was the policy the members wanted, when, in fact, the evidence was rarely conclusive; or else, like all ideologues, they paid little attention to what the rank and file desired, simply insisting that their policy should be acted upon. The Webbs, in particular, were scathing in their criticisms of the Parliamentary Committee and of the T.U.C. In the first edition of their justly famous *History of Trade Unionism*, they condemned the Parliamentary Committee for 'its failure to help in the solution of the problems of industrial organisation or to give an intellectual lead to the rank and file'. They repeated these charges in the last edition of this work which appeared in 1920, stating, 'As an institution it [the T.U.C.] can hardly be said to have shown, between 1890 and 1917, at least, any development at all.'[1]

These judgments reflected the philosophy of the Webbs, which was antipathetic to the Liberal State. They held the Trades Union Congress in contempt because it did not sweep away what they regarded as old shibboleths, and adopt a new 'scientific' basis of organisation. The very things which had made the T.U.C. a success were what they despised most; its loose method of organisation; its lack of central control, and the adoption of *ad hoc* policies to meet situations as they arose, instead of a clear-cut plan of campaign to achieve the kind of society they held to be desirable.

One criticism advanced by the Webbs was certainly valid. They emphasised that if the T.U.C. wanted its work done well, it should engage an expert staff to assist its Parliamentary Committee, but it took the trade unions a long time to see this necessity. However, their view that the influence of the Parliamentary Committee on social reform had been negligible hardly accords with the facts. In his book, *Labour Legislation, Labour Movements and Labour Leaders*, Mr. George Howell gives a list of 123 Acts of Parliament, placed on the Statute Book between 1868 and 1901, with the passing of which the Parliamentary Committee had been in some way involved. He writes, 'In the series of Congresses—1868 to 1901 inclusive—every measure, of importance affecting workmen has been considered, and the Parliamentary Committee initiated, promoted, advocated, and supported Bills introduced.'[2] This list, when extended to 1921, shows a truly impressive record of achievement. It would, of course, be silly to claim that the Parliamentary Committee alone was responsible for all the measures of social reform that were made; it is often difficult to establish the originator of any particular reform, or exactly what part the Parliamentary Committee played in its promotion, but it is clear that it exercised an important and growing influence on Government policy. Nor is it true to say that the T.U.C. failed to help in finding a solution of the problem of industrial organisation. The Parliamentary Committee assisted in settling inter-union disputes, as many annual reports testify. It did not and could not provide a final solution to the problems which arose from the variety of different types of trade union in existence. It attempted to secure some rationalisation of the structure of the trade union movement by assisting unions to achieve amalgamation, and everyone would have liked this process to go further. This, however, depended on the willingness of the unions to amalgamate, and there was nothing which the Parliamentary Committee could do to force them to take this step. Had the Parliamentary Committee been foolish enough to attempt to reshape the trade union movement on neat, planned lines by some show of force, the Trades Union Congress would have been rent by discord, and it would have destroyed itself. It is odd that the Webbs should have made this criticism when they had shown so clearly the factors which limited the development of trade union structure and organisation.[1]

Another criticism made by the Webbs was that 'the Parliamentary Committee has continued to regard itself almost entirely as a Parliamentary Committee, just as if the Trade Unions had not united in a distinct political organisation and had not created their own Parliamentary Labour Party'.[2] The Webbs wanted the T.U.C. to confine itself to industrial functions only. It had, they believed, plenty of work to do in reorganising the trade union movement so as to prevent trade unions from over-lapping; in assisting the unions to maintain the 'standard rate'; and in improving workshop organisation. These were matters over which the member unions would permit the T.U.C. to exercise only the most limited influence. Wages and collective bargaining were precisely those functions which the unions guarded most jealously from any interference from the T.U.C. They might ask for material and technical assistance when preparing a wage claim, but even that was rare, and on no account would they permit the T.U.C. to exercise any authority over them in this field. As for helping them in matters of workshop organisation, the unions regarded this aspect of their activities as entirely their own domestic affair, and any suggestion that the T.U.C. should extend its work in this direction would have met with the most emphatic opposition.

The splitting-off of the Labour Party from the T.U.C. as an entirely separate and independent political organisation has been of profound importance to the development of political democracy in Britain. It enabled the trade union movement to secure the benefits of increased Labour representation in the House of Commons, while

[1] Webb, S. and B., *Industrial Democracy*, Ch. IV, pp. 104 *et seq.*
[2] Webb, S. and B., *The History of Trade Unionism*, p. 570.

at the same time it allowed the T.U.C. to remain independent and exercise its influence on all Governments whatever their party colour might be. Had the T.U.C. abdicated all its political functions to the Labour Party, as the Webbs desired, it would have been completely dependent on the Parliamentary Labour Party for obtaining legislative reforms, and would have been shorn of its ability to bring pressure to bear through direct negotiations with Liberal or Tory ministers. The Webbs were scornful of 'the futile annual deputations to Ministers' and the presentation to them of 'the crude resolutions of the Trades Union Congress, without regard to the contemporary situation in the House of Commons, or the action taken by the Parliamentary Labour Party. . . .'[1] These deputations may not, on many occasions have succeeded in securing for the trade unions all that they demanded, but they often did produce modifications in Government policy. Moreover, they were of great value in so far as they acquainted ministers at first hand with the views of the trade union movement on a wide variety of subjects, and materially helped to develop the consultative relationship between the T.U.C. and the Government which was an important feature of the emerging social democracy in Britain.

The Webbs' objection arose from their conception of the socialist State and of the tactics necessary to achieve it. They assumed that the unions were bent on achieving socialism and they saw little good coming from the Trades Union Congress acting as a pressure group without a long-term plan of campaign closely co-ordinated with that of the Labour Party. It was true that sometimes the political activities of the Parliamentary Committee were out of step with the policy of the Labour Party, though this did not occur very often. However, the trade unions, even though they were the main element in the Labour Party, could not afford simply to wait for success at the polls, or to place their fate entirely in the hands of the Parliamentary Labour Party. They were concerned with influencing legislation and policy as it was made, there and then as the opportunity offered. Had they handed over these functions to the Labour Party, they would have been in a very weak position when Liberal and Conservative Governments were in office, and unable to exercise any important influence when a Labour Government came into power. It was just as essential, as experience proved, for the trade union movement to be independent of the Labour Party, when that party formed the Government, as when any other party was in power. This was completely alien to the Webbs' idea of the socialist State. They did not believe that the trade unions should have power to put pressure on a Labour Government which was carrying out a socialist policy. In their 'Constitution

[1] Webb, S. and B., *The History of Trade Unionism*, p. 570.

for a Socialist Commonwealth' the Webbs found little part for the Trades Union Congress to play. Important industrial decisions would be taken by the industrial parliament and political decisions by the political parliament. Pressure group activities would be neither necessary nor desirable, as they would lead to the perversion of public policy by sectional interests. By their definition of socialism, this was something to be avoided.

The Webbs had nothing good to say about the Parliamentary Committee, but they acknowledged that the annual Congress served a useful purpose in so far as it brought together the leaders of the different trades, and gave them an opportunity of exchanging views and information, and also gave publicity to matters that were agitating the unions. Here, again, in their eyes, the Parliamentary Committee failed, because it did not present to the delegates a carefully worked out long-term programme. 'From first to last there is no sign of a "Front Bench" of responsible leaders.'[1] This analogy with cabinet government was, however, wholly misapplied in relation to the Parliamentary Committee. There was no party discipline among the unions, and they retained so much autonomy, that the Parliamentary Committee had no means of enforcing its policy. The analogy implied a completely different type of trade union organisation; one in which there was a high degree of central control and bureaucratic rule. It was just this type of Trades Union Congress that the unions absolutely refused to accept; and in any case, though cabinet government might have been good for the country, it did not follow that it would have been good for the unions.

Although the Webbs saw some value in the annual Congress they summed it up, contemptuously, as 'rather a parade of the Trade Union forces than a genuine Parliament of Labour'.[2] It certainly was a parade of forces, but to say that 'As a business meeting the whole function of the Congress is discharged in the election of the Parliamentary Committee' was completely to distort the facts. It was true that important questions were sometimes either not discussed at all, or were passed over with inadequate consideration, but on matters that touched the vital interests of the unions debates were usually full and animated and the Committee was given a clear instruction. Part of the problem lay in the fact that the Congress was too large, and that too many resolutions appeared on the agenda. There were obvious limits to what a conference of this kind could achieve in a session lasting five days. These defects arose, primarily, out of the nature of the trade union movement. No union would forfeit the right to submit resolutions or send delegates; however attempts were made through the General Purposes Committee to

[1] *Ibid.*, p. 566. [2] *Ibid.*, p. 564.

reduce the resolutions to manageable proportions, by compositing them, but there were limits to what could be achieved in this direction. The Parliamentary Committee was allowed to table three of its own resolutions, and, in case of emergency, with the approval of Congress, standing orders could always be suspended to permit the urgent consideration of any question. Had the Parliamentary Committee attempted to dictate the contents of the agenda Congress would simply have refused to accept its ruling. In these circumstances, it was quite impossible for the Parliamentary Committee to behave like a 'Front Bench', dominating the delegates. An opposite criticism might have been made that the Congress failed to exercise sufficient control over the Parliamentary Committee, which could always rely upon one section of the unions being against another. Also, resolutions tended inevitably to be framed in a general manner, which gave the Parliamentary Committee a good deal of latitude when trying to carry them out. Again, Congress could not foresee the future, and the Parliamentary Committee had to be left free to take what action it considered necessary in the light of circumstances; but, as already explained, it was at all times fully alive to the fact that ultimately it would have to obtain the approval of Congress for what it had done.

The Annual Trades Union Congress was something more than a business meeting. It was an affirmation of the spirit of the trade union movement. Good fellowship and pleasurable entertainment there was in plenty, and though this often gave the puritanical members of the Labour movement an opportunity for cynical and lofty amusement, some diversion from the serious business of debate and discussion was a necessary leavening that helped to keep the occasion a sane and balanced demonstration of trade union aims and aspirations. It must be admitted, however, that the Congress did not always allow itself enough time to discuss all the items on its agenda. Before the First World War the Congress did not really get down to business until the second day of the week. After the presidential address on the Monday morning the Congress adjourned, and the afternoon was spent on excursions that had been previously arranged. There was considerable competition to entertain the T.U.C. and some curious invitations were accepted by the Reception Committee of the local Trades Council, on whom responsibility fell for making arrangements of a social character. On one occasion the delegates were taken for a trip down the Mersey, as guests of the Cunard Company, and returned feeling the effects of the weather, which had made most of the party violently sea-sick. In 1899, when the Congress met at Plymouth, it was arranged that the delegates should visit the estate of Lord Mount Edgcumbe. One of the members of the party allowed his satirical talents full rein in commenting on the outing in the columns of the *Clarion*. He described how their host had arranged for their safe conduct round the estate, 'having them escorted like the convicts at Dartmoor, by his Lordship's agent in front, armed with a hunting crop, the rear being brought up by retainers who were instructed to see them safely off the premises the back way, and lock the gates after them'. Even in 1920, when the agenda had grown very much longer, and the Parliamentary Committee's report had vastly expanded, time was still found for the delegates to spend the Wednesday afternoon sightseeing at places of local interest. In addition to the excursions, delegates were always invited to a succession of teas given by prominent persons, and by such diverse organisations as the Bi-metallic League, the Proportional Representation Society, and the Labour Officials' Temperance Fellowship.

The annual reports of the Parliamentary Committee to Congress provide an impressive record of the multifarious and ever-growing range of activities of the Committee. In the early years of the T.U.C. they were slim documents, but by the end of the First World War they numbered one hundred and fifty pages of close print. Naturally they do not give the full record of the work of the Committee, and though they often present verbatim reports of deputations and conferences, they usually summarise the conclusions and decisions. One rarely finds in the reports of the work of any committee more than a record of its collective decisions. The way in which decisions are arrived at, the protagonists of different points of view and their arguments and manœuvres are not set out, and can be deduced only by additional evidence. The lengthy annual reports of the debates in Congress reveal much that might otherwise be obscure in the work of the Parliamentary Committee. These debates give a vivid picture of working men, and a tiny band of women, making their contribution, through a great national institution of their own creation, to the development of a social democracy. Often of a high quality, sometimes appallingly bad, their speeches reveal the strength and weakness of the trade union movement, with its broad vision of a better society in which to live, and its narrow, selfish sectionalism, as conservative and reactionary as any group in the community.

Many of those who made their mark in the debates of Congress, and served its interests on the Parliamentary Committee had notable public careers. These included—to mention but a few—Alexander Macdonald, George Howell, Henry Broadhurst, Thomas Burt, John Burns, David Shackleton, C. W. Bowerman, Harry Gosling, Will Thorne, J. H. Thomas, J. R. Clynes and Margaret Bondfield. The trade union movement was a hard school of experience, which produced men who were self-reliant, wise with a wisdom not learnt from books, perhaps egotistical and over-cautious, but not lacking in courage. The trade union movement produced its visionaries and dreamers and cultured men, to whom Congress always listened with interest and respect, but it never placed its fate in their hands. Those who rose to the top and held the confidence of Congress were the practical, capable men. The ability to make a telling speech was a necessary part of their equipment; without it they would have been unarmed, but alone this was not enough—the other qualities had to be there as well.

These were the men who had built the Trades Union Congress, and no matter what criticisms may be brought against them the longevity of their creation amply demonstrates that they laid firm foundations. They knew the value of the tried and traditional and moved ahead slowly and empirically adjusting their ideas as events made fresh demands upon them. If, sometimes, crude and bureaucratic, they also had a strong streak of Liberalism and were tolerant to those who were impatient and idealistic. That is why there were no splits in the trade union movement of Britain to compare with those on the Continent. The revolutionaries and dissidents were, perhaps, allowed to have more than their share of the limelight, but the resilience, ability to compromise, and diplomatic skill of those who rose to the top turned revolutions into a gradual process of change with honours shared.

What had the trade union movement achieved through its Trades Union Congress under the leadership of these men? In its fifty-three years of existence it had played a tremendous part in laying the legal foundations upon which the future of the trade union movement depended. The right of working men and women to organise, the right to strike, the right to play a full part as citizens in the social and political life of the nation had been its constant preoccupation. From its beginning the T.U.C. had been associated with almost every movement of social reform which affected the daily lives of working men and women. Through its work, the harsh conditions of toil generated by the Industrial Revolution were lightened and sweetened as it secured better conditions in the factories and mines, on ships at sea and on the land. Through its work, towns were better governed, the health of the nation improved, housing standards raised, the judicial system overhauled, the cultural facilities provided by museums and libraries extended for the benefit of working men and women, the educational system advanced, and greater leisure secured to permit the enjoyment of a higher standard of life.

All this was not accomplished by the T.U.C. alone, but it did make a great contribution to the vast social changes that occurred in the last quarter of the nineteenth century, and the first two decades of the twentieth. Above all, the immense changes were achieved within the framework of a continuously developing society without bloodshed and revolution, without the destruction of values fundamental to a democracy, and without a legacy of bitterness to sour politics for generations. There was no finality in the work of the T.U.C., and the new constitution promised that it would be carried on more efficiently in the future, whatever Government was in power, and whatever social conditions existed.

APPENDIX 1

THE NATIONAL FEDERATION OF ASSOCIATED EMPLOYERS OF LABOUR

STATEMENT AS TO FORMATION AND OBJECTS

We beg to call attention to the enclosed Rules of this Federation, and to explain why it has been formed, what are its objects, and how it proposes to attain them.

It has been formed in consequence of the extraordinary development—oppressive action—far-reaching, but openly-avowed designs—and elaborate organisation of the Trade Unions.

Its object is, by a defensive organisation of the employers of labour, to resist these designs so far as they are hostile to the interests of the employers, the freedom of the non-unionist operatives, and the well-being of the community.

Few are aware of the extent, compactness of organisation, large resources, and great influence of the Trade Unions. They have their annual Congress, at which an increasing number of Unions are represented each year. Last year, at the congress held at Leeds, nearly 700,000 unionists were represented, and since then their power has been largely developed.

They have the control of enormous funds, which they expend freely in furtherance of their objects, and the proportion of their earnings which the operatives devote to the service of their leaders is startling. The "Friendly Society of Stonemasons" spent between 1833 and 1873 £344,000; and the "Amalgamated Carpenters and Joiners", between October, 1862, and January, 1871—a period of little more than eight years—expended £80,000, and created a reserve fund of £18,000! This was done by a society which commenced with only 805 members and ended with not more than 10,500. Whilst the "Amalgamated Society of Engineers", having 33,474 members, spent £109,809 in 1868 alone! When these and numberless other societies are federated together, acting in common accord under able leaders, it will be seen that their operations will be sustained by adequate funds.

They have a well-paid and ample staff of leaders, most of them experienced in the conduct of strikes, many of them skilful as organisers, all forming a class apart, a profession, with interests distinct from, though not necessarily antagonistic to, those of the workpeople they lead; but, from their very raison d'être, hostile to those of the employers and the rest of the community.

Without disputes, whether as to the rate of wages, the hours of work, the employment of non-union men, the mode of calculating wages, the number of apprentices, or the materials worked—without aggressive schemes for the assumption of power, flattering to their followers—their influence would wane, their exchequer would languish, and their order would cease to exist as a power in the community.

The inducements of their position to keep the industrial world in a state of chronic confusion are almost irresistible, and the natural consequence is that they are incessantly engaged in keeping the relations between employers and employed in a state of irritation and hostility, and in fomenting dissatisfaction with all the laws which are intended to protect the employer. the employed, and especially the non-unionist from their overbearing interference.

This course of procedure tends not only to secure the permanence of their special order, but to gratify the not unnatural ambition of several of them to obtain seats in Parliament as advocates of the policy of the Unions.

They have, through their command of money, the imposing aspect of their organisation; and partly also, from the mistaken humanitarian aspirations of a certain number of literary men of good standing, a large array of literary talent, which is *prompt* in their service on all occasions of controversy. They have their own press as a field for these exertions. Their writers have free access to some of the leading London journals.

They organise frequent meetings, at which paid speakers inoculate the working classes with their ideas, and urge them to dictate terms to candidates for Parliament.

Thus they exercise a pressure upon members of Parliament, and those aspiring to that honour, out of all proportion to their real power, and beyond belief excepting to those who have had the opportunity of witnessing its effects.

They have a standing Parliamentary Committee, and a programme, and active members of Parliament are energetic in their service.

They have the attentive ear of the Ministry of the day, and their communications are received with instant and respectful attention.

They have a large representation of their own body in London whenever Parliament is likely to be engaged in the discussion of the proposals they have caused to be brought before it.

Thus, untrammelled by pecuniary considerations, and specially set apart for this peculiar work, without other clashing occupations, they resemble the staff of a well-organised, well-provisioned army, for which everything that foresight and pre-occupation in a given purpose could provide is at command.

The necessary and legitimate result of this powerful organisation—of the sacrifices, pecuniary and otherwise, which the workpeople make in its support—of the skilful and ceaseless energy with which it is directed—must be to give it to a large extent the control of the elections, and consequently Parliament; the power to dictate terms everywhere between employers and employed, and the mastery over the independence of the workmen, as well as over the operations of the employers.

These results are the deserved reward of the superiority of the trades unionists over the employers in those high qualities of foresight, generalship, and present self-sacrifice for the sake of future advantage, which form necessary elements in the success of every organised society.

It is more than time for the employers to emulate the example thus set in energy and devotion, but in pursuit of more legitimate and less selfish ends.

The following passages are extracted from leading articles in the trades union organ, the *Beehive*:

April 19th, 1873.

"But where peaceful and rational means fail, and war is declared—
"because we can look upon strikes and lockouts as nothing less than
"industrial civil war—then *the Central Council ought to interpose its*
"*authority in the name of the whole federated trades, and put their veto*
"*upon any unjustifiable act of aggression* upon the part of either workmen
"or employers. If labour is to hold its own, and the masses continue to
"raise themselves in the social and industrial scale, they must make their
"trade organisations as perfect as energy, prudence, and discretion can
"make them, which we believe will be best accomplished by adopting
"the principle of amalgamation in the first place, followed by a national
"federation of all the organised trades throughout the country."

July 12th, 1872.

"But the gigantic movements which have taken place lately show that
"the present age will more or less be characterised by national struggles,
"not the isolated struggles of small bodies of one section of industry
"against their immediate employers, but movements affecting the interests
"of thousands, and in which some recognised principle of the rights of
"labour has been infringed."

July 12th, 1872.

"No state of society can be just that does not bring into more equal
"position the producers of wealth and the possessors of it. To effect this
"the co-operation of the working classes is necessary, not only in the
"formation of trade unions for the watching over of their individual
"interests, BUT THE COMBINATION OF THOSE UNIONS INTO A KIND OF
"IMPERIAL GOVERNMENT FOR THE WORKING MAN, which, while careful
"not to be aggressive, protects the various industries of the nation from
"the oppression of capital, and lays down those general principles, which,
"while recognising the rights of capital as one of the essential elements
"of the wealth-producing power of the country, does not overlook the
"fact that skill and labour united are worthy of even greater considera-
"tion, and ought to take a higher position in laying down those laws by
"which capital and labour and social interests are governed."

These extracts serve to show the avowed designs to the promotion of which this vast machinery is devoted.

Look, on the other hand, at the position in which the employers find themselves to combat this organisation, either industrially, legislatively, or educationally as regards public opinion.

They have in some trades, associations, originating mostly in the necessity to resist some special operative demand, concerning wages or some other question of dispute; but these are mostly confined to one town, or to one branch of trade in a town, and rarely display any sign of vitality except under the influence of urgent local necessity.

In a few trades—notably in the iron and building trades—the employers' organisations embrace a larger area, but their objects are equally limited.

The only employers' association having wider objects is that of the factory occupiers of the four counties of Lancaster, York, Derby, and Chester, whose special function it is to watch over the interests of the textile trades in Parliament.

But the success of all these associations depends upon the *voluntary* and *intermittent* efforts of individual employers, whose thoughts and time are engrossed with the conduct of their own affairs.

The disadvantage of there being no adequate organisation charged with the special duty of vindicating employers' interests is made prominent when the Trades Union seek to force through Parliament some desired change in the law, such as the Fifty-four Hours Bill, the repeal of the Criminal Law Amendment Act, the Mines Regulation Bill. Their staff—literary, parliamentary, and agitative—is always ready for work. But employers, if any among them are vigilant enough, have first to create an association to defend the particular interest assailed. They have then to frame as best they may, by voluntary effort, answers to the professional publications in the form of "cases", "pamphlets", "reports", speeches and newspaper articles, which are rapidly issued on the other side. In this way they have put before the public generally, and members of the legislature in particular, answers to the report of Messrs. Bridges and Holmes upon the sanitary aspects of factory labour, and to Mr. Mundella's speech on introducing the Nine Hours Bill. They have also arranged deputations to confer with the Home Secretary and members of Parliament.

But if, in particular instances, this voluntary and fitful action has been tolerably efficient, yet in many cases, equally requiring decisive action, none whatever has been taken; and the Trades Unions have now before Parliament many proposals which are not receiving from employers the attentive consideration which they imperatively demand, and concerning which the public has heard only the statements of one side. Such are: 1st, the repeal of the Criminal Law Amendment Act; 2nd, the repeal of all penal laws affecting workmen; 3rd, the Conspiracy Law Amendment Bill; 4th, the revision of the Masters and Servants' Act; 5th, the promotion of the Payment of Wages Bill; 6th, the promotion of the Compensation to Workmen's Bill; and 7th, the promotion of the Factories Nine Hours Bill.

Should the unions be unresisted in these efforts, a period of legislative change adverse alike to the employers, to the liberty of the independent workman, and to the interests of the whole community, will be brought in with the new Parliament.

To supply the want which the preceding statement clearly indicates—to offer a centre of action for associated employers—to instruct public opinion—to conciliate electoral support—to acquire that parliamentary influence which is indispensable if legislation is not to become restrictive and destructive in its operation upon our industry—are the peculiar objects of the National Federation of Associated Employers. It will have its efficient literary staff, ever watchful and ready in defence of its policy. It will have extensive communication with the press. It will examine and take such measures as are necessary with reference to every parliamentary proposal. It will be watchful of every trades union or other effort affecting employers' interests. It will be its duty, as defined in rule 2a, "to watch over, with a view to influence, all legislation affecting industrial questions and the relations of employers and employed." This it will endeavour to do in a large and imperial spirit, weighing maturely the advantages and disadvantages of every legislative proposal from whatever quarter it may come—supporting that which is for the common good, and steadily opposing that which is adverse to industrial interests.

It will, according to rule 2b, "collect and disseminate throughout the country information bearing upon industrial questions." This will be done by the usual well-known and recognised means, and to this the council attaches the highest degree of importance. Upon the spread of sound information reliance is placed to neutralise the one-sided teaching of the Trades Union leaders—to encourage the independence of non-unionists—and to give to education, intelligence, and capital their fair share of influence in the constituencies.

A prominent part of its functions will be the encouragement and assistance, by the aid of its staff, and occasionally by that of members of its council, of the formation of local associations of employers with a view to their affiliation with the federation.

It will bring employers of every trade and every part of the United Kingdom into communication and active sympathy with each other, by means of its annual meetings, the action of its staff, its publications, its constant attention to the interests of employers, and to the promotion of freedom of labour, through the instrumentality of its council composed of representatives of associations of every trade and every district. And should the measures indicated by paragraphs a and b of rule 2 fail of their purpose—should the "industrial civil war" waged by the Trades Union leaders continue to gather head and increase in intensity, and the employers be driven to the exercise of all their defensive powers—then it will be the office of the Council to guide and to lead them, with patience, prudence, and moderation, but with firmness and unflinching decision, in the use of such measures as—having first been voluntarily acquiesced in by the associations and firms composing the Federation—shall appear necessary to defeat the organised aggression which threatens the national prosperity.

It will be no part of its duty to interfere with the management of local associations, or with questions affecting local trade disputes; neither is it proposed to emulate the trades unions in expenditure. On this head we refer you to rules iv. and v., which regulate the basis of the local subscriptions to the Federation, and we invite you, if you are a member of some local body, to take steps to secure its affiliation with the Federation; and if the employers in your district are not united, then to lose no time in endeavouring to form an association. Should you think it would either assist you in forming an association, or be advantageous in promoting affiliation with the Federation, that some members of our staff or council should attend a meeting of the employers of your district, arrangements shall be made to meet the requirements of the case, on your desire to that effect being signified to the secretary.

On behalf of the Council of the Federation,

JOHN ROBINSON, President.
STEPHEN A. MARSHALL, Treasurer.
HENRY WHITWORTH, Secretary.

TEMPORARY OFFICES:

96, King Street, Manchester.
December 11th, 1873.

APPENDIX 2

DETAILS OF TRADES UNION CONGRESSES 1868–1921

No.	Date	Place of Meeting	Name of President
1.	1868	Manchester	W. H. Wood (Manchester Trades Council)
2.	1869	Birmingham	T. J. Wilkinson (Flint Glass Makers)
3.	1871	London	George Potter (Working Men's Association)
4.	1872	Nottingham	W. H. Leatherland (Organised Trades Assn.)
5.	1873	Leeds	W. Lishman (Leeds Trades Council)
6.	1874	Sheffield	W. Rolley (President, Trades Council)
7.	1875	Liverpool	J. Fitzpatrick (Secretary, Trades Council)
8.	1875	Glasgow	J. Battersby (Compositors)
9.	1876	Newcastle	J. C. Laird (President, Trades Council)
10.	1877	Leicester	D. Merrick (Boot and Shoe Finishers)
11.	1878	Bristol	G. F. Jones (Secretary, Trades Council)
12.	1879	Edinburgh	D. Gibson (President, Trades Council)
13.	1880	Dublin	J. Murphy (Ironfounders)
14.	1881	London	E. Coulson (Bricklayers)
15.	1882	Manchester	R. Austin (Engineers)
16.	1883	Nottingham	T. Smith (Boot and Shoe Riveters)
17.	1884	Aberdeen	J. C. Thompson (President, Trades Council)
18.	1885	Southport	T. R. Threlfall (Typographical Association)
19.	1886	Hull	F. Maddison (Typographical Association)
20.	1887	Swansea	W. Bevan (Carpenters and Joiners)
21.	1888	Bradford	S. Shaftoe (Basket Makers)
22.	1889	Dundee	R. D. B. Ritchie (Dundee Trades Council)
23.	1890	Liverpool	W. Matkin (Carpenters and Joiners)
24.	1891	Newcastle	T. Burt (Miners)
25.	1892	Glasgow	J. Hodge (Steel Smelters)
26.	1893	Belfast	S. Munro (Typographical Association)
27.	1894	Norwich	F. Delves (Engineers)
28.	1895	Cardiff	J. Jenkins (Shipwrights)
29.	1896	Edinburgh	J. Mallinson (Edinburgh Trades Council)
30.	1897	Birmingham	J. V. Stevens (Tin Plate Workers)
31.	1898	Bristol	J. O'Grady (Cabinet Makers)
32.	1899	Plymouth	W. J. Vernon (Typographical Association)
33.	1900	Huddersfield	W. Pickles (House and Ship Painters)
34.	1901	Swansea	C. W. Bowerman (London Compositors)
35.	1902	London	W. C. Steadman (Barge Builders)
36.	1903	Leicester	W. B. Hornidge (Boot and Shoe Operatives)
37.	1904	Leeds	R. Bell (Railway Servants)
38.	1905	Hanley	J. Sexton (Dock Labourers)
39.	1906	Liverpool	D. C. Cummings (Boilermakers)
40.	1907	Bath	A. H. Gill (Cotton Spinners)

No.	Date	Place of Meeting	Name of President
41.	1908	Nottingham	D. J. Shackleton (Weavers)
42.	1909	Ipswich	D. J. Shackleton (Weavers)
43.	1910	Sheffield	J. Haslam (Miners)
44.	1911	Newcastle	W. Mullin (Cotton Spinners)
45.	1912	Newport	W. Thorne (Gasworkers)
46.	1913	Manchester	W. J. Davis (Brassworkers)
47.	1915	Bristol	J. A. Seddon (Shop Assistants)
48.	1916	Birmingham	H. Gosling (Watermen)
49.	1917	Blackpool	J. Hill (Boilermakers)
50.	1918	Derby	J. W. Ogden (Weavers)
51.	1919	Glasgow	G. H. Stuart-Bunning (Postmen's Federation)
52.	1920	Portsmouth	J. H. Thomas (Railwaymen)
53.	1921	Cardiff	E. L. Poulton (Boot and Shoe Operatives)

Date	Chairman of Parliamentary Committee and General Council	Secretary to Congress, Parliamentary Committee and General Council
1868	. . . .	P. Shorrocks
1869	Geo. Potter	R. McRae
1871	Geo. Potter	G. Howell
1872	A. Macdonald	G. Howell
1873	A. Macdonald	G. Howell
1874	A. W. Bailey	G. Howell
1875	R. Knight	G. Howell
1875	J. Kane and J. D. Prior	H. Broadhurst
1876	J. D. Prior	H. Broadhurst
1877	J. D. Prior	H. Broadhurst
1878	A. W. Bailey	H. Broadhurst
1879	J. D. Prior	H. Broadhurst
1880	H. Slatter	H. Broadhurst
1881	W. Crawford	H. Broadhurst
1882	T. Birtwistle	H. Broadhurst
1883	J. Inglis	H. Broadhurst
1884	A. W. Bailey	H. Broadhurst
1885	J. S. Murchie	Geo. Shipton
1886	J. Mawdsley	H. Broadhurst
1887	J. M. Jack	H. Broadhurst
1888	W. Crawford	H. Broadhurst
1889	J. Swift	H. Broadhurst
1890	E. Harford	C. Fenwick
1891	John Wilson	C. Fenwick
1892	J. Havelock Wilson	C. Fenwick
1893	J. Burns	C. Fenwick
1894	D. Holmes	S. Woods
1895	E. Cowey	S. Woods
1896	W. Thorne	S. Woods
1897	A. Wilkie	S. Woods
1898	W. J. Davis	S. Woods
1899	F. Chandler	S. Woods
1900	C. W. Bowerman	S. Woods
1901	W. C. Steadman	S. Woods
1902	W. B. Hornidge	S. Woods
1903	R. Bell	S. Woods
1904	J. Sexton	S. Woods
1905	D. C. Cummings	W. C. Steadman
1906	A. H. Gill	W. C. Steadman
1907	D. J. Shackleton	W. C. Steadman
1908	D. J. Shackleton	W. C. Steadman
1909	J. Haslam	W. C. Steadman
1910	W. Mullin	W. C. Steadman
1911	W. Thorne	C. W. Bowerman

Date	Chairman of Parliamentary Committee and General Council	Secretary to Congress, Parliamentary Committee and General Council
1912	W. J. Davis	C. W. Bowerman
1913	J. A. Seddon	C. W. Bowerman
1915	H. Gosling	C. W. Bowerman
1916	J. Hill	C. W. Bowerman
1917	J. W. Ogden	C. W. Bowerman
1918	G. H. Stuart-Bunning	C. W. Bowerman
1919	J. H. Thomas	C. W. Bowerman
1920	E. L. Poulton	C. W. Bowerman
1921	R. B. Walker	C. W. Bowerman

Date	No. of Delegates	No. of Societies Represented	No. of Members	Total Income £ s. d.		
1868	34	—	118,367	—		
1869	47	40	250,000	—		
1871	57	49	289,430	41	10	0
1872	77	63	255,710	287	8	1
1873	132	140	750,000	438	0	2
1874	169	153	1,191,922	579	16	4
1875	151	107	818,032	—		
1875	139	109	539,823	616	9	11
1876	140	113	557,823	646	19	11
1877	152	112	691,089	704	19	5
1878	136	114	623,957	751	3	1
1879	115	92	541,892	687	1	4½
1880	120	105	494,222	727	4	4
1881	157	122	463,899	711	9	8
1882	153	126	509,307	788	15	7
1883	166	134	520,091	853	19	7
1884	142	126	598,033	837	8	4
1885	161	136	580,976	848	17	9
1886	143	122	635,580	770	17	4
1887	156	131	674,034	703	16	5
1888	165	138	816,944	825	8	6
1889	211	171	885,055	908	5	3
1890	457	211	1,470,191	1,166	8	9
1891	552	213	1,302,855	1,489	14	10
1892	495	225	1,219,934	1,118	6	1
1893	380	226	900,000	1,177	2	9
1894	378	179	1,100,000	1,444	16	0
1895	330	170	1,000,000	1,473	18	4
1896	343	178	1,076,000	1,572	5	10
1897	381	180	1,093,191	1,496	18	1
1898	406	188	1,184,241	1,928	16	6
1899	384	181	1,200,000	2,060	17	2
1900	386	184	1,250,000	1,570	19	7
1901	407	191	1,200,000	1,947	2	2
1902	485	198	1,400,000	2,010	19	1
1903	460	204	1,500,000	2,716	5	0
1904	453	212	1,422,518	2,691	14	11
1905	457	205	1,541,000	2,813	16	0
1906	491	226	1,555,000	3,034	12	10
1907	521	236	1,700,000	3,298	8	4
1908	522	214	1,777,000	3,379	8	1
1909	498	219	1,705,000	3,328	14	9
1910	505	212	1,647,715	3,029	19	3

Date	No. of Delegates	No. of Societies Represented	No. of Members	Total Income £ s. d.		
1911	523	202	1,662,133	[1] 6,928	2	1
1912	495	201	2,001,633	[1] 5,289	12	9
1913	560	207	2,232,446	3,691	16	9½
1915	610	215	2,682,357	[2] 2,712	4	5
1916	673	227	2,850,547	5,381	6	4
1917	697	235	3,082,352	6,131	19	11½
1918	881	262	4,532,085	8,823	14	4½
1919	851	266	5,283,676	8,969	2	10
1920	955	215	6,505,482	[3] 18,720	7	6
1921	810	213	6,417,910	[4] 37,137	8	2½

[1] Inclusive of Levy *re* Osborne Case.

[2] Affiliation fee reduced to 10s. per 1,000 members in consideration of the fact that the full fee had been paid for the 1914 Congress (postponed on account of the war), the total income for that year amounting to £5,286 10s. 1½d.

[3] Inclusive of £1 per 1,000 towards expenses of International Trade Union Bureau.

[4] Affiliation fee increased to 1d. per member, and inclusive of £9,344 4s. 7½d. Special Levy (Council of Action).

Note.—From 1868 to 1894 inclusive the numbers in the membership column contain an element of duplication by the inclusion of trades councils.

APPENDIX 3

MEMBERS OF THE PARLIAMENTARY COMMITTEE 1869-1921

Allan, W., 1871–4.
Anderson, J., 1892.
Arch, J., 1874, 1876.
Arrandale, M., 1908–12
Bailey, A. W., 1869, 1872, 1874, 1876–86.
Ball, J. M., 1877–80.
Barnes, G. N., 1906–7
Battersby, J., 1876.
Beard, J., 1920.
Bell, R., 1899, 1902–9.
Birtwistle, T., 1877–89, 1891.
Boa, A., 1874.
Bondfield, M., 1917–21.
Boothman, H., 1919–21.
Bowerman, C. W., 1897–1921.
Bramley, F., 1916–17
Broadhurst, H., 1874–89, 1893–4.
Brown, W., 1875
Burnett, J., 1876–85
Burns, J. 1890, 1893–4
Chandler, F., 1895–9, 1901–3, 1905–10, 1916.
Cooper, B., 1907–8.
Coulson, E., 1869.
Cowey, E., 1893–1903.
Crawford, W., 1878–80, 1882–9.
Cumming, D. C., 1901–8.
Davis, W. J., 1881–3, 1896–1901, 1903–20.
Edwards, G., 1912.
Emery, H., 1909–11.
Evans, A., 1911–15.
Fenwick, C., 1890–3.
Ferguson, G., 1895.
Fitzpatrick, H., 1878.
Flynn, T. A., 1916–17.
Gill, A. H., 1903–7, 1913–14.
Gosling, H., 1908–21.
Greenall, T., 1918.
Guile, D., 1871–5.
Hall, F., 1917.

Halliday, T., 1872, 1875–6.
Harford, E., 1887–92, 1894–7.
Haslam, J., 1904–12.
Hicking, W., 1872.
Higham, D., 1872.
Hill, J., 1909–21.
Hobson, C., 1900–1.
Hodge, J., 1892–3, 1895.
Holmes, D., 1892–1900, 1902–3.
Hornidge, W. B., 1899–1907.
Howell, G., 1869–75.
Hudson, W., 1898.
Inglis, J., 1877–85, 1887–9, 1891.
Inskip, W., 1887–98.
Jack, J. M., 1884–8, 1890, 1892–6.
Jenkins, J. H., 1909–17.
Jones, L., 1871, 1872.
Judsen, E., 1917.
Kane, J., 1869, 1872–3, 1875.
Kelley, G. D., 1871, 1883, 1887, 1890–1.
Knight, R., 1875–82, 1896–1900.
Leatherland, W. H., 1883.
Leicester, J., 1871.
Leigh, W., 1871.
Macdonald, A., 1871–4.
Matkin, W., 1871, 1890–1, 1911–15.
Mawdsley, J., 1882, 1884–9, 1891–6.
Mitchell, I. H., 1897.
Mosses, W., 1907–11, 1913–17.
Mottershead, T., 1874.
Mullin, W., 1897–1902, 1908–12, 1915.
Murchie, J. S., 1883–6, 1888.
Odger, G., 1872–6.
Ogden, J. W., 1911–21.
Onions, A., 1917–18.
Owen, W., 1873.
Patterson, W., 1881–2.

APPENDIX 4

TRADES UNION CONGRESS STANDING ORDERS
ADOPTED IN 1920

Date of Meeting

1. The annual meeting of the Congress shall be held during the first week in September, commencing on the first Monday.

Duration of Sittings

2. On the first day Congress shall assemble at 12 o'clock noon prompt; on each succeeding day at 9.30 a.m., and adjourn at 1 p.m., reassemble (Wednesday excepted) at 2 p.m., and adjourn for the day at 5 p.m.

Delegates' Qualification

3. The Congress shall consist of delegates who are or have been bona fide workers at the trade which they represent, and are legal members of trade societies; but no person can be a delegate to the Trades Union Congress unless he is actually working at his trade at the time of appointment, or is a permanent paid working official of his Trade Union.

No representative shall be accepted as bona fide other than direct representation from Trade Unions.

The delegate's name, the number of members in the society, together with the amount of the society's contribution shall be forwarded to the Secretary of the General Council fourteen days prior to the meeting of Congress.

Basis of Representation

4. Trade Societies, by whatever name they may be known, shall be entitled to one delegate for every 5,000 members or fraction thereof, provided always that they have paid an annual affiliation fee of 1d. per member upon the full numerical strength of the society—probationary, free, or otherwise —towards the expenses of the General Council for the past year, and 10s. for each delegate attending Congress. The names and addresses of the delegates must be forwarded to the Secretary fourteen days prior to the date fixed for the meeting of Congress.

A credential card shall not be issued to any society which has failed to comply with the foregoing conditions.

Congress Officials

5. The Chairman of the General Council for the past year shall be President of the Congress, and the Vice-Chairman, the Vice-President, and the Secretary of the General Council shall be the Secretary of the Congress. The Chairman shall deliver the opening address, which shall not exceed thirty minutes.

Appointment of Committees

6. Special committees shall be appointed to deal with questions affecting the different industries, and where the propositions are of a technical character they shall be remitted to committees composed of representatives from the societies whose members are engaged in the industry to which the proposition refers, who shall fully consider the same and report to Congress.

Tellers and Ballot Scrutineers

7. The General Council shall nominate six or more Tellers and seven Ballot Scrutineers from the names of delegates received not later than July 31st in each year. The Nominations shall be submitted to Congress for approval.

Voting

8. The method of voting shall be by card to be issued to the delegates of trades societies according to membership, and paid for (as per Standing Order No. 4) on the basis of one vote for every 1,000 members or fraction thereof represented.

Such cards to be issued to delegates by the General Council before the meeting of Congress.

(It will only be necessary to resort to this method of voting in divisions that may be challenged by delegates to Congress.)

Qualification for Parliamentary Committee

9. No candidate shall be eligible for election on the General Council unless he is a delegate (as per Standing Order No. 3), and the Society so represented must have contributed towards the payment of the expenses of that Council, in accordance with Standing Order No. 4, during the year previous to his election.

No candidate shall be eligible for election to the General Council who has privately assisted, during the year preceding Congress, in the production of anything made by non-union labour or, by such firms as may be declared unfair by the interested trade society, or has continued to assist privately in the production of anything made by non-union labour or by such firms as may be declared unfair by the interested trade society, after such matters have been pointed out to him.

Election of General Council

10. The General Council of Congress shall be composed of 32 members, representing 18 trade groups, as follows: Mining and quarrying, 3 representatives; railway, 3; transport (other than railways) 2; ship-building, 1; engineering, founding, and vehicle building, 3; iron and steel, enginemen, and minor metal trades, 2; building and woodworking, and furnishing, 2; printing and paper, 1; cotton, 2; textiles (other than cotton), 1; clothing, 1; leather, boot and shoe, and hatmaking, 1; glass, pottery, chemicals, food, drink, tobacco, brushmaking, and distribution, 1;

agriculture, 1; public employees, 1; non-manual workers, 1; general workers, 4; women workers, 2.

That each union affiliated to Congress shall be allocated to its appropriate Group by the General Council when appointed, subject to the right of appeal by the unions concerned, such appeals to be considered, and decisions thereon to be given, by an Allocation Committee set up for the purpose, which shall act pending the election of the General Council.

Each union shall have the right to nominate candidates to represent it in its Group on the General Council.

The General Council shall be elected by the Trades Union Congress the nominee or nominees in each Group securing the highest number of votes to be elected.

In the event of the death or resignation of any member of the General Council, the candidate who secured the next highest number of votes in the same Group shall be eligible to fill the vacancy.

The General Council, at its first meeting after each Congress, to subdivide the Council into five Groups or Sub-Committees, in general accordance with the following plan: Group A: mining, 3; railways, 3; transport, 2–8. Group B: shipbuilding, 1; engineering, 3; iron and steel, 2; building, 2–8; Group C: cotton 2; other textiles, 1; clothing, 1; leather 1–5. Group D: glass, pottery, distribution, etc., 1; agriculture, 1; general workers, 4–6. Group E: printing, 1; public employees, 1; non-manual workers, 1; women workers, 2–5.

Canvassing and bartering of votes for any position or purpose shall be strictly forbidden. Any candidate on whose behalf such means are employed shall be held responsible, and upon it being proved to the satisfaction of the General Council, he shall be disqualified for election and his society debarred from representation on the general Council or any other position for three years. This notification to be printed at the foot of all ballot papers issued.

The ballot papers shall be issued by the Scrutineers, and after being filled up shall then be immediately placed in the box without inspection by the delegates other than those of the society voting. Any delegate or delegates found guilty of violating this Standing Order shall at once be reported to Congress, named by the President, and expelled. Such delegate or delegates shall not be eligible to attend Congress again for three years.

Duties of the General Council

11. The General Council shall elect from among themselves a Chairman, Vice-Chairman, and Treasurer for the ensuing year.

Subject to the necessary safeguards to secure the complete autonomy of the unions and Federations affiliated to Congress.

The General Council shall keep a watch on all industrial movements, and shall attempt to co-ordinate industrial action.

It shall promote common action by the Trade Union movement on general questions, such as wages and hours of labour, and any matter of general concern that may arise between Trade Unions and employers or between the Trade Union movement and the Government, and shall have power to assist any union which is attacked on any vital question of Trade Union principle.

Where disputes arise, or threaten to arise, between Trade Unions it shall use its influence to promote a settlement.

It shall also enter into relations with the Trade Union and Labour movements in other countries with a view to promoting common action and international solidarity.

In the event of a legal point arising, which in the opinion of the General Council (after consultation with counsel) should be tested in the House of Lords in the general interest of Trade Unionism, the Council shall be empowered to levy the affiliated societies pro rata to provide the necessary expenses. Any society failing to pay the levy shall be reported to Congress.

In all Parliamentary Constituencies where any Labour candidates are seeking election to the House of Commons, the General Council shall endorse and support such candidates, providing the following conditions are complied with:

1. That such candidates are in favour of the reforms that may be advocated by the Trades Union Congress.

2. That their candidature is endorsed by a bona fide Trade Union, the General Federation of Trade Unions, or the Labour Party.

In all Parliamentary elections where no Labour candidate is running, the General Council shall question candidates as to whether they are in favour of Government contracts being given only to those firms recognised as fair by the Trade Unions, and shall submit to them any other test questions that may be considered expedient at the time, such questions and the replies thereon to be given immediate publicity in the Press.

Programme of Business

12. Propositions for the Congress agenda must be signed by the secretary and chairman of the society sending them, and must reach the Secretary of the General Council at least twelve weeks before the time fixed for the meeting of Congress.

Such propositions shall be printed and sent to the official correspondents of recognised Trade Unions not less than eight weeks before the meeting of Congress. The order in which these subjects are to be discussed shall be decided by ballot conducted by the General Council.

A Trade Union shall not be allowed more than three resolutions but in order that important Labour questions may not be omitted from the discussions at Congress, the General Council are empowered to place not more than three propositions on the Congress agenda.

The agenda compiled by the General Council shall be taken as the first business of Congress.

All amendments to the propositions submitted by the various trades must reach the Secretary of the General Council four weeks before the opening of Congress, such amendments to be signed by the president and secretary and also bear the stamp of the society.

A complete agenda of the propositions and amendments shall be printed and sent, not less than fourteen days before the meeting of Congress, to the official correspondents of the Trade Unions who have sent delegates' fees in accordance with Standing Order No. 3.

General Council's Report

13. The Congress having been duly opened, the General Council shall present their report for the past year, which shall be laid on the table for discussion. The report shall be discussed en seriatim, and not as a whole. Each speaker to be limited to five minutes. The report shall contain a list of the General Council meetings with dates, also the names of those members who were present at such meetings.

The Standing Orders of Congress and General Council shall be published with each Annual Report of the proceedings of Congress.

Secretary Ex-Officio Member of Congress

14. The Secretary shall be elected by Congress, and be ex-officio a member of the Congress and the General Council. Should a vacancy occur between the annual meetings of the Congress, the General Council shall have power to fill up the vacancy. The Secretary shall devote his whole time to the work (but this shall not prevent him being a candidate for or a member of Parliament), and he shall remain in office so long as his work and conduct give satisfaction to the General Council and the representatives attending Congress.

No future candidate for the office of Secretary shall be eligible unless he is prepared to sign the constitution of the Labour Party in the event of his becoming a candidate for a seat in Parliament.

Nomination of Secretary and General Council

15. All nominations for the office of Secretary and General Council shall be sent to the Secretary at least twelve weeks prior to the meeting of Congress, and the list of names shall be published on the agenda paper containing the propositions that are to be discussed at Congress. Individual ballot papers containing the names of each candidate shall be supplied to delegates on the day of election.

Limitation of Speeches

16. The mover of a proposition shall be allowed ten minutes, the seconder seven, and any or each succeeding speaker five minutes. A delegate shall not speak more than once on a question, except the mover of the original proposition, who shall have the right of reply.

All amendments to propositions must be taken in the order in which they are printed.

Should the President of the Congress consider there is no practical difference of opinion among the delegates, he shall have power to stop the discussion and submit the proposition to Congress.

Arrangements for Congress

17. The General Council shall assist the local committee of the place where the next Congress is to be held, for the purpose of making the arrangements as complete as possible, and shall have power to invite the following persons to attend the sittings of the Congress (subject to the approval of Congress), viz., deputations, Labour Members of Parliament, members of the city or borough, the Mayor or Provost, and the members of the Corporation of the place in which the Congress is held.

The General Council shall meet during the week prior to the date of each Congress for the purpose of attending to these matters.

General Purposes Committee

18. A General Purposes Committee of five members for the ensuing Congress shall be nominated and elected by ballot. If any member elected is not a delegate to the ensuing Congress, or a vacancy arises from any other cause, the highest unsuccessful candidate shall be called upon to fill the vacancy.

They shall appoint from their body a chairman and a secretary. Their duties shall be:

(a) To co-operate with the movers of propositions and amendments in order that composite propositions may be obtained wherever possible.

(b) To have printed and circulated to the delegates copies of the composite propositions they have approved.

(c) To submit to the President of Congress a programme of all propositions and amendments approved by them as being in accordance with Standing Orders, together with all suggestions for the proper conduct of the business of the Congress.

(d) To report to the General Council any violation of the Standing Orders that may be brought to their notice, together with any recommendation agreed upon.

Auditors.

19. Two Auditors shall be elected by ballot, who shall have access to all papers and documents relating to income and expenditure of the General Council.

Accounts for the Year.

20. In order that affiliated societies may have an opportunity of perusing the financial statements prior to Congress assembling, the financial year shall close on July 31st. The audit shall then take place, and printed balance sheets, duly certified by the Auditors, shall be sent with the complete agenda to the official correspondents of the trades not less than fourteen days before the meeting of Congress.

All surplus moneys after payment of the expenses of Congress shall be used for the general purposes of the General Council.

Dealing with Disputes.

21. Any society engaged in a dispute and considering themselves aggrieved by reason of the members of another society assisting to defeat those on strike, may report the circumstances to the General Council, who may then take such steps as the circumstances may warrant, and should the charge be proved, the offending society shall be charged with all costs.

Should any society make a charge against another society, and after the investigation fail to prove the same, it shall bear the whole cost of the investigation, including the expenses incurred by the defendant society; and if in the opinion of the General Council the charge be a false one, wilfully and knowingly made, the society shall, in addition to bearing the expense, be liable to a fine not exceeding £20.

Should any society make a charge against another society, and the society against whom the charge is made refuses to have the same investigated, such society shall be deemed guilty, and be reported to Congress.

Amendment of Standing Orders

22. Should any amendment of the Standing Orders of the Congress be proposed by any society, such amendment must be forwarded to the General Council at least twelve weeks before the meeting of Congress.

In no case shall the Standing Orders be suspended unless agreed to by two-thirds of the delegates voting.

Delegates Leaving Congress

23. No delegate shall leave Congress without the consent of the Vice-President, and delegates absent one whole sitting without leave of absence shall be named by the President.

Foreign Delegations

24. In the event of Congress deciding upon any foreign, American, or Annual Co-operative Congress or other delegation, nominations for such delegations must be sent to the Secretary not later than twelve weeks prior to the meeting of Congress.

Secretary's Salary

25. The Secretary's salary shall be £500 per annum, and over and above this allowance the General Council shall provide reasonable remuneration on a Trade Union basis for his clerical assistant or assistants.

International Trade Union Bureau

26. An annual contribution of £1 per 1,000 of the affiliated membership shall be payable towards the expense of maintaining the International Trade Union Bureau.

APPENDIX 5

T.U.C. EDUCATIONAL POLICY

That this Congress affirms that an educational system under which every child obtains full and equal opportunities of developing its faculties, intellectual, physical and moral, is the indispensable formation of a healthy and democratic society; protests against the obstacles to the creation of such a system which are offered by the overwork of children and young persons in industry, by obsolete class barriers, by the misuse of educational endowments, and by the short-sighted parsimony of the State and local authorities, declares that the primary aim of education is the training of boys and girls for independent and self-respecting citizenship. To that end, we press for the revision of the curriculum now obtaining in the elementary and secondary schools, especially in the teaching of history and allied subjects, so that in training the children of the working class in the ideals of citizenship they may have presented to them a clear view of the real life and development of the population of this and other countries; and instructs the Parliamentary Committee to impress upon the Government the immediate adoption of the following programme:

1. *Nursery Schools.*

That the establishment of a sufficient number of nursery schools be made obligatory upon all local educational authorities administering an area with a population of 20,000 or upwards, and that such nursery schools shall be open to all children under six years of age when parents desire them to attend.

2. *Universal Full-time Education.*
   (a) That the maximum number of children allowed on the register of any class in a public elementary school be reduced to forty, and within a period not exceeding five years to thirty.
   (b) That the age of compulsory full-time attendance be raised to sixteen years.
   (c) That local authorities be required to provide adequate maintenance allowance on account of all children attending school above the age of fourteen.
   (d) That the employment of children out of school hours by way of trade or for purposes of gain be prohibited.
   (e) That the salaries of elementary school teachers be raised to the level needed to attract and retain the services of the ablest men and women available, and that candidates should be required to complete a course of education in a university before entering on their professional training.

3. *Full-time Secondary Education.*

That all fees for attendance at State-aided secondary schools be abolished, and that secondary education be made freely accessible to all children desirous and capable of taking advantage of it.

4. *Part-time Continued Education.*

   (*a*) That the education given in continuation schools be directed primarily to the strengthening of character, physique, and intelligence, and only secondarily, and after the age of sixteen, to imparting training for industry.

   (*b*) That continuation classes held on the premises of employers be not recognised as continuation schools within the meaning of the Act.

   (*c*) That the hours of labour of young persons under eighteen be limited by law to not more than twenty-five per week.

5. *Physical Training and Medical Treatment.*

   (*a*) That it be made obligatory upon all local education authorities to make adequate provision for medical and dental treatment for all children attending public elementary schools.

   (*b*) That it be made obligatory upon all local education authorities to make adequate provision for physical training and organised games, including school playing fields and school baths.

   (*c*) That the Board of Education inform local education authorities that physical training given in elementary, secondary, or continuation schools must not be of a military bias or intention, and that no grant be paid on account of time spent in training which is military in intention or character.

6. *University Education.*

   That with a view to making university education accessible to all classes of the population:

   (*a*) A generous system of State maintenance scholarships be established tenable at universities and university colleges, and financed from State funds.

   (*b*) That the Exchequer grants to universities and university colleges be increased, and their payments be made conditional upon the provision at the universities of scholarships for students of small means and of extra part-time university classes of a university character for students unable to attend the university full-time.

   (*c*) That a Royal Commission be appointed to inquire into and report upon the constitution, government, endowments, and finance of the universities, including the Universities and Colleges of Oxford and Cambridge.

   (*d*) That a report should be periodically issued by the Board of Education showing the source, value, control and expenditure of the endowments of secondary schools, universities, and other educational institutions and trusts.

7. *Finance.*

   That not less than 75 per cent of the total average expenditure of local authorities upon education be defrayed from the National Exchequer, provided that the education given by the local authorities is approved as efficient.

   Moved by C. T. Cramp, National Union of Railwaymen.
   T.U.C. Annual Report, 1918.

INDEX

393